WHAT IF WE COULD REIMAGINE
COPYRIGHT?

WHAT IF WE COULD REIMAGINE
COPYRIGHT?

EDITED BY REBECCA GIBLIN & KIMBERLEE WEATHERALL

PRESS

Published by ANU Press
The Australian National University
Acton ACT 2601, Australia
Email: anupress@anu.edu.au
This title is also available online at press.anu.edu.au

National Library of Australia Cataloguing-in-Publication entry

Title: What if we could reimagine copyright? / Rebecca Giblin
                (editor) ; Kimberlee Weatherall
                (editor).

ISBN: 9781760460808 (paperback) 9781760460815 (ebook)

Subjects: Copyright, International.
                Copyright--Economic aspects.
                Copyright--Political aspects.

Other Creators/Contributors:
                Giblin, Rebecca, editor.
                Weatherall, Kimberlee, editor.

Dewey Number: 346.0482

Cover design and layout by ANU Press. Cover image adapted from FreeImages.com.

This book is dedicated to everyone who believes we can fix copyright (including François and David, who are already convinced, and Linus who one day will be).

With thanks to Monash University for funding the project via a Research Accelerator Grant, our workshop hosts at the Centre d'Etudes Internationales de la Propriété Intellectuelle, and our reviewers. We're very grateful also to our contributing authors for tackling a difficult thought experiment with courage and perseverance.

Contents

Foreword

Peter Drahos

In the opening chapter, of this volume the editors invite the reader
to imagine that he or she has a blank slate when it comes to drawing
up a new copyright law. One supposes that there would be a lot of
interesting proposals, especially from the non-lawyers whose minds
would be less trammelled by copyright's technicality. Some readers
might keep the slate blank. The freedom of a blue sky should allow
one to conclude that commodification by copyright should play no
role in a social system. Anarchists, as well as those libertarians who
do not extend natural property rights to intangible objects, might
arrive at such a conclusion from first principles. Alternatively, one
might conclude on consequential grounds, as Machlup did about
the patent system, that if one did not have a copyright law it would
be irresponsible to implement one.

None of the contributors to this volume argue for the abolition of
copyright. Instead, they suggest feasible changes to copyright systems
based on the assumption of a world in which copyright design issues
are not settled by a global political economy dominated by the variable
of power. The upshot is a set of stimulating and highly readable essays
that reflect upon the rules, principles, doctrines and interpretations
that would help to draw copyright law into the service of *civitas*
rather than the *imperium* of factions or nations.

Aside from the service of bringing these essays into public circulation,
the editors show us both the need for and the difficulty of imagining
alternatives to existing institutional designs. Social scientists tend to
ground their explanations for institutional change in structure or some
combination of structure and agency. Obviously a foreword is not the

place to begin an argument about the role of imagination, but perhaps one can agree with the editors that imagination has an important role to play in copyright reform.

Aristotle in *De Anima* suggests that 'imagination is that in virtue of which an image arises for us' and importantly 'imagining lies within our own power whenever we wish' (see Book III, Part 3 in one of the handily available ebook versions of *De Anima*). When we speak of alternative visions of things we are harking back to this old view of imagination as a capacity or perhaps faculty of being able to see images of how things might be otherwise.

My guess, and it is only a guess, is that copyright and intellectual property more generally have been the object of at least some reimagining. In the early 1990s, my colleague John Braithwaite and I interviewed a small number of Washington policy entrepreneurs and lobbyists who had been working for more than a decade on something the world has come to know as the *Agreement on Trade-Related Aspects of Intellectual Property Rights* (TRIPS). At that time most of them replied to our questions in terms of the need for a new vision and creative approach to the problems of insufficient protection for investors in intellectual property. Whatever might be said of their vision for the world, and much has been said, perhaps there is some plausibility in the claim that the origin of TRIPS lies in acts of individual imagination, a picture of what else might be. Of course, these individuals had access to resources that allowed them to seed their proposals in think tanks like the Heritage Foundation and the Brookings Institution, and they were part of networks of capital that made the kind of campaign contributions that brought the practiced empathetic eye contact and firm handshake from Congressional representatives.

It is worth focusing for a moment on Aristotle's observation concerning our power to use imagination whenever we wish. It is a power available to us all. If we do not exercise the power of imagination then legal structures, much like the Berlin Wall, look permanent, immovable, a restraint on our freedom from which there seems little hope of escape. Through the act of picturing another world we inject the first element of contingency into structure, a brick begins to look removable, a structure begins to look indeterminate, a wall comes down.

Acts of imagining alternatives to structures of domination are also acts of power. TRIPS, and the era of trade-driven intellectual property that it ushered in, represents the imagining of a powerful elite. It was always a vision of *imperium*. If it is service to *civitas* that we seek from our institutions of intellectual property then we must begin to imagine that possibility.

The final paragraphs of the final chapter by the two editors suggest that they see reimagining as a method for moving debates about copyright reform in more constructive directions. In this they are surely right. As they say, this project has been a challenging exercise for them, but as the reader of this innovative volume will see it has also been a very worthwhile one.

Peter Drahos
The Australian National University and
Queen Mary University of London

1

If we redesigned copyright from scratch, what might it look like?

Rebecca Giblin and Kimberlee Weatherall

What if we could start with a blank slate, and write ourselves a brand new copyright system? If we could scrap the existing structure entirely and design a law to encourage creativity, remunerate and support creators, and increase the size of cultural markets to ensure broad access to new knowledge and creativity; in short, if we could draw up a new copyright law that genuinely furthered the public interest, what might it look like? Would we opt for radical overhaul? Or would we keep our current fundamentals? What parts of the system would we jettison? What would we keep?

Most critical and academic commentary on copyright takes current law as a given.[1] Not uncommonly, commentators lament the way that the current copyright system was conceived in very different technological and economic conditions, and built on foundations that

---

1   This is true even of projects that aim to rethink the copyright system: e.g. Jessica Litman, *Digital Copyright* (Prometheus Books, 2nd ed, 2006); Pamela Samuelson, 'The Copyright Principles Project' (2010) 25 *Berkeley Technology Law Journal* 1175. The explicit goal of the Copyright Principles project was to 'improve' and 'refine' copyright law by seeking to explore the level of possible 'consensus': Samuelson at 1175, 1176. Another project along similar lines was the Wittem Project, which aimed to develop a model copyright law designed to operate within the international obligations of the European Union (and thus be consistent with both the Berne Convention and TRIPS (*Berne Convention for the Protection of Literary and Artistic Works*, opened for signature 9 September 1886 (amended in 1914, 1928, 1948, 1967, 1971, and 1979) 25 UST 1341, 828 UNTS 221, entered into force 5 December 1887; and *Marrakesh Agreement Establishing*

have been undermined by technological, economic and social change. Much *has* changed in the decades since copyright's foundational frameworks were settled. Perhaps most fundamental is the way in which the advent of digital technologies has driven the marginal cost of distributing many kinds of cultural and informational work towards zero, which, at least in some senses and for some people, has eliminated scarcity.[2] At the same time, we have also come to know more than ever before about how the *theory* of how copyright was supposed to work actually matches up with practice.[3]

But treaty obligations, political realities and existing economic interests and business models all combine to lock in the status quo. And so most discussion of possible copyright reform is pragmatic, and tinkers at the margins: it aims for achievable change within the confines of the existing international frameworks.

This collection does something bolder. Contributors were asked to apply these new realities and knowledge advances to key areas of copyright policy: to imagine what copyright law might look like if we designed it from scratch in today's sociotechnological environment, unconstrained by existing international treaties and other law and practice.[4]

There is an urgent need for this thought experiment. Even as we write, the international framework is becoming incrementally more constraining. International treaties in intellectual property are increasingly framed not in statements of general principles, but as an ever more detailed reflection of domestic legislation. This is particularly notable in recent (albeit, at the time of publication, stalled) trade negotiations, particularly for the Trans-Pacific Partnership (TPP) and the Transatlantic Trade and Investment Partnership (TTIP). There are serious questions about the appropriateness of locking in specific details of the current system. We live in a fast-changing social and technological environment. Only 20 years ago few people were even

---

the World Trade Organization, opened for signature 15 April 1994, 1867 UNTS 3 (entered into force 1 January 1995), annex IC (*'Agreement on Trade-Related Aspects of Intellectual Property Rights'*), respectively): see <www.copyrightcode.eu>.

2   See generally Mark A Lemley, 'IP in a world without scarcity' (2015) 90 *NYU Law Review* 460.

3   Mark A Lemley, 'Faith-Based Intellectual Property' (2015) 62 *UCLA Law Review* 1328.

4   By treaties, we are referring generally to supranational legal instruments, including the various EU Directives. When we talk about 'copyright', we include the civil law notion of author's rights (*droit d'auteur* or *urheberrecht*).

online. Now, even if large swathes of the world's population still lack that opportunity, many of us routinely carry the means of accessing most of the world's knowledge and culture with us in our pockets. If we don't know what technology will look like 20 years from now, or how society will have changed, how can we possibly know what system of regulation we will need? There is also a risk that, if we view the possibilities for systemic change wearing the blinkers of existing international constraints, we'll miss identifying better ways of achieving our aims. Incremental thinking that merely proposes small changes at the margins is not, in and of itself, sufficient.

And so, drawing inspiration from Jessica Litman,[5] we invite you to join in our thought experiment: if we could draw up a new copyright law, from a blank slate, ignoring current international legal constraints, what might it look like? As a starting point, any attempt at such fundamental rethinking needs at least *some* guiding principles or goals. We turn therefore to our guiding principle – the aim of furthering the public interest.

The 'public interest' (please don't stop reading)

The organising principle we have used as our springboard is that copyright should serve the public interest. But this does not necessarily mean what you think it means – assuming you think it has a meaning at all.

Your first instinct might be to dismiss the concept of the public interest as 'vacuous, deceptive and generally useless'.[6] As a concept, the public interest may have been around for thousands of years, but generations of philosophers, economists, political scientists, lawyers and regulators have made little progress in determining precisely what we mean by it,[7] leaving many sceptical about (or even vexed by)

---

5   In 2001, Jessica Litman asked readers to engage in a thought experiment: imagining that they were the US public's copyright lawyer asked to advise whether the public should agree to the deal; Litman, above n 1, 70.

6   Virginia Held, *The Public Interest and Individual Interests* (Basic Books, 1970) 1.

7   As a result it is often left 'totally undefined': Robert A Dahl and Charles E Lindblom, *Politics, Economics, and Welfare: Planning and Politico-Economic Systems Resolved Into Basic Social Processes* (Harper & Row, 1963) 501.

its usage. Sorauf nominated it to head a list of ambiguous phrases that would 'never be missed',[8] complaining that, not only was there no current or emerging consensus about its meaning, but scholars don't even agree 'about what they are trying to define: a goal, a process, or a myth'.[9] That lack of substantive content means that:

> any detailed inquiry about its exact meaning plunges the inquiry into a welter of platitudes, generalities, and philosophic arguments. It soon becomes apparent that no general agreement exists about whether the term has any meaning at all, or, if it has, what the meaning is, which specific actions are in the public interest and which are not, and how to distinguish between them.[10]

The term's amorphousness also renders it susceptible to hijack; 'hopelessly vulnerable to annexation or colonization by those who exercise power in society'.[11] Dahl and Lindblom find that '[o]ften enough a precise examination would show that it can mean nothing more than whatever happens to be the speaker's own view as to a desirable public policy'.[12] As Flathman laments, 'the misuse of the concept (and its ancestors) is as old as politics'.[13] Alexander further captures the slipperiness of the concept:

> The notion of 'public interest' is not a single or unified concept –
> its content will vary depending upon who is considered to make up
> 'the public' and who is articulating its interests. At times different
> interests may come into conflict, and at other times they may be
> complementary.[14]

---

8   Frank Sorauf, 'The Conceptual Muddle' in Carl J Friedrich (ed), *Nomos V: The Public Interest* (Atherton Press, 1962) 190. See also Glendon Schubert, *The Public Interest: A Critique of the Theory of a Political Concept* (Free Press, 1960) 224, arguing that the concept 'makes no operational sense, notwithstanding the efforts of a generation of capable scholars'.

9   Sorauf, above n 8, 186; see also Mike Feintuck, *'The Public Interest' in Regulation* (Oxford University Press, 2004) 3, noting that anything more than the most superficial examination of the term 'the public interest' reveals enormous difficulties in defining this 'deceptively familiar concept.'

10   Anthony Downs, 'The public interest: Its meaning in a democracy' (Spring 1962) 29 *Social Research* 1.

11   Feintuck, above n 9, 33.

12   Dahl and Lindblom, above n 7, 501. See also Richard C Box, 'Redescribing the Public Interest' (2007) 44(4) *The Social Science Journal* 585, 585–586, arguing that its uncertain meaning 'allows it to be used to justify individual or group preferences or undemocratic use of public power'.

13   Richard E Flathman, *The Public Interest: An Essay Concerning the Normative Discourse of Politics* (John Wiley & Sons, 1966) 9.

14   Isabella Alexander, *Copyright Law and the Public Interest in the Nineteenth Century* (Hart Publishing, 2010) 16.

Perhaps more encouragingly, Alexander describes the concept's opacity as both strength and weakness: 'strength because the simpler a rhetorical appeal can be made, the more likely it will resonate with its audience; weakness because it can be used as a cloak for private interests and thereby discredited'.[15]

These shortcomings are well and truly evident when people debate copyright. In this context, the public interest is sometimes treated as synonymous with the current law as enacted – perhaps on the assumption that whatever the legislature has decided to do is, by definition, 'in the public interest'.[16] But more often, copyright's various constituencies will give the concept of the public interest *in copyright* a meaning consistent with their own visions of copyright, or using it to promote specific policy or law reform goals or a particular outcome in a dispute.

For example, the public interest in copyright is sometimes used synonymously with the interests of those protected by copyright – namely, authors and owners. That is how the Berne Convention appears to have treated concepts of the 'public interest' and 'public good'; so too did US Copyright Register Maria Pallante when she described authors' interests being 'not a counterweight to the public interest but … at the very centre of the equation'.[17]

On the other hand, in recent times the 'public interest' has also been increasingly used as a proxy for 'user' (or even 'consumer') interests. This leads to its being invoked 'in favour of free and unfettered access by the public to copyright works combined with the means of copying them for personal use'.[18] Along similar lines, the public interest is sometimes used as the counterweight to author interests or, in other words, the interests of everyone *but* authors and owners. For example, the preamble to the WIPO Copyright Treaty emphasises 'the need to

---

15   Ibid.

16   Sherwin Siy, 'Two Halves of the Copyright Bargain: Defining the Public Interest in Copyright' (2012–2013) 31(3) *Cardozo Arts & Entertainment Law Journal* 683, 684 citing *eBay Inc v MercExchange LLC*, 547 US 388, 391 (2006).

17   Pallante's comments are in her testimony to Congress at 3: Maria A Pallante Statement to the Register of Copyrights of the United States Subcommittee on Courts, Intellectual Property and the Internet Committee on the Judiciary, United States House of Representatives 113th Congress, 1st Session, 'The Register's Call for Updates to U.S. Copyright Law' <web.archive.org/web/20130418013229/http://judiciary.house.gov/hearings/113th/03202013/Pallante%20032013.pdf>.

18   Gillian Davies, *Copyright and the Public Interest* (Sweet & Maxwell, 2nd ed, 2002) 7.

maintain a balance between the rights of authors and the larger public interest, particularly education, research and access to information'.[19] Davies has suggested that 'from the inception of the copyright system, there has been a built-in tension between the interests of the author on the one hand and those of the public on the other'.[20] The US Copyright Principles Project expresses a richer conception of the public interest but still places it in opposition to the interests of copyright owners:

> A well-functioning copyright law carefully balances the interests of the public in access to expressive works and the sound advancement of knowledge and technology, on the one hand, with the interests of copyright owners in being compensated for uses of their works and deterring infringers from making market-harmful appropriations of their works, on the other.[21]

There are obvious problems with conflating 'the public interest' with one specific interest group or another. Such conceptions will rarely convince others in the context of the perennial copyright debate. As Alexander argues, it is simply unrealistic to treat the public interest as synonymous with ever-stronger intellectual property (IP) rights, or to treat every other interest (including access to works for both the broader public and second generation authors) as being somehow outside the copyright system. Equally, however, taking authors out of the equation entirely takes the heart out of copyright law, and fails to recognise the public's interest in the creation of a diversity of cultural material.

We can avoid these problems by recognising that the public interest must encompass a range of goals. Thus Barbara Ringer, a former Register of the US Copyright Office, once defined the public interest as 'the *aggregate* of the fundamental goals that the society seeks to achieve for *all* of its members — not for a majority of its members or for any large and powerful group, but for all of the people within

---

19   *World Intellectual Property Organisation Copyright Treaty*, opened for signature 20 December 1996, 36 ILM 65 (entered into force 6 March 2002) ('WIPO Copyright Treaty').
20   Davies, above n 18, 235.
21   See also G Dworkin, 'Copyright, The Public Interest and Freedom of Speech: A UK Copyright Lawyer's Perspective' in J Griffiths and U Suthersanen (eds), *Copyright and Free Speech: Comparative and International Analysis* (Oxford University Press, 2005) 154, stating that '[c]opyright and the public interest are inextricably linked. All copyright systems seek to strike a balance between the rights of the owner and the public interest'.

the society'.[22] The fundamental societal goals commonly described as constituting the public interest in copyright include the promotion of creativity,[23] learning and progress,[24] the widest possible creation, dissemination and access to works[25] (including space to 'produce new works by building on the ideas and information contained in the works of others'),[26] freedom of expression,[27] the preservation of culture[28] and a robust public domain.[29] Alternatively, descending below grand social goals to focus on something more personal and specific, we might argue, with Ginsburg among many others,[30] that '[t]he public interest comprises the goals and aspirations of authors *and* users, of publishers *and* educators, and so forth'.[31]

This, however, takes us back to platitudes; such general aspirations provide no real guidelines for deciding what a copyright law in the public interest would look like.

---

22   Barbara Ringer, 'Authors' rights in the electronic age: Beyond the Copyright Act of 1976' (1981) 1(1) *Loyola Entertainment Law Journal* 2 (first emphasis added).

23   Neil Netanel, 'Why has Copyright Expanded? Analysis and Critique' in F Macmillan (ed), *New Directions in Copyright Law, Volume 6* (Edward Elgar, 2008) 4; 'The Washington Declaration on Intellectual Property and the Public Interest' (2013) 28(1) *American University International Law Review* 19, 21.

24   See e.g. Davies, above n 18, 12; Preamble to WIPO Copyright Treaty emphasising 'the need to maintain a balance between the rights of authors and the larger public interest, particularly education, research and access to information'; Sam Ricketson, 'The Copyright Term' (1992) 23(6) *International Review of Intellectual Property & Competition Law* 753, 755.

25   See e.g. Davies, above n 18, 7, 16; 'Intellectual Property and Innovation', CMnd 9712, HMSO, 1986 (UK government white paper from 1986) 35, [4].

26   *CCH Canadian v Law Society of Upper Canada* [2004] 1 SCR 339 [23].

27   *Ashdown v Telegraph Group Ltd* [2001] EWCA Civ 1142, in which the UK Court of Appeal suggested that the UK's fair dealing exceptions 'will normally afford the Court all the scope that it needs properly to reflect the public interest in freedom of expression and, in particular, the freedom of the press', at [66]. See also [71], explaining how essential it is to remember that 'considerations of public interest are paramount' and thus not to apply tests inflexibly. Also 'The Washington Declaration on Intellectual Property and the Public Interest' (2012) 28(1) *American University International Law Review* 19, 25; Ricketson, above n 24, 753, 755.

28   See e.g. Australian Law Reform Commission, *Copyright and the Digital Economy Final Report*, Report No 122 (2013) 278; Laura N Gasaway, 'America's Cultural Record: A Thing of the Past?' (2003) 40(3) *Houston Law Review* 643–671.

29   'The Washington Declaration on Intellectual Property and the Public Interest', above n 27, 19, 21.

30   Caron also describes the rights of authors and the public as being 'indissociable in nature': Christophe Caron, 'Abuse of Rights and Author's Rights' (1998) 176 *Revue Internationale du Droit d'Auteur*, 2, 54.

31   Jane C Ginsburg, 'Authors and Users in Copyright' (1997) 45(1) *Journal of the Copyright Society of the USA* 1, 4.

We still need this concept

If leading thinkers have trouble defining the public interest, and if the term can be hijacked, why shouldn't it simply be abandoned? The answer is because it captures something important about the goals of public policy, and because abandoning the concept simply leaves a void that something else must fill:

> The problems associated with 'public interest' are among the crucial problems of politics. Determining justifiable governmental policy in the face of conflict and diversity is central to the political order; it is a problem which is never solved in any final sense but which we are constantly trying to solve. The much-discussed difficulties with the concept are difficulties with morals and politics. We are free to abandon the *concept*, but if we do so we will simply have to wrestle with the *problems* under some other heading.[32]

Held agrees, suggesting that concepts such as the public interest are 'indispensable' in enabling evaluations of government decisions.[33] Thus, while we don't exactly know what the public interest means, and will debate its content forever, we have a keen intuition that it is important – hence former US Supreme Court Justice Felix Frankfurter's description of it as a 'vague, impalpable but all-controlling consideration'.[34] We need the *concept* of the public interest because its absence would leave lacunae in policy development and evaluation. As Colm observes, 'it is difficult to imagine that politicians, statesmen, judges, and officials concerned with the formulation of government policies could do without this concept'.[35]

Fundamentally, the concept of the public interest stands for something central to our democratic system: the idea that 'we' are not just a welter of self-interested individuals out to further our own specific interests regardless of the impact on others, but rather, that we make up a society, in which guise we can have a shared set of interests. It also suggests that, on occasion, furtherance of those shared interests can

---

32   Flathman, above n 13, 13.
33   Held, above n 6, 9–10.
34   Quoted in Gerhard Colm, 'The Public Interest: Essential Key to Public Policy' in Carl J Friedrich (ed), *Nomos V: The Public Interest* (Atherton Press, 1962) 115.
35   Ibid 127.

and should take precedence over individual or group self-interest.[36] Thus, although 'its fuzziness makes it awkward as a practical guide to daily affairs',[37] the concept invokes considerations that cannot be ignored.[38]

For our purposes in this book, too, the other most common trope in copyright policy discussions – the concept of 'balancing interests' – is deeply unsatisfactory.[39] 'Balance' helps define what is politically feasible, but not what is socially desirable.[40] A policy change is seen as being 'unbalanced' if it favours one existing stakeholder more than another, regardless of its objective merits. Thus the notion of 'balance' favours existing ways of doing things, business models and interests. We want to move past that constraint to consider what good policy would actually look like, regardless of how it might impact the slices of those who currently divide up the pie.

Methods for giving content to 'the public interest': The tools of philosophy

If we want to reimagine copyright to better further the public interest, we need to be able to give that concept some content. Thankfully, we are not the first to attempt to do so. Generations of social and political philosophers have already wrestled with this problem, and they have produced some tools that can help.

---

36   Charles J Fox and Hugh Theodore Miller, *Postmodern Public Administration: Toward Discourse* (Sage Publications, 1995) 123–124.

37   Box, above n 12, 585, 586.

38   For example, Feintuck, above n 9, 3, 25; Held, above n 6, vii; Downs, above n 10, 1–2.

39   See Story's review of the literature, which found references to various copyright systems providing '"a just balance", "a good balance", "a weak balance", "the proper balance", "the appropriate balance", "an unfair balance", and an "equitable balance"'; '[c]ommentators on copyright often worry that some legal change has "tilted the balance" or "upset [the balance] unnecessarily" and that we need to "redress the balance."' Alan Story, *'Balanced Copyright': Not a Magic Solving Word* (27 February 2012) Intellectual Property Watch <www.ip-watch.org/2012/02/27/%E2%80%98balanced%E2%80%99-copyright-not-a-magic-solving-word/>. See also Carys Craig, reminding us that 'the idea of "balancing" competing interests is no more than a metaphor itself, albeit one that is a pervasive and persuasive presence in modern legal discourse': Carys J Craig, 'The Evolution of Originality in Canadian Copyright Law: Authorship, Reward and the Public Interest' (2005) 2(2) *University of Ottawa Law & Technology Journal* 425, 441.

40   Lok Sang Ho, *Public Policy and the Public Interest* (Routledge, 2012).

Held's typology divides public interest conceptions in general legal and political philosophy into three main categories: 'preponderance theories', 'common interest theories', and 'unitary theories'.[41] 'Interest' can itself have different meanings,[42] but here we adopt Held's approach of limiting ourselves to interests 'in something being *done*, or enacted, or brought about, or maintained'.[43]

Preponderance theories suggest that the public interest 'cannot be in conflict with a *preponderance* or *sum* of individual interests'.[44] Epitomised by the work of Hobbes, Hume and Bentham, such aggregationist theories suggest that 'something might be in the public interest where it's not in an individual's interest, as long as it's in the interests of sufficient individuals'.[45] Davies seems to have adopted a preponderance conception in *Copyright and the Public Interest*:

> Whether a particular act is 'in the public interest' is probably not subject to any objective tests. Inherent in the noble motive of the public good is the notion that, in certain circumstances, the needs of the majority override those of the individual, and that the citizen should relinquish any thoughts of self-interest in favour of the common good of society as a whole.[46]

One unanswered and vexing question concerns how this preponderance is to be judged. Is it by simple majority of numbers, or weighted by political strength? Is it 'to be judged in empirical or behavioral terms, as a higher degree of force, or a greater weight of actual opinion, or a superior group strength'?[47] And of course there is the obvious problem: how to factor in minority interests.[48]

---

41   Held, above n 6, 42–46. Alternative typologies have also been established by a number of other scholars. See e.g. EC Banfield, 'Note on Conceptual Scheme' in M Meyerson and EC Banfield, *Politics, Planning and the Public Interest* (Free Press, 1955); Schubert, above n 8; CE Cochran 'Political science and the public interest' (1974) 36(2) *Journal of Politics* 327; Wayne AR Leys and Charner Marquis Perry, 'Philosophy and the Public Interest: A document' (Paper presented at the Symposium of the Western Division of the American Philosophical Association, University of Wisconsin, 1 May 1959).

42   See e.g. Flathman, above n 13, 14–31.

43   Held, above n 6, 19.

44   Ibid 43.

45   Ibid (emphasis added).

46   Davies, above n 18, 4.

47   Held, above n 6, 83.

48   Feintuck suggests a 'counter majoritarian' response would be needed: Feintuck, above n 9, 12 (internal note omitted).

Common interest theories avoid these difficulties by requiring unanimity. That is, they suggest that something will only be in the public interest where it is in the interests of *all* members of a polity.[49] As Barry observes, interests common to all members of society are rare,[50] but do exist: operational monetary systems, sustainable access to breathable air and drinkable water, and community firefighting facilities are all in the common interest. Rousseau, a leading proponent of this view, rejected preponderance theories on the grounds that simply following the preponderance of opinion might mean yielding to force, acting out of necessity rather than inclination.[51] Common interest theories suggest that where a policy triggers conflict between individual interests it cannot be in the public interest. But given the near impossibility of persuading all voters to favour a given policy, common interest theories are unlikely to provide a mechanism for effective decision-making involving large groups. Common interest theories seem even less likely to be a helpful guide to copyright policymaking, given the contentiousness arising from its multitude of often competing private interests.

Preponderance and common interest theories are sometimes described as **process theories**, because they provide a *process* for determining where the public interest lies without purporting to give it normative content. This has led to criticism for lack of usefulness. For example, in the context of preponderance theories, Held has noted that:

> to assert that '*x* is in the interests of a preponderance of individuals' implies only that '*x* is in the interests of a preponderance of individuals.' ... [I]f we want to know whether a given *x* is in the public interest, we want to know something else than the empirical fact that it is in the interests of a preponderance of individuals, although being in the interests of a preponderance of individuals may well be among the possible good reasons for believing that such an *x* is in the public interest.[52]

---

49   Held, above n 6, 44.
50   BM Barry, 'The Use and Abuse of the Public Interest' in Carl J Friedrich (ed), *Nomos V: The Public Interest* (Atherton Press, 1962) 199.
51   Held, above n 6, 100, citing Jean Jacques Rousseau, *The Social Contract: Book 1* (Charles Frankel, New York, 1947) ch 3, 8–9.
52   Held, above n 6, 84.

In reality however, process theories *must* involve some normative content being given to the concept of the public interest. That is because a determination as to whether a given policy is in the interests of either a majority or all of a polity cannot be made without identifying where those interests actually lie. For example, whenever it is argued that a given policy is in the public interest because it is in everybody's interest, a normative judgment is being made that is in fact that case – that it is indeed desirable to have a robust national defence force or independent judiciary or stable currency or whatever the policy might be. Thus, before process conceptions of the public interest can be applied there must at least be some implicit normative basis for deciding that certain things are desirable while others are not. Sometimes this is clear-cut; for example, most people would argue that a policy to criminalise murder is in all or most individuals' interests. When it comes to copyright policy, however, it can be much more difficult to determine where all or a preponderance of individuals' interests lie. Are they better served by policies that facilitate access but risk certain kinds of new content being underproduced, or those that incentivise the creation of more or particular kinds of content but result in overall less use?

The third category in Held's typology can be described as **'unitary' theories**. In this conception, which can be traced to the work of Plato and Aristotle, and later Hegel and Marx, if something is in the public interest as a matter of 'valid' judgment, it must also be in each individual's interest. Equally, if something is not in the interest of an individual as a matter of such judgment, then it cannot be in the public interest either.[53] Unlike the process conceptions, unitary theories give explicit normative content to the concept of the public interest. Validity or justifiability are conferred by the universal moral order, and whether something is in the public interest is determined on that basis.[54] The obvious difficulty with such a formulation is in reaching agreement on where this 'objective good' actually lies. Plato and Aristotle differed significantly on this question,[55] and the subsequent 2,000 years have not brought the world any closer to moral unanimity. There is widespread disagreement about whether the moral content of the public interest aligns with the interests of the state (as posits the

---

53   Ibid 45.
54   Ibid 136.
55   Ibid 142–143.

Hegelian view), the Church, the society or some other benchmark.[56] Also problematic is the refusal of unitary theories to permit the existence of any justifiable conflict between the public interest and individual interests.[57] That is, any individual's disagreement with the morally valid 'public interest' would itself, by definition, be invalid. While moral validity may sometimes be clear, in the case of copyright policy the wide range of genuinely held yet contradictory views as to what it is seeking to achieve make it difficult to identify any moral 'right' without dismissing core philosophical and cultural concerns. For example, for Tang, writing on the public interest in copyright in China, a key consideration is whether the act 'stimulates a socialist spirit and values'.[58] That this is not a consideration that would necessarily animate the concept elsewhere hints at the difficulty of defining a morally valid 'public interest' in copyright. The fundamental debates over instrumentalist versus naturalist copyright traditions, discussed below, make it more difficult still.

More recently, Ho has put forward a method for determining the public interest using a familiar *ex ante* perspective:

> The public interest is the interest of 'the representative individual' – an imaginary person who forgot his identity and who imagined that he had equal chance of being anyone in society. By pondering policy options using this *ex ante* perspective impartially, the most preferred option is the one that is deemed to maximize the public interest. With the public interest defined this way, policy decisions should be made on the basis of comparing benefits in terms of enhancement of the public interest on the one hand, and costs on the other hand.[59]

As well as having roots in work by Mill and Harsanyi, this *ex ante* framework evokes the Rawlsian 'invisible veil', which suggests that the principles of justice must be determined by individuals in a 'hypothetical situation of equal liberty':

---

56   Ibid 154–156.
57   Ibid 156–158.
58   Guan H Tang, *Copyright and the Public Interest in China* (Edward Elgar, 2011) 122.
59   Ho, above n 40, 8.

Among the essential features of this situation is that no one knows his place in society, his class position or social status, nor does any one know his fortune in the distribution of natural assets and abilities, his intelligence, strength, and the like. I shall even assume that the parties do not know their conceptions of the good or their special psychological propensities. The principles of justice are chosen behind a *veil of ignorance*. This ensures that no one is advantaged or disadvantaged in the choice of principles by the outcome of natural chance or the contingency of social circumstances. Since all are similarly situated and no one is able to design principles to favor his particular condition, the principles of justice are the result of a fair agreement or bargain.[60]

Of course, analyses carried out via Ho's framework or under cover of the Rawlsian veil are unlikely to be truly representative: they will always be shaped to some extent by the attitudes of the wielders. If these devices are predominantly employed by white, liberal, middle-class individuals, the results will disproportionately reflect white, liberal, middle-class world views. What the representative individual framework is very effective in stripping away, however, in common with its predecessors in the work of Mill, Harsanyi and Rawls, is *privilege*. This attribute is essential given the need to reflect the full range of voices and interests impacted by copyright policies. The representative individual might not be truly and universally representative, but, by stripping away privilege and its associated benefits, such as political strength, the framework at least enables fuller consideration to be given to the breadth of individual and group interests at play. Vested interests tend to dominate and distort policy thinking in copyright.[61] In thinking about what the law *should* be, *or would be if we designed it today*, it is clearly vital to divorce ourselves from such positions. If we want to think outside existing frameworks, we need to think in terms of policy goals rather than the tools or institutional or market structures we currently use to achieve those goals. This is of course easier said than done, but one of the main

---

60   John Rawls, *A Theory of Justice* (Belknap Press, 2005) 11–12 (emphasis added).
61   As Litman has observed, '[a]ny given copyright law will be more hospitable to some sorts of technological change than to others. Interests who find themselves, usually more by reason of accident than design, in a favorable legal position will naturally resist proposals to tinker with it'. Litman, above n 1, 36.

attractions of Ho's conception is that it does help to free the mind from self-interest and traditional ways of doing things, and ensure representation of a broader range of interests.

Like the preponderance, common interest and unitary conceptions of the public interest already identified, Ho's 'representative individual' approach requires some normative judgments to be made before the tool can be of any use. The representative individual would be unable to determine the best policy unless she knows broadly what she wants it to achieve. Before she designs a copyright policy, she needs to know whether she is trying to design a content creation and cultural/knowledge advancement copyright policy, a copyright policy for the protection and promotion of artist's inherent and inalienable interests in their creations, or something else altogether. To the extent that she has a combination of aims, she needs to understand their interrelationships with one another, and, to the extent that they're inconsistent, have an idea about how they should be subordinated to one another.

Although Ho is an economist, we do not read his formulation as limiting the representative individual's considerations to the purely economic. This would be a shortcoming indeed; conceptions of the public interest dominated by a focus on allocative efficiencies have been justly criticised for being too narrow.[62] Instead, the 'representative individual' could take into account any relevant moral, ethical or philosophical beliefs and considerations in determining whether any given policy is in the public interest. This is an essential feature when considering copyright policy, which is nowhere purely a creature of instrumentalism. The representative individual ought also be sufficiently generous and wise to include the interests of future generations in forming her view, something that existing process-based conceptions of the public interest do not necessarily take into account,[63] but which is vital given the impact of copyright policies on future generations.

---

62   See e.g. Feintuck, above n 9, 13–21; M Blitz, 'Public Interest' in NJ Smelser, James Wright and PB Baltes (eds), *International Encyclopedia of the Social & Behavioural Sciences* (Pergamon, June 2014) 12546. ('There are, however, limits to this perspective. They are evident in the narrowness of the economic view of the public when it is compared to other notions of what is potentially common in common goods.')
63   See e.g. Feintuck, above n 9, 13.

In summary, the above-described conceptions give guidance about various ways in which a copyright law that is actually in the public interest might be shaped:

1. by formulating it to be consistent with the *preponderance* of individual interests within a polity (which requires identifying where those interests lie, as well as how that preponderance is to be determined – by weight of numbers, political strength or some other factor);

2. by formulating it to be consistent with everyone's individual interests, or at least, as unanimously agreed by members of the polity (which requires the making of that same determination);

3. by formulating it to be 'valid', that is, morally justified (which assumes that moral validity is capable of determination – and of course, that determination of what is 'right' must depend on what is intended to be achieved);

4. by formulating it using a constructed, impartial *ex ante* perspective to determine the policy that maximises the public interest (which also requires determination of what the policy is intended to achieve).

What *do* we want copyright law to achieve?

The above analysis provides a vital lesson: that, regardless of which conception is adopted, it is impossible to argue sensibly that any copyright policy is in the public interest without explicitly identifying what it seeks to achieve. That sounds obvious, and in fields where policy aims are clear, presents few problems. Here, however, it leads us directly into what Alexander describes as copyright's 'heart of darkness: the justification for its existence'.[64]

Historical rationales for the grant of copyright can be broadly clustered into 'naturalist' and 'instrumentalist' theories. Instrumentalist approaches justify the grant of copyright as a way of achieving certain social and economic aims, such as the dissemination of knowledge and culture. In this view, copyright laws are justified only to the extent they further public interest considerations. By contrast, naturalist

---

64   Alexander, above n 14, 3.

approaches assume that authors have expansive rights over their creative outputs as of right. Those rights are most commonly explained as springing from the output being brought about by the author's labour (the Lockean approach) or because it is a materialisation of her personality (per Kant and Hegel). In these conceptions, 'the author acquires a property right in his work by virtue of the mere act of creation. This has the corollary that nothing is left to the law apart from formally recognising what is already inherent in the "very nature of things"'.[65]

At their extremes, the two approaches are fundamentally inconsistent. Instrumentalist justifications have public interest considerations squarely at the fore, while in naturalism the public's role is secondary.[66] One treats authors' rights as a means to an end, and the other as an end in and of themselves.

The reality is that considerations traceable to both rationales can be found alongside one another within both international treaties and domestic laws.[67] Countries operating within ostensibly instrumentalist traditions have often adopted policies that are clearly motivated by naturalist considerations, and vice versa.[68] For example, the US Constitution limits Congressional power to grant intellectual property rights to where it 'promote[s] the progress of science and the useful arts'.[69] But despite that express utilitarian focus, such considerations

---

65   Martin Senftleben, *Copyright, Limitations and the Three Step Test* (Kluwer Law International, 2004) 6.

66   Alexander, above n 14, 3; also Davies, above n 18, 171; Ricketson, above n 24, 753, 755. This perhaps explains why the copyright discourse so often conceptualises the 'public interest' in opposition to authors' interests.

67   See e.g Senftleben, above n 65, especially at 6–10; Alain Strowel, *Droit d'auteur et copyright, Divergences et Convergences* (Bruylant, 1993); Davies, above n 18, 348–351; Jerome Reichman, 'Duration of Copyright and the Limits of Cultural Policy' (1996) 14(3) *Cardozo Arts & Entertainment* 625, 643–644, Ricketson, above n 24, 753, 755.

68   As Senftleben argues, it's inaccurate to conceive of the two traditions, European and Anglo-American, as incompatible and separate. Instead, 'the two traditions of copyright law can be described as mixtures of a shared set of basic ideas derived from natural law theory and utilitarian notions alike': Senftleben, above n 65, 10.

69   *United States Constitution* Art IV § 8.

are not always given primacy.[70] Similarly, the European Copyright Directive, created in the heartland of continental naturalism, emphasises instrumentalist aims like 'foster[ing] substantial investment in creativity and innovation', which would 'lead in turn to growth and increased competitiveness of European industry', in order to 'safeguard employment and encourage new job creation'.[71] Multilateral treaties, too, contain elements of both: property rights accompanied by explicit mention of authors' moral rights and a term tied to the life of the author. It is not unusual for a particular policy to be explainable *only* through a combination of instrumentalist and naturalist approaches.[72]

This is not surprising. Extreme manifestations of the two dominant philosophical approaches are unattractive and unrealistic. A purely economic approach in which we aim for a legal system that gives the absolute minimum reward to creators to ensure an adequate level of culture and knowledge is just as difficult to swallow as an extreme conception of author's rights in which creators get total control and dominion over their creative products forever. The juxtaposition of rationales, uneasy as it may sometimes be, is inescapable.

Perhaps this is, ultimately, the argument for using, defining and defending the public interest as an organising principle for thinking about how we might reimagine copyright. Whatever conception of the public interest we use, at base, it is about recognising that we have an overall shared set of interests as a society beyond individual self-interest. In the copyright context, we have a shared interest in encouraging and supporting creativity; in recognising the rights and interests of creators, in a rich and accessible culture, and in technological and economic progress. We can and will differ on the

---

70   As Jaszi has observed, 'over the history of Anglo-American copyright, Romantic "authorship" has served the interests of publishers and other distributors surprisingly well': Peter Jaszi, 'On the Author effect: Contemporary Copyright and Collective Creativity' (1992) 10(2) *Cardozo Arts & Entertainment Law Journal* 293, 298. Goldstein also notes that '[w]hile congressional committees will episodically invoke the utilitarian rhetoric of cost and benefit, the legislative record in fact reveals a regular expansion of copyright with little empirical inquiry into a particular measure's costs and benefits'; Paul Goldstein, Aspen Publishers Inc., *Goldstein on Copyright*, 1.13.2.

71   *Directive 2001/29/EC of the European Parliament and of the Council of 22 May 2001 on the Harmonisation of Certain Aspects of Copyright and Related Rights in the Information Society* [2001] L 167/10, recital 4.

72   See e.g. Peter Drahos, *A Philosophy of Intellectual Property* (ANU Press, 2016) 96–97.

details of how to get there, but, in common with Ginsburg, we would argue that the public interest in copyright comprises the goals and aspirations of authors *and* users, of publishers *and* educators, and so forth.[73]

But still, in using this concept, it is important to avoid the pitfalls recognised in the philosophical literature above. Having recognised that all too often 'the public interest' either stands instead for one stakeholder or another, or worse, is simply used with no meaning at all, it is beholden on anyone undertaking a reimagining of any aspect of copyright 'in the public interest' to be explicit about how they are conceiving the public interest; the specific goals they are trying to achieve, and why their proposals are a good way of achieving them.

What could copyright law look like if we were not constrained by existing treaty obligations?

This book draws together a set of sometimes provocative imaginings for a public interest–furthering copyright law freed of the constraints of existing frameworks. In the contributions that follow, we and our international colleagues explore what copyright should hope to achieve, and imagine ways in which copyright frameworks could be redesigned to further those aims. Since they come from lawyers, these proposals will look different than those that would be put forward by sociologists, psychologists, creators or any other group. However, they are informed by a rich mixture of experience within a wide variety of copyright traditions and philosophies, and though grounded in law, benefit from significant expertise across such diverse fields as technology, economics, philosophy and international trade. The topics covered in the book span issues relating to subsistence, scope and duration of rights, how systems might better facilitate the remuneration of creators, whether and how copyright systems should incorporate formalities, how to solve problems of orphan works, what role copyright might have as a tool for achieving distributive

---

73 Ginsburg, above n 31, 4.

justice, and what enforcement mechanisms might look like in a world where the copyright's structural and institutional problems have been largely solved.

Sometimes the contributors fundamentally disagree. For example, the reader will find very different visions here of the role of copyright. De Beer imagines a copyright that is almost purely market facilitative, leaving other goals to be addressed elsewhere in the legal system. By contrast, Senftleben challenges the appropriateness of leaving so much to the market: copyright is often presented as being intended to serve the individual interests of creators, but the reality is that many creators (especially those identified as 'autonomous' in Bourdieu's sociological analysis) may never achieve a bargaining position that could allow them to effectively exploit their rights. Both Ncube and Geiger argue that copyright law itself must be framed more explicitly around social goals and dimensions. Ncube highlights the failure of existing market-based copyright systems to incentivise the production of works for economically disadvantaged language populations, arguing for the incorporation of distributive justice as a goal (something de Beer acknowledges is neglected by the market). Geiger argues for the centrality of copyright's role in enabling access to science and culture, through, for example, the recognition of explicit obligations for copyright holders and the recognition that users have rights.

Another area where our colleagues have disagreed relates to what should fall within the scope of the copyright system. In a chapter primarily dealing with subsistence, Reese argues for a relatively low threshold of creativity for protection, and puts a case that the legislature is the appropriate gatekeeper in deciding what forms of creativity warrant copyright protection, with categories as clearly expressed as possible (though technology neutral). Geiger, on the other hand, imagines a higher threshold for protection expressed as a standard rather than a rule: in which case judges might be the ones to decide whether given material is sufficiently creative to warrant protection, and granting it only if it will not unduly interfere with future creation nor cause unjustified harm to legitimate public interests such as cultural participation.

In various places the contributions touch upon similar issues. For example, Gangjee's contribution draws upon his expertise in registration-based trademark systems to flesh out how and why formalities could also help copyright. Giblin's chapter argues that we ought to disaggregate copyright's various goals in order to consider how they might best be achieved, and proposes an approach to duration that would not simply involve tinkering with term length, but would also need to integrate appropriate formalities (and compulsory licences and exceptions as well). Both Gangjee and Giblin suggest a kind of 'phased' copyright, with different rights (and obligations) at different points in the duration of copyright.

The importance of exceptions is addressed in a number of other chapters too. Ncube situates them as being essential in helping to rectify the failure of the market to produce a socially optimal amount of creative and informational works for neglected populations. Geiger and Senftleben both argue that some exceptions should be elevated to the status of user rights, with Geiger arguing that it is necessary to further copyright's essential access goals and Senftleben seeing certain rights of use as an essential part of the author's right to create. However, we made a deliberate choice not to incorporate a chapter focusing exclusively on exceptions. Though that is where the debate about where the public interest in copyright has long been centred, our intention is to highlight the wider public interest in other aspects of copyright. As Craig has persuasively argued, the public has interests vitally at stake in all aspects of drafting copyright law, and leaving public interest considerations until exceptions analyses – until a person has perhaps already been branded a free-rider and prima facie infringer – might well be leaving it too late.[74]

Each contribution adopts the unifying principle of the public interest, but here too there is rich divergence. Ncube and Reese adopt preponderance conceptions, defining the 'preponderance of interests' as one determined by sheer weight of numbers, rather than by political strength. Giblin takes Ho's representative individual and explores how that framework might change the way we think about duration policy. Weatherall adapts the representative individual approach in order to assess the public interest in copyright *enforcement*. Her chapter puts

---

74   Craig, above n 39, 425, 435–436.

the reader in the shoes of a public regulator tasked with ensuring appropriate enforcement of copyright and considers the tools and approaches such a regulator would take in order to promote the broader societal interest in copyright. Geiger argues that there is in fact a common interest in copyright – an interest shared by society at large. The contribution from Senftleben proceeds on the assumption that it is necessary to first identify the interests of authors in order to meaningfully develop a public interest-furthering copyright; Gangjee too sets about identifying a series of specific public goals that formalities can either promote or harm. The assumption underlying de Beer's chapter is that the proper functioning of the capitalist market economy is itself in the public interest, with additional nuance coming from his recognition that further mechanisms can be necessary to mitigate the potential distributive injustices of the free market.

At other times there is a convergence of goals or ideas (or at least common themes). A number of contributors, including Ncube, Giblin and Weatherall, emphasise the importance of serving the interests of individual creators, although this is most explicitly at the fore in Senftleben's detailed exploration of the question – what do authors really want? Another common theme is the importance of access, albeit from different directions. Ncube highlights the dearth of genuine access to literature in neglected languages. Weatherall imagines tying at least the use of public resources in enforcement to access, raising doubts about whether strong rights of enforcement ought to be available to right holders who have not made their creations accessible, at a reasonable price. Geiger is concerned with something similar, arguing that copyright should come with a positive duty to disseminate.

We welcome all of this contestation. The aim in this collection is not to attempt to compile a new proposed Copyright Act, or one single, coherent whole, but to present some alternative visions and some specific proposals and ideas across the full scope of the copyright system. The range of ideas here should encourage us to remove our blinkers, and to start thinking through broader possibilities for achieving copyright's aims.

There is, however, one thing that all of these chapters have very much in common. Namely, not one of the proposals that the reader will find in these chapters could actually be implemented, at least in full, given the constraints of the existing international legal framework. And that is precisely why this thought experiment and these ideas are important, right now – every one of these chapters illustrates what possibilities we lose when existing rules become set in concrete. We'll have some more to say about that in the conclusion.

2

Copyright, creators and society's need for autonomous art – the blessing and curse of monetary incentives

Martin Senftleben[1]

1. The field of literary and artistic production

Refining Niklas Luhmann's concept of relatively closed social systems with a distinct identity and a boundary between them and their environment,[2] Pierre Bourdieu developed the concept of 'fields' in society. Although constituting an autonomous social space with its own rules, dominance structures and established set of opinions, a field is not isolated from other social spaces and processes surrounding it. The structure of a field results from constant internal

---

1   PhD; Professor of Intellectual Property and Director, Kooijmans Institute for Law and Governance, VU University Amsterdam; Of Counsel, Bird & Bird, The Hague. I would like to thank Jeremy de Beer, Graeme Dinwoodie, Dev Gangjee, Christophe Geiger, Rebecca Giblin, Caroline Ncube, Tony Reese, Kimberlee Weatherall, Alexander Peukert and the participants of the workshop 'Social Science Approaches to Copyright' at the University of Frankfurt for their valuable comments on a previous draft.
2   N Luhmann, *Soziale Systeme: Grundriss einer allgemeinen Theorie*, (Suhrkamp, 1984).

fights of competing players for predominance and leadership.[3] A field's degree of autonomy, then, depends on the extent to which external players can influence these internal fights. External factors may have a deep impact on a field's constitution.[4] Given the continuous change of power relations, the structure of a social field is not static and fixed. By contrast, a field has its own history reflecting different stages of development – from the field's genesis as a social space with far-reaching autonomy to the potential loss of this autonomous position as a result of powerful external influences.[5] For the analysis of a given field, it is thus necessary to examine its relationship with the social environment in which it is embedded at a given point in time.

Applying this theoretical model to the field of literary and artistic production, Bourdieu assumes that the field's autonomy rests on the rejection of the capitalism of the bourgeoisie. The field of literature and art militates against the bourgeois logic of profit maximisation by developing its own, independent logic. This specific 'nomos' of the literary and artistic field lies in the independence from economic and political powers.[6] Instead of striving for commercial success, an autonomous literary or artistic production aims at internal recognition within the field. It emancipates itself from the focus on monetary success and honours awarded by the bourgeois society.[7] As a result of this nomos, the consecration mechanisms in the literary and artistic field – the power to set quality standards and dominate the internal discourse – become self-referential: *l'art pour l'art*. The field of literature and art becomes a universe countering the profit logic that impregnates the economic and political discourse. The break with the ruling powers constitutes the basis of an artist's independent, autonomous existence.[8] Autonomous literature and art is a provocation. It challenges the pervasive 'economism' in society.[9]

---

3   P Bourdieu, 'Die Logik der Felder' in P Bourdieu and LJD Wacquant (eds), *Reflexive Anthropologie* (Suhrkamp 1996) 124, 134–135; P Bourdieu, *Die Regeln der Kunst. Genese und Struktur des literarischen Feldes*, (Suhrkamp, 1999) (French original: P Bourdieu, *Les règles de l'art. Genèse et structure du champ littéraire*, (Éditions du Seuil, 1992)), 253–255, 368.

4   P Bourdieu, R Chartier and R Darnton, 'Dialog über die Kulturgeschichte' (1985) 26 *Freibeuter – Vierteljahreszeitschrift für Kultur und Politik* 22, 28.

5   Bourdieu, 'Die Logik der Felder', above n 2, 134; J Jurt, *Bourdieu* (Reclam, 2008) 91–92.

6   Bourdieu, *Die Regeln der Kunst*, above n 2, 103–105.

7   Ibid 344.

8   Ibid 105.

9   Ibid 342.

It follows from this configuration of the literary and artistic field that an artist seeking to gain recognition among peers must not align her work with the tastes of the masses and produce mainstream works in the hope of commercial success. This would be perceived as a concession to the predominant profit orientation of society. By contrast, the renunciation of commercial interests and the focus on the internal quality standards within the literary and artistic field testify to an artist's genuinely literary and artistic orientation. In consequence, the field generates a peculiar reverse economy. An artist can only win recognition in the field of literature and art by losing on the territory of monetary rewards: the one who loses (in economic terms), wins (in artistic terms).[10]

This reverse economy also determines the structure of the field of literature and art. As long as the field is autonomous, the highest positions will be held by those artists turning their back on the bourgeois economy and the prospect of commercial gains. The degree of the field's autonomy, in other words, depends on whether independent artists striving for recognition within the field (limited production for other independent artists), or dependent artists striving for recognition outside the field (mainstream production for the masses), hold the highest hierarchical positions.[11]

Accordingly, the fight for predominance and leadership in the literary and artistic field is a fight between autonomous/independent and bourgeois/dependent artists for the power to set quality standards and dictate the internal discourse.[12] The stronger the position of dependent, profit-oriented artists in this fight, the bigger the influence of external economic and political players on the structure of the literary and artistic field, and the lower the field's autonomy.[13]

On the basis of this analysis of the power relations in the literary and artistic field, Bourdieu paints an alarming picture of the field's current degree of autonomy. In the light of reduced state subsidies

---

10   Ibid 136, 344–345.
11   Ibid 344–345.
12   Ibid 198–203. Within the group of autonomous, independent artists, Bourdieu also describes a further fight between established artists presently holding the consecration and discourse power, and upcoming avant-garde artists challenging this established position: 198, 253–255, 379–380.
13   Ibid 344.

for cultural productions and the rise of culture sponsoring by enterprises, he warns of an increasing mutual penetration of the world of art and the world of money: more and more literary and artistic productions become subject to entrepreneurial marketing strategies and commercial pressures.[14] With the growing influence of external players and profit rationales, the distinction between autonomous, independent productions and commercial, dependent productions is increasingly blurred. To a growing extent, the profit logic of commercial productions also prevails in avant-garde works.[15] Therefore, the autonomy of the field of literature and art is currently at risk.[16]

2. The rationales of copyright revisited

In the light of this analysis, the role of copyright in the field of literary and artistic production seems ambiguous. Utilitarian copyright theory regards copyright as a vehicle to encourage the creation of literary and artistic works by providing an economic stimulus: the promise of monetary rewards is offered to authors as an incentive to create new works.[17] From the perspective of Bourdieu's analysis, this utilitarian incentive rationale is questionable. It may enhance the productivity of dependent artists who share the profit orientation of the bourgeois society. Artists following the specific *l'art pour l'art* nomos of the literary and artistic field, by contrast, are primarily interested in reputational rewards. They aim at recognition among peers. The incentive scheme underlying copyright law thus appears as a risk factor. It may entice autonomous artists away from the independent *l'art pour l'art* logic of the literary and artistic field.

---

14   Ibid 530.

15   Ibid 531.

16   Ibid 533.

17   FI Michelman, 'Property, Utility, and Fairness: Comments on the Ethical Foundations of "Just Compensation" Law' (1967) 80 *Harvard Law Review*, 165, 1211; SP Calandrillo, 'An Economic Analysis of Property Rights in Information: Justifications and Problems of Exclusive Rights, Incentives to Generate Information, and the Alternative of a Government-Run Reward System' (1998) 9 *Fordham Intellectual Property Media & Entertainment Law Journal*, 301, 310–312; PE Geller, 'Must Copyright Be For Ever Caught Between Marketplace and Authorship Norms?' in B Sherman and A Strowel, *Of Authors and Origins*, (Clarendon Press, 1994) 159, 159, 164–166.

The offer of copyright seems to be not only a bait to spur creativity but also an attempt to persuade autonomous artists to spend time and effort on the production of mainstream works.

A less critical picture can be drawn on the basis of the natural law argument. This copyright theory posits that the author acquires a property right in her work by virtue of the mere act of creation.[18] As the author spends time and effort on the creation of a work, it is deemed right and just to afford her the opportunity to reap the fruit of this creative labour.[19] Copyright law merely recognises formally what has already occurred in the course of the act of creation. This approach is less directly linked with an incentive scheme. Continental European *droit d'auteur* systems following the natural law approach do not only provide strong economic rights but also strong moral rights allowing an author to safeguard the unbreakable bond with her work as a materialisation of her personality.[20] Nonetheless, the concept of recognising copyright as a reward for creative labour leads to a comparable dilemma. It implies that the author derives financial benefits from the exclusive entitlement to exploit a work. This reward mechanism favours commercially exploitable productions. It seems tailored to the interests of profit-oriented, dependent artists. Autonomous authors striving for reputational rewards within their own community are less likely to create works that generate substantial royalty revenue. Accordingly, the exploitation opportunity secured by copyright law offers much less support for their creative efforts.

Finally, even the freedom of expression argument for copyright protection appears doubtful in the light of Bourdieu's analysis. According to this line of reasoning, copyright protection ensures authors' independence from any kind of patronage potentially seeking to restrict their freedom of expression. With the grant of copyright,

---

18   H Desbois, *Le droit d'auteur en France* (Dalloz, 2nd ed, 1978) 538; H Hubmann, 'Die Idee vom geistigen Eigentum, die Rechtsprechung des Bundesverfassungsgerichts und die Urheberrechtsnovelle von 1985' (1988) *Zeitschrift für Urheber- und Medienrecht* 4, 5.

19   FW Grosheide, *Auteursrecht op Maat*, (Kluwer, 1986) 128 (argument B).

20   As to continental European moral rights theory, see Geller, above n 16, 169–170; A Strowel, 'Droit d'auteur and Copyright: Between History and Nature' in B Sherman and A Strowel, *Of Authors and Origins* (Clarendon Press, 1994) 235, 236–237; B Edelman, 'The Law's Eye: Nature and Copyright' in B Sherman and A Strowel, *Of Authors and Origins* (Clarendon Press, 1994) 79, 82–87; E Ulmer, *Urheber- und Verlagsrecht* (Springer, 1980) 110–111. See Desbois 1978, above n 17, 538: 'L'auteur est protégé comme tel, en qualité de créateur, parce qu'un lien l'unit à l'objet de sa création.'

authors obtain the opportunity to exploit their works and acquire a source of income that is independent of patronage and other forms of sponsoring.[21] Truly independent authors in the sense of Bourdieu's analysis, however, aim at recognition among other independent authors who also renounce the profit orientation of the bourgeoisie. At the crucial early stage of a career in the area of literary and artistic production, the contribution of copyright to an autonomous artist's individual freedom of expression is thus likely to remain limited. In many cases, autonomous artists will have difficulty to derive substantial financial benefits from copyright protection. Dependent artists with a commercial mainstream orientation, by contrast, will have much less difficulty to generate a solid income. This bourgeois group of artists, however, follows market dictates anyway. Their production is not independent in the sense of the specific *l'art pour l'art* nomos of the literary and artistic field. Strictly speaking, market-oriented artists would not even need copyright to ensure freedom of patronage because they are not striving for independence of commercial influences in the first place. For autonomous artists requiring an extra income to keep their focus on independent productions, however, copyright has little to offer unless their fame within the group of autonomous artists allows them to translate this internal reputation into monetary rewards on the art market.

Hence, it seems difficult to reconcile the standard rationales of copyright protection with the maxim of *l'art pour l'art* in the field of literary and artistic production. By definition, monetary rewards cannot support autonomous artists in their efforts to gain recognition among their peers. Instead of supporting independent creations, the prospect of commercial exploitation is likely to further mainstream productions that may erode the autonomy of the literary and artistic field.[22]

---

21   NW Netanel, 'Copyright and a Democratic Civil Society' (1996) 106 *Yale Law Journal* 283, 288: 'Copyright supports a sector of creative and communicative activity that is relatively free from reliance on state subsidy, elite patronage, and cultural hierarchy.' For an in-depth analysis of this argument, see generally NW Netanel, *Copyright's Paradox* (Oxford University Press, 2008).
22   With regard to the impact of continuous expansions of copyright on different kinds of creation strategies, see also Y Benkler, 'Free as the Air to Common Use: First Amendment Constraints on Enclosure of the Public Domain' (1999) 74 *New York University Law Review* 354.

The corrosive effect of this configuration of copyright law must not be underestimated. In particular, it would be wrong to assume that the group of autonomous artists and the impact of the problem are only marginal. Bourdieu's analysis – distinguishing between autonomous artists creating art for art's sake and bourgeois artists seeking to make money – is a theoretical model that Bourdieu developed to shed light on the power relations in the field of literary and artistic productions. His strict theoretical distinction between two prototypes of creators, however, need not be applied with the same rigidity when examining real-life implications of the incentives offered in copyright law.

In reality, creators are not unlikely to strive for both monetary and reputational rewards. To varying degrees, creators of flesh and blood are not unlikely to display characteristics of both independent, autonomous artists and market-oriented, bourgeois artists. The central question, then, is whether a creator's profit orientation is so strong that she is prepared to compromise her own aesthetic (scientific, journalistic, etc.) convictions when this is necessary to derive more profit from a work.

Once this more practical standard is applied, a creator can be qualified as autonomous as long as her interest in sufficient monetary rewards does not corrupt her aesthetic (scientific, journalistic, etc.) convictions and does not dilute her genuine, artistic expression. Viewed from this broader, more practical perspective, Bourdieu's analysis brings to light a core problem of copyright law – a problem that does not remain limited to marginal side effects on a specific group of creators and a small fraction of literary and artistic productions. Bourdieu's theory raises the general question of the desired degree of autonomous aesthetic (scientific, journalistic, etc.) expression in literary and artistic works. How truthful are literary and artistic productions that benefit from the incentive scheme of copyright law?

Arguably, copyright law should not only be in favour of profit-oriented mainstream productions. It should also encourage artists to cultivate their own, independent way of expressing themselves – without interference of market dictates. Hence, the examination of copyright law in the light of Bourdieu's analysis must not end here. It would be wrong to jump to the conclusion that copyright has nothing to offer autonomous art and artists. From the perspective of economic theory, it is even indispensable to explore copyright's potential to contribute to the production of autonomous literature and art. At the core of the incentive rationale in copyright law lies the economic insight that literary and artistic works constitute 'public goods'. Because of non-rivalry in consumption[23] and non-excludability in use,[24] they are unlikely to be created in sufficient quantities in the absence of appropriate incentives.[25] The grant of intellectual property rights, however, is only one strategy for providing the required incentives. A system of public subsidies could solve the problem as well.[26] As pointed out by Bourdieu, this alternative solution of state subsidies is currently unavailable. Therefore, the remaining option of recalibrating the copyright system in a way that strengthens the autonomy of literature and art is of central importance. To safeguard the autonomy of the field, copyright law should become an engine of autonomous *l'art pour l'art* productions.

Before embarking on a survey of potential measures seeking to achieve this goal on the basis of copyright law, however, it is necessary to explain why this recalibration of the copyright system is desirable from the perspective of society as a whole. The proposal of introducing a bias in favour of autonomous literature and art in copyright law lacks power of persuasion in the absence of a clear indication of benefits for society. Therefore, the question arises how a recalibration of copyright law in favour of autonomous literary and artistic productions can be justified. The aesthetic theories of Friedrich Schiller and Theodor Adorno yield important insights in this respect.

3. Need for a bias in favour of autonomous literature and art

While Schiller sees works of art as catalysts paving the way for an ethical and free society (as discussed in section 3.1), Adorno describes the task of art to challenge reality and suggest necessary societal changes (3.2). Against this background, it becomes apparent

---

23   Use by one actor does not restrict the ability of another actor to benefit as well.

24   Unauthorised parties ('free riders') cannot be prevented from use.

25   WW Fisher, 'Reconstructing the Fair Use Doctrine' (1988) 101 *Harvard Law Review* 1659, 1700; WM Landes and RA Posner, 'An Economic Analysis of Copyright Law' (1989) 18 *Journal of Legal Studies* 325, 326; Netanel, *Copyright's Paradox*, above n 20, 84–85.

26   RA Posner, 'Intellectual Property: The Law and Economics Approach' (2005) 19 *Journal of Economic Perspectives* 57, 58–59; Calandrillo, above n 16, 310–312.

that a copyright system focusing on the furtherance of autonomous literature and art is of particular importance. It functions as an engine of alternative visions of society that can serve as a reference point for necessary changes of social and political conditions (3.3).

3.1. Schiller's aesthetic theory

Disillusioned by the French Revolution, which had culminated in chaos and violence instead of leading to a free and equal society, Schiller wrote his letters about mankind's aesthetic education to explore the possibility of a transition from an absolutist, authoritarian state to a purified, ethical state that is founded on human reason.[27] As a precondition for this transition, Schiller emphasises the need to harmonise human desires with the rules of reason. As it is not the destiny of mankind to renounce its natural senses in favour of moral laws,[28] support for an ethical, reasonable state must come from the totality of human dispositions: desire and reason alike. Individuals should not only feel an obligation to follow the rules of reason, they should feel a desire to do so. If human desires are brought in line with the postulates of reason, a revolution will no longer end in chaos and violence. It will lead to the establishment of a moral state instead.[29]

To align human desires with the rules of reason, a catalyst is required that brings moral laws not only to people's heads but also to their hearts. Schiller solves this problem by positing that art can serve as such a catalyst. Even though incapable of changing mankind directly, art can point the way to a change for the better by focusing people's thoughts on the 'necessary and eternal', and make them strive for this ideal.[30] Art is predestined to accomplish this task because it satisfies the desire to play and enjoy. Instead of openly criticising people's actions and attitudes, art can improve society in a subtle way by making visions of ethical behaviour part of people's play and pleasure:

---

27 F Schiller, *Über die ästhetische Erziehung des Menschen*, edited by KL Berghahn, (Reclam, 2000) 11–14 [Letter 3].

28 Ibid 28 [Letter 6].

29 Ibid 120–121 [Letter 27].

30 Ibid 36 [Letter 9].

> In vain will you combat their maxims, in vain will you condemn their
> actions; but you can try your moulding hand on their leisure. Drive
> away caprice, frivolity, and coarseness, from their pleasures, and you
> will banish them imperceptibly from their acts, and length from their
> feelings. Everywhere that you meet them, surround them with great,
> noble, and ingenious forms; multiply around them the symbols of
> perfection, till appearance triumphs over reality, and art over nature.[31]

Schiller relies on art as a vehicle to let people experience an ideal
balance between desire and reason until they finally orient their
actions by moral laws instead of following mere physical necessities.
A person succumbing to a temptation while knowing that it is against
the rules of reason feels overpowered by nature. A person fulfilling
a moral obligation in spite of inner resistance feels forced by reason.
The aesthetic play, however, reconciles reason with desire, neutralises
physical and moral constraints and, in consequence, allows mankind
to enjoy full freedom.[32] It enables the individual to experience a state
of perfection in which neither the power of nature nor the postulates
of reason restrict possible courses of action: in the aesthetic play,
mankind experiences humanity in its entirety.[33]

A true work of art is capable of evoking this equilibrium between
reason and desire, and this freedom of the mind through appearances
of beauty that neither reflect nor require reality.[34] To accomplish this
task, the artist must not be a protégé of her time. She must leave the
realm of reality behind and employ the techniques of art to depict
a vision of the ultimate ideal.[35] In Schiller's view, the experience
and enjoyment of this ultimate perfection can pave the way for the
establishment of a moral society in which individual freedom no
longer follows from the restriction of the freedom of others but from
a consensus on ethical norms that corresponds with people's desires
– as refined in the aesthetic play.[36] An individual driven by physical
necessity must first experience beauty – the aesthetical balance

---

31   Ibid 37 [Letter 9, English translation taken from: 'Literary and Philosophical essays: French,
German and Italian. With Introductions and Notes', *The Harvard Classics*, vol 32, (Collier, 1910)
available at the Internet Modern History Sourcebook: <legacy.fordham.edu/halsall/mod/schiller-
education.asp>].

32   Schiller, above n 26, 57–58 [Letter 14].

33   Ibid 60–64 [Letter 15] and 105–106 [Letter 25].

34   Ibid 111–112 [Letter 26].

35   Ibid 34–35 [Letter 9].

36   Ibid 120–121 [Letter 27].

between desire and rules of reason – before she can actively and freely opt for moral norms and moral actions.[37] It is thus the task of art to prepare mankind for the transition from the physical state of desire to the moral state of reason.[38]

3.2. Adorno's aesthetic theory

In his aesthetic theory, Theodor Adorno also underlines the societal relevance of art. Against the background of the alienation which the individual faces in a fully rationalised, efficiency-driven world, he warns of the affirmative nature of art. An artwork bringing a conciliatory reflection of enchantment into the disenchanted, empirical reality offers comfort in the rationalised world and supports the unbearable status quo.[39] In the light of the inhumanity of the real world, art would make itself an accomplice of present and coming disasters if it sustained positive visions of society and obscured the defects and poorness of reality.[40] With the prospect of a better world that, as an ultimate truth,[41] shimmers through each genuine artwork,[42] art may falsely pretend that existing societal conditions are acceptable. Therefore, art is constantly at risk of becoming guilty of supporting the inhuman *status quo* and fortifying present ideologies.[43]

On the other hand, art must not be condemned altogether as long as true art is capable of unmasking the negativity of present societal conditions. Showing visions of a better, happier life, art can rouse opposition against the existing reality and contribute to necessary societal changes.[44] True art can play a decisive role in society because it generates utopian views of a better life that may become drivers of a change for the better. This role of authentic art defines its social character: art is the 'social antithesis' of society.[45] Given this delicate position in the social fabric of modern societies, there is a fine line to be walked: the artist must relentlessly expose the inhumanity of reality

---

37   Ibid 90–91 [Letter 23].
38   Ibid 92 [Letter 23].
39   TW Adorno, *Ästhetische Theorie*, edited by G Adorno and R Tiedemann, (Suhrkamp, 1970) 10, 34.
40   Ibid 28, 503.
41   Ibid 128, 196–197.
42   Ibid 199–200.
43   Ibid 203.
44   Ibid 25–26, 56.
45   Ibid 9–10, 19, 53.

without offering any prospect of reconciliation. In doing so, the artist creates genuine works that, by their very nature, offer shining visions of a better life and a better society in spite of the hopelessness reflected in the artworks themselves.[46] As an antithesis of the total disaster in the real world, art becomes the messenger of an ideal, utopian world.[47]

There is thus an inescapable dualism in contemporary authentic art: the sadness of presenting a happier life as a goal that remains unattainable under present societal conditions.[48] To accomplish this task, art must seek to escape tendencies to undermine and neutralise its critical and irrational impetus, such as the efforts of the cultural industry to commercialise and canonise even the most rebellious and resistant works.[49] Reacting to the growing demand for enchantment in the disenchanted, rationalised reality,[50] the cultural industry offers artworks as consumer goods – abstract objects that function as a *tabula rasa* into which the bourgeois purchaser can project her own feelings and aspirations.[51] As a result, an artwork becomes an echo and confirmation of the viewer's own hopes and attitudes. It becomes an escape from the unbearable real world. This, however, leads to the 'disartification' of art. Once it is consumed as an object of pleasure that offers comfort in an inhuman world, its critical impetus – the exposure of the ugliness of reality as an impulse for societal changes – is negated. The purchaser who only projects her own aspirations into the artwork can no longer experience the underlying truth. Instead of assimilating oneself to the artwork and exploring its genuine meaning,[52] a person consuming a work of art as an object for the projection of her own emotions only seeks to ignore the shameful difference between the utopia shimmering through the artwork and the poorness of her own life.[53] Instead of seeing the artwork as a subject and disappearing in the utopian vision of a radical change of society offered by the artwork,[54] the art consumer simply annexes the artwork to other objects of possession and deprives it of its genuine meaning by replacing the

---

46   Ibid 127, 199.
47   Ibid 55–56.
48   Ibid 204–205.
49   Ibid 32.
50   Ibid 34.
51   Ibid 33.
52   Ibid 27–28.
53   Ibid 32.
54   Ibid 27.

unpleasant critique of the empirical reality with her own projections. The cultural industry initiates and exploits this process leading to the neutralisation of art.[55]

To escape this threat of disqualification, art must insist on its difference and autonomy by refusing claims for rule obedience and resisting the temptation to fulfil societal expectations. It must preserve its opposition and dissonance by producing works of a non-identical and fragmentary nature that negate the unity of traditional productions, fall outside aesthetical categories and bring chaos in the established order.[56] To mirror the ugliness and futility of present society in an authentic way, artworks must become ugly and futile themselves. The world of art must become a closed counter universe: the last refuge of humanity in an inhuman world that is disfigured by deal and profit maxims.[57] Remaining alien to the world, true art, by definition, is puzzling and gives rise to conflicting interpretations based on internal tension in the work or its connection to conflicts in society.[58] For the final resolution of these tensions and conflicts, society as a whole would have to be transformed. It would have to decipher the contradictions reflected in authentic works of art and extrapolate the underlying ultimate truth that is expressed by simultaneously challenging reality and suggesting improvements.[59]

3.3. Importance of autonomous art

By no means do these two aesthetic theories exhaust the possibilities of describing the role of autonomous literary and artistic productions in society. Nonetheless, the two examples of an assessment of the societal relevance of independent art already show that by presenting alternative visions of society, art can play a crucial role in the improvement of social and political conditions. Providing this additional insight, Schiller's and Adorno's aesthetic theories – despite obvious conceptual differences – offer answers to questions that go beyond Bourdieu's description of the field of literary and artistic production. With the outlined aesthetic theories, Bourdieu's analysis

---

55   Ibid 33.
56   Ibid 41.
57   Ibid 337–338.
58   Ibid 197–198.
59   Ibid 55, 193–196.

can be supplemented with an assessment of the value and importance of artworks for society as a whole: what would be lost if the field of literary and artistic production was no longer autonomous? If it were dominated by commercial considerations? If literature and art did no longer follow its own, independent logic – its 'nomos' of self-referential *l'art pour l'art*?

Considering Schiller's and Adorno's theories, the answer to these questions lies in the potential of art to mirror shortcomings of present society and raise a desire for changes for the better. As an independent, autonomous observer, the artist is capable of depicting alternatives to an insufficient and unacceptable reality. An artwork can unmask defects of existing societal conditions and prepare society for the transition to a better community. Once the field of literary and artistic production loses its autonomy, this constant challenge of reality and indispensable training for a better world would be lost. Society would remain in a lamentable state of imperfection without the impulses necessary to improve the situation. Hence, there is substantial reason to recalibrate copyright law and make it an engine of autonomous, independent works of true art in the sense of Schiller's and Adorno's theories.

4. Recalibration of copyright law

Given the threat to the autonomy of literature and art that follows from the reduction of state subsidies for independent productions, copyright law must take a position in the fight between autonomous/independent and bourgeois/dependent authors for predominance, leadership and consecration power in the literary and artistic field. It must seek to support autonomous art productions in order to preserve the autonomy of the field and its potential to generate alternative visions of society that can pave the way for necessary social and political changes. This need to recalibrate copyright law leads to the question: which features of the system are of particular importance to autonomous artists following the *l'art pour l'art* nomos of the literary and artistic field? The aforementioned moral rights of authors, including the right of attribution and the right to prevent derogatory actions,[60] can serve as a first example of rules that may be of particular relevance to autonomous authors seeking to preserve the integrity of their artistic creations. Commercially oriented authors may have less difficulty to accept modifications of their works as long as they increase exploitation revenues.

Other copyright rules that offer support for autonomous productions enter the picture once Bourdieu's description of fights for power and predominance within the community of autonomous artists is taken into consideration. Apart from the competition between autonomous and bourgeois artists that defines the level of autonomy of the literary and artistic field as a whole, Bourdieu also describes internal fights within the group of autonomous artists. This description shows that freedom to transform pre-existing works is essential to the constant evolution of new avant-garde movements (4.1).

In the light of decreasing state subsidies, copyright law must also ensure a redirection of money flows within the field of literary and artistic productions – a redirection in favour of autonomous *l'art pour l'art* productions. Therefore, it is necessary to also reconsider and refine remuneration mechanisms within the copyright system. A first question arising in this context concerns the introduction of a right to fair remuneration that can be invoked in the context of contractual agreements about the exploitation of literary and artistic works (4.2). As autonomous artists may have difficulty to find a publisher, producer or art gallery willing to invest in their works, however, a direct redistribution of copyright revenue in favour of autonomous literature and art must also be considered (4.3).

4.1. Recognition of a right to transformative use

According to Bourdieu's analysis, newcomers in the community of autonomous artists can only establish a new school of thought by rebelling against the rules established by the generation of autonomous artists that is presently in power. The new generation must challenge existing convictions to obtain the power to set its own

---

60   See the international recognition of moral rights in Berne Convention, article 6*bis*. As to the recognition of these rights in Anglo-American countries, see G Dworkin, 'The Moral Right of the Author: Moral Rights and the Common Law Countries' (1995) 19 *Columbia-VLA Journal of Law & the Arts*, 229.

quality standards and dictate the discourse. It must degrade the ruling avant-garde to an arrière-garde.[61] The constant evolution of fresh, autonomous avant-garde productions thus depends on mechanisms that allow new generations of autonomous authors to legitimise their unorthodox, new approach by criticising the dogmata of the predominant school of thought.

For a new generation to challenge the leading avant-garde, it must detect the structural gaps within the texture of already known aesthetic positions. It must formulate an alternative artistic position in the light of the weaknesses and contradictions of the present state of the art.[62] The room between the positions that have already been taken in the literary and artistic field thus constitute potential starting points for an artistic revolution.

Copyright law can support this constant process of renewal within the group of autonomous artists by guaranteeing certain user freedoms.[63] To be capable of challenging established positions, an autonomous artist must be free to dissociate herself from the dogmata set forth by her predecessors. The law can thus enable a new generation of artists to destruct an established order and erect a new one by exempting the use of protected, pre-existing works for the formulation of a new aesthetic position. The idea/expression dichotomy[64] ensures that the ideas and concepts underlying literary and artistic works remain free for this purpose. The freedom to refer to earlier creations, for example in quotations and parodies,[65] allows a new generation to criticise the currently prevailing school of thought. In this way, new autonomous

---

61   Bourdieu, above n 2, 253–255.

62   Ibid 372.

63   For a discussion of Bourdieu's approach in the context of identifying patterns of permissible fair use in the sense of US legislation, see MJ Madison, 'A Pattern-Oriented Approach to Fair Use' (2004) 45 *William and Mary Law Review* 1525, 1627–1642.

64   *Marrakesh Agreement Establishing the World Trade Organization*, opened for signature 15 April 1994, 1867 UNTS 3 (entered into force 1 January 1995), annex 1C (*Agreement on Trade-Related Aspects of Intellectual Property Rights*) ('TRIPS'), Art 9(2); *World Intellectual Property Organization Copyright Treaty* ('WIPO Copyright Treaty'), opened for signature 20 December 1996, 36 ILM 65, entered into force 6 March 2002, Art 2.

65   See the international recognition of the right of quotation in Berne Convention, article 10(1). As to the inclusion of parody in this broad quotation concept, see AA Quaedvlieg, 'De parodiërende nabootsing als een bijzondere vorm van geoorloofd citaat' (1987) *RM Themis*, 279. For an example of the development of the right of quotation in a national copyright system, see MRF Senftleben, 'Quotations, Parody and Fair Use' in PB Hugenholtz, AA Quaedvlieg and DJG Visser (eds), *A Century of Dutch Copyright Law – Auteurswet 1912–2012* (deLex, 2012) 359, online available at <ssrn.com/abstract=2125021>.

artists can demarcate their new position from previous ones. They can lay the foundations for a new avant-garde movement by defining their own position in relation to pre-existing works.

Apart from the freedom to use and criticise pre-existing works in the process of defining and demarcating a new aesthetic position, Bourdieu's analysis highlights a further freedom of use that is crucial to the process of constant renewal in the area of autonomous *l'art pour l'art* productions. To allow a new generation of autonomous authors to formulate a new aesthetic position, these newcomers must first learn of the positions that have already been taken by previous independent artists. Unless they master the history of their particular art and know the heritage of former generations of artists, they are inhibited from detecting structural gaps that allow them to take a legitimate and plausible next step in the evolution of literary and artistic productions.[66] Therefore, the guarantee of freedom to use pre-existing material for the creation of new avant-garde works is only one way in which copyright law can support the process of aesthetic renewal. In addition, copyright law can support the evolution of new avant-garde movements by exempting the use of existing works for educational purposes and private study – exemptions that allow new generations of autonomous artists to explore the cultural landscape and find starting points for the articulation of new positions that challenge and supersede established convictions.

Hence, freedom to learn of pre-existing works and freedom to use and criticise them for the purpose of establishing a new avant-garde movement are of particular importance to authors with an autonomous, independent orientation.[67] This insight necessitates a change in the understanding of the rights to be guaranteed in copyright law. In fact, the term 'copyright' as such becomes doubtful and appears misleading. 'Copyright' must not content itself with safeguarding an author's

---

66   Bourdieu, above n 2, 385.
67   It must not be overlooked in this context that Bourdieu's analysis – with the two poles of purely bourgeois authors on one side of the spectrum, and purely autonomous authors on the other – is a theoretical model. The conclusion drawn here, accordingly, is based on this strict theoretical distinction between the two groups. In reality, creators of both camps are not unlikely to appreciate the existence of both rights and freedoms to varying degrees. Depending on their individual position between the two poles of purely bourgeois and purely autonomous authors, they will attach more importance to exploitation rights than user freedoms and *vice versa*. For an analysis of copyright law as an engine of cultural diversity that supports this assumption, see Netanel, *Copyright's Paradox*, above n 20, 195–199; Benkler, above n 21, 400–412.

exploitation interests. This traditional concept of exclusive rights focuses on the profit orientation of bourgeois authors and the creative industry. However, it neglects the dependence of autonomous artists on freedom to use pre-existing works for the purpose of developing a new avant-garde. Therefore, the concept of authors' rights must be extended to use privileges: a right to make transformative use.[68] The present copyright system already complies with this broader conception of authors' rights when drawing a boundary line between protected individual expression on the one hand, and unprotected ideas and concepts on the other.[69]

However, the outlined broader concept of authors' rights, including a right of transformative use, challenges the approach to limitations of exclusive exploitation rights in the present copyright system. Insofar as broad, flexible exploitation rights are regarded as the rule, and limitations of these rights are perceived as exceptions that must be construed and applied restrictively,[70] the envisaged broader concept of authors' rights requires substantial changes:[71] use privileges supporting the creative destruction of works, such as the exemption of quotations and parodies, must not be qualified as copyright limitations in the first place. They are an author's right to criticise pre-existing literary and artistic expression to create room for the formulation of a new artistic position. Hence, certain use privileges that are seen as copyright limitations in the present system would have to be redefined as authors' rights[72] to avoid an impediment of the process of creative destruction in the area of autonomous literary and artistic productions.

---

68   Transformative use is understood here in the sense of a productive use that aims to employ a protected work in a different manner or for a different purpose, such as the critique of the work or its adaptation to achieve a different artistic effect. It is use transforming the original in new information, new aesthetics, new insights and understandings. For a similar concept developed in the context of the US fair use doctrine, see PN Leval, 'Toward a Fair Use Standard' (1990) 103 *Harvard Law Review* 1105, 1111.

69   Art 9(2) TRIPS; Art 2 WIPO Copyright Treaty.

70   This traditional dogma of the restrictive interpretation of copyright limitations can be found, for instance, in EU copyright systems. For instance, see *Infopaq International v Danske Dagblades Forening* (CJEU, C-5/08, 16 July 2009) [56]–[58].

71   On the basis of similar considerations, C Geiger, 'Promoting Creativity through Copyright Limitations: Reflections on the Concept of Exclusivity in Copyright Law' (2010) 12 *Vanderbilt Journal of Entertainment and Technology Law* 515, 532–533, argues for introducing a wider limitation for creative uses and converting traditional exploitation rights to prohibit the use of copyrighted works into a right to receive a fair remuneration.

72   Cf C Geiger, 'Die Schranken des Urheberrechts im Lichte der Grundrechte – Zur Rechtsnatur der Beschränkungen des Urheberrechts' in RM Hilty and A Peukert, *Interessenausgleich im*

Interestingly, international copyright law can serve as a point of departure for this redefinition. With regard to quotations, the Berne Convention, in its prevailing French version,[73] states: '[s]ont licites les citations tirées d'une œuvre ...'.[74] This formulation can be understood as an obligation of Berne Union members to exempt quotations from the control of the owner of copyright in the underlying work. A mere option to limit copyright in certain respects is expressed differently in the Convention: '[e]st réservée aux législations des pays de l'Union la faculté de permettre ...'.[75] The English text confirms this analysis. Stating that '[i]t shall be permissible to make quotations from a work ...', the English version leaves little doubt about the nature of the quotation right. The exemption is mandatory and not optional. If parody is qualified as a particular species of quotation,[76] it also falls within the scope of this guarantee of a right to transformative use in the Berne Convention.

In spite of this international framework, the use privilege of making quotations and parodies is still qualified and treated as a regular copyright limitation in national copyright laws. EU legislation, for instance, does not make it clear that the adoption of the right of quotation and the right of parody is mandatory for all member states.[77] Moreover, the EU legislator saw no need to ensure that these rights prevail over the protection of technological protection measures,[78] and escape further scrutiny in the light of the three-step test.[79]

Urheberrecht (Nomos, 2004) 143, 147–150; MRF Senftleben, 'Die Bedeutung der Schranken des Urheberrechts in der Informationsgesellschaft und ihre Begrenzung durch den Dreistufentest' in RM Hilty and A Peukert, *Interessenausgleich im Urheberrecht* (Nomos, 2004) 159, 167–170.

73   According to Berne Convention, Art 37(1)(c), the French text prevails in case of differences of opinion on the interpretation of the various language versions.

74   Berne Convention, Art 10(1).

75   This formulation is used in Berne Convention, Arts 9(2), 10(2) 10*bis*(1) and (2).

76   In this sense Quaedvlieg, above n 64, 285, 288; Senftleben, above n 64, 363.

77   In contrast to the mandatory exemption of transient copying in Art 5(1) of the Information Society Directive 2001/29, the adoption of Art 5(3)(d) and (k) of the Directive is not mandatory.

78   By contrast, Art 6(4) of the Information Society Directive 2001/29 fails to shield the right of quotation and the right of parody from the potential corrosive effect of technological protection measures.

79   Art 5(5) of the Information Society Directive 2001/29. For a discussion of the role of the three-step test in EU copyright law, see MRF Senftleben, 'Comparative Approaches to Fair Use: An Important Impulse for Reforms in EU Copyright Law' in GB Dinwoodie (ed) *Methods and Perspectives in Intellectual Property* (Edward Elgar, 2013) 30; J Griffiths, 'The "Three-Step Test" in European Copyright Law – Problems and Solutions' (2009) *Intellectual Property Quarterly*, 489; C Geiger, 'The Three-Step Test, a Threat to a Balanced Copyright Law?' (2006) *International Review of Intellectual Property and Competition Law*, 683. As to guidelines for the

According to article 13 of the *Agreement on Trade-Related Aspects of Intellectual Property Rights* (TRIPS) and article 10 of the *World Intellectual Property Organization Copyright Treaty* (WIPO Copyright Treaty), the scope of the three-step test is confined to limitations imposed on the exclusive rights of copyright owners:

> Members shall confine limitations or exceptions to exclusive rights to certain special cases which do not conflict with a normal exploitation of the work and do not unreasonably prejudice the legitimate interests of the right holder.[80]

The redefinition of the exemption of quotations and parody as an author's right to transformative use would thus have the effect of excluding these use privileges from the ambit of operation of the three-step test altogether. However, existing copyright statutes, such as EU copyright legislation, do not support this more comprehensive conception of authors' rights.

---

appropriate application of the test, see C Geiger, J Griffiths and RM Hilty, 'Declaration on a Balanced Interpretation of the "Three-Step Test" in Copyright Law' (2008) *International Review of Intellectual Property and Competition Law*, 707; Senftleben, above n 64.

80   Art 13 TRIPS. The provision was modelled on the first three-step test in international copyright law enshrined in Berne Convention, Art 9(2). After the TRIPS Agreement, the test reappeared in Art 10 WIPO Copyright Treaty. For a discussion of the test's development in international copyright law and its interpretation by WTO Panels, see C Geiger, D Gervais and MRF Senftleben, 'The Three-Step Test Revisited: How to Use the Test's Flexibility in National Copyright Law' (2014) 29 *American University International Law Review*, 581; D Gervais, 'Fair Use, Fair Dealing, Fair Principles: Efforts to Conceptualize Exceptions and Limitations to Copyright' (2009–2010) 57 *Journal of the Copyright Society of the U.S.A.* 499, 510–511; A Kur, 'Of Oceans, Islands, and Inland Water – How Much Room for Exceptions and Limitations Under the Three-Step Test?' (2009) 8 *Richmond Journal of Global Law and Business* 287, 307–308; MRF Senftleben, 'Towards a Horizontal Standard for Limiting Intellectual Property Rights? – WTO Panel Reports Shed Light on the Three-Step Test in Copyright Law and Related Tests in Patent and Trademark Law' (2006) 37 *International Review of Intellectual Property and Competition Law* 407; S Ricketson and JC Ginsburg, *International Copyright and Neighbouring Rights – The Berne Convention and Beyond* (Oxford University Press, 2006) 759–763; Senftleben, above n 64, 43–244; M Ficsor, 'How Much of What? The Three-Step Test and Its Application in Two Recent WTO Dispute Settlement Cases' (2002) 192 *Revue Internationale du Droit d'Auteur*, 111; J Oliver, 'Copyright in the WTO: The Panel Decision on the Three-Step Test' (2002) 25 *Columbia Journal of Law and the Arts*, 119; DJ Brennan, 'The Three-Step Test Frenzy: Why the TRIPS Panel Decision might be considered Per Incuriam' (2002) *Intellectual Property Quarterly* 213; J Reinbothe and S von Lewinski, *The WIPO Treaties 1996 – The WIPO Copyright Treaty and the WIPO Performances and Phonograms Treaty – Commentary and Legal Analysis* (Butterworths, 2002); M Ficsor, *The Law of Copyright and the Internet – The 1996 WIPO Treaties, their Interpretation and Implementation* (Oxford University Press, 2002); J Ginsburg, 'Toward Supranational Copyright Law? The WTO Panel Decision and the "Three-Step Test" for Copyright Exceptions' (2001) 190 *Revue Internationale du Droit d'Auteur* 13.

Nonetheless, the courts may provide considerable breathing space for certain forms of transformative use, in particular quotations and parody. In the decision *Infopaq/DDF*, the Court of Justice of the European Union (CJEU) adhered to the traditional dogma of a strict interpretation of copyright limitations. Scrutinising the mandatory exemption of transient copies in article 5(1) of the Information Society Directive (ISD),[81] the Court pointed out that for the interpretation of each of the cumulative conditions of the limitation, it should be borne in mind:

> that, according to settled case-law, the provisions of a directive which derogate from a general principle established by that directive must be interpreted strictly … This holds true for the exemption provided for in Article 5(1) of Directive 2001/29, which is a derogation from the general principle established by that directive, namely the requirement of authorisation from the rightholder for any reproduction of a protected work.[82]

According to the Court:

> [t]his is all the more so given that the exemption must be interpreted in the light of Article 5(5) of Directive 2001/29, under which that exemption is to be applied only in certain special cases which do not conflict with a normal exploitation of the work or other subject-matter and do not unreasonably prejudice the legitimate interests of the rightholder.[83]

---

81 Directive 2001/29/EC of the European Parliament and of the Council of 22 May 2001, on the harmonisation of certain aspects of copyright and related rights in the information society [2001] OJ L 167, 10.

82 *Infopaq International v Danske Dagblades Forening* (CJEU, C-5/08, 16 July 2009) [56]–[57].

83 Ibid [58].

The CJEU thus established the rule that copyright limitations had to be construed narrowly. In *Football Association Premier League*, however, this decision did not hinder the Court from emphasising with regard to the same exemption – transient copying in the sense of article 5(1) ISD – the need to guarantee the proper functioning of the limitation and ensure an interpretation that takes due account of the exception's objective and purpose. The Court explained that, in spite of the required strict interpretation, the effectiveness of the limitation had to be safeguarded.[84] On the basis of these considerations, the Court concluded that the transient copying at issue in *Football Association Premier League*, performed within the memory of a satellite decoder and on a television screen, was compatible with the three-step test of article 5(5) ISD.[85]

For the purposes of the present inquiry, it is of particular interest that in *Painer/Der Standard*, the Court confirmed this line of argument with regard to the right of quotation laid down in article 5(3)(d) ISD. The Court underlined the need for an interpretation of the conditions set forth in article 5(3)(d) that enables the effectiveness of the quotation right and safeguards its purpose.[86] More specifically, it clarified that article 5(3)(d) was:

> intended to strike a fair balance between the right of freedom of expression of users of a work or other protected subject-matter and the reproduction right conferred on authors.[87]

In its further decision in *Deckmyn/Vandersteen*, the CJEU followed the same path with regard to the parody exemption in article 5(3)(k) ISD. As in *Painer/Der Standard*, the Court bypassed the dogma of a strict interpretation of copyright limitations by underlining the need to ensure the effectiveness of the parody exemption[88] as a means to balance copyright protection against freedom of expression.[89]

---

84   *Football Association Premier League v QC Leisure* (CJEU, C-403/08 and C-429/08, 4 October 2011) [162]–[163].

85   Ibid [181].

86   *Eva Maria Painer v Standard VerlagsGmbH* (CJEU, C-145/10, 1 December 2011) [132]–[133].

87   Ibid [134].

88   *Deckmyn and Vrijheidsfonds VZW v Vandersteen* (CJEU, C-201/13, 3 September 2014) [22]–[23].

89   Ibid [25]–[27].

In practice, the courts may thus give copyright limitations that support transformative use a status that comes close to an author's right – even though the underlying copyright statute, such as the Information Society Directive in the EU, does not qualify these limitations as rights but includes them in the catalogue of exceptions to exclusive rights instead. As the examples taken from CJEU jurisprudence demonstrate, the fundamental guarantee of freedom of expression plays a crucial role in this context.[90] Relying on article 11 of the EU Charter of Fundamental Rights and article 10 of the European Convention on Human Rights, the CJEU could interpret the quotation right and the parody exemption less strictly than limitations without a comparably strong freedom of speech underpinning. In both the *Painer* and the *Deckmyn* decision, the Court emphasised the need to achieve a 'fair balance' between, in particular, 'the rights and interests of authors on the one hand, and the rights of users of protected subject-matter on the other.'[91] The Court thus referred to quotations and parodies as user 'rights' rather than mere user 'interests'.

Does this mean that there is no need for reforms? Does it mean that, in practice, the right of transformative use already exists by virtue of court decisions, even though it is hidden in the catalogue of exceptions in many national copyright statutes? For at least two reasons, the answer to these questions can hardly be in the affirmative. First, a legislative reform that removes use privileges for transformative use from the catalogue of exceptions and openly redefines them as authors' rights – with the same status as traditional exploitation rights – would make the particular importance of these use privileges visible within the copyright statute itself. It would allow an internal balancing of different rights when the courts have to decide on quotations and parodies. This seems more satisfactory

---

90   As to the influence of freedom of speech guarantees on copyright, cf C Geiger, '"Constitutionalising" Intellectual Property Law? The Influence of Fundamental Rights on Intellectual Property in the European Union' (2006) 37 *International Review of Intellectual Property and Competition Law*, 371; A Strowel, F Tulkens and D Voorhoof (eds), *Droit d'auteur et liberté d'expression* (Editions Larcier, 2006); PB Hugenholtz, 'Copyright and Freedom of Expression in Europe' in N Elkin-Koren and NW Netanel (eds), *The Commodification of Information* (Kluwer, 2002) 239; S Macciacchini, *Urheberrecht und Meinungsfreiheit* (Stämpfli, 2000); Benkler, above n 21, 355; Netanel, 'Copyright and a Democratic Civil Society', above n 20, 283.

91   *Eva Maria Painer v Standard VerlagsGmbH* (CJEU, C-145/10, 1 December 2011), case C-145/10, Eva Maria Painer/Standard VerlagsGmbH, para. [132]; *Deckmyn and Vrijheidsfonds VZW v Vandersteen* (CJEU, C-201/13, 3 September 2014, case C-201/13, Deckmyn and Vrijheidsfonds VZW/Vandersteen, para.) [26].

than the present practice of balancing copyright against freedom of expression as an external influence factor leading to an exceptionally broad application of a copyright limitation that, in principle, would have to be construed narrowly.[92]

Second, it must not be overlooked that quotations and parodies are longstanding and well-established copyright limitations. The courts may have much more difficulty to arrive at satisfactory solutions when it comes to other cases of transformative use that are not, or at least less clearly, reflected in the catalogue of copyright limitations. With the constant evolution of new artistic practices, it cannot be ruled out that an impediment of autonomous art productions comes to the fore and that copyright law, in the absence of a formal recognition of a right to transformative use, becomes an obstacle to the evolution of new independent art. Sound sampling artists, for instance, face copyright claims as well as neighbouring rights claims of phonogram producers. The more snippets of pre-existing sound recordings they use, the higher will be the risk of infringement. The focus on the protection of exploitation interests in existing sound recordings may thus have a deterrent, corrosive effect on their creativity. In particular, this bias is likely to impede so-called 'collage sampling' using layers of quantitatively or qualitatively insignificant parts of pre-existing recordings to create new musical works.[93] In contrast to traditional quotation and parody cases, the courts seem much more reluctant to make particular efforts to offer room for transformative use in sound sampling cases.[94] In Germany, for example, sampling artists had to argue their case all the way up to the German Federal Constitutional

92   With regard to the question of internal and external balancing exercises, see T Dreier, 'Balancing Proprietary and Public Domain Interests: Inside or Outside of Proprietary Rights?', in R Dreyfuss, D Leenheer-Zimmerman and H First (eds), *Expanding the Boundaries of Intellectual Property. Innovation Policy for the Knowledge Economy* (Oxford University Press, 2001) 295.

93   See DM Morrison, 'Bridgeport Redux: Digital Sampling and Audience Recording' (2008) 19 *Fordham Intellectual Property Media and Entertainment Law Journal* 75, 96, who warns of a corrosive effect on the so-called 'collage paradigm' in sampling.

94   As to the preference given to exploitation interests instead, see, for instance, *Metall auf Metall II*, Bundesgerichtshof [German Federal Court of Justice], I ZR 182/11, 13 December 2012, reported in [2013] *Gewerblicher Rechtsschutz und Urheberrecht*, 614; *Metall auf Metall*, Bundesgerichtshof [German Federal Court of Justice], I ZR 112/06, 20 November 2008, reported in [2009] *Gewerblicher Rechtsschutz und Urheberrecht*, 403. For a translation of the latter case into English, see N Conley and T Braegelmann, 'Metall auf Metall: The Importance of the Kraftwerk Decision for the Sampling of Music in Germany' (2009) 56 *Journal of the Copyright Society of the U.S.A.*, 1017. For case comments, see BHM Schippers, 'Het chilling effect van Kraftwerk I/II op sound sampling: pleidooi voor zelfregulering ter bevordering van samplegebruik' (2014) *Tijdschrift voor auteurs-, media- en informatierecht*, 105; FJ Dougherty, 'RIP, MIX and

Court to receive the confirmation that, besides the property interests of copyright holders and phonogram producers, their right to freedom of art had to be given sufficient room as well.[95] Other forms of collage art, such as film and photo compositions, are likely to raise similar problems. The formal recognition of a right to transformative use in copyright law could thus make a difference in these cases – not only on paper but also in practice.

A last question concerns the scope of the right to transformative use that should be recognised in copyright law. As pointed out above, Bourdieu's analysis does not only highlight the importance of freedom to use and criticise pre-existing works in the process of defining and demarcating a new aesthetic position. It also sheds light on the need to allow artists of a new generation to learn of the positions that have already been taken by predecessors. Therefore, the question arises whether a right to transformative use should only cover core areas, such as the making of quotations, parodies and collages, or be extended to peripheral areas, such as educational use, library use, and private studying.[96]

The problem with these latter categories is that, unlike the freedom of quotation, parody and collage, they do not lie at the core of the creative process as such. Use privileges for educational and cultural heritage institutions are crucial to the dissemination of information and the guarantee of equal access to information in the information society. However, they are not directly linked with the process of creation. It is unclear whether an art student or a library user will sooner or later embark on the creation of a literary or artistic work. Use privileges for educational and cultural heritage institutions are investments in *potential* acts of creation that may take place in the future. They increase the likelihood of users receiving sufficient inspiration for the creation of a new literary or artistic work. However, they operate in a preliminary, preparatory phase. Moreover, it can hardly ever be ascertained whether the use of services of educational

---

BURN: Bemerkungen zu aktuellen Entwicklungen im Bereich des digitalen Sampling nach US-amerikanischem und internationalen Recht' (2007) *Gewerblicher Rechtsschutz und Urheberrecht – Internationaler Teil*, 481.

95   Bundesverfassungsgericht [German Federal Constitutional Court], 1 BvR 1585/13, 31 May 2016 available at <www.bundesverfassungsgericht.de/SharedDocs/Entscheidungen/DE/2016/05/rs20160531_1bvr158513.html>.

96   For a discussion of this question, see also Senftleben, above n 64, 39–41.

institutions, archives, museums and libraries, is consumptive or transformative. This dilemma clearly comes to the fore in the case of private copying. It is difficult, if not impossible, to conceive of contextual factors that could reliably indicate whether the copying takes place for mere entertainment and enjoyment purposes, or for the studying of aesthetic positions that will finally lead to a new literary or artistic production.

Given these conceptual and practical difficulties, it seems advisable to confine the recognition of a right to transformative use to use privileges that directly support the process of creation, such as a quotation right that permits the taking of parts of a pre-existing work to make a comment, a parody right that permits the evocation of a pre-existing work to express humour or mockery, a collage right that permits the composition of a new work on the basis of fragments of pre-existing works.

4.2. Refinement of remuneration mechanisms

As explained above, Bourdieu's analysis casts doubt upon standard justifications of copyright protection. In particular, the focus on the motivating power of monetary rewards in current copyright law is questionable. As autonomous authors attach more importance to reputational rewards, the prospect of copyright protection does not necessarily spur their creativity. Taking Bourdieu's assumptions to the extremes, it could be said that autonomous authors, by definition, have no interest in monetary rewards. As winning in economic terms implies losing in artistic terms, commercial success may even be seen as undesirable. Hence, one might be tempted to assume that autonomous authors need not be remunerated for their work.

This cynical line of reasoning, however, follows from a misunderstanding of the above critique of the standard rationales of copyright protection in the light of Bourdieu's analysis. It is correct to say that the reliance of traditional copyright theories on the power of monetary incentives is questionable. Authors with an independent *l'art pour l'art* orientation are unlikely to be more creative and more productive when copyright protection is offered as a bait. However, it would be incorrect to infer from these doubts about a standard argument for copyright protection that autonomous authors should not receive any remuneration for their work. The reason for securing this remuneration, however, is not the utilitarian incentive rationale. By contrast, an appropriate remuneration must be guaranteed because of social considerations and the need for equal treatment.

As market-oriented authors, autonomous authors have to earn a living. Therefore, it is a matter of fairness and equality to remunerate not only bourgeois authors but also autonomous authors for their creative work. From a social perspective, it may be added that the need to take measures to ensure an appropriate remuneration is even more pressing in the case of autonomous authors because this group may fail to attach sufficient importance to revenue streams when it comes to negotiations with producers and disseminators seeking to exploit their works (exploiters). As long as a certain mode of exploitation is likely to yield attractive reputational rewards, autonomous authors may be tempted to give their works away at a price that does not appropriately reflect their market value. Hence, the question arises how copyright law can ensure that autonomous creators receive a fair remuneration for their creative labour. The answer to this question can hardly be found in the very nature of copyright itself. Copyright law ensures that authors' exploitation rights are marketable. However, autonomous artists in the sense of Bourdieu's sociological analysis may never attain a bargaining position that allows them to ensure a decent income on the basis of copyright because their works are not made for the tastes of the masses in the first place. While these consequences may be seen as a normal result in a market economy driven by supply and demand, they become problematic when it is considered that copyright, as pointed out above, is often presented as a right that serves the individual interests of creators. If the whole group of creators with a *l'art pour l'art* orientation does not have the bargaining power to derive substantial economic benefit from copyright,[97] this problem may discredit the protection system as

---

97   In this regard, see the analyses of the bargaining position and income situation of individual creators by M Kretschmer et al, *2011 Copyright Contracts and Earnings of Visual Creators: A Survey of 5,800 British Designers, Fine Artists, Illustrators and Photographers* (Centre for Intellectual Property Policy & Management (CIPPM), 2011) available at <ssrn.com/abstract=1780206>; J Weda et al, *Wat er speelt – De positie van makers en uitvoerend kunstenaars in de digitale omgeving*, (SEO Economisch Onderzoek, 2011), available at <www.rijksoverheid.nl/documenten-en-publicaties/rapporten/2011/04/11/rapport-wat-er-speelt.html>; PB Hugenholtz and L Guibault, *Auteurscontractenrecht: naar een wettelijke regeling?*, (Institute for Information Law (IViR), 2004) available at <www.ivir.nl/publicaties/overig/auteurscontractenrecht.pdf> (unavailable from original source but accessible via archive.org; copy on file with editors).

a whole.[98] If copyright only serves as a vehicle to vest the creative industries with strong rights in information products while these rights are defended as a means to remunerate authors, the creators of literary and artistic works – including the group of autonomous artists that is often depicted as the prototype of the 'romantic author' – only function as a dummy to conceal the industry's insatiable appetite for continuously expanding exclusive rights. As a result, the arguments advanced in favour of copyright can be unmasked as false rhetoric[99] and the protection system is in danger of losing its support in society. The system's social legitimacy is put at risk.

To avoid this erosion of copyright's acceptance in society, the lawmaker can seek to reduce the exposure to market forces and adopt measures that strengthen the position of creators vis-à-vis exploiters. In 2002, an example of legislation in this area – an *Act on Copyright Contract Law* – entered into force in Germany. This legislation confers upon authors a right to fair remuneration besides the traditional exploitation rights. By virtue of § 32(1) of the German *Copyright Act* (UrhG), as amended by the *2002 Copyright Contract Act*, authors have the right to demand the modification of a contract about a work's exploitation that fails to provide for a fair remuneration. § 32(2) UrhG complements this right to fair remuneration by making it clear that so-called 'common remuneration rules' established in negotiations between a representative association of authors on the one hand, and an individual exploiter or an association of exploiters on the other hand (§ 36 UrhG), are to be deemed 'fair' in this sense by virtue of the law.

---

98   For empirical evidence of the precarious income situation of creators (not limited to the group of autonomous artists), see, for example, Kretschmer et al, above n 96. As to the need for a strengthening of the bargaining position of authors, see Weda et al, above n 96.

99   Cf SE Sterk, 'Rhetoric and Reality in Copyright Law' (1996) 94 *Michigan Law Review* 1197, 1197–1198, pointing out that 'although some copyright protection indeed may be necessary to induce creative activity, copyright doctrine now extends well beyond the contours of the instrumental justification. The 1976 statute and more recent amendments protect authors even when no plausible argument can be made that protection will enhance the incentive for authors to create'.

Although the German *Copyright Contract Act* has now been in effect for more than 10 years, it has not led to the envisaged general improvement of the income situation of authors.[100] Authors seem hesitant to assert their remuneration right in court. As an exception to this rule, translators started court procedures that finally led to first decisions of the German Federal Court of Justice on the fair remuneration question.[101] On balance, however, the determinants of what constitutes a fair remuneration in an individual case still seem too vague to allow the effective use and enforcement of the new right. As the party invoking the right to fair remuneration, the burden of proving that a contractually agreed remuneration falls short of the legally guaranteed fair remuneration rests on the author. Hence, she also carries the risk and costs of showing that a certain remuneration is to be deemed fair in the relevant sector of the creative industry, and that the concluded contract does not provide for this fair remuneration.[102]

For cases in which no common remuneration rules are available, § 32(2) UrhG indicates that a remuneration can be considered fair when it complies with the remuneration that, according to the customary practices in the sector concerned, an author could reasonably expect in light of the scope and reach of the granted right, the duration and time of the use, and other circumstances relevant to the individual case.[103] These flexible factors, however, can hardly clarify the conceptual contours of the fair remuneration right. In the absence of model contracts or other customary remuneration schemes that come close to common remuneration rules in the sense of § 36 UrhG, an author will still have difficulty to prove that a contractually agreed

---

100 See the recent analyses by H Maas, 'Kulturelle Werke – mehr als nur ein Wirtschaftsgut' (2016) *Zeitschrift für Urheber- und Medienrecht*, 207, 209, and K-N Peifer, 'Urhebervertragsrecht in der Reform: Der „Kölner Entwurf"' (2015) *Gewerblicher Rechtsschutz und Urheberrecht – Praxis im Immaterialgüter- und Wettbewerbsrecht*, 1, 1–2; as well as earlier comments by G Schulze, 'Vergütungssystem und Schrankenregelungen' (2005) *Gewerblicher Rechtsschutz und Urheberrecht*, 828, which in principle were shared by A Dietz, 'Das Urhebervertragsrecht in Deutschland' in RM Hilty and C Geiger (eds), *Impulse für eine europäische Harmonisierung des Urheberrechts* (Springer, 2007) 465. However, Dietz qualified the first common remuneration rule that had been established under the new German legislation as a success of the system as a whole. See Dietz at 473–474.
101 See Bundesgerichtshof [Federal Court of Justice], I ZR 38/07 and I ZR 230/06, 7 October 2009, reported in (in German) <www.bundesgerichtshof.de>. This case law will be discussed in more detail below.
102 Schulze, above n 99, 829–830; Dietz, above n 99, 469.
103 Schulze, above n 99, p. 595.

remuneration is not fair on the basis of this vague definition of fairness based on the custom in a given sector.[104] Similarly, the author will have difficulty in assessing the risk of litigation about the remuneration question as long as there is no reliable information on the customary remuneration.

Against this background, the additional option to invoke § 36 UrhG and formally establish common remuneration rules in collective negotiations between an association of authors and industry representatives is of particular practical importance. By virtue of § 32(2) UrhG, a standard remuneration scheme of this type constitutes a legally binding definition of the fair remuneration in the industry sector concerned. A standard remuneration scheme in the sense of § 32(2) thus provides the legal certainty necessary to assess the chances of court procedures. It can also serve as a yardstick for proving the unfairness of a remuneration that does not comply with the standard described in the remuneration scheme.

In Germany, the Common Remuneration Rules for Writers of German Fiction[105] constitute a prominent example of remuneration rules that were concluded on the basis of the German *Copyright Contract Act* in negotiations between the Association of German Writers in the United Services Trade Union Ver.di and several publishers.[106] As no representative association of publishers entered the negotiations,[107] it was difficult to foresee the impact of this standard remuneration rule on the sector as a whole. The fact that the German Ministry of Justice itself finally decided to mediate informally between the parties to ensure the adoption of the remuneration rules mirrors the difficulty of the negotiations.[108]

---

104 Schulze, above n 99, 829–830; AA Wandtke, 'Der Anspruch auf angemessene Vergütung für Filmurheber nach § 32 UrhG' (2010) *Gewerblicher Rechtsschutz und Urheberrecht Internationaler Teil* 704, 707.

105 These common remuneration rules are available (in German) at <www.bmj.de/media/archive/962.pdf>.

106 The rules were signed, for instance, by Rowohlt, S Fischer and Random House. See A Dietz in G Schricker, *Urheberrecht – Kommentar* (CH Beck, 3rd ed, 2006) 797.

107 See Deutscher Bundestag, 3 May 2004, Kurzprotokoll der 14. Sitzung (öffentlich) der Enquete-Kommission 'Kultur in Deutschland', Protokoll Nr 15/14, 13/4–13/5.

108 The mediation was informal in the sense that it was no formal mediation procedure with a dispute commission under § 36a UrhG. See Dietz, above n 99, 797; Schulze, above n 99, 830.

Given the scarcity of common remuneration rules in the sense of § 36 UrhG,[109] it is tempting for the courts to make extensive use of existing rules. As already indicated above, the German Federal Court of Justice had the opportunity to clarify the scope of common remuneration rules in two cases that had been initiated by translators. A collectively agreed remuneration rule for translators in the sense of § 36 UrhG was not available for a decision in these cases. Moreover, the Federal Court of Justice had serious doubts about the customary remuneration in the translation sector. Referring to the aforementioned general definition of 'fair remuneration' in § 32(2) UrhG, the Court pointed out that compliance with customary remuneration practices in a particular sector may nonetheless be insufficient in the light of the general fairness criteria formulated by the legislator:

> Even if a particular honorarium – as in this case – is customary in the sector, this does not necessarily mean that it is fair. By contrast, a given remuneration is only fair when it equally takes account of the interests of the author besides those of the exploiter.[110]

Having neither a common remuneration rule in the sense of § 36 UrhG nor an appropriate customary remuneration scheme in the sense of § 32(2) UrhG at its disposal, the Federal Court of Justice finally turned to the Common Remuneration Rules for Writers of German Fiction as a point of departure for determining the fair remuneration of translators.[111] By analogy, the Court used these Common Remuneration Rules as a guideline for its decision on a fair level of remuneration for translators. This widening of the field of application of common remuneration rules is remarkable because the Common

---

109 In Germany, the number of common remuneration rules in the sense of § 36 UrhG is growing. Cf A Dietz, 'Schutz der Kreativen (der Urheber und ausübenden Künstler) durch das Urheberrecht oder Die fünf Säulen des modernen kontinentaleuropäischen Urheberrechts' (2015) *Gewerblicher Rechtsschutz und Urheberrecht – Internationaler Teil* 309, 315–316. The scope of these rules, however, is often limited to specific groups of authors and exploiters. For example, see the initiatives in the area of public broadcasting described by P Weber, 'Rahmenverträge und gemeinsame Vergütungsregeln nach Urhebervertragsrecht – aus der Praxis des ZDF' (2013) *Zeitschrift für Urheber- und Medienrecht* 740, 742–745. On balance, the result can thus still be seen as unsatisfactory. See G Spindler, 'Reformen der Vergütungsregeln im Urhebervertragsrecht' (2012) *Zeitschrift für Urheber- und Medienrecht* 921, 921.
110 German Federal Court of Justice, 7 October 2009, I ZR 38/07, 11, with case comment by R Jacobs at (2009) *Gewerblicher Rechtsschutz und Urheberrecht* 1148, 1150; German Federal Court of Justice I ZR 230/06, 12, available (in German) at <www.bundesgerichtshof.de>.
111 German Federal Court of Justice, 7 October 2009, I ZR 38/07, 16; German Federal Court of Justice, 7 October 2009, I ZR 230/06, 15–16; both reported in (in German) <www.bundesgerichtshof.de>.

Remuneration Rules for Writers of German Fiction explicitly exclude applicability to translated works.[112] In addition, the Federal Court of Justice was unimpressed by the fact that only one of the two cases brought by translators concerned fiction works. The second case was about translations of non-fiction books. The Court, however, also surmounted this hurdle of 'double' analogy. It did not matter that the case concerned translators instead of writers, and it did not matter that it concerned non-fiction instead of fiction books:

> Even though the remuneration rules ... are not directly applicable to publication contracts for non-fiction books, there are no prevailing concerns against their use for the purpose of determining a fair remuneration for the translation of a non-fiction book. According to the findings of the Court of Appeals, none of the parties argued and no other circumstances suggest that the conditions of publication contracts for non-fiction books differ from those of contracts over fiction works to such an extent that the remuneration rules for writers could not be taken into account.[113]

Using the Common Remuneration Rules for Writers of German Fiction as a guideline for the development of a fair remuneration standard for translators, the Court finally ruled that translators are entitled to 2 per cent of the net retail price of hardcover editions and 1 per cent in the case of paperback editions. This amounts to one-fifth of the remuneration which, according to the Common Remuneration Rules for Writers of German Fiction, is due to writers. If the publisher guarantees an honorarium that can be deemed reasonable in light of the custom in the sector, this right to fair remuneration is reduced to 0.8 per cent for hardcover sales and 0.4 per cent for paperback sales. Moreover, this reduced royalty only needs to be paid as of the 5,000th copy sold. In addition, translators are entitled to 50 per cent of the net profits from the commercialisation of ancillary rights.[114]

---

112 See Gemeinsame Vergütungsregeln für Autoren belletristischer Werke in deutscher Sprache, available at <www.bmj.de/media/archive/962.pdf>, 1 n 1, on the one hand, and German Federal Court of Justice, 7 October 2009, I ZR 38/07, 17, and German Federal Court of Justice, 7 October 2009, I ZR 230/06, 16, <www.bundesgerichtshof.de>, on the other hand.

113 See German Federal Court of Justice, 7 October 2009, I ZR 230/06, [34], <www.bundesgerichtshof.de>.

114 See German Federal Court of Justice, 7 October 2009, I ZR 38/07, 18–23, and German Federal Court of Justice, 7 October 2009, I ZR 230/06, 18–23, both <www.bundesgerichtshof.de>. Nonetheless, this level of fair remuneration did not meet the expectations of translators. Cf Dietz, above n 99, 469.

This jurisprudence of the Federal Court of Justice shows that common remuneration rules established under § 36 UrhG can have a broad field of application. In particular, the courts may extend the scope of these rules to parties who have not been involved in the underlying negotiations. A common remuneration rule may become a general yardstick for the establishment of fair remuneration standards in a given sector even though it was only concluded between specific parties and for a specific group of creators. On its merits, this jurisprudence transforms common remuneration rules into generally binding legal instruments with a considerable impact on remuneration standards in the respective segment of the creative industry.

On the one hand, this approach can have positive effects for authors in a sector where no agreement on a common remuneration rule can be reached. By invoking remuneration rules of a related sector or a related group, German courts can still arrive at a fair remuneration standard in these cases and improve the income situation of authors by reference to remuneration standards in a comparable field. On the other hand, the jurisprudence of the Federal Court of Justice can easily become an additional obstacle to negotiations on common remuneration rules in the sense of § 36 UrhG. If it is at all possible to find individual exploiters or business associations that are willing to speak about common remuneration rules in a particular branch, these exploiters and associations may be reluctant to enter into formal negotiations because of the risk of resulting fair remuneration standards being declared applicable to the whole sector afterwards by the courts. Given this risk of generalisation, interested enterprises and associations may also face pressure from other players in the relevant sector who fear that the establishment of common remuneration rules in one particular branch may finally affect remuneration standards in the entire sector.

In spite of these problems, the underlying recipe – the combination of a right to fair remuneration with the possibility of establishing common remuneration standards in negotiations between authors and the creative industry – served as a model for other countries also seeking to enhance the credibility of the copyright system by strengthening the position of individual authors vis-à-vis commercial exploiters of their works. In the Netherlands, for instance, legislation that copies the core elements of the German system was adopted in 2015.[115] Regardless of this export success, however, the question remains how fair remuneration legislation could be rendered more effective in practice. A clearer definition of the underlying concept of fairness, a reversal of the burden of proof with regard to evidence of remuneration standards in a given sector, extra incentives for the creative industry to enter into collective negotiations with associations of authors and, as a last resort, the imposition of a legal obligation to establish common remuneration rules could be considered in this context.

In the drafting process underlying the present German legislation, a far-reaching obligation to accept common remuneration standards was contemplated with regard to situations where the parties involved in negotiations, finally, could not reach agreement. A common remuneration rule could then also have been established in compulsory settlement procedures or through a court decision.[116] This proposal, however, was rejected because of fears that it would encroach upon fundamental freedoms of enterprises and business associations, in particular the general freedom of action and the negative freedom of not being obliged to enter into coalitions guaranteed in the German constitution.[117] Legislation that imposes a de facto obligation

---

115 See the Law of 30 June 2015 changing the *Dutch Copyright Act* and the *Neighbouring Rights Act* in connection with the strengthening of the position of authors and performing artists in contracts concerning copyright and neighbouring rights (*Copyright Contract Act*), *Staatsblad* 2015, 257, which led to a new section in the *Dutch Copyright Act* (Arts 25b–25h) dealing specifically with authors' contract rights. As to the preparatory work for this new legislation, see Ministerie van Veiligheid en Justitie, 12 June 2012, 'Wetsvoorstel auteurscontractenrecht', *Kamerstukken II* 2011/12, 33 308, (2013) *Tijdschrift voor auteurs-, media en informatierecht*, 23; B J Lenselink, 'Auteurscontractenrecht 2.0 – Het wetsvoorstel inzake het auteurscontractenrecht' (2013) *Tijdschrift voor auteurs-, media- en informatierecht*, 7; E Wybenga, 'Ongebonden werk – Is de literaire sector gebaat bij het voorontwerp auteurscontractenrecht?' (2011) *Tijdschrift voor auteurs-, media- en informatierecht*, 41; D Peeperkorn, 'De lange geschiedenis van het auteurscontractenrecht' (2010) *Tijdschrift voor auteurs-, media- en informatierecht*, 167; JP Poort and JJM Theeuwes, 'Prova d'Orchestra – Een economische analyse van het voorontwerp auteurscontractenrecht' (2010) *Tijdschrift voor auteurs-, media- en informatierecht*, 137; MRF Senftleben, 'Exportschlager deutsches Urhebervertragsrecht? Het voorontwerp auteurscontractenrecht in Duits perspectief' (2010) *Tijdschrift voor auteurs-, media- en informatierecht*, 146; H Cohen Jehoram, 'Komend auteurscontractenrecht' (2008) *Intellectuele eigendom en reclamerecht*, 303; PB Hugenholtz and L Guibault, above n 96.

116 See Deutscher Bundestag, 26 June 2001, 'Entwurf eines Gesetzes zur Stärkung der vertraglichen Stellung von Urhebern und ausübenden Künstlern', *Drucksache* 14/6433, 4 [§ 36(3), (5)–(8)], 17.

117 See *Grundgesetz* [German Basic Law], Arts 2(1), 9, available online at <www.bundestag.de/bundestag/aufgaben/rechtsgrundlagen/grundgesetz/gg_01/245122>; Cf H Schack, 'Neuregelung des Urhebervertragsrechts' (2001) *Zeitschrift für Urheber- und Medienrecht* 453, 462. See also NP Flechsig

to establish common remuneration rules thus seems excessive.[118] The current discussion about an amendment of the German system, however, includes the proposal to make the concept of fairness more concrete by pointing out that a fair remuneration, in principle, requires more than a one-time 'buy out' payment. Instead, the author should continuously receive a share of the revenue accruing from the exploitation of her work.[119]

Given the various problems identified in the ongoing debate, copyright legislation seeking to improve the income situation of creators should not exclusively rely on the recognition of a right to fair remuneration and the vague hope that agreements on appropriate remuneration standards will evolve from negotiations between authors and the creative industry. By contrast, additional instruments are necessary to ensure that authors receive a fair monetary reward for their creative work.

Again, Bourdieu's analysis can offer important impulses in this regard. While a general right to fair remuneration *ex ante* may be of particular importance to bourgeois authors whose works are likely to be commercially successful in the marketplace, the difficulty of providing evidence for a certain level of standard remuneration in a specific field of art is likely to constitute an almost insurmountable hurdle for autonomous authors. As their works do not follow market dictates and may be avant-garde productions not following known patterns, a remuneration concept presupposing the existence of a customary level of fair remuneration seems inapt from the outset. Autonomous artists may also fear negative reactions in the art sector concerned when they insist on the right to fair remuneration. Facing a relatively small circle of investors and producers, an autonomous artist may be concerned about seeing her name being added to a 'black list' of creators with whom exploiters do not want to work because of past disputes about an adequate level of remuneration.

---

and K Hendricks, 'Zivilprozessuales Schiedsverfahren zur Schließung urheberrechtlicher Gesamtverträge – Zweckmäßige Alternative oder Sackgasse?' (2000) *Zeitschrift für Urheber- und Medienrecht*, 721, for an assessment of the pros and cons of a formal settlement procedure.

118 For a detailed discussion of this point, see Spindler, above n 108, 925–928.

119 Cf K-N Peifer, 'Der Referentenentwurf zum Urhebervertragsrecht' (2016) *Gewerblicher Rechtsschutz und Urheberrecht* 6, 8, and J Kreile and E Schley, 'Reform der Reform – Wie viel vom Kölner und Münchner Entwurf steckt im Referentenentwurf zum Urhebervertragsrecht?' (2015) *Zeitschrift für Urheber- und Medienrecht* 837, 837, for a discussion of a proposed new sentence in § 32(2) UrhG.

However, once the work of an autonomous creator has attained the status of an important avant-garde production within the circle of independent artists and generates considerable monetary revenue on the art market because of this status, the author may have a particular interest in a remuneration rule that ensures a fair profit sharing *ex post*. If the work becomes successful on the art market to such an extent that the remuneration originally received appears disproportionally low, an *ex post* remuneration rule would ensure that the author can demand an adjustment of the contract in the light of changed circumstances.

Again, experiences with copyright legislation in Germany can serve as an example in this context. Prior to the introduction of the above-described 2002 *Act on Copyright Contract Law*, the German *Copyright Act* already contained a safeguard against remuneration schemes that turn out to be disproportionate in the course of a work's exploitation: the so-called 'bestseller clause' was regarded as an important addition to the general rule on *imprévision* in the German Civil Code. It softened the requirement that new circumstances justifying an adjustment of the remuneration had to be unforeseeable for contracting parties at the time of concluding the exploitation contract. The strict application of this requirement had rendered the general *imprévision* rule in the German Civil Code ineffective in many copyright cases.[120] Against this background, the traditional bestseller clause in the German copyright system was based on an alternative threshold for requesting an adjustment of the remuneration: a showing of 'gross' disproportionality. This condition was deemed to be fulfilled when the honorarium received by the author amounted to only one-third of what would have constituted a usual royalty revenue when taking into account the work's success.[121]

In the 2002 *Act on Copyright Contract Law*, the German legislator replaced this bestseller clause with an even more elastic 'fairness clause'. In § 32a(1) UrhG, it was stated explicitly that this new clause could be invoked regardless of whether the parties could have foreseen the disproportionality between remuneration and revenue when entering into the exploitation contract. The condition of

---

120 For instance, see German Federal Court of Justice, 'Horoskop-Kalender' (1991), *Gewerblicher Rechtsschutz und Urheberrecht* 901, 902; German Federal Court of Justice, 'Comic-Übersetzungen' (1998) *Zeitschrift für Urheber- und Medienrecht* 497, 502.

121 See German Federal Court of Justice, 'Horoskop-Kalender' (1991), *Gewerblicher Rechtsschutz und Urheberrecht*, 903.

'gross' disproportionality was attenuated by setting forth a threshold of 'striking' disproportionality instead. In the official materials accompanying the 2002 Act, the German legislator explained that this new requirement could be deemed to be met when the author had received an honorarium amounting to less than half of the income that could have been expected considering the work's success.[122] In literature, it is argued that even one-fifth should already be sufficient to assume a striking disproportionality.[123] German courts, however, have not had sufficient opportunities to fix this new threshold requirement yet.[124]

As with the traditional bestseller clause, the new fairness clause covers all kinds of contracts awarding exploitation entitlements. Its scope of application ranges from transfers and exclusive licenses to non-exclusive licenses and specific permissions of use, such as a permission to translate or adapt a work.[125] Moreover, the new provision makes it clear that in the case of a license chain, the author can assert the right to *ex post* adjustment of the contractually agreed remuneration against every license holder (§ 32a(2) UrhG). It is thus irrelevant whether a licensee was involved in the original honorarium negotiations and received the exploitation entitlement directly from the author.

---

122 See Deutscher Bundestag, 23 January 2002, 'Gesetz zur Stärkung der vertraglichen Stellung von Urhebern und ausübenden Künstlern – Beschlussempfehlung und Bericht des Rechtsausschusses', *Drucksache* 14/8058, 19.

123 Cf the overview provided by Schulze in Th Dreier and G Schulze, *UrhG – Kommentar* (CH Beck, 3rd ed, 2008) 616.

124 Court decisions based on the new fairness clause are still scarce. See Schulze, above n 122, 617. As to the practical difficulties of court procedures seeking to clarify the fairness of the remuneration received by the authors under the new fairness clause, see N Reber, 'Der "Fairnessparagraph", § 32a UrhG' (2010) *Gewerblicher Rechtsschutz und Urheberrecht – Internationaler Teil* 708, 709.

125 See Schulze, above n 122, 613.

Arguably, *ex post* adjustment measures of this type are more effective than attempts to secure a fair remuneration *ex ante* – at a stage where a work's exploitation has not yet started. Support for *ex post* remuneration mechanisms can also be found in international copyright law. The optional *droit de suite* recognised in article 14ter(1) of the Berne Convention grants the author and her heirs an interest in any sale of original works of art and original manuscripts subsequent to the work's first transfer. As bestseller and fairness legislation seeking to ensure an additional income in case of disproportionality between initial remuneration and later revenues, this international provision aims to ensure that the author receives a share of profits accruing from a work's successful exploitation at a later stage.

For lawmakers aiming at appropriate remuneration mechanisms for individual creators, the debate on fair remuneration also yields more general guidelines. In particular, exploitation contracts offering authors a revenue share seem more desirable than fixed one-time honoraria in 'buy out' contracts. With a remuneration scheme ensuring a continuous royalty stream, the risk of disproportionality between remuneration and revenue can be reduced from the outset. As a legislative measure, it may thus be advisable to encourage remuneration in the form of royalty percentages and discourage agreements based on lump sum honoraria as the only form of remuneration.

A final aspect of the debate on a fair remuneration for the work of creators concerns the cross-financing of productions. When *ex post* measures are taken to adjust the remuneration in the case of works having huge market success, exploiters may warn of shrinking budgets for the financing of less successful works. The income from bestsellers, so runs the argument, is needed to compensate for the losses stemming from unsuccessful productions. If the creative industry must share profits accruing from bestsellers with the authors, the potential of bestseller productions for levelling out losses resulting from investment in commercially insecure productions is reduced. This may limit the willingness of the creative industry to invest in unorthodox works of unknown artists from the outset.

Revisiting Bourdieu's analysis, a line can be drawn between this cross-financing argument and the ongoing fight between bourgeois and autonomous authors for predominance in the field of literary and artistic production. If it was true that the creative industry used the income from successful mainstream productions to finance less promising autonomous productions, *ex post* adjustments of revenue streams leading to a higher income for bourgeois bestseller authors may have the effect of reducing the budget available for less secure art productions of autonomous authors. In other words: the potential of mainstream productions of bourgeois authors serving as a subsidy for *l'art pour l'art* productions of autonomous authors would be reduced.

In the absence of an economic analysis confirming this alleged interdependence of investment decisions in bourgeois and autonomous productions in the creative industry, however, it cannot readily be assumed that the alleged cross-financing of art productions is taking place, and that it would be frustrated by *ex post* adjustments of remuneration schemes for bestsellers. These *ex post* adjustments would only occur when a work's market success has not already been factored into the equation at the time of concluding the exploitation contract. Once a creator is known as a bestseller author, however, she will have the bargaining power to negotiate an adequate remuneration in the initial exploitation contract. Hence, *ex post* adjustments only impact the calculations of the creative industry in case a work was not expected to have outstanding commercial success so that the creator had limited bargaining power. Even if the alleged practice of cross-financing exists, it is thus unclear whether these cases would minimise industry profits to such an extent that the alleged subsidising of art productions becomes unfeasible.

4.3. Redistribution of copyright revenue

Copyright legislation that aims to strengthen the position of creators vis-à-vis exploiters by awarding a right to fair remuneration presupposes that the creative industry is willing to invest in a creator's work. Otherwise, the creator will have no opportunity to assert remuneration rights in the first place. The central problem of autonomous art, then, is its limited potential to generate profit. As independent artists do not strive for market success, refuse to align their works with the tastes of the masses and are unlikely to create bestsellers, the grant of a right to fair remuneration – *ex ante* or *ex post* – may fail to yield tangible results. If no exploiter can be found for a true work of art, the autonomous artist will simply have no chance of invoking her right to fair remuneration. Hence, the grant of a right to fair remuneration does not change the position of an autonomous artist for the better in these circumstances.

Therefore, it is necessary, as a last resort, to also consider the room in copyright law for a direct redistribution of copyright revenue in favour of autonomous artists. Is it possible to subsidise independent literature and art with income accruing from dependent, profit-oriented productions? At the level of individual, commercially successful authors or industries, the introduction of a direct subsidy of autonomous art is hardly conceivable. Out of solidarity, financially successful creators or exploiters may be prepared to sponsor autonomous art projects on a case-by-case basis. However, a statutory obligation to systematically deposit a share of the revenues accruing from successful productions in a fund for less successful autonomous productions would most likely be seen as an act of expropriation.

The situation is different, however, at the level of collective copyright management. In the EU, the *Amazon* case about the payment and repartitioning of private copying levies in Austria showed that far-reaching mechanisms for the use of collected funds for social and cultural purposes may already be in place. One of the prejudicial questions asked by the Austrian Supreme Court was whether a collecting society lost its right to the payment of fair compensation if, in relation to half of the funds received, the collecting society was required by law not to pay the levy income to the persons entitled to compensation but to distribute it to social and cultural institutions.[126]

Answering this question, the CJEU held the view that EU law did not contain an obligation to pay all the fair compensation collected on the basis of private copying legislation directly to rights owners in cash. By contrast, a member state was free to provide that part of the compensation for the damage caused by private copying be distributed in the form of indirect compensation through social and cultural institutions set up for the benefit of authors and performing artists.[127] The fact that the fair compensation had to be regarded as recompense for the harm suffered by holders of the exclusive right of reproduction by reason of the introduction of the private copying exception did

---

126 *Amazon v Austro-Mechana* (CJEU, C-521/11, 11 July 2013) [15].
127 Ibid [49].

not constitute an obstacle to the establishment of such an indirect payment mechanism through the intermediary of social and cultural institutions.[128] In the light of the objectives underlying the Information Society Directive, the Court even stated that such a system of indirect distribution of collected funds was conducive to ensuring that European cultural creativity and production received the necessary resources. It also safeguarded the independence and dignity of artistic creators and performers.[129] The Court made it a condition, however, that the social and cultural establishments involved actually benefit those entitled to fair compensation for private copying. Moreover, it was necessary that the detailed arrangements for the operation of social and cultural institutions were not discriminatory. Benefits had to be granted to those persons entitled to fair compensation and the system had to be open to nationals and foreigners alike.[130]

At the level of collecting societies, there might thus be room to adopt measures to offer extra support for autonomous artists and independent art productions. If it is legitimate to use half of the funds of collecting societies for social and cultural purposes, it also seems possible to devote particular attention to the furtherance of independent literature and art when taking decisions on the distribution of this substantial share of the collected money. However, the decision of the CJEU in *Amazon* sheds light on two hurdles to be surmounted in this context.

Firstly, the Court made it clear that the use of funds by social and cultural institutions must constitute an indirect form of payment for those entitled to the collected remuneration. In the *Amazon* case, the remuneration was the result of private copying legislation providing for the payment of fair compensation for the damage caused by acts of private copying.[131] Hence, the question arises to which extent the partitioning of collected funds must directly relate to the losses of

---

128 Ibid [50].

129 Ibid [52].

130 Ibid [53]–[54].

131 Art 5(2)(b) ISD. As to the criterion of harm which the CJEU established in this context, see *Padawan v SGAE*, (CJEU, C-467/08, 21 October 2010) [40], [42]. As to the underlying debate on private copying in the EU, see DJG Visser, 'Private Copying' in PB Hugenholtz, AA Quaedvlieg and DJG Visser (eds), *A Century of Dutch Copyright Law – Auteurswet 1912–2012* (deLex, 2012) 413; JN Ullrich, 'Clash of Copyrights – Optionale Schranke und zwingender finanzieller Ausgleich im Fall der Privatkopie nach Art 5 Abs. 2 lit. B) Richtlinie 2001/29/EG und Dreistufentest' (2009) *Gewerblicher Rechtsschutz und Urheberrecht – Internationaler Teil*, 283; C Geiger, 'The Answer to the Machine Should not be the Machine: Safeguarding the Private Copy Exception in the

individual groups of authors. If a strict alignment with individual damage is necessary, the requirement of an indirect compensation via social and cultural institutions would replicate the general problem of a focus on monetary incentives in copyright law. As profit-oriented mainstream productions are likely to be copied more often than independent avant-garde productions, it seems difficult to spend a higher share of the collected remuneration on programs supporting *l'art pour l'art* productions and artists. By contrast, the lion's share of the collected remuneration would have to benefit those authors presumably suffering most from private copying: profit-oriented mainstream artists.

In *Amazon*, however, the CJEU referred to the fact that it was very difficult, if not impossible, to calculate the damage caused by private copying. Against this background, the Court underlined that member states enjoyed wide discretion in determining the form, the detailed arrangements and the possible level of fair compensation.[132] In the exercise of this wide discretion, member states were free to establish a system of indirect compensation via social and cultural institutions.[133] Hence, the Court itself does not seem to insist on a system that distributes collected money meticulously on the basis of the individual harm suffered by individual authors because such a detailed calculation of individual damage is hardly possible. The Austrian provision underlying the *Amazon* decision read as follows:

1. Collecting societies may create institutions for social and cultural purposes for the beneficiaries which they represent and for their family members.

2. Collecting societies that exercise the right to remuneration for blank cassettes shall create institutions for social or cultural purposes and pay to them 50 per cent of the funds generated by that remuneration, minus the relevant administration costs ...

3. Collecting societies must establish strict rules concerning the sums paid by their institutions for social and cultural purposes.

Digital Environment' (2008) *European Intellectual Property Review*, 121; C Geiger, 'Right to Copy v. Three-Step Test, The Future of the Private Copy Exception in the Digital Environment' (2005) *Computer Law Review International*, 12.
132 *Amazon v Austro-Mechana*, (CJEU, C-521/11, 11 July 2013) [20], [40].
133 Ibid [49].

4. As regards the funds paid to social and cultural institutions deriving from remuneration in respect of blank cassettes, the federal Chancellor may determine, by regulation, the circumstances to be taken into account by the rules to be established under subparagraph 3. That regulation must ensure, inter alia, that:

    1. there is a fair balance between the sums allocated to social institutions and those allocated to cultural institutions;

    2. in the case of social establishments, it is possible, primarily, to provide support for rightholders suffering hardship;

    3. the sums allocated to cultural establishments are used to promote the interests of rightholders.[134]

In subsection 4(2), this provision explicitly leaves room to focus on 'rightholders suffering hardship'. Therefore, it seems that the indirect compensation mechanism following from the Austrian system is not strictly based on individual harm suffered by individual right holders. By contrast, particular support for creators in a precarious financial situation is possible. The criterion of harm underlying the remuneration system for private copying in the EU, therefore, does not constitute an insurmountable hurdle when seeking to set up social and cultural institutions with a particular focus on support for independent art and artists.

Secondly, the CJEU made it clear in *Amazon* that a system of indirect compensation via social and cultural institutions must not be discriminatory. This further requirement could also be seen as an obstacle to the establishment of a system favouring autonomous creators. Particular support for *l'art pour l'art* productions could be regarded as an unfair discrimination against bourgeois mainstream authors. This conclusion, however, need not be the last word on the matter. Cultural institutions can support autonomous art while basing their sponsoring decisions on objective criteria, such as a need to provide financial support because of missing opportunities to find a commercial investor. As autonomous art has lower chances of attracting the interest of commercial exploiters, the application of such a general criterion could de facto have the effect of offering

---

134   § 13 of the Austrian Law on Collecting Societies (Verwertungsgesellschaftengesetz) of 13 January 2006, *Bundesgesetzblatt* I, 9/2006, as in force at the time of the *Amazon* case. The translation is taken from *Amazon v Austro-Mechana*, (CJEU, C-521/11, 11 July 2013), [8].

stronger support for independent *l'art pour l'art* productions than for profit-oriented mainstream productions. Moreover, it must be considered that even if discrimination in favour of autonomous art was found, this discrimination could be justified. Given the above-described fundamental importance of autonomous art as an engine of alternative visions of society that may pave the way for necessary social and political changes, there is a sound justification for lending stronger support to independent productions and autonomous artists.

Hence, the discussion of redistribution mechanisms in the field of collective management of copyright revenue, such as the Austrian system of indirect compensation for private copying via social and cultural institutions, shows that mechanisms for the partitioning of collected funds in line with specific social and cultural objectives are possible. To offer stronger support for autonomous art and artists, it would be necessary to employ these redistribution mechanisms systematically to support autonomous artists and finance the production of independent art capable of offering alternative visions of society.

5. Towards a copyright system supporting autonomous art

Bourdieu's sociological analysis provides an important theoretical model that sheds light on the motivations and expectations of different groups of creators. It explains how the ongoing fight between bourgeois and autonomous creators for predominance in the field of literary and artistic production impacts the quality standards and the internal discourse in the art community, and how it influences the degree of autonomy of the social space in which works of literature and art are created. Bourdieu highlights the plurality of factors influencing the decision to create a work. With a spectrum of driving forces ranging from monetary to reputational rewards, the analysis confirms previous research pointing out that the focus on the motivating power of pecuniary incentives in copyright law is incomplete and doubtful. In the area of autonomous *l'art pour l'art* productions, Bourdieu identifies a peculiar reverse economy contradicting the reliance on the grant of exploitation rights as a reward and incentive scheme: a creator winning in economic terms loses in artistic terms. Artists striving for monetary success are unlikely to acquire a reputation as an autonomous, independent artist in the art community. From this perspective, copyright law may even be accused of enticing authors away from an autonomous *l'art pour l'art* orientation. Considering Bourdieu's description of the ongoing fight of bourgeois and autonomous creators for predominance in the field of literary and artistic production, it may also be said that copyright is not impartial in the power struggle. Focusing on monetary incentives, it offers more support for bourgeois authors than for autonomous authors.

As state subsidies for autonomous art and artists are continuously reduced, it is indispensable to remove this bias of copyright law in favour of profit-oriented mainstream productions. In the absence of public funds for the creation of independent literature and art, it would be disastrous not to take measures supporting autonomous productions in copyright law. Works of true art fulfil a function of particular importance in society. They offer alternative visions of life and society that can pave the way for necessary changes of social and political conditions. Without these impulses provided by independent, autonomous art, society has less chances to evolve and overcome imperfections. Hence, it is of particular importance to identify those features of copyright law that are capable of compensating for the loss of state subsidies and functioning as a driver of autonomous art.

The analysis of copyright law from this perspective leads to a broader understanding of authors' rights. Apart from traditional exploitation rights that allow an author to prohibit the unauthorised use of literary and artistic works (right to control consumptive use), copyright law should also recognise an author's right to use pre-existing material for the purpose of creating new works (right of transformative use of protected material). Limitations that are central to this transformative process, such as the idea/expression dichotomy and the freedom to make quotations, parodies and remixes, would have to obtain the same status as traditional exploitation rights. This would exclude a strict, narrow interpretation. It would also require the development of appropriate enforcement mechanisms, for instance with regard to works protected through technological measures.

The analysis of copyright law in the light of Bourdieu's theory also leads to the question how copyright law can ensure a fair remuneration for bourgeois and autonomous authors alike. It is contradictory when the law justifies the grant of broad exploitation rights in the light of the difficult income situation of creators, while at the same time condoning the practice of imposing 'buy out' contracts upon authors with insufficient bargaining power. Again, Bourdieu's analysis can offer guidelines in this regard. While a general right to fair remuneration *ex ante* may be of particular importance to bourgeois authors whose works are likely to be commercially successful in the marketplace, independent artists may have a particular interest in a remuneration rule that ensures a fair profit sharing *ex post*.

Accordingly, legislative measures seeking to ensure that creators receive a fair remuneration for their creative work should not be confined to mechanisms focusing on an appropriate reward *ex ante* – at the time the exploitation contract is concluded. By contrast, fair remuneration legislation must necessarily include an *ex post* remuneration rule giving authors the right to demand an adjustment of the exploitation contract if a work has outstanding success. If the paid honorarium appears disproportionately low in the light of a work's later success, such an *ex post* rule ensures an appropriate remuneration against the background of verifiable sales and income figures. The introduction of an *ex post* remuneration mechanism may also encourage the conclusion of exploitation contracts which, instead of merely providing for a one-time 'buy out' honorarium, offer continuous royalty payments based on a predefined revenue share.

Finally, the present analysis yields the insight that a direct redistribution of money in the creative sector is advisable to support autonomous art and artists. Such a redistribution of financial resources is possible in the area of collective copyright management. The schemes of collecting societies for the partitioning of collected funds can systematically be aligned with the need to support the production of independent art. For this purpose, the distribution of copyright revenue that is available for autonomous art should be left to designated bodies of collecting societies with a particular focus on furthering the production of autonomous literature and art.

As a critical comment on this latter point, it is to be added that the recommendation of a direct redistribution of copyright revenue via designated bodies of collecting societies is inspired by Bourdieu's conclusion that, as a result of reduced state subsidies for independent art, the autonomy of the field of literary and artistic productions is currently at risk. Against this background, the direct redistribution of remuneration in favour of autonomous art and artists must be seen as an extraordinary measure. It culminates in the cross-financing of independent art through income accruing from dependent mainstream productions. On its merits, this concept imposes an obligation on the cultural sector to finance its own autonomy. Given the crucial importance of autonomous art for society as a whole, however, this may be deemed an unfairly heavy burden. On the one hand, measures based on partitioning schemes of collecting societies that favour autonomous art must not become a cheap escape strategy for state authorities seeking to rid themselves of the responsibility to ensure an intact system of autonomous art and provide financial support for underlying societal goals. On the other hand, the implementation of support strategies for autonomous art by the cultural sector itself has the advantage of avoiding the shortcomings of direct state patronage.[135] Funding via repartitioning schemes of collecting societies allows creators to establish criteria for the distribution of available funds themselves. The discussion about an appropriate framework for supporting autonomous art may be a particularly challenging task for the different groups of artists who are members of a given collecting society. Once it is clear that a certain percentage of collected revenue must be available for autonomous art, however, the necessity to find workable solutions for the distribution of resulting funds is not unlikely to lead to the establishment of a procedure for appropriate decision-making. The funding decisions taken by the designated bodies of collecting societies, in turn, can be qualified as acts of self-regulation. Once this self-regulation is in place, the state can contribute to the funding of autonomous art without interfering with the decision-making process. For this purpose, the state can simply make additional funds available to the designated bodies of collecting societies (which have been established by the artists in the collecting society themselves).

---

135 For a detailed discussion of potential shortcomings, see SA Pager, 'Beyond Culture vs. Commerce: Decentralizing Cultural Protection to Promote Diversity Through Trade' (2011) 31 *Northwestern Journal of International Law & Business* 63, 75–97. However, the shortcomings listed by Pager are not fully applicable in the present context because he focuses on market-based incentives and commercial productions.

Finally, the limitations of the present analysis must not be concealed. Bourdieu focuses on professional authors devoting time and effort to the creation of literary and artistic works. Hence, the rights and remuneration infrastructure that would be needed to support the creativity of amateur creators falls outside the scope of the present inquiry from the outset. Guidelines for the application of copyright rules to amateur producers of user-generated content can hardly be inferred from Bourdieu's theoretical model. Therefore, the various questions[136] raised by the increased participation of users in the creation of literary and artistic works remain open.

---

136 For an exceptional case of a specific use privilege for user-generated content, see Art 29.21 of the *Copyright Act* of Canada, as introduced by Bill C-11, *Copyright Modernization Act*, adopted 18 June 2012. As to the debate on user-generated content and its impact on copyright law, see SD Jamar, 'Crafting Copyright Law to Encourage and Protect User-Generated Content in the Internet Social Networking Context' (2010) 19 *Widener Law Journal* 843; N Helberger et al, *Legal Aspects of User Created Content* (Institute for Information Law, 2009) available at <ssrn.com/abstract=1499333>; MWS Wong, 'Transformative User-Generated Content in Copyright Law: Infringing Derivative Works or Fair Use?' (2009) 11 *Vanderbilt Journal of Entertainment and Technology Law* 1075; E Lee, 'Warming Up to User-Generated Content' (2008) *University of Illinois Law Review* 1459; B Buckley, 'SueTube: Web 2.0 and Copyright Infringement' (2008) 31 *Columbia Journal of Law and the Arts* 235; TW Bell, 'The Specter of Copyism v. Blockheaded Authors: How User-Generated Content Affects Copyright Policy' (2008) 10 *Vanderbilt Journal of Entertainment and Technology Law* 841; S Hechter, 'User-Generated Content and the Future of Copyright: Part One – Investiture of Ownership' (2008) 10 *Vanderbilt Journal of Entertainment and Technology Law* 863; G Lastowka, 'User-Generated Content and Virtual Worlds' (2008) 10 *Vanderbilt Journal of Entertainment and Technology Law* 893.

3

Copyright as an access right: Securing cultural participation through the protection of creators' interests

Christophe Geiger[1]

It is never too late to give up our prejudices. No way of thinking or doing, however ancient, can be trusted without proof. What everybody echoes or in silence passes by as true today may turn out to be falsehood tomorrow, mere smoke of opinion, which some had

---

1   Professor of Law, Director General and Director of the Research Department of the Centre for International Intellectual Property Studies (CEIPI), University of Strasbourg; Affiliated Senior Researcher, Max Planck Institute for Innovation and Competition, Munich; and Spangenberg Fellow in Law & Technology at the Spangenberg Center for Law, Technology & the Arts, Case Western Reserve University School of Law, Cleveland, US. This paper draws for some parts on previous research published by the author on the social function of intellectual property and the relationship between human rights and copyright, in particular: 'The Social Function of Intellectual Property Rights, Or how Ethics can Influence the Shape and Use of IP law' in GB Dinwoodie (ed), *Intellectual Property Law: Methods and Perspectives* (Edward Elgar, 2014) 153; '"Constitutionalising" Intellectual Property Law?, The Influence of Fundamental Rights on Intellectual Property in Europe' (2006) 37(4) *International Review of Intellectual Property and Competition Law*, 371; 'Flexibilising Copyright – Remedies to the Privatisation of Information by Copyright Law' (2008) 39(2) *International Review of Intellectual Property and Competition Law*, 178; 'Implementing Intellectual Property Provisions in Human Rights Instruments: Towards a New Social Contract for the Protection of Intangibles' in C Geiger (ed), *Research Handbook on Human Rights and Intellectual Property* (Edward Elgar, 2015), 661. The author is thankful to Elena Izyumenko, PhD Candidate at the CEIPI, for her great research assistance and editorial support.

trusted for a cloud that would sprinkle fertilizing rain on their fields. What old people say you cannot do, you try and find that you can. Old deeds for old people, and new deeds for new.

Henry David Thoreau, *Walden; or, Life in the Woods*, Boston, Ticknor and Fields, 1854, p 11.

Introduction

Copyright, originally conceived as a tool to protect the author and to provide incentives for him to create for the benefit of society, is nowadays more and more perceived as a mechanism to the advantage of 'large, impersonal and unlovable corporations'.[2] As the results of a major recent study on the intellectual property (IP) perceptions of Europeans demonstrate, more than 40 per cent of EU citizens, when asked who benefits the most from IP protection, mention large companies and famous artists,[3] and not creators or the society at large.

The inherent social dimension of copyright law has hence progressively been lost of sight by policymakers to the benefit of strictly individualistic, even egotistic conceptions. In the recent discourse on the strengthening of legal means of protection, copyright is more frequently presented as an investment-protection mechanism[4] than a vehicle of cultural and social progress. In this context, the society's enrichment and future creativity are often portrayed in the rhetoric of the major economic players only as 'a fortunate by-product of private

---

2   JC Ginsburg, 'How Copyright Got a Bad Name for Itself' (2002) 26(1) *Columbia Journal of Law & the Arts* 61, 61.
3   'European Citizens and Intellectual Property: Perception, Awareness and Behaviour' (OHIM Report, November 2013) 66.
4   See e.g. M Vivant, 'Propriété intellectuelle et nouvelles technologies, À la recherche d'un nouveau paradigm' in *Université de tous les savoirs* (Odile Jacob, 2001) vol 5: *Qu'est ce que les technologies?* 201 *et seq*. This conclusion can equally be reached for patent law, where the protection of creativity and innovation seems to become subordinate to the protection of investment. As B Remiche, 'Marchandisation et brevet' in M Vivant (ed), *Propriété intellectuelle et mondialisation* (Dalloz, 2004) 127, correctly emphasises, we have been witnessing for several years a change in the centre of interest of the law 'turning from the inventor's person to the investing company'. This change of paradigm can already be considered worrying since the perception of investment does not contain any human or ethical dimension. Compensation of the investment is not systematically a synonym for progress, and as Professor Remiche recalls, 'to accent the investment – or even to make the nearly single element out of it – means to incite the research and the investment only there where they are the most cost-effective and profitable!' (at 128). The interest of society cannot be reduced to economic interest; the social justification for intellectual property is larger and should take into account certain fundamental values.

entitlement'.[5] A good example of this discourse can be found in the huge advertisement campaigns that were launched a few years ago by the music industry, showing young internet users behind bars for having engaged in music file sharing and using classical analogy with the theft of tangible goods, according to which illegal downloading amounts to going into a shop and stealing.[6] This has provoked some important counter-reactions: as copyright is perceived mainly as a right to forbid, to sanction and punish, infringing copyright has evolved, predominantly among the young generations, to an act of protest,[7] leading to a serious crisis of legitimacy.[8] Even among creators, copyright is increasingly perceived as a hurdle in the creative process, as the success of so-called 'open content' models clearly demonstrates.

These developments urgently attest the need to rethink copyright in order to adapt its rules to its initially dual character: 1) of a right to secure and organise cultural participation and access to creative works (access aspect); and 2) of a guarantee that the creator participates fairly in the fruit of the commercial exploitation of his works (protection aspect). Avoiding the privatisation of information by copyright law[9] and assuring that cultural goods are still available for future innovations

---

5   CJ Craig, 'Locke, Labour and Limiting the Author's Right: A Warning against a Lockean Approach to Copyright Law' (2002) 28 *Queen's Law Journal* 1, at 14–15.

6   On this rhetoric, see more generally PL Loughlan, '"You Wouldn't Steal a Car …" Intellectual Property and the Language of Theft' (2007) 401 *European Intellectual Property Review*.

7   'European Citizens and Intellectual Property', above n 2, 55.

8   Further on this crisis, see e.g. N Kroes, Vice-President of the European Commission responsible for the Digital Agenda from 9 February 2010 until 1 November 2014, 'Our Single Market is Crying Out for Copyright Reform', Speech delivered at the opening of Information Influx, the 25th anniversary International Conference of the Institute for Information Law (IViR), Amsterdam, 2 July 2014 (European Commission - SPEECH/14/528): 'Every day citizens … across the EU break the law just to do something commonplace. And who can blame them when those laws are so ill-adapted … Technology moves faster than the law can, particularly in the EU. Today, the EU copyright framework is fragmented, inflexible, and often irrelevant. It should be a stimulant to openness, innovation and creativity, not a tool for of obstruction, limitation and control.'

9   Further on this tendency, see C Geiger, 'Flexibilising Copyright – Remedies to the Privatisation of Information by Copyright Law' (2008) 39(2) *International Review of Intellectual Property and Competition Law*, 178.

might mean (re)conceiving copyright as an 'access right',[10] and not as the right to forbid, exclude or sanction, thus emphasising the inclusive rather than the exclusive nature of copyright protection.[11]

Before turning to the consequences of such an understanding for the shape and use of copyright law (II), it will however be necessary to examine, first, the rationales underlying the often neglected nature of copyright as an 'access right' (I).

1. Rationales for copyright to be conceived as an access right

1.1. The social function of copyright law and the philosophical link with the common interest[12]

Even though the demand for an access aspect of copyright has only been made for a relatively short time, the idea is not completely new. Already in the 13th century, the theologian and philosopher Thomas

---

10   The term 'access right' in the context of this chapter needs to be clearly differentiated from its past, diametrically opposite understanding. In fact, the term 'access right' has been used in previous scholarly work to describe the right to control, even forbid, access to copyright works, which resulted from technical protection measures (TPM) and their legal protection by copyright law: see e.g. JC Ginsburg, 'From Having Copies to Experiencing Works: The Development of an Access Right in U.S. Copyright Law' (2003) 50 *Journal of the Copyright Society of the USA*, 113; T Hoeren, 'Access Right as a Postmodern Symbol of Copyright Deconstruction?' in JC Ginsburg and JB Besek (eds), *Adjuncts and Alternatives to Copyright, Proceedings of the ALAI Congress June 13–17, 2001* (Kernochan Center for Law Media and the Arts, 2002), 360; T Heide, 'Copyright in the E.U. and the United States: What "Access Right"?' (2001) *European Intellectual Property Review*, 476; S Olswang, 'Accessright: An Evolutionary Path for Copyright in the Digital Era?' (1995) *European Intellectual Property Review* 215. See however for an interesting attempt to define and conceptualise the access right in the digital world, Z Efroni, *Access- Right: The Future of Digital Copyright Law* (Oxford University Press, 2011). This author distinguishes 'access rights' and 'rights to access' and proposes a stimulating 'theoretical framework for a discussion on an information property system based on the concept of access' (at Introduction, xxi).

11   On the idea of inclusivity in IP, see also G van Overwalle, 'Smart Innovation and Inclusive Patents for Sustainable Food and Health Care: Redefining the Europe 2020 objectives' in C Geiger (ed), *Constructing European Intellectual Property: Achievements and New Perspectives* (Edward Elgar, 2013) EIPIN Series, vol 1; S Dusollier, 'Du gratuit au non-exclusif: Les nouvelles teintes de la propriété intellectuelle' in *Vers une rénovation de la propriété intellectuelle?, 30e anniversaire de l'IRPI* (Litec, 2014) 29; and from the same author: 'The commons as a reverse intellectual property- from exclusivity to inclusivity' in H Howe and J Griffiths (eds), *Concepts of Property in Intellectual Property Law* (Cambridge University Press, 2013) 258.

12   Throughout this chapter, the philosophical notion of the 'common interest', reflecting the interests of society at large, will be preferred to the terms 'public interest'. The 'public interest' terminology has in fact been already heavily used in past copyright legal discourse, especially

Aquinas expressed an opinion that 'positive right' (*jus positivum*) could be regarded as fair and legitimate only inasmuch as it aims at the common wellbeing: put differently, if the right fulfils its so-called 'social function'. This idea has been hereafter reiterated by many legal philosophers.[13] It was first confined to the context of private law in general (1) and then extended more specifically to the sphere of intellectual property (2).

1.1.1. The social function of law

Balance is the key concept that lies behind the social function. If law is a question of balance, there cannot be an 'absolute' right that can be exercised in a totally self-reflective manner with no consideration for the consequences that this exercise involves. As has been aptly put by Du Pasquier, 'the role of the law is to assure the peaceful coexistence of the human group or, as is often said, to harmonise the activity of members of society. In a word, it is the basis for the social order, which could only be achieved through a balance between opposing interests'.[14]

In France, this idea was developed in the 1930s by Louis Josserand. So far as concerns the right to property, he wrote that 'there is no need to investigate deeply to notice that this right that claims to be unlimited involves, above all in the field of real estate, a multitude of obstacles, barriers, frontiers that restrain its movements and oppose its expansion.' He further adds: 'This is fortunate, since if this tyrannical

---

in common law countries, both as an argument to extend *and* to limit protection. See G Davies, *Copyright and the public interest*, (Sweet and Maxwell, 2nd ed, 2002) 236, 'It is seen to be in the public interest that authors and other right owners should be encouraged to publish their works so as to permit the widest possible dissemination of works to the public at large … Thus, while copyright protection is justified by the public interest, the States imposes certain limitations thereto, again in the public interest.' Thus, there is already an important legal background and understanding attached to this terminology, which does not favour the 'blue-sky thinking' encouraged by the editors of this volume when rethinking and redesigning copyright law. The terms 'public interest', when used in this chapter, will thus refer only to situations when this wording has been employed by legislators of courts (for example in quotes) or will be put in brackets.

13   Further on this, see C Geiger, 'The Social Function of Intellectual Property Rights, Or how Ethics can Influence the Shape and Use of IP law' in GB Dinwoodie (ed), *Intellectual Property Law: Methods and Perspectives* (Edward Elgar, 2014) 153.

14   C Du Pasquier, *Introduction à la théorie générale et à la philosophie du Droit* (Delachaux et Nestlé, 4th ed, 1967), 19. See also JH Drake, Editorial Preface of R von Ihering, *Der Zweck im Recht* [Law as a Means to an End] (Boston Book Company, 1913) 188: 'Law is not the highest thing in the world, not an end in itself; but merely a means to an end, the final end being the existence of society.'

right was left to itself, to its specific nature, it would invade everything and end up by destroying itself'.[15] In the field of contract law, this social concept has been more recently developed by a number of legal scholars. Denis Mazeaud, for example, advocates 'the definitive recognition of a principle of 'loyalty, solidarity and fraternity' as a main and guiding principle of contemporary contract law'.[16]

In Germany, the theory of the social function of private law (*Sozialbindung des Privatrechts*)[17] made its appearance at the end of the 19th century, subsequently becoming a fundamental principle of German private law.[18] This theory insists on the idea that private rights are limited by social constraints. It underlines the social nature of the legal system and the function of private law, which is to regulate the relationships between individuals within society. The function of the legal system is thus to find a compromise between the interests of the individual and the interests of the community. It must, on the one hand, ensure the grant of subjective rights to individuals but at the same time, on the other hand, ensure that these are compatible with the interests of the rest of the community. The rights of the individual are not seen as an absolute right but rather as rights limited in social terms. This theory is implemented, moreover, in the extremely rich judicial practice developed on the basis of Section 242 of the German Civil Code concerning good faith – a general clause that in the hands of the judge has become a veritable balancing instrument.[19]

---

15   L Josserand, *De l'esprit des droits et de leur relativité* (Dalloz, 2nd ed, 1939, re-edited 2006) 16.

16   D Mazeaud, 'Loyauté, solidarité, fraternité: La nouvelle devise contractuelle?' in *L'avenir du droit, Mélanges en hommage à François Terré* (Dalloz/PUF/Éditions du Jurisclasseur, 1999) 603.

17   Literally translated: 'The social bounds of private law'.

18   O Von Gierke, *Die soziale Aufgabe des Privatrechts* (Berlin, 1889; republished by Klosterman, 1943); J Kohler, *Das Autorrecht, eine zivilrechtliche Abhandlung* (Verlag von G Fischer, Jena, 1880), 41. On this theory, see more recently T Repgen, *Die soziale Aufgabe des Privatrechts: Eine Grundfrage in Wissenschaft und Kodifikation am Ende des 19. Jahrhundert* (Mohr Siebeck, 2001).

19   WF Ebke and BM Steinhauer, 'The Doctrine of Good Faith in German Contract Law' in J Beatson and D Friedman (eds), *Good Faith and Fault in Contract Law* (Clarendon Press/Oxford University Press, 1997) 171.

1.1.2. The social function of copyright law and the common interest

The idea that copyright must serve a social function has its origins in the philosophy of the Enlightenment.[20] It rests upon the idea that intellectual property law is the product of a type of 'social contract' between the author and society.[21] According to this concept, copyright is justified because it encourages creativity. Society has a need for intellectual productions in order to ensure its development and cultural, economic, technological and social progress and therefore grants the creator a reward in the form of an intellectual property right, which enables him to exploit his work and to draw benefits from it. In return, the creator, by rendering his creation accessible to the public, enriches the community. Copyright law is hence 'conditioned' by the achievement of certain objectives and its use can be (or rather *must be*) measured in the light of the results obtained. This particularly strong focus on the interests of society very soon led numerous German scholars to extend the theory of the social function to intellectual property rights.[22] Julius Kopsch as early as the 1920s even evoked the idea of an 'increased' social function with respect to intellectual property.[23]

One key aspect that derives from the social function is thus that the objectives and conditions of the exercise of copyright should always be examined in the light of the interest of society and the common interest. However, what exactly is this *common interest*? Most of the time, this notion is closely related to utilitarian doctrines, but philosophically speaking, there are several different versions of Utilitarianism.[24] Mireille Buydens identifies three different philosophical conceptions.[25] In a first understanding, the common interest is the *interest of the Nation/State* (Aristotle, Hegel, Fichte):[26] whatever the state defines

---

20   See, for example, A Strowel, *Droit d'auteur et copyright, Divergences et Convergences* (Bruylant/LGDJ, 1993), 86 *et seq*; C Geiger, *Droit d'auteur et droit du public à l'information* (Litec, 2004) 27 *et seq*; 'Copyright and Free Access to Information, For a Fair Balance of Interests in a Globalised World' (2006) *European Intellectual Property Review*, 366.

21   For more details on this issue, see Geiger, above n 19, 27 *et seq*.

22   Kohler, above n 17, 40; E Riezler, *Deutsches Urheber- und Erfinderrecht* (Schweitzer, 1909), 430.

23   J Kopsch, 'Zur Frage der gesetzlichen Lizenz' (1928) (1) *ArchFunkR* 201.

24   For a fascinating analysis in the context of intellectual property, see M Buydens, *La propriété intellectuelle, Evolution historique et philosophique* (Bruylant, 2012), 351.

25   M Buydens, 'L'intérêt général, une notion protéiforme' in M Buydens and S Dusollier (eds), *L'intérêt général et l'accès à l'information en propriété intellectuelle* (Bruylant, 2008), 1.

26   Ibid 8 *et seq*.

as the common interest has to be reflected by law. In a second interpretation, the notion is understood in exactly the opposite way: the common interest is defined according to the *particular interests of the individual* (Bentham, Adam Smith, John Stuart Mill);[27] from the sum of the individual interests, acting in their own advantage, emerges the common interest. The common interest is the one that maximises profits of the majority of individuals. The third understanding of the notion is Christian in its inspiration. *The common interest is defined as the 'good of Mankind'* (Thomas Aquinas, Hume);[28] in this conception, the reference is the human being. The role of society is to define a framework for human development and happiness, according to universal human values (including immaterial benefits such as social cohesion, solidarity, education, health, culture, sustainable development, etc.). This common interest has to originate from the 'Human' and be implemented by legislators. The link to human rights is here easily made and it is therefore not surprising to find human rights and constitutional law obligations among the second category of rationales for copyright as an 'access right'.

1.2. Copyright through the lens of international human rights law and domestic constitutional law

The common interest rationales behind IP protection are envisaged in numerous international and regional human rights treaties and national constitutions worldwide. This is done, first, through incorporation of certain[29] copyright aspects in the universally recognised right to culture and science[30] (1.2.1). Second, the access aspect of copyright can be traced in likewise internationally binding 'expressive' foundations of IP (in accordance with which copyright is

---

27   Ibid 22 *et seq.*

28   Ibid 37 *et seq.*

29   Further on the distinction that exists between the standard IP rights and the human rights protection given to creators in accordance with the right to science and culture, see UN Committee on Economic, Social and Cultural Rights (CESCR), *General Comment No. 17: The Right of Everyone to Benefit from the Protection of the Moral and Material Interests Resulting from any Scientific, Literary or Artistic Production of Which He or She is the Author (Art. 15, Para. 1 (c) of the Covenant)*, UN Doc E/C.12/GC/17 (12 January 2006); UN General Assembly, Report of the Special Rapporteur in the field of Cultural Rights, F Shaheed, *Copyright Policy and the Right to Science and Culture*, Human Rights Council, Twenty-eighth session, A/HRC/28/57, 24 December 2014.

30   See, on the international level, article 27 of the *Universal Declaration of Human Rights* (UDHR) (see below n 32) and article 15 of the *International Covenant on Economic, Social and Cultural Rights* (ICESCR) (see below n 34).

to be regarded as an exception to the generic right to freely express oneself, impart and receive information)[31] (1.2.2). Finally, inclusion of copyright within the protection of property at constitutional level[32] often guarantees that the social function of property is extended to intellectual property (1.2.3).

1.2.1. Copyright as enabling an access to science and culture

The best example of an access-safeguarding framework for copyright protection is offered by article 27 of the Universal Declaration of Human Rights (UDHR).[33] According to its first paragraph, everyone has 'the right freely to participate in the cultural life of the community, to enjoy the arts and to share in scientific advancement and its benefits', while according to the second paragraph of the same provision, everyone has the right to the protection of the moral and material interests resulting from any scientific, literary or artistic production of which he is the author.[34] Although it is true that the UDHR does not have a direct binding effect, the same does not apply to article 15(1) of the International Covenant on Economic, Social and Cultural Rights (ICESCR),[35] adopting the wording of the UDHR almost verbatim.[36] On the regional level, copyright is in a similar manner conceived as enabling access to science and culture in article 14 of the Additional

---

31   See article 19 of the UDHR and article 19 of the *International Covenant on Civil and Political Rights* (ICCPR).

32   At the international level, see article 17 of the UDHR. Note, however, that neither ICESCR nor ICCPR enshrine a similar guarantee of property within their human rights catalogues.

33   *Universal Declaration of Human Rights*, GA Res 217A, UN Doc A/810 (10 December 1948).

34   For further analysis of article 27 of the UDHR, see inter alia E Stamatopoulou, *Cultural Rights in International Law: Article 27 of the Universal Declaration of Human Rights and Beyond* (Martinus Nijhoff Publishers, 2007), 110.

35   *International Covenant on Economic, Social and Cultural Rights*, opened for signature 16 December 1966, 993 UNTS 3.

36   See, for further discussion of this provision, C Sganga, 'Right to Culture and Copyright: Participation and Access' in C Geiger (ed), *Research Handbook on Human Rights and Intellectual Property* (Edward Elgar, 2015), 560; L Shaver and C Sganga, 'The Right to Take Part in Cultural Life: On Copyright and Human Rights' (Winter 2010) 27 *Wisconsin International Law Journal*, 637; L Shaver, 'The Right to Science and Culture' (2010) (1) *Wisconsin Law Review*, 121. See also the forthcoming proceedings of international roundtable organised by the Centre d'Etudes Internationales de la Propriété Intellectuelle (CEIPI) on the topic 'Intellectual Property and Access to Science and Culture: Convergence or Conflict?', CEIPI, University of Strasbourg, 11 May 2015, especially the papers presented by Lea Shaver, Rebecca Giblin and Christophe Geiger, CEIPI-ICTSD publication series, number 3, *Global Perspectives and Challenges for the Intellectual Property System*, 2016.

Protocol to the American Convention on Human Rights (ACHR)[37] and article 13 of the American Declaration of the Rights and Duties of Man[38] – the latter being in fact a precursor to the UDHR.[39]

The classical foundations of IP are placed in a stable balance in these international human rights instruments: on the one hand, the foundation of natural law by acknowledging an exploitation right and a *'droit moral'* for the creator; and, on the other hand, the utilitarian foundation, because this acknowledgement has the promotion of intellectual variety and the spread of culture and science throughout society as a goal.[40] Further, both the UDHR and the ICESCR emphasise the link to the 'author', namely the creator, also referring to the words such as 'he' and 'everyone', thereby excluding protection of the legal entities' entitlements on the level of human rights.[41]

So far as concerns the domestic constitutional level, an impressive number of national primary law instruments mirror the UDHR and the ICESCR in safeguarding creators' rights within the scope of the right to science and culture.[42] Most of such clauses are characterised

---

37   *Additional Protocol to the American Convention on Human Rights in the Area of Economic, Social and Cultural Rights* (*'Protocol of San Salvador'*), Organization of American States, opened for signature 17 November 1988, OASTS 69 (ACHR).

38   *American Declaration of the Rights and Duties of Man*, Inter-American Commission on Human Rights, 2 May 1948, OAS Res XXX, adopted by the Ninth International Conference of American States, reprinted in *Basic Documents Pertaining to Human Rights in the Inter-American System*, OAS/Ser.L/V/I.4 Rev 9 (2003) (*'American Declaration'*).

39   Since the discussed provisions of the UDHR, the ICESCR, the ACHR and the American Declaration closely correspond to each other, this paper mainly focuses on the provisions of only the UDHR and the ICESCR as instruments of universal coverage.

40   For further discussion of the classical foundations of IP law, see C Geiger, '"Constitutionalising" Intellectual Property Law? The Influence of Fundamental Rights on Intellectual Property in Europe' (2006) 37(4) *International Review of Intellectual Property and Competition Law* 371, 377 *et seq.*

41   See CESCR, above n 28, [7].

42   For examples of such constitutional provisions, see article 54(3) of the *Constitution of the Republic of Bulgaria* (1991); article 69 of the *Constitution of the Republic of Croatia* (1990); article 34(1) of the Czech *Charter of Fundamental Rights and Freedoms* (1993); article 113 of the *Constitution of Latvia* (1922); article 42 of the *Constitution of the Republic of Lithuania* (1992); article 43(1) of the *Constitution of Slovakia* (1992); article 42 of the *Constitution of the Portuguese Republic* (1976); article 36 of the *Constitution of the Republic of Armenia* (1995); article 44(1) of the *Constitution of the Russian Federation* (1993); article 73(2) of the *Constitution of the Republic of Serbia* (2006); article 58 of the *Constitution of the Republic of Albania* (1998); article 64 of the *Constitution of the Republic of Turkey* (1982); article 2(8) of the *Political Constitution of Peru* (1993); article 98 of the *Constitution of the Bolivian Republic of Venezuela* (1999); article I, section 8, clause 8 of the *United States Constitution* (1787); articles 125 and 127 of the *Political Constitution of the Republic of Nicaragua* (1987); article 29 of the *Constitution of the Republic of the Congo* (2002); article 46 of the *Constitution of the Democratic Republic of Congo* (2006); article 94 of the

by a balanced wording, directly referring to the 'public interest' dimension of copyright. To give just a few examples, article 42 of the Lithuanian Constitution of 1992, for instance, ensures that the State *'supports culture and science'* while 'protecting and defending the spiritual and material interests of an author which are related to scientific, technical, cultural, and artistic work'.[43] A similar wording is adopted by many other constitutions worldwide, including article 73 of the Constitution of Serbia of 2006, article 98 of the Constitution of Venezuela of 1999, article 46 of the Constitution of the Democratic Republic of Congo of 2006, and article 40 of the Constitution of Tajikistan of 1994. Nevertheless, perhaps the most famous constitutional provision, explicitly referring to the interests of society as a legislative motive behind copyright protection, is article 1, section 8, clause 8 of the US Constitution of 1787,[44] which reads as follows: 'The Congress shall have Power … *To promote the Progress of Science and useful Arts* by securing for limited Times to Authors and Inventors the exclusive Rights to their respective Writings and Discoveries.'[45]

The common interest considerations behind the grant of protection are made salient here: exclusive rights are conferred *insofar and inasmuch* as they facilitate cultural progress. The interests of society are a reason for granting protection but also a reason for limiting it – a premise that has been further interpreted and completed by the established judicial practice of the US Supreme Court. For instance, a decision dating from 1932 laid down that the 'sole interest of the United States and the primary object in conferring a monopoly lie in the general benefits

---

Constitution of the Republic of Mozambique (2004); article 26 of the *Constitution of the Republic of Madagascar* (1992); article 47 of the *Constitution of the Islamic Republic of Afghanistan* (2004); article 49 of the *Constitution of the Kyrgyz Republic* (2010); article 16 of the *Constitution of the People's Republic of Mongolia* (1992); article 22 of the *Constitution of the Republic of Korea* (1948); article 40 of the *Constitution of the Republic of Tajikistan* (1994); article 60 of the *Constitution of the Socialist Republic of Vietnam* (1992); Part 9, Section 86 of the *Constitution of the Kingdom of Thailand* (2007). For further discussion, see C Geiger, 'Implementing Intellectual Property Provisions in Human Rights Instruments: Towards a New Social Contract for the Protection of Intangibles' in C Geiger (ed), *Research Handbook on Human Rights and Intellectual Property*, (Edward Elgar, 2015).

43   Emphasis added. For an excellent analysis of the Lithuanian Constitutional Court's interpretation of article 42 intellectual property provision, see V Mizaras, 'Issues of Intellectual Property Law in the Jurisprudence of the Constitutional Court of the Republic of Lithuania' (2012) 19(3) *Jurisprudence*.

44   The so-called 'Progress Clause'.

45   Emphasis added.

derived by the public from the labour of authors'.[46] In addition, the 'Progress-Clause' explicitly refers to 'authors' as beneficiaries of copyright protection, thereby reinforcing, on a constitutional level, the primary role of the creator.

1.2.2. Copyright as an exception to freedom of expression

In direct link with its capacity to enable cultural access is the constitutional perception of copyright as an integral part of the right to freedom of expression and information.

Since its inception copyright has maintained close links with freedom of expression and its corollary, the public's right to receive and impart information.[47] In fact, the access to information and copyright fully converge regarding both the rationale and the principles involved.[48]

A good illustration of this convergence is article 20 of the Spanish Constitution of 1978, where IP is protected within the framework of the right to freedom of expression and information (paragraph 1(b)).[49] As put succinctly by F Bondia in a comment on this provision:

---

46   *Fox Film Corp v Doyal*, 286 US 123, 127 (1932). Many cases reiterate the reference to the public interest and the public good. See, for example, *Fogerty v Fantasy Inc*, 510 US 517, 526 (1994): 'We have often recognized the monopoly privileges that Congress has authorized, while "intended to motivate the creative activity of authors and inventors by the provision of a special reward," are limited in nature and *must ultimately serve the public good*' (referring to the landmark *Sony Corp of America v Universal City Studios Inc*, 464 US 417, 429 (1984), emphasis added). See also *Harper & Row Publishers Inc v Nation Enterprises*, 471 US 539, 558 (1985): 'The economic philosophy behind the clause empowering Congress to grant patents and copyrights is the conviction that encouragement of individual effort by personal gain is the best way to *advance public welfare* through the talents of authors and inventors in "Science and useful Arts"' (quoting *Mazer v Stein*, 347 US 201, 219 (1954), emphasis added); *NY Times Co v Tasini*, 533 US 483, 524 n 20 (Stevens J, dissenting) (2001): 'Copyright law is not an insurance policy for authors, but a *carefully struck balance* between the need to create incentives for authorship and *the interests of society in the broad accessibility of ideas*' (emphasis added).

47   See Geiger, above n 19, 27 *et seq.*

48   On the double-sided nature of the right to freedom of expression, see an interesting document published recently by the Freedom of Expression on the Internet Initiative of the Center for Studies on Freedom of Expression and Access to Information, *Freedom of Expression versus freedom of expression: Copyright protection invokes internal tension* (Palermo University, 2013).

49   For further discussion of this provision, see JM Otero, 'La protección constitucional del derecho de autor: Análisis del artículo 20.1 b/ de la Constitución española de 1978' (1986) Part 2 *La Ley* 370.

[f]reedom of expression belongs to intellectual property, as its lack kills artistic creativity, scientific research as well as the philosophical search for the truth. Besides, intellectual property is the river bed or the iter where freedom of expression passes by, and that is perfectly understood in our Constitution when it gathers both rights at the same legal article ...[50]

In fact, one can infer from article 20 of the Spanish Constitution that the goal of IP is, at least partly, to guarantee freedom of expression and the public's right to information – a logic that could be traced further in article 15(e) of the Liberian Constitution of 1984, when it refers to 'the commercial aspect of expression in ... copyright infringement', and article 13 of the Central African Constitution of 2004, incorporating the protection of 'freedom of intellectual, artistic and cultural creation' within the broader right to freedom of expression and information.

Apart from domestic constitutions, in Europe, the European Convention on Human Rights (ECHR) codifies the principle of freedom of expression and communication in article 10(1),[51] while article 10(2) provides for restrictions in the protection of the rights of others, which include the rights of creators.[52]

This recognition of creators' rights as an exception to the general rule of freedom of expression protection dovetails with the recent case law of the European Court of Human Rights (ECtHR), the body in charge of interpreting and enforcing the ECHR.[53] In particular, two

---

50   F Bondia, *Propiedad intelectual. Su significado en la Sociedad de la Información* (Trivium, 1988), 94, 105, cited in J Rodriguez, 'A Historical Approach to the Current Copyright Law in Spain' (2006) 28(7) *European Intellectual Property Review* 389, 393.

51   On the level of the EU, analogous guarantee of free expression protection is enshrined in article 11 of the EU Charter of Fundamental Rights, the scope and meaning of which are the same as of article 10 ECHR (see Note from the Praesidium, *Draft Charter of Fundamental Rights of the European Union*, Text of the Explanations Relating to the Complete Text of the Charter as set out in CHARTE 4487/00 CONVENT 50 (Brussels, 2000), 13–14).

52   On the cases in which copyright was considered as falling under the 'rights of others' within the meaning of article 10(2) European Convention on Human Rights (ECHR), see e.g. *Neij and Sunde Kolmisoppi v Sweden* (dec) (European Court of Human Rights, no. 40397/12, 19 February 2013); *Ashby Donald and Others v France* (European Court of Human Rights, no. 36769/08, 10 January 2013); *Société Nationale De Programmes FRANCE 2 v France* (dec) (European Commission of Human Rights, no. 30262/96, 15 January 1997); *N V Televizier v The Netherlands* (report) (European Commission of Human Rights, no. 2690/65, 3 October 1968).

53   Further on this, see C Geiger and E Izyumenko, 'Copyright on the Human Rights' Trial: Redefining the Boundaries of Exclusivity Through Freedom of Expression' (2014) 45(3) *International Review of Intellectual Property and Competition Law* 316.

important rulings from the Court rendered in 2013, *Ashby Donald*[54] and *'The Pirate Bay'*,[55] clearly demonstrated the major change of perspective on copyright as being traditionally regarded immune from any external freedom of expression review. In both cases the ECtHR held that the use of a copyrighted work could be considered as an exercise of the right to freedom of expression, even if the use qualifies as an infringement and is profit-motivated. Therefore, by verifying if in the given situation the interference can be justified with regard to other conflicting rights, the ECtHR advanced the idea that freedom of expression has to be considered as the point of departure and that no predetermined answer can be given by copyright law.[56] This goes in line with the freedom of expression-compliant principle that the exclusive right constitutes an exception to a broader principle of freedom of use.[57]

1.2.3. Copyright as property – extension of the social function

Apart from article 10, there is however yet another provision under the ECHR that can help to fill the missing link between copyright protection and its 'public-interest' justifications. Article 1 of the First

---

54   *Ashby Donald and Others v France* (European Court of Human Rights, no. 36769/08, 10 January 2013); Comment, '*Ashby Donald and others v France*' (2014) 45(3) *International Review of Intellectual Property and Competition Law* 354; P Torremans, '*Ashby Donald and others v France*, application 36769/08, EctHr, 5th section, judgment of 10 January 2013' (2014) 4(1) *Queen Mary Journal of Intellectual Property* 95.

55   *Neij and Sunde Kolmisoppi v Sweden* (dec), (European Court of Human Rights, no. 40397/12, 19 February 2013); Comment, 'Pirate Bay' (2013) 44(6) *International Review of Intellectual Property and Competition Law* 724. For a comment, see J Jones, 'Internet Pirates Walk the Plank with Article 10 Kept at Bay: Neij and Sunde Kolmisoppi v Sweden' (2013) 35(11) *European Intellectual Property Review* 695.

56   For a joint comment of *Ashby Donald* and '*The Pirate Bay*', see Geiger and Izyumenko, above n 52. See also D Voorhoof, 'Freedom of Expression and the Right to Information: Implications for Copyright' in C Geiger (ed), *Research Handbook on Human Rights and Intellectual Property* (Edward Elgar, 2015) 331.

57   C Geiger, 'Fundamental Rights, a Safeguard for the Coherence of Intellectual Property Law?' (2004) 35(3) *International Review of Intellectual Property and Competition Law* 268, 272, stating that 'intellectual property rights constitute islands of exclusivity in an ocean of liberty'. Further on the important implications of the right to freedom of expression for copyright law, see Voorhoof, above n 55; Geiger and Izyumenko, above n 52. For trademarks, M Senftleben, 'Free Signs and Free Use: How to Offer Room for Freedom of Expression within the Trademark System', and for domain names, J D Lipton, 'Free Speech and Other Human Rights in ICANN's New Generic Top Level Domain Process: Debating Top-down versus Bottom-up Protections', both in *Research Handbook on Human Rights and Intellectual Property* (Edward Elgar, 2015).

Protocol to the ECHR (guaranteeing the general protection of property) in fact extends, in the absence of a specific Convention clause on IP, to the protection of intellectual property rights.[58]

The inclusion of intellectual property within the protection of property at the constitutional level is important because it expands the social function of property to intellectual property. In fact, the right to property protected by the Convention is inherently limited by its social function.[59] The first paragraph of article 1 of the First Protocol to the ECHR provides for the possibility of restrictions of the right 'in the public interest', while the second paragraph of the same provision allows the State 'to enforce such laws as it deems necessary to control the use of property *in accordance with the general interest ...*'.[60]

Unlike the ECHR, yet another principal European human rights instrument, the Charter of Fundamental Rights of the European Union (EU Charter), explicitly places intellectual property within its catalogue of fundamental rights. In particular, article 17, dealing with the general right to property under its first paragraph, also contains a second paragraph specifying in a somewhat laconic

---

58   For the case law of the Court, in accordance with which different intellectual property rights have been attached to the Convention property provision, see, in the field of copyright: *Neij and Sunde Kolmisoppi v Sweden* (dec) (European Court of Human Rights, no. 40397/12, 19 February 2013); *Ashby Donald and Others v France* (European Court of Human Rights, no. 36769/08, 10 January 2013); *Balan v Moldova* (European Court of Human Rights, no. 19247/03, 29 January 2008); *Melnychuk v Ukraine* (dec) (European Court of Human Rights, no. 28743/03, 5 July 2005, Reports of Judgments and Decisions 2005-IX); *Dima v Romania* (dec) (European Court of Human Rights, no. 58472/00, 26 May 2005); *Aral, Tekin and Aral v Turkey* (dec) (European Commission of Human Rights, no. 24563/94, 14 January 1998); *A D v the Netherlands* (dec) (European Commission of Human Rights, no. 21962/93, 11 January 1994). In the field of trademarks: *Paeffgen Gmbh v Germany* (dec) (European Court of Human Rights, nos. 25379/04, 21688/05, 21722/05 and 21770/05, 18 September 2007; *Anheuser-Busch Inc v Portugal* (European Court of Human Rights, Grand Chamber, no. 73049/01, 11 January 2007, Reports of Judgments and Decisions 2007-I). In the field of patent law: *Lenzing AG v the United Kingdom* (dec) (European Comission of Human Rights, no. 38817/97, 9 September 1998); *Smith Kline & French Lab. Ltd v the Netherlands* (dec) (European Comission of Human Rights, no. 12633/87, 4 October 1990, Decisions and Reports 66) 70. For a detailed analysis of the intellectual property case law of the ECHR, see LR Helfer, 'The New Innovation Frontier? Intellectual Property and the European Court of Human Rights' (2008) 49 *Harvard International Law Journal* 1; DS Welkowitz, 'Privatizing Human Rights? Creating Intellectual Property Rights from Human Rights Principles' (2013) 46 *Akron Law Review* 675.

59   See, for details on this issue, Geiger, above n 12.

60   Emphasis added.

way: 'Intellectual property shall be protected'.[61] Even though not devoid of a considerable amount of controversy, this clause needs to be analysed through the prism of the provision within which it is incorporated. Thus, article 17(1) of the EU Charter on the general guarantee of property clearly safeguards the social limits of the right: it reiterates that '[t]he use of property may be regulated by law *in so far as is necessary for the general interest*'.[62]

This limited nature of the right to property was clearly envisaged by the drafters of both the Charter and the ECHR. As the *travaux préparatoires* of the First Protocol to the ECHR demonstrate, a newly introduced property paradigm was viewed as being of a 'relative' nature as opposed to the absolute right to own property in a sense it was understood by Roman law.[63] A similar logic, clearly excluding an 'absolutist' conception of IP, accompanies the preparatory documents of the EU Charter, insofar as the drafters took care to specify that 'the guarantees laid down in paragraph 1 [of article 17] shall apply as appropriate to intellectual property' and that 'the meaning and scope of Article 17 are the same as those of the right guaranteed under Article 1 of the First Protocol to the ECHR'.[64] Article 17(2) of the Charter could then be considered to be nothing more than a simple clarification of article 17(1), with the consequence that there would be absolutely no justification to expand protection on this ground.

---

61   On this provision, see C Geiger, 'Intellectual Property Shall be Protected!? Article 17(2) of the Charter of Fundamental Rights of the European Union: A Mysterious Provision with an Unclear Scope' (2009) 31(3) *European Intellectual Property Review* 113; C Geiger, 'Intellectual "Property" after the Treaty of Lisbon, Towards a Different Approach in the New European Legal Order?' (2010) 32(6) *European Intellectual Property Review* 255. See also J Griffiths and L McDonagh, 'Fundamental Rights and European Intellectual Property Law – The Case of Art 17(2) of the EU Charter' in C Geiger (ed), *Constructing European Intellectual Property* (Edward Elgar, 2013) EIPIN Series, vol 1, 75.

62   Emphasis added.

63   Council of Europe, *Preparatory work on Article 1 of the First Protocol to the European Convention on Human Rights*, CDH(76)36, Strasbourg, 13 August 1976 (see e.g. presentation of Mr de la Vallée-Poussin (Belgium), 12; consider also the statement made by Mr Nally (United Kingdom), 16, that the 'basis of Europe's fight for survival is a struggle for the subordination of private property to the needs of the community').

64   Note from the Praesidium, above n 50, 19–20.

It is this 'restrictive' understanding of IP protection that has clearly accompanied the recent case law of the CJEU.[65] According to the latter:

the protection of the right to intellectual property is indeed enshrined in Article 17(2) of the EU Charter of Fundamental Rights of the European Union. There is, however, nothing whatsoever in the wording of that provision or in the Court's case-law to suggest that that *right is inviolable and must for that reason be absolutely protected.*[66]

---

65 See e.g. *Productores de Música de España (Promusicae) v Telefónica de España SAU* ('*Promusicae*') (C-275/06) [2008] ECJ, Judgment of the Court (Grand Chamber) of 29 January 2008, ECR I-00271, [65]–[68]; *LSG-Gesellschaft zur Wahrnehmung von Leistungsschutzrechten GmbH v Tele2 Telecommunication GmbH* ('*Tele2*') (C-557/07) [2009] ECJ, Order of the Court (Eighth Chamber) of 19 February 2009, ECR I-01227, [28], [29]; *Bonnier Audio and Others v Perfect Communication Sweden AB* (C-461/10) [2012] CJEU, Judgment of the Court (Third Chamber) of 19 April 2012, published in the electronic Reports of Cases, [56]; *Painer v Standard VerlagsGmbH and Others* ('*Painer*') (C-145/10) [2011], CJEU, Judgment of the Court (Third Chamber) of 1 December 2011, ECR I-12533, [105], [132]; *Scarlet Extended SA v Société belge des auteurs, compositeurs et éditeurs SCRL (SABAM)* ('*Scarlet Extended*') (C-70/10) [2011] CJEU, Judgment of the Court (Third Chamber) of 24 November 2011, ECR I-11959, [53]; *Belgische Vereniging van Auteurs, Componisten en Uitgevers CVBA (SABAM) v Netlog NV* ('*SABAM v Netlog*') (C-360/10) [2012], CJEU, Judgment of the Court (Third Chamber) of 16 February 2012, published in the electronic Reports of Cases, [51]; *UPC Telekabel Wien GmbH v Constantin Film Verleih GmbH and Wega Filmproduktionsgesellschaft mbH* ('*UPC Telekabel*') (C-314/12) [2014] (CJEU, Judgment of the Court (Fourth Chamber) of 27 March 2014) [46]; and *Johan Deckmyn and Vrijheidsfonds VZW v Helena Vandersteen and Others* ('*Deckmyn*') (C-201/13) [2014] (CJEU, Judgment of the Court (Grand Chamber) of 3 September 2014) [26], [27]. On some of these cases, see C Geiger and F Schönherr, 'Limitations to Copyright in the Digital Age' in A Savin and J Trzaskowski (eds), *Research Handbook on EU Internet Law* (Edward Elgar, 2014), 110, and, from the same authors: 'Defining the Scope of Protection of Copyright in the EU: The Need to Reconsider the Acquis Regarding Limitations and Exceptions' in T Synodinou (ed), *Codification of European Copyright Law, Challenges and Perspectives* (Kluwer Law International, 2012), 142; J Griffiths, 'Constitutionalising or Harmonising? The Court of Justice, the Right to Property and European Copyright Law' (2013) 38 *European Law Review* 65; C Geiger, 'The Role of the Court of Justice of the European Union: Harmonizing, Creating and sometimes Disrupting Copyright Law in the European Union' in I Stamatoudi (ed), *New Developments in EU and International Copyright Law* (Kluwer Law International, 2016) 441; see also the Opinion of the European Copyright Society (ECS), 'Limitations and Exceptions as Key Elements of the Legal Framework for Copyright in the European Union: Opinion on the Judgment of the CJEU in Case C-201/13 *Deckmyn*' (2015) 37(3) *European Intellectual Property Review* 129, and J Griffiths et al, 'The European Copyright Society's "Opinion on the Judgment of the CJEU in Case C-201/13- *Deckmyn*"' (2015) 37(3) *European Intellectual Property Review* 127.

66 *UPC Telekabel* (C-314/12) [2014] (CJEU, Judgment of the Court (Fourth Chamber) of 27 March 2014) [61]; *SABAM v Netlog*, (C-360/10) [2012], CJEU, Judgment of the Court (Third Chamber) of 16 February 2012, published in the electronic Reports of Cases, [41]; *Scarlet Extended*, (C-70/10) [2011] CJEU, Judgment of the Court (Third Chamber) of 24 November 2011, ECR I-11959, [43] (emphasis added).

Moreover, to remove any ambiguity, in *Luksan v Petrus* the CJEU directly referred to article 17(1) of the Charter in the context of IP protection, *before* discussing article 17(2) – an explicit illustration on the part of the Court that IP clause of the Charter benefits from the more general wording of article 17(1).[67]

The right to property in the Charter and in the ECHR is thus considered as a right having strong social bounds and its scope of protection is therefore limited by nature,[68] leaving the states a large margin of appreciation to regulate property.[69] This means that copyright – just like the right to physical property – can be limited in order to safeguard the interests of society at large.

2. Consequences for the shape and use of copyright as an access right

2.1. The need to secure the balance of interests within copyright law: The social contract implies duties for authors and rights for users

Admitting that intellectual property law has a social purpose and is grounded on human rights obligations should, in principle, lead the legislature to check that copyright rules actually reflect their access aspect and, if not, to correct them. As Professor Schricker aptly noted, if account is taken of the cultural, economic and social consequences of copyright, one might wonder whether the legislature (and the judges interpreting the provisions of copyright law) should not be expected to take account of the general interest in the positive sense: copyright should be conceived of in such a way that it contributes as much as

---

67   *Martin Luksan v Petrus van der Let* (C-277/10) [2012] (CJEU, Judgment of the Court (Third Chamber) of 9 February 2012) [68].

68   See in this sense, C Calliess, 'The Fundamental Right to Property' in D Ehlers (ed), *European Fundamental Rights and Freedoms* (De Gruyter, 2007) 456, stating that the social function 'serves as a justification for and limitation of the restrictions imposed on property utilisation'.

69   For example, in the *Smith Kline* case (*Smith Kline & French Lab Ltd v the Netherlands*, (European Commission of Human Rights, no. 12633/87, 4 October 1990, Decisions and Reports 66)), the European Commission of Human Rights stated that the grant under Dutch law of a compulsory licence for a patented drug was not a violation of article 1 of the First Protocol. It considered that the compulsory licence was lawful and pursued the legitimate aim of encouraging technological and economic development.

possible to the development of intellectual, cultural and economic progress.[70] This would require a legislator to first justify convincingly the grant of intellectual property rights (which seems difficult where the rule is the pure result of pressure from certain interest groups), and then to exercise subsequently a sort of 'self-monitoring'. In this sense, the social function with its integral access aspect could imply a duty to demonstrate why legislation is passed and what results are to be obtained, by means of reliable data and impact studies that will make it possible to measure the probable consequences of the legislative activity.[71] This would have a very important consequence, since the legislator would have *an obligation to justify any extension of intellectual property law*. Moreover, this could imply that the legislator periodically evaluates the results of past copyright legislations and verifies that they have led to the desired results, with the logical consequence of having to modify them when this is found not to be the case.[72] A good example is the steady increase over time of the term of protection of copyright and neighbouring rights, which has regularly caused heated debates among scholars and copyright experts,

---

70   G Schricker, 'Introduction' in G Schricker (ed), *Urheberrecht Kommentar* (Beck, 2nd ed, 1999) 7.
71   See in this sense, in the context of the EU, C Geiger, 'The Construction of Intellectual Property in the European Union: Searching for Coherence' in C Geiger (ed), *Constructing European Intellectual Property: Achievements and New Perspectives* (Edward Elgar, 2013) EIPIN Series, vol 1, 5, advocating that future initiatives by the European legislature need to be based more frequently on serious (and above all independent) economic data and on impact studies that will make it possible to measure the probable consequences of the legislative activity. See also the report of Professor I Hargreaves, 'Digital Opportunity, A Review of Intellectual Property and Growth', May 2011, 1, inviting the legislature 'to ensure that in the future, policy on Intellectual Property issues is constructed on the basis of evidence, rather than weight of lobbying'. More generally on the importance of evidence-based policies in copyright law, see recently J Poort, *Empirical Evidence for Policy in Telecommunication, Copyright and Broadcasting* (Amsterdam University Press, 2015) 9: 'Increasingly, politicians, judges and stake holders require economic analysis and economic evidence to make informed decisions about new policy measures, to make optimal decisions within the legal boundaries and to fathom the proposed consequences of proposed legal interventions. Without empirical evidence *they may simply assume the effects of a policy measure as an article of faith*' (emphasis added).
72   At present in the EU, it is true that the Commission sometimes undertakes evaluations of past directive. However, an unsatisfying result of past legislation hardly leads to any action. A good example has been the negative evaluation of the legal protection for databases, implemented in the EU through a very complicated legal instrument, which according to the Commission's own admission did not had the expected success (see the evaluation of Directive 96/9/EC on the legal protection of databases published by the European Commission on 12 December 2005. On this text, see A Kur et al, 'First Evaluation of Directive 96/9/EC on the Legal Protection of Databases - Comment by the Max Planck Institute for Intellectual Property, Competition and Tax Law' (2006) *International Review of Intellectual Property and Competition Law*, 551). Despite the evaluation, the legal instrument has not been modified or abolished.

criticising this extension as being detrimental to the public domain and leading rather to rent-seeking than to an increase of creation of new works.[73]

The question then arises: how to oblige the legislature to respect copyright as an access right? This could be the case if an access aspect of intellectual property is established at a supra-legislative level. The problem is that in the European Union and some of its member states, unlike in the United States, there is no constitutional clause regulating the activity of the legislature when it comes to passing intellectual property legislation. However, as emphasised above, intellectual property has been raised to the supra-legislative level by attaching it to the constitutional protection of the right to property, which may be subjected to restrictions that are justified by the general interest. In this spirit, the German Constitutional Court has laid down very clearly in the context of copyright that while the protection of property rights:

> implies that the economic benefits of the work are in principle owed to the author, the constitutional protection of property rights does not extend to all these benefits. It is for the legislature to set out the contours of copyright by imposing appropriate criteria that take account of the nature and *social function* of copyright and to ensure that the author participates in the exploitation of the work fairly.[74]

73　See e.g. R Pollock, 'Optimal Copyright Over Time: Technological Change and the Stock of Works' (2007) vol 4, no 2, *Review of Economic Research on Copyright Issues*, 51; C Buccafusco and PJ Heald, 'Do Bad Things Happen When Works Enter the Public Domain?: Empirical Tests of Copyright Term Extension' (2013) vol 21, issue 1, *Berkeley Technology Law Journal*, 1. A recent example in the EU for a strongly criticised measure in this regard has been the Directive extending the term of neighbouring rights from 50 to 70 years (*Directive 2011/77/EU of the European Parliament and of the Council of 27 September 2011 amending Directive 2006/116/EC on the term of protection of copyright and certain related rights* [2011] OJ L 265, 1–5), which was based on no independent economic study and has been massively rejected by the majority of European academics: 'Creativity stifled? A Joint Academic Statement on the Proposed Copyright Term Extension for Sound Recordings' (2008) *European Intellectual Property Review* 341; C Geiger, J Passa and M Vivant, 'La proposition de directive sur l'extension de la durée de certains droits voisins: Une remise en cause injustifiée du domaine public' [2009] No 31, *Propriété intellectuelle*, 146; C Geiger, 'The Extension of the Term of Copyright and Certain Neighbouring Rights – A Never Ending Story?' (2009) *International Review of Intellectual Property and Competition Law*, 78.
74　German Constitutional Court, 'Schoolbook' decision, 7 July 1971 (1972) *Gewerblicher Rechtsschutz und* Urheberrecht, 481 (emphasis added); W Rumphorst, Comment, (1972) *International Review of Intellectual Property and Competition Law*, 394.

The legislature is thus subjected to an obligation of moderation. This obligation of balance is accentuated by the fact that the legislature is required, when laying down the contours of the right, to respect other fundamental rights of equal value;[75] it is for this reason, moreover, that all legislation on intellectual property rights imposes a certain number of limitations and exceptions on the exclusive right. To a large extent, attaching intellectual property rights to fundamental rights thus guarantees respect for the social function of these rights.[76] In practical terms, it can even be asked if the obligation to protect competing fundamental rights and values when implementing new intellectual property legislation should not oblige the legislator also to implement *legal duties for right holders*.[77] Philosophically speaking, this would clearly be in line with the idea of the social contract underlying the social function, which implies counterparts. As one scholar has interestingly stated, 'the grant of a right in the intellectual property may itself be derivative of a duty to others; that is, when the intellectual property owner acquires a legal intellectual property right, a duty to the public is simultaneously imposed on the intellectual property owner'.[78]

Such obligations imposed on right holders could for example result in a duty to disseminate as widely as possible protected creations and to exploit them. This could result in a prohibition to prevent the dissemination of any protected creation: for example, by securing access to orphan, out of print works, forbidding the use of contracts or TPMs (technological protection measures) that are blocking access through exceptions and limitations, and other analogous obligations.[79]

---

75   C Geiger, 'Reconceptualizing the Constitutional Dimension of Intellectual Property' in P Torremans (ed), *Intellectual Property and Human Rights* (Kluwer Law International, 3rd ed, 2015), 115; C Geiger, 'Copyright's Fundamental Rights Dimension at EU Level' in E Derclaye (ed), *Research Handbook on the Future of EU Copyright* (Edward Elgar, 2009), 27; Geiger, 'Intellectual "Property" after the Treaty of Lisbon', above n 60; C Geiger, 'Fundamental Rights as Common Principles of European (and International) Intellectual Property Law' in A Ohly (ed), *Common Principles of European Intellectual Property Law* (Mohr Siebeck, 2012), 223.

76   C Geiger, 'Fundamental Rights, a Safeguard for the Coherence of Intellectual Property Law?', above n 56.

77   For details on the legal consequences of the 'constitutionalisation' of intellectual property for legislators, see Geiger, above n 39, 397 *et seq*.

78   EF Judge, 'Intellectual Property Law as an Internal Limit on Intellectual Property Rights and Autonomous Source of Liability for Intellectual Property Owners' (2007) 27(4) *Bulletin of Science, Technology & Society*, 311. On the idea of duties of authors in the field of copyright law, see C Colin, 'The Author's Duty' (2010) (224) *Revue Internationale du Droit d'Auteur*, 160.

79   For further proposals resulting from the obligation to secure access, see C Geiger, 'The Future of Copyright in Europe: Striking a Fair Balance between Protection and Access to Information'

The right holders' duties would also envisage allowance of a public discourse about a certain creation through parody, quotations, creative reuse and alike. As can be seen, some of these duties clearly result from fundamental rights such as freedom of expression, freedom of information, artistic freedom or freedom to conduct a business, and the positive obligation of the State to protect those rights could imply that mechanisms are inserted in intellectual property law to secure these values.

One such mechanism would be to grant *users' rights* which could be enforced in courts.[80] Limitations to intellectual property rights, which are based on fundamental rights and thereby represent basic democratic values within IP law, could be elevated to *rights* of the users (and not mere interests to be taken into account), which are of equal value as the exclusive right.[81] The consequence of this is that they should be considered mandatory (which means the user's exercise of statutory limitations cannot be restricted by contract)[82] and should prevail over technical measures. The national legislatures could introduce into their acts a prohibition of technical devices that

---

(2010) *Intellectual Property Quarterly*, 1. One of the duties of right holders could be to guarantee that access is granted under fair conditions (pricing issue) and that the business models are adapted to the needs of consumers (easy to use, diversity of content, usable on a variety of devices etc.). In fact, granting access under unfair conditions or at too high a price results often in hindering access for a majority of people. Libraries and archives have a particular role to play here, and there could be a duty to make the work available also through these channels.

80   Favouring the granting of positive rights to users, see also e.g. R Burell and A Coleman, *Copyright Exceptions: The Digital Impact* (Cambridge University Press, 2005) 279; T Riis and J Schovsbo, 'User's Rights, Reconstructing Copyright Policy on Utilitarian Grounds' (2007) *European Intellectual Property Review* 1; Geiger, above n 19, 371 *et seq*. In the context of technical measures, see A Ottolia, 'Preserving Users' Rights in DRM: Dealing with "Judicial Particularism" in the Information Society' (2004) 35 *International Review of Intellectual Property and Competition Law*, 491.

81   See for a more detailed analysis, C Geiger, 'Promoting Creativity through Copyright Limitations: Reflections on Concept of Exclusivity in Copyright Law' (2010) 12(3) *Vanderbilt Journal of Entertainment & Technology Law* 515. See also *CCH Canadian Ltd v Law Society of Upper Canada* [2004] 1 SCR 339.

82   The Belgian law states this imperative character of copyright exceptions explicitly (see article 23*bis* of the Belgian Act of 30 June 1994, inserted by an Act of 31 August 1998, which implemented the Database Directive in Belgian law). The mandatory character of the exceptions was maintained in the new Belgian Act of 22 May 2005 (M.B., 27 May 2005, 24997; on this Act, see M-C Janssens, 'Implementation of the 2001 Copyright Directive in Belgium' (2006) 37 *International Review of Intellectual Property and Competition Law* 50), except for the works made available to the public on agreed contractual terms (article 7). In France, the imperative nature of copyright exceptions could be deduced from the wording of article L 122-5 of the Intellectual Property Code, as it specifies that 'the author cannot prohibit' the uses there stated. The Paris District Court in its decision of 10 January 2006 (2006) 13 *Revue Lamy Droit De L'immatériel*, 24, even held explicitly that the private copy exception was '*d'ordre public*', meaning mandatory,

prevent a use privileged by law, or at least grant the user judicial means to 'enforce' his exceptions (this would lead to the creation of a 'subjective right' to the exception). In the European context, such action could even be deduced from the InfoSoc Directive.[83] According to article 6(4) of the Directive, member states shall take 'appropriate measures' to ensure the functioning of certain limitations when technical measures are implemented. However, the Directive does not specify what these measures could consist of. Arguably, it would be contrary to the states' obligations under article 15 ICESCR, article 10 ECHR and to the social function of copyright if it is not assured that the beneficiaries of exceptions listed in article 6(4) are able to benefit from them.

Importantly, the idea of users' rights as enforceable rights of equal value appears to have found its way into the recent practice of the CJEU.[84] In particular, in its decision in *UPC Telekabel* from March 2014, the Court clearly adopted the language of users' rights as a counterbalance to the disproportionally extensive enforcement of copyright.[85] The Court, by *obliging* the national authorities (albeit under the limited range of circumstances) to avail the users of the procedural opportunity to challenge copyright enforcement measures

---

and therefore that a technical measure should not hinder the making of a copy of a CD. But the French Supreme Court has since then taken a different position (28 February 2006 (2006) *Recueil Dalloz* 784).

83   *Directive 2001/29/EC of the European Parliament and of the Council of 22 May 2001 on the harmonisation of certain aspects of copyright and related rights in the information society (InfoSoc)* [2001] OJ L 167, 10.

84   See *Technische Universität Darmstadt v Eugen Ulmer KG* ('*Ulmer*') (C-117/13) [2014] (CJEU, Judgment of the Court (Fourth Chamber) of 11 September 2014) [43]; CJEU, Case C-201/13, *Deckmyn,* (C-201/13) [2014] (CJEU, Judgment of the Court (Grand Chamber) of 3 September 2014) [26]; *UPC Telekabel,* (C-314/12) [2014] (CJEU, Judgment of the Court (Fourth Chamber) of 27 March 2014) [57]; *Padawan SL v Sociedad General de Autores y Editores de España (SGAE)* ('*Padawan*') (C-467/08) [2010], CJEU, Judgment of the Court (Third Chamber) of 21 October 2010, ECR I-10055, [43]; *Painer,* (C-145/10) [2011], CJEU, Judgment of the Court (Third Chamber) of 1 December 2011, ECR I-12533, [132]. For the further discussion of these cases, see ECS, above n 64.

85   *UPC Telekabel* (C-314/12) [2014] (CJEU, Judgment of the Court (Fourth Chamber) of 27 March 2014). For a comment see C Geiger and E Izyumenko, 'The Role of Human Rights in Copyright Enforcement Online: Elaborating a Legal Framework for Website Blocking' (2016) 32 *American University International Law Review* 43.

before the courts,[86] accepts the idea that fundamental right (in the instant case – freedom of expression) may be invoked as not a mere defence but as a right on which an action in the main case is based. Since *UPC Telekabel*, the idea of users' rights has already reoccurred in *Ulmer* from September 2014. Notably, the CJEU referred in that case to the *'ancillary right'* of users to digitise works contained in publicly accessible libraries' collections.[87] In the Court's opinion, such a *right* of communication of works enjoyed by establishments such as publicly accessible libraries would stem from the exception in article 5(3)(n) InfoSoc for the purpose of research and private study. In the light of this recent case law of the CJEU, it can be argued that the Court moves towards understanding human rights as an integral part of the European copyright order in full recognition of the above-examined social function of IP law and its underlying human rights rationales.

On the other side of the Atlantic, an analogously liberal stance has been taken by the Supreme Court of Canada, which, since its groundbreaking *Théberge*[88] and *CCH*[89] decisions, was increasingly emphasising 'a move away from an earlier, author-centric view' towards 'promoting the public interest' and the 'users' rights [as] an essential part of furthering the public interest objectives of the Copyright Act'.[90] Interestingly, the Court explicitly referred in these cases to the 'proper balance between protection and access' as an ultimate goal of any copyright law regulation. As we have seen, the same dual rationale underlines the protection of creators under article 27 UDHR and article 15 ICESCR – provisions intrinsically integrating the access and protection aspects of copyright.

---

86   *UPC Telekabel*, (C-314/12) [2014] (CJEU, Judgment of the Court (Fourth Chamber) of 27 March 2014) [57]: '[I]n order to prevent the fundamental rights recognised by EU law from precluding the adoption of an injunction such as that at issue in the main proceedings, the national procedural rules *must provide* a possibility for internet users to assert their rights before the court once the implementing measures taken by the internet service provider are known' (emphasis added).

87   *Ulmer*, (C-117/13) [2014] (CJEU, Judgment of the Court (Fourth Chamber) of 11 September 2014) [43].

88   *Théberge v Galerie d'Art du Petit Champlain Inc*, [2002] 2 SCR 336.

89   *CCH Canadian Ltd v Law Society of Upper Canada*, [2004] 1 SCR 339.

90   *SOCAN v Bell Canada*, [2012] 2 SCR 326, [9]–[11]. See also *Alberta (Minister of Education) v Canadian Copyright Licensing Agency (Access Copyright)*, [2012] 2 SCR 345. For an excellent analysis of the Canadian Supreme Court's jurisprudence on users' rights, see D Vaver, 'User Rights' (2013) 25 *Intellectual Property Journal* 105. See also P Chapdelaine, 'The Ambiguous Nature of Copyright Users' Rights' (2013) 26 *Intellectual Property Journal* 1.

In short, it can be stated that the legislator should secure that the human rights implementation within the intellectual property regimes is safeguarded from private ordering. This implies for example that at least the exceptions and limitations that are justified by human rights rationales are declared mandatory[91] and that mechanisms are implemented to secure their effectiveness, especially in the digital environment (where they are endangered by technical protection measures and online contracts).[92]

2.2. The revision of the balance of interests within copyright law: Towards a new paradigm?

2.2.1. A more restrictive understanding of the conditions of protection

If one considers intellectual property rights as exceptions to a major principle of the freedom of use,[93] then this implies also some changes in positive law. Very simply, this could imply that the exclusive rights would have to be conceived restrictively and the limitations broadly, at least in a flexible manner. This could for example be achieved by changing the perspective and introducing a sort of three-step test to determine access to protection.

2.2.1.1. Towards a three-step test to gain access to copyright protection?

The idea of having a 'test' to qualify for protection is commonly accepted in countries such as the UK, where the judges for a long time used to appeal to the 'skill-and-labour-test' to decide whether a creation can be protected or not.[94]

---

91   Not all the exceptions and limitations have the same justification and importance with regard to securing access. The limitations that necessitate particular attention include exceptions for libraries and archives, for teaching and research purposes, for news reports, for press reviews, for quotations and parodies and, more incidentally, exception for people with disabilities, as well as private copying when it allows access to information and is not covered by one of the exceptions already mentioned.

92   See C Geiger, 'The Answer to the Machine should not be the Machine, Safeguarding the Private Copy Exception in the Digital Environment' (2008) *European Intellectual Property Review* 121.

93   See Geiger, 'Fundamental Rights, a Safeguard for the Coherence of Intellectual Property Law?', above n 56.

94   For just a few examples, see High Court of Justice, Chancery Division, 7 April 2006, 2006 EWHC 719; and Court of Appeal, Civil Division, 28 March 2007, WC2A 2LL.

Therefore, it would be interesting to elaborate a certain number of criteria that an expression would need to satisfy in order to enjoy protection. For this, the American conception of fair use or the three-step test, which sets criteria for exempted use, could serve as a model, except that such a test would not circumscribe the limitations but provide for the conditions of access to protection.

Now, what would be these criteria? First, in order to have a uniform approach (between continental and common law), the criterion of creativity is to be preferred to 'originality', usually defined as the 'print of the author's personality'. The second is too difficult to determine and involves the risk of arbitrariness. Moreover, referring to the function of law as an instrument to promote creativity, property should only be granted if there is any creative contribution or collective enrichment. Thus, henceforth, it should be the *degree* of creativity that separates protected from unprotected forms.

In this context, Professor Mireille Buydens of the University of Brussels has suggested a very interesting distinction between creation protected by copyright law and 'quasi-creation', which would benefit from a different type of protection. According to her, the freedom of which the creator disposes constitutes the distinctive criterion.[95] Consequently, in order to decide whether a work may enjoy copyright protection or protection by some *sui generis* right (meaning a kind of investment protection), the court will assess whether the originator has been *essentially* free during the process of creation or if, on the contrary, his freedom has been accessory because he had to observe all sorts of necessities. For example, the creative freedom of a designer who creates a furniture design is most often limited by functional necessities (a chair must have several characteristic features), by necessities due to the method of production (series production, costs) and by public taste (trends of style).[96]

---

95 M Buydens, 'La protection de la quasi-création' (Larcier, 1989), 252. See also M Buydens, 'The Conditions and Scope of Copyright Protection' in R M Hilty and C Geiger (eds), 'The Balance of Interests within Copyright Law' (2006) Proceedings of the conference organised in Berlin by the Max Planck Institute for Intellectual Property, 4–6 November 2004, Munich, available online at <www.intellecprop.mpg.de>.

96 Buydens, 'La protection de la quasi-création', above n 94, 276. The criterion of freedom of the designer is used to determine the scope of protection in the field of design law (see article 9(2) of *Directive 98/71/EC of 13 October 1998 on the legal protection of designs*, OJ EC L 289 of 28 October 1998, 28: 'In assessing the scope of protection, the degree of freedom of the designer in developing his design shall be taken into consideration').

The distinctive criterion concerning creation and quasi-creation is whether the freedom of the creator has been accessory or principal. If necessities concerning function, type, current style and methods of production are predominant, the work will be excluded from copyright protection. Concerning the protection of all the creations that are consequently excluded, Mireille Buydens suggests creating a specific system of quasi-creation that is meant to complement existing legal instruments (design law in particular). Evidently, there is a need to envisage new solutions or to improve existing instruments. This is not the place to specify details, but it shows that it is possible to find more objective criteria for deciding whether a form is protected or not by copyright. Furthermore, the judge could also take into consideration the consequences that copyright protection might have on creations in the future as well as the impact of the right on the availability of information and the common interest. This would mean that courts should also take into account some fundamental-rights rationales when deciding whether the work enjoys protection or not.[97] In fact, public interest objectives such as competition law and certain fundamental rights, generally a justification for exempting a certain use, could already be taken into consideration at the protection level. Hence, certain forms could be excluded from protection because of their importance to society, following the example of article 2(4) of the Berne Convention of 1886.[98] This would result in giving the public domain a positive definition.[99] Let us take, for example, the case of a photograph capturing the assassination of a famous person, or a letter from an important politician who has been involved in a corruption scandal. It would be possible to take into account the freedom of expression and the public's right to information (article 10

---

97   See in this sense Geiger, above n 39.

98   *Berne Convention for the Protection of Literary and Artistic Works*, opened for signature 9 September 1886 (amended in 1914, 1928, 1948, 1967, 1971, and 1979) 25 UST 1341, 828 UNTS 221, entered into force 5 December 1887 ('Berne Convention'), article 2(4): 'It shall be a matter for legislation in the countries of the Union to determine the protection to be granted to official texts of a legislative, administrative and legal nature, and to official translation of such texts'.

99   The notion and the content of the public domain are still not really clarified in legal literature. On this issue, see e.g. J Litman, 'The Public Domain' (1990) 39 *Emory Law Journal* 965; J Boyle (ed), 'The Public Domain' (2003) 66(1)–(2) *Law & Contemporary Problems*; PB Hugenholtz and L Guibault (eds), *The Public Domain of Information* (Kluwer Law International, 2006); S Dusollier and V-L Benabou, 'Draw Me a Public Domain' in P Torremans (ed), *Copyright Law: A Handbook of Contemporary Research* (Edward Elgar, 2007) 161. Unlike in the environmental sector, the preservation of informational resources has not been legally secured so far.

ECHR) already when deciding whether the expression is protected or not, and refuse to grant copyright protection due to important public interest motives.

Incidentally, certain decisions seem to indicate a change of approach in this direction. For example, in Germany the Düsseldorf District Court in its decision of 25 April 2007[100] refused copyright protection to a simple presentation of news information in default of individuality. Likewise, in the Netherlands, the Court of Appeal of Amsterdam[101] refused to protect a recorded conversation of a person reprinted in a book on the grounds that the person answering the questions did not have the intention to create a work.[102] Even if the court did not refer to article 10 ECHR, it seems that the court implicitly balanced the interest of the right holders with those of the public to be informed about the conversation already at the protection level and let the freedom of information prevail. In a similar vein, when the French courts exclude in a very radical way perfume from copyright protection, this is certainly likewise part of an effort to restrain the field of protection.[103]

---

100 Düsseldorf District Court, Case No 12 0 194/06, 25 April 2007.

101 The Amsterdam Court of Appeal, *Endstra's Sons v Middelburg, Vugts and Nieuw Amsterdam*, 8 February 2007, (2007) (4) *AMI*.

102 Note, however, that this ruling was subsequently referred back to appeal by the Dutch Supreme Court, concluding that copyright protection without an intention to create was not impossible by definition. The Supreme Court stated that though it is true that there must be human labour and therefore creative choices, it is however not important whether the author has intentionally wanted to create a work and has intentionally wanted to make particular original choices (Dutch Supreme Court, *Endstra's Sons v Middelburg, Vugts and Nieuw Amsterdam*, Case No C07/131HR, 30 May 2008. For a comment, see B Beuving, 'Endstra's Final Work? Dutch Copyright: Scope of Protection Remains Very Wide' (February 2009) *Bird & Bird Copyright Update* 24, 26). For the second (and final) appeal decision on this case, see The Amsterdam Court of Appeal, *Endstra's Sons v Middelburg, Vugts and Nieuw Amsterdam*, 16 July 2013.

103 See French Supreme Court, 1st Civil Division, 13 June 2006, (2006) 37 *International Review of Intellectual Property and Competition Law* 988: 'The fragrance of a perfume, which results from the simple implementation of know-how, does not constitute the creation of a form of expression capable of benefiting from the protection provided by copyright for works of the mind within the meaning of Arts. L. 112-1 and L. 112-2 of the Intellectual Property Code'. However, since then the lower courts have refused to follow the approach of the Supreme Court and continued to accept copyright protection: District Court of Bobigny, 28 November 2006, *Communication Commerce électronique*, at 13, comment by C Caron; and Paris Court of Appeal, 4th chamber A (February 2007) 14 February 2007, (2008) 39 *International Review of Intellectual Property and Competition Law* 113.

2.2.1.2. Formulating a three-step test to access copyright protection

The above-examined considerations would lead to the following general clause: 'Only expressions that are the result of a creational process in which the freedom of the creator has been superior to imposed necessities and which neither interfere unduly with future creation nor cause unjustified harm to legitimate public interests such as cultural participation may enjoy copyright protection'. Thus, access to copyright protection would be determined by a proper 'three-step test', serving as a guiding rule to the judges. Of course, the first criterion would be preponderate, but the two further criteria would serve as correctives, particularly by excluding a form from protection if there is no sufficient dissemination enabling cultural participation,[104] or, if granted, the protection would lead to a strong risk of predominantly negative consequences for innovation. The last might be the case, for example, if a form is to be considered an essential facility, that is, that its use constitutes the condition to accede to a certain market. Of course, all these criteria can also be taken into account at the level of copyright limitations. The objective of the second step, for example, could be reached by the implementation of an exception for creative use.[105] However, it might seem unsatisfying to grant protection where the consequence on innovation and creativity could be harmful and then take it back by a complicated exemption mechanism. If the function of copyright law with its inalienable access aspect is taken seriously, protection that could be detrimental to future creativity should not be granted in the first place. Of course, even though the judges could already use such criteria when deciding on the eligibility of a work for copyright protection, a legal implementation of this new three-step test would be desirable in order to have more transparency for the economic players.

It worth noting that by following this procedure, the French theory of the 'unité de l'art' would probably have to be abandoned. This theory, according to which copyright protection is not excluded because

---

104 On the duty of right holders to disseminate a copyrighted work as a counterpart of copyright protection, see earlier discussion in this chapter, under subheading II A: 'The need to secure the balance of interests within copyright law: The social contract implies duties for authors and rights for users.'

105 On the implementation of such an exception to foster creativity, see C Geiger, 'Copyright and the Freedom to Create, A Fragile Balance' (2007) 38 *International Review of Intellectual Property and Competition Law* 707.

of the utility of a work, would lose all its interest. In fact, either the creator has enjoyed sufficient freedom during the creation process and will thus enjoy copyright protection, or the creative factor has only been accessory because of numerous necessities, in which case he will have access to another system of protection (e.g. design law). Consequently, one would need to distinguish whether a utility work is predominantly creative or functional. It is true that there is a certain risk that certain peripheral creations might be 'declassed' to functional objects. This, however, is the price to pay in order to 'purify' copyright law from certain forms and to guarantee a certain availability of information (which represents nothing more than ideas 'put into form'). It must also be specified that this does not mean that these works will go unprotected. They will merely not be protected by such a strong and enduring protection as copyright, but by other existing protection mechanisms (or mechanisms that would have to be created).[106]

2.2.2. An extensive/flexible understanding of copyright limitations

As demonstrated above, in view of the approach that free use (freedom of expression, freedom of science and arts) represents the principle, and exclusive rights the exception, limitations to exclusivity cannot be considered as 'exceptions' to the principle of exclusivity. At the end, the demand for a more extensive and rigorous protection,[107] as well as the postulate of a narrow interpretation of copyright limitations, represents a purely political statement. In this context, what would matter is only whether copyright regulation achieves the desired purpose, not what legal technique (exclusive right or limitation) is used. In fact, 'exceptions'[108] are no more than simple tools for the

---

106 Advocating the creation of a special investment-protection mechanism, see RM Hilty, 'The Law Against Unfair Competition and its Interfaces' in RM Hilty and F Henning-Bodewig (eds), *Law Against Unfair Competition, Towards a New Paradigm in Europe* (Springer, 2007), 1.

107 See in this sense, in the context of Europe, e.g. recital 11 to *Directive 2001/29/EC of the European Parliament and of the Council of 22 May 2001 on the harmonisation of certain aspects of copyright and related rights in the information society (InfoSoc)* [2001] OJ L 167,; recital 16 to *Directive 2006/115/EC of the European Parliament and of the Council of 12 December 2006 on rental right and lending right and on certain rights related to copyright in the field of intellectual property* (codified version), OJ No L 376 of 27 December 2006, 28. See also the Commission of the European Communities, *Green Paper: Copyright in the Knowledge Economy* (COM, 2008, 466 final), 4.

108 As limited to our specified interpretation of it, the term 'limitation' appears more appropriate. On the distinction between the terms 'exception' and 'limitation', see C Geiger, 'Promoting Creativity through Copyright Limitations: Reflections on Concept of Exclusivity in Copyright

legislators to delimit the scope of the right, in order to maintain the balance of right holders' and users' rights.[109] Hence, they should be interpreted in accordance with their underlying justification. Starting out from the assumption that copyright serves the interest of society by encouraging creation of new works, it is necessary to permit sufficient free space for creativity.

Furthermore, even in economic terms, the value of limitations can be measured in various forms, typically showing the benefits of such a system.[110] There are, in fact, numerous businesses that use 'free' material – meaning material where uses are permitted by a limitation (so-called 'added value services') – to generate income and economic growth.[111] Even if the limitation provides for the payment of remuneration, the absence of costs related to finding the right holder and the negotiation of a license (not to mention, in case of problems, the costs related to litigation), also has a measurable value, and therefore facilitates the creative reuses of existing works.[112]

In some cases, changes in technical or social circumstances might yet require extensive interpretation and even the creation of new exceptions by analogy (i.e. without legal basis).[113] Otherwise,

---

Law' (2010) 12(3) *Vanderbilt Journal of Entertainment & Technology Law* 515, 518 *et seq*.

109 See in particular PB Hugenholtz, 'Adapting Copyright to the Information Superhighway' in PB Hugenholtz (ed), *The Future of Copyright in a Digital Environment* (Kluwer, 1996), 94; M Vivant, 'La limitation ou "réduction" des exceptions au droit d'auteur par contrats ou mesures techniques de protection. De possibles contrepoids?' (General Report presented at the ALAI Study Days, Barcelona, 19–20 June 2006); C Geiger, 'Der urheberrechtliche Interessensausgleich in der Informationsgesellschaft' (2004) *Gewerblicher Rechtsschutz und Urheberrecht, Internationaler Teil* 815.

110 See L Gibbons, 'Valuing Fair Use' (Paper presented at the Conference on Innovation and Communication Law, University of Turku, Finland, 17 July 2008).

111 T Rogers and A Szamosszegi, *Fair Use in the U.S. Economy: Economic Contribution of Industries Relying on Fair Use* (Computer & Communications Industry Association, 2011); L Gibbons and XL Wang, 'Striking the Rights Balance Among Private Incentives and Public Fair Uses in the United States and China' (2008) 7 *John Marshall Review of Intellectual Property Law* 488, 494; B Gibert, 'The 2015 Intellectual Property and Economic Growth Index: Measuring the Impact of Exceptions and Limitations in Copyright on Growth, Jobs and Prosperity' (The Lisbon Council, 2015); K Erickson et al, 'Copyright and the Value of the Public Domain: An Empirical Assessment', Study for the UK Intellectual Property Office, January 2015.

112 See further C Geiger, 'Statutory Licenses as an Enabler of Creative Uses' in RM Hilty and K-C Liu (eds), *Remuneration of Copyright Owners: Regulatory Challenges of New Business Models* (Springer, forthcoming 2017).

113 See in this sense, e.g. M Buydens and S Dusollier, 'Les exceptions au droit d'auteur: Évolutions dangereuses' (September 2001) *Communication Commerce électronique*, 11; C Geiger, 'Creating Copyright Limitations Without Legal Basis: The 'Buren' Decision, a Liberation?' (2005) 36 *International Review of Intellectual Property and Competition Law*, 842; J-C Galloux,

'freezing' the *status quo* of exceptions would prevent any adaptability of the system. It is necessary to bear in mind that the system of exceptions has not changed much in most European countries, and, where it has, such changes have never lived up to the expectations raised by a real adaptation of copyright law to the 'information society'. Many authors have pointed out that the 2001 Directive on the harmonisation of copyright in the information society failed in this matter[114] by only providing a list of facultative exceptions, so that the European legislature did not oblige national legislatures to modernise their copyright laws.[115] Therefore, there are justifiable doubts that current legislations are still 'up to date'. By this token, courts are now tending towards renouncing the principle of restrictive interpretation by sometimes permitting a reasoning by analogy[116] or creating exceptions beyond legal statutes. By way of example, even in France – a country that is known to have a very restrictive understanding of copyright limitations – judges have created an exception of accessory reproduction[117] without a statutory basis.

It is true that, unlike those countries that have the exception of fair use at their disposal, the continental system does not provide the judge with any suitable instrument concerning limitations. The three-step test incorporated in the InfoSoc Directive, however, might enable judges in the future to apply exceptions in a more flexible

---

'Les exceptions et limitations au droit d'auteur: Exception française ou paradoxe français?' in RM Hilty and C Geiger (eds), *Impulse für eine europäische Harmonisierung des Urheberrechts* (Springer, 2007), 329 *et seq.* However, it has to be admitted that there are numerous voices urging in the opposite direction, too.

114 See e.g. RM Hilty and M Vivant, 'La transposition de la directive sur le droit d'auteur et les droits voisins dans la société de l'information en Allemagne et en France, Analyse critique et prospective' in RM Hilty and C Geiger (eds), *Impulse für eine europäische Harmonisierung des Urheberrechts* (Springer, 2007) 51, 71.

115 See in this sense the study conducted by Instituut voor Informatierecht (IViR) of the University of Amsterdam, 'The Recasting of Copyright and Related Rights for the Knowledge Economy', November 2006 <www.ivir.nl>, 75, which recommends that certain limitations should be declared obligatory in order to assure an effective harmonisation.

116 See for example in this sense the decision by the Supreme Court of the Netherlands of 20 October 1995 in the proceeding *Dior v Evora* (1996 NJ 682), where the Court estimates that it is not forbidden to judge by analogy in a situation the legislature could not have foreseen.

117 French Supreme Court, 1st Civil Division, 15 March 2005, (2005) 36 *International Review of Industrial & Copyright* 869. See on this decision also Geiger, 'Creating Copyright Limitations Without Legal Basis', above n 112. See also Bordeaux Court of Appeal, 13 June 2006, (2007) (238) *Légipresse* 5, comment by A Maffre-Baugé, on the reproduction of an image for a reportage about the audience of a famous court case.

way.[118] According to article 5(5) of the Directive, 'exceptions and limitations ... shall only be applied in certain special cases which do not conflict with a normal exploitation of the work or other subject-matter and do not unreasonably prejudice the legitimate interests of the rightholder'.[119] The judge – being the person who generally *applies* the exception – will henceforth be able to use this legal instrument in order to adapt exceptions to circumstances that have not been provided for by copyright law.[120] In fact, this flexibility need not lead to a reduction of the exceptions. With a certain free hand granted generally to the judge, this freedom of action should logically not only be used to restrict but also to extend.[121] It is true that this fact might be slightly detrimental to legal certainty. Yet this is the price to be paid in order to achieve a refined application of exceptions (in both senses) and, thus, an adaptation of the system to new circumstances. Otherwise, the entire test should be rejected, for the lack of legal

---

118 In this sense, see M Senftleben, 'The International Three-Step Test: A Model Provision for EC Fair Use Legislation' (2010) 1(2) *Journal of Intellectual Property, Information Technology and E-Commerce Law,* 67; and M Senftleben, 'Comparative Approaches to Fair Use: An Important Impulse for Reforms in EU Copyright Law' in G B Dinwoodie (ed), *Intellectual Property Law: Methods and Perspectives* (Edward Elgar, 2014); C Geiger, 'The Role of the Three-Step Test in the Adaptation of Copyright Law to the Information Society' (January–March 2007) *e-Copyright Bulletin.*

119 The three-step test is known under a similar (but not identical) composition in numerous international agreements relating to copyright law and intellectual property, such as article 9(2) of the Berne Convention (for the right of reproduction), article 13 TRIPS (for all exploitation rights) (*Marrakesh Agreement Establishing the World Trade Organization,* opened for signature 15 April 1994, 1867 UNTS 3 (entered into force 1 January 1995), annex IC (*Agreement on Trade-Related Aspects of Intellectual Property Rights*)), and article 10 and article 16, respectively, of the WIPO treaties concerning copyright law (*World Intellectual Property Organization Copyright Treaty,* opened for signature 20 December 1996, 36 ILM 65, entered into force 6 March 2002, 'WIPO Copyright Treaty') and the right of the performers or producers of phonograms (*World Intellectual Property Organization Performances and Phonograms Treaty* ('WPPT'), opened for signature 20 December 1996, 36 ILM 76, entered into force 20 May 2002). Further on this, see C Geiger, D Gervais, and M Senftleben, 'The Three-Step-Test Revisited: How to Use the Test's Flexibility in National Copyright Law' (2014) 29(3) *American University International Law Review* 581.

120 This is especially the case since some legislatures have implemented the three-step test in their national copyright law (in France for example in article L 122-5 IPC). Since then, it is incontestable that the three-step test will be used by courts when applying the exceptions (see C Geiger, 'From Berne to National Law, via the Copyright Directive: The Dangerous Mutations of the Three-Step Test' (2007) *European Intellectual Property Review* 486).

121 Anyhow, it seems that the ECJ in its *Infopaq* decision of 16 July 2009 understood the three-step test of article 5(5) as implying a restrictive interpretation of copyright exceptions (*Infopaq International v Danske Dagblades Forening* (C-5/08) [2009] ECJ, Judgment of the Court (Fourth Chamber) of 16 July 2009 ECR I-06569, [56]–[58]).

certainty cannot, on the one hand, be acceptable when it benefits the right owner and, on the other hand, be considered unacceptable if it is of advantage to the user.

In fact, the third step of the test deals with the justification that underlies the limitation. Therefore, it is by far the most important part of the test. According to it, application of limits to copyright must not be to any 'unjustified' disadvantage of the copyright owner. The rationale is that the author should not be in the position to control *all* sorts of use of his work, but he has to tolerate certain interferences as long as they are justified by values that are superior to the copyright owner's interests.[122] This formula will enable the judge to apply a sort of control of proportionality such as is used in cases of conflict between different fundamental rights.[123] In such cases, the judge takes into consideration the justification underlying the limitation concerned in order to achieve a refined balance of the different interests and fundamental rights involved. Thus combining the security of the closed system of exceptions with the flexibility of the fair-use method, this approach would have an interesting outcome: henceforth, the judge would be able to adjust the application of limitations not only with regard to the economic interests of the right holder but also by taking into consideration divergent interests of the users, as well as the interests of the author in case they are different from those of the exploiter.[124] Unfortunately, in some cases the application of the three-step test by the courts has been rather restrictive,[125] because the criteria have been interpreted to the clear advantage of the right holders. Nevertheless,

---

122 The Constitutional Court of Germany clarified it very clearly in its 'Schoolbook' decision, 7 July 1971 (1972) *Gewerblicher Rechtsschutz und* Urheberrecht.

123 M Senftleben, *Copyright, Limitations and the Three-Step Test* (Kluwer, 2004), 226; S Dusollier, 'L'encadrement des exceptions au droit d'auteur par le test des trois étapes' (2005) *Intellectuele Rechten – Droit Intellectuels* 213, 221; C Geiger, 'The Three-Step Test, A Threat to a Balanced Copyright Law?' (2006) 37 *International Review of Intellectual Property and Competition Law* 683, 696; T Sinodinou, 'Voyage des sources du test des trois étapes aux sources du droit d'auteur' (2007) (30) *Revue Lamy Droit De L'immatériel*, at 67.

124 In fact, the authors and the exploiters may have very different interests, especially when it comes to the adoption of technical protection measures. In this sense, it is important to consult the wording of the three-step test to clarify the perspective. As a matter of fact, in the Berne Convention and the WIPO Treaty of 1996, it is 'the legitimate interests of the author' that have to be taken into account, while in the TRIPS Agreement and in the Directive it is 'the legitimate interests of the rightholder'. If it is really the author who is at the centre of interest, as is so often declared in author's-right countries, it should be the interests of the authors that prevail over those of the right holders when interpreting the test.

125 French Supreme Court, 1st Civil Division, 28 February 2006, (2006) 37 *International Review of Intellectual Property and Competition Law* 760, with comment by C Geiger, 683.

in the future judges will be free to interpret the test in another way. In this way, they could draw inspiration from the suggestions of some scholars who have proposed other interpretations[126] in order to render the three-step test an efficient instrument of flexibility, so that limitations provided by the legal statutes could finally be interpreted more extensively.

2.3. Securing the material interests of creators: A crucial aspect of copyright as an access right

Establishing copyright as an access right and a right to participate in the cultural life does not necessarily mean that this access will be for free. In fact, one essential feature of a copyright system conceived as an access right is that in the spirit of the international human rights provisions that secure access to culture, the material and moral interests of the creators are safeguarded. This certainly implies that the copyright system benefits the creators in a better way, meaning that they must participate more effectively in the exploitation of their works. How this can finally be reached is secondary. One could, of course, imagine a better contract law[127] (with some mandatory rules, like the copyright contract rules of some European countries), but also an increase of statutory licences if these offer financially more favourable solutions for the creators than the exclusive right.[128] This latter course has so far remained relatively unexplored and still requires

---

126 See Geiger, Gervais and Senftleben, above n 118; Senftleben, 'The International Three-Step Test', above n 117; and Senftleben, 'Comparative Approaches to Fair Use' above n 117; Geiger, above n 117; KJ Koelman, 'Fixing the Three-Step Test' (2006) *European Intellectual Property Review* 407.

127 See e.g. RM Hilty, 'Five Lessons About Copyright in the Information Society: Reaction of the Scientific Community to Over-Protection and What Policy Makers Should Learn' (2006) 53 *Journal of the Copyright Society of the USA* 127, 137.

128 See the very interesting article by J C Ginsburg, 'Fair Use for Free, or Permitted-but-Paid?' (2014) vol 29, *Berkeley Technology Law Journal*, 1384, favouring the development in the US of statutory licenses or privately negotiated accords within a statutory framework, as they can ensure that 'uses the legislator perceives to be in the public interest proceed free of the copyright owner's veto, but with compensation—in other words: permitted-but-paid'. According to this author, 'whichever method employed to set the rates for permitted-but-paid uses, the copyright law should ensure that authors share in any statutory or privately ordered remuneration scheme' (at 1446).

closer investigation.[129] In fact, from an international human rights perspective, neither the UDHR nor the ICESCR determine *the way* in which the protection of the relevant material and immaterial interests has to be achieved. There is no mention of the exclusive rights or even of property: that means that within the scope of these treaties, other means of protection are equally conceivable.[130] This leaves countries a good deal of room to manoeuvre, while at the same time guaranteeing creators a just remuneration for their work, which makes these legal instruments particularly modern and flexible means of regulating intellectual property matters.[131]

In summary, the copyright regimes should secure that creators participate fairly in the earnings generated by the commercial exploitation of their creations. This does not have to be necessarily through the implementation of an exclusive property right. Legislators should have the freedom to choose the legal means to secure the right for creators to receive a fair remuneration for the commercial exploitation of their works.[132]

Conclusion

An investigation of the basis of intellectual property shows that the classical justifications have been displaced in favour of protection of investment and that the balance within the system is threatening to break in favour of the exploiters of IP rights. This conclusion is

---

129 Such ideas have in fact been formulated for the field of copyright. See Geiger, above n 80, 515; Geiger, above n 19, 318 *et seq.*; RM Hilty, 'Verbotsrecht vs. Vergütungsanspruch: Suche nach den Konsequenzen der tripolaren Interessenlage im Urheberrecht' in A Ohly et al (eds), *Festschrift für Gerhard Schricker* (Beck, 2005), 348 *et seq.* In the context of the levy for private copying, see also K Gaita and AF Christie, 'Principle or Compromise? Understanding the Original Thinking Behind Statutory License and Levy Schemes for Private Copying' (2004) *Intellectual Property Quarterly* 426; A Dietz, 'Continuation of the Levy System for Private Copying also in the Digital Era in Germany' (2003) *Auteurs et Médias*, 348 *et seq.*

130 The General Comment No 17 confirmed, for example, that IP protection, not excluding the property entitlement in the majority of cases, may still, under certain circumstances guided by public-interest considerations, be reduced to 'compensatory measures, such as payment of adequate compensation': CESCR, above n 28, [24]. See also Geiger, 'Fundamental Rights as Common Principles of European (and International) Intellectual Property Law', above n 74, 227.

131 See also in this sense, T Mylly, 'Intellectual Property and Fundamental Rights: Do they Interoperate?' in N Bruun (ed), *Intellectual Property Beyond Rights* (WSOY, 2005), 197; Geiger, 'Fundamental Rights as Common Principles of European (and International) Intellectual Property Law', above n 74, 227.

132 See Geiger, 'Statutory Licenses as an Enabler of Creative Uses', above n 111.

not new, this 'paradigm shift' already having been stressed by the literature in the 1980s,[133] but no real conclusions were drawn at the time. Assuming, however, that the foundations of the system have changed, the same solutions cannot apply and establishing copyright as a 'right to access' rather than a 'right to forbid or sanction' has become absolutely necessary.

Of course, as we have seen, both the protection and access aspects of copyright are closely linked. However, the current overprotective tendencies might require an emphasis on cultural participation and on the inclusive function of copyright law in order to re-establish the fair balance of interests within the system. It is thus not without importance whether copyright is understood as a cultural right or as an investment-protection mechanism, and the massive rejection of intellectual property in the public opinion is a clear indicator of this. As we have shown, (re)conceiving IP, and in particular copyright, as an access right[134] will help avoiding the privatisation of information by IP law[135] and assure that cultural and scientific creations are still available for future innovations.

---

133 See e.g. A Dietz, 'Transformation of Authors' Rights, Change of Paradigm' (1988) 138 *Revue Internationale du Droit d'Auteur*, 22.

134 In this spirit, see the thematic report of December 2014 by the UN Special Rapporteur in the field of cultural rights, which is devoted to the issue of the impact of intellectual property regimes on the enjoyment of right to science and culture, as enshrined in particular in article 15 ICESCR (UN General Assembly, Report of the Special Rapporteur in the field of Cultural Rights, F Shaheed, *Copyright Policy and the Right to Science and Culture*, Human Rights Council, Twenty-eighth session, A/HRC/28/57, 24 December 2014).

135 Further on this tendency, see Geiger, above n 8.

4

What should copyright protect?

R Anthony Reese

Introduction

This project aims to imagine what copyright law might look like if it were designed anew, from scratch. In Chapter 1, the editors ask what it would look like if we could 'design a law to encourage creativity, remunerate and support creators, and increase the size of cultural markets to ensure broad access to new knowledge and creativity'.[1] These goals seem to me to reflect the 'preponderance of individual interests' approach to the public interest that the editors have described.[2] After all, virtually every member of society is a creator – for example, in the age of cell phones, almost all of us take photographs. And almost all of us enjoy access to some informational and/or cultural products. Again, to take a simple and widespread example, virtually all of us sing or hum other people's songs (perhaps in the shower, or to our beloved), or tell jokes we have heard from other people. These dual roles as creator and enjoyer of informational and cultural products undergird each individual's interest in the copyright system, and result in what the

---

1   Rebecca Giblin and Kimberlee Weatherall, 'If we redesigned copyright from scratch, what might it look like?', this volume, [1].
2   Giblin and Weatherall, above n 1, [10]–[11].

editors describe as our *'shared* interest in encouraging and supporting creativity[,] in recognising the rights and interests of creators, in a rich and accessible culture, and in technological and economic progress.'[3]

An early task in reimagining a redesigned copyright law that seeks to achieve those goals will be defining *which* kinds of creativity this copyright law will encourage, *which* creators it will protect and support, and *which* informational and cultural products will come within its ambit. In recent years, current law has repeatedly faced questions about what material copyright protects. Is an artistically planted flowerbed a copyrightable work?[4] What about a yoga pose, or a series of such poses?[5] Or a genetically modified fish?[6] Can a perfume be protected by copyright?[7] Can a sporting event?[8] While a motion picture can be copyrighted under current law, is an actor's five-second performance in a film itself protected as a copyrighted work?[9] Is a list of names and phone numbers of everyone in a particular geographic locality, organised alphabetically by surname, copyrightable?[10] The answers given to these questions have not always been consistent or convincing. A reimagined copyright system must address these questions and, ideally, provide a framework for answering the additional questions about the availability of copyright protection that will inevitably arise going forward.

---

3   Giblin and Weatherall, above n 1, [19] (emphasis added).

4   See *Kelley v Chicago Park District*, 635 F 3d 290 (7th Cir, 2011).

5   See *Bikram's Yoga College of India LP v Evolation Yoga LLC*, 803 F 3d 1032 (9th Cir, 2015); Copyright Office, *Registration of Claims to Copyright*, 77 Fed Reg 37,605 (22 June 2012).

6   US Copyright Office, *Re: GloFish Red Zebra Danio Glowing in Artificial Sunlight* (5 September 2013) <ipmall.law.unh.edu/sites/default/files/hosted_resources/CopyrightAppeals/2013/GloFish RedZebraDanioGlowing.pdf> (rejecting copyright claim in 'a living Red Zebra Danio fish that the Applicant has genetically altered so that the fish "fluoresces" when it is exposed to artificial light').

7   See Kamiel Koelman, *Copyright in the Courts: Perfume as Artistic Expression?*, (2006) September *WIPO Magazine*; see also Charles Cronin, *Genius in a Bottle: Perfume, Copyright, and Human Perception*, (2009) 56 *Journal of the Copyright Society of the USA* 427; Thomas G Field, Jr, *Copyright Protection for Perfumes*, 45 (2004) *IDEA: The Journal of Law and Technology*, 19.

8   See *Premier League Ltd v QC Leisure*, (C-403/08 and C-429/08 (joined cases)) [2011] ECR-I-9083; *National Basketball Association v Motorola Inc*, 105 F 3d 841 (2nd Cir, 1997). See also Instituut voor Informatierecht (IViR), *Study on sports organisers' rights in the European Union: Final Report*, 29–30 (2014).

9   *Garcia v Google Inc*, 786 F 3d 733 (9th Cir, 2015) (en banc), *superseding* 766 F 3d 929 (9th Cir, 2014).

10   *Feist Publications Inc v Rural Telephone Service Co Inc*, 499 US 340 (1991); *Telstra Corporation Limited v Phone Directories Company Pty Ltd* [2010] FCAFC 149.

The question of what copyright protects has at least two components.[11] The first issue is which type of material copyright will cover – that is, what is the *subject matter* of copyright law? Defining copyright's subject matter results in including and excluding entire categories of material from protection. So, for example, someone who breeds a new flower will not be able to obtain copyright protection for that flower if plants are not within copyright's subject matter, but the breeder's photograph of one of her new flowers in bloom will be eligible for copyright protection if photographs are within copyright's subject matter. The second issue concerns any particular item within copyright's subject matter for which protection is sought. Simply falling within copyright's subject matter is not enough – the item in which copyright is claimed must also meet copyright's *standards* in order to actually qualify for protection. So, for example, while paintings are within the subject matter of copyright,[12] a painting of one of the new flowers will be protected only if it meets the law's requirements, such as being independently created by the painter and embodying minimal creativity (or, in another formulation, being the painter's 'own intellectual creation'). Figuring out what a reimagined copyright law should protect involves defining both copyright's subject matter and the standards required for protection.

The fundamental public interest aims identified in Chapter 1 do not offer much direct guidance on the questions of subject matter and standards. The reimagined copyright system may aim to provide incentives for the production of creative works, to enable creators to obtain a fair return on their creative works, and to promote the preservation and dissemination of creative works that make up our cultural heritage. But these aims do not tell us *which* creative works we want to promote, reward and preserve, or just *how creative* those works should be.

---

11 A potential third component of the question is the *scope* of protection granted to any item that comes within copyright's subject matter and meets the standards for protection. This chapter largely does not take up that aspect of a reimagined copyright law.

12 At least for any copyright system that complies with the obligations of the Berne Convention (*Berne Convention for the Protection of Literary and Artistic Works*, opened for signature 9 September 1886 (amended in 1914, 1928, 1948, 1967, 1971, and 1979) 25 UST 1341, 828 UNTS 221, entered into force 5 December 1887).

Determining what a reimagined copyright system would protect is important for at least two reasons. First, the decision has significant implications for all other aspects of copyright law. The articulations of copyrightable subject matter and of the standards for protection serve as the gatekeepers for copyrightability. The wider the gate is opened, the more – and more varied – will be the creations that are copyrightable.

To the extent that this volume's project is to try to design a copyright system from scratch, how broadly the scope of copyright's subject matter should extend, and what standards for protection the law should impose, depends to some degree on other elements of the redesigned copyright system. Take the question of whether the text of an entirely ordinary short and routine email message should qualify for copyright protection. If qualifying for copyright gives the writer of the message a robust set of rights to exclude others for a very long period of time[13] with generous remedies against infringers[14] and no obligation to comply with any formalities,[15] then the public might well want copyright law to impose a relatively demanding standard of creativity for a work to receive protection. In such instances, the public does not seem well served by granting copyrights that would potentially give the copyright owner broad power to interfere with other people's expression – even when they draw on the original writer's expression. On the other hand, if the email qualifies for a copyright that includes narrower exclusionary rights that last for a relatively short term, and only if the email's author complies with useful formalities, then the public might not be particularly concerned that the writer could receive copyright protection even though her product displays very little creativity.

While the chapters elsewhere in this volume address many of those other aspects of a redesigned copyright system, in this chapter I do not attempt to imagine how to calibrate copyright's subject matter and standards to all of the possible permutations of these other aspects. Instead, I assume for purposes of argument that the other aspects

---

13   See Rebecca Giblin, 'Reimagining copyright's duration', this volume.
14   See Kimberlee Weatherall, 'A reimagined approach to copyright enforcement from a regulator's perspective', this volume.
15   See Dev S Gangjee, 'Copyright formalities: A return to registration?', this volume.

of copyright law would remain largely as they are today, and then attempt to rethink the questions of subject matter and standards for protection in light of the current system.

Second, the decision of what copyright law will protect reflects the principles animating the purpose of copyright itself. In the instrumentalist view,[16] the decision embodies an answer to the question of which products of human creativity society determines that the law needs to protect against copying so that creators will produce those products at the level that society wants and will be rewarded for doing so. Determining the 'optimal' level of production of any particular product of human creativity may be an insoluble empirical question. It may well be possible, though, for a society to decide that the populace would prefer, in comparison to current levels, to have a greater, a lower, or about the same level of production of certain creative products, and copyright law could reflect that decision. On the naturalist view, decisions about protectability reflect determinations of desert – specifically, whether the author has produced the kind of creation that deserves the kind of protection offered by copyright law.

In this chapter, my primary aim is not to produce a complete enumeration of what particular subject matter copyright law should protect or a complete articulation of the standards any item of protectable subject matter should have to meet in order to actually acquire copyright protection. Instead, with respect to subject matter, I focus largely on *how* a reimagined copyright system should articulate what is and is not protected, rather than identifying *what* should be protected. With respect to standards for protectability, I suggest four specific areas in which imposing a standard in order for a creation to achieve copyright protection would seem justified, though for the most part I do not seek to identify detailed standards in these four areas.

---

16   Throughout this chapter, I use the terms 'instrumentalist' and 'naturalist' in the sense they are explicated in Chapter 1.

1. Subject matter

1.1. Defining what copyright's subject matter includes

1.1.1. The need to define subject matter boundaries

A copyright system demands some identification of the universe of material to which copyright law does and does not apply. At the very least, such boundary definition is necessary to separate the legal regime governing copyright from other legal regimes that govern different types of subject matter, such as land, tangible personal property, financial instruments, bodily organs and so forth.

At the most basic level, copyright protection might be thought to extend to any product of human creativity. Copyright's fundamental impetus, after all, as identified in the goals discussed above, is to spur and reward human creativity. In the instrumentalist view, copyright does this by granting the creator enforceable rights to exclude others from using her creation in order to give the author (and those who assist her in disseminating that creation) the opportunity to earn a return on the resources they have invested in it. In the naturalist view, copyright does this by recognising the creator's rights to control the products of her creativity. Perhaps, then, copyright's subject matter boundaries should be defined simply by reference to human creativity, so that if something is a product of human creativity it could be protected by copyright.[17]

Granting copyright to any product of human creativity, though, would produce a copyright law with overly broad coverage. First, the law's coverage would overlap with other legal regimes. For example, many inventions that are subject to patent protection result from human creativity, but it is hard to see how the public would benefit by protecting those inventions by copyright law instead of, or in addition to, protecting them by patent law. The standards for protection, the rights granted, the term length, and many other features of the

---

17   See Christophe Geiger, 'Copyright as an access right: Securing cultural participation through the protection of creators' interests', this volume.

copyright regime are ill-suited for a system governing the kinds of industrial property traditionally protected under patent law, even though those inventions are usually the products of human creativity.

In addition, extending copyright to all products of human creativity would bring within copyright's subject matter a wide variety of those products that have traditionally (though not necessarily universally) not been eligible for copyright protection. A partial list of such creative products would include yoga poses and sequences of yoga poses;[18] artistically planted flower beds,[19] and garden or landscape design more generally (including, for example, the design of golf courses);[20] new breeds of plants or animals; perfumes[21] as well as digital recordings of smells;[22] culinary dishes, or perhaps the particular set of dishes available on a particular restaurant's menu;[23] particular varieties of created food products such as beer, wine or cheese; fireworks displays;[24] typography;[25] clothing and other fashion design; tactile enhancements to books;[26] sports plays or routines,

---

18　See e.g. *Bikram's Yoga College of India LP v Evolation Yoga LLC*, 803 F 3d 1032 (9th Cir, 2015); Copyright Office, *Registration of Claims to Copyright*, 77 Fed Reg 37,605 (2012).

19　See e.g. *Kelley v Chicago Park District*, 635 F 3d 290 (7th Cir, 2011).

20　Cf *Pebble Beach Co v Tour 18 I Ltd*, 155 F 3d 526 (5th Cir, 1998) (finding trade dress protection in appearance of golf holes).

21　See Koelman, above n 7; see also Cronin, above n 7; Field, above n 7.

22　See e.g. Stephen Williams, 'Plug-and-Play Aromas at Your Keyboard', *NY Times* (online), 20 January 2011; William Grimes, 'Now on the PC Screen: Scent of a Kitchen', *NY Times* (online), 13 September 2000, F1; Charles Platt, 'You've Got Smell!', *Wired* (online), November 1999.

23　See e.g. Christopher J Buccafusco, 'On the Legal Consequences of Sauces: Should Thomas Keller's Recipes Be Per Se Copyrightable?' (2007) 24 *Cardozo Arts and Entertainment Law Journal* 1121; Caroline Reebs, 'Sweet or Sour: Extending Copyright Protection to Food Art' (2011) 22 *DePaul Journal of Art, Technology & Intellectual Property Law* 41. See also *Kim Seng Co v J & A Importers Inc*, 810 F Supp 2d 1046 (CD Cal 2011) (claiming protection on a traditional Vietnamese dish of a bowl of rice sticks topped with egg rolls, grilled meat, and assorted garnishes as a 'food sculpture'). Note that the 'sculptural' (or pictorial, in the case of, for example, decorated cakes or cookies) aspects of the *presentation* of a particular culinary dish might be protectable under current copyright law in many jurisdictions.

24　See Bobby Kerlik, 'Judge tosses lawsuit between fireworks rivals Zambelli, Pyrotecnico', *Pittsburgh Tribune-Review* (online), 11 November 2010, <www.pittsburghlive.com/x/pittsburghtrib/news/pittsburgh/s_708880.html> (site discontinued) (reporting on dispute over alleged violation of non-compete clause when employee of one fireworks company left to work for a rival company).

25　See Robert A Gorman, Jane C Ginsburg, and R Anthony Reese, *Copyright: Cases & Materials* (Foundation Press, 8th ed, 2011) 250–252.

26　See e.g. Elise Hu, 'Sensory Fiction: Books That Let You Feel What The Characters Do', *NPR All Tech Considered* (6 February 2014), <www.npr.org/blogs/alltechconsidered/2014/02/06/272044748/sensory-fiction-books-that-let-you-feel-what-the-characters-do>.

or even sporting events;[27] parades;[28] amusement park rides (such as rollercoasters); body parts altered by cosmetic surgery;[29] the patterns of liquid created by fountains;[30] the arrangement and positioning of objects and people to be photographed;[31] and invented languages.[32] It is not clear that a preponderance of citizens would want a significantly greater level of production of all of these types of creative works than we currently have, or would want that greater production enough to grant exclusive rights in all of these products of creativity. At the very least, experience to date does not suggest that society suffers from a serious deficit in production of these creations because they lack the possibility of obtaining reward by means of copyright protection. Nor does there appear to be a social consensus that those who create these types of products of human creativity deserve the protection as 'authors' that has so far largely been withheld from them.

A reimagined copyright regime that would automatically offer protection to all products of human creativity would thus seem to recognise copyrightable subject matter more broadly than the identified goals for the regime would justify. As discussed below, human creativity may be *necessary* to produce a copyrightable work, but the fact that a creation is a product of human creativity is likely not *sufficient* to justify protecting that creation by copyright. Many products of human creativity seem likely to lie outside the scope of a copyright system designed to further the public interest. At the very least, it seems impossible to say that the public interest would be best served by making all of these products protectable by copyright based merely on the fact that they can be described as products of

---

27   See e.g. *Premier League Ltd v QC Leisure*, (C-403/08 and C-429/08 (joined cases)) [2011] ECR-I-9083; *National Basketball Association v Motorola Inc*, 105 F 3d 841 (2nd Cir, 1997). See also IViR, *Study on sports organisers' rights in the European Union: Final Report* (2014) 29–30.

28   See e.g. *Production Contractors Inc v WGN Continental Broadcasting Co*, 622 F Supp 1500 (ND Ill 1985).

29   See e.g. Guy Trebay, 'The Man Behind the Face', *NY Times* (New York), 30 March 2014, ST 1, 15, 17 (Dr Frederic Brandt, cosmetic dermatologist, noted that 'I approach each face with a visual perception, an *artistic* perception and a medical perception') (emphasis added).

30   See e.g. *In re Hruby*, 373 F 2d 997 (CCPA 1967) (holding design of fountain spray to be an 'article of manufacture' subject to design patent protection).

31   See e.g. *Creation Records Ltd and Others v News Group Newspapers Ltd*, [1997] EWHC (Ch) 370.

32   See e.g. *SAS Institute Inc v World Programming Ltd*, [2013] EWHC (Ch) 69, [33]. See also Ben Hancock, 'Copyright Klingon? Not Quam Ghu'vam, IoD!', (2016) *The Recorder* (online), 28 April 28, 2016 (discussing litigation over claims of copyright in invented Klingon language from *Star Trek* works); Amy Chozick, 'Athhilezar? Watch Your Fantasy World Language', *NY Times* (New York), 12 December 2011, A1, A3.

human creativity. Copyright law needs some further filter or filters to determine *which* products of human creativity should be subject to copyright protection.

1.1.2. Subject matter boundaries should be defined legislatively[33]

I do not propose in this chapter to attempt to identify the precise boundaries of *which* products of human creativity should and should not be subject to copyright protection. The decision whether to protect any particular type of work will depend on fact-specific questions, involving the issue of whether copyright protection for that particular type of work will, overall, advance the public interest or not. Whether copyright protection for a particular kind of subject matter will advance the public interest may well change over time,[34] making it impossible to define in the abstract a complete list of which types of work copyright should protect. This is particularly true given that technological developments will likely create hitherto unknown forms of creative expression, and that views of what constitutes 'creativity' or 'authorship' are likely to evolve over time.

Weighing the costs and benefits of extending copyright protection to any particular form of human creativity requires deliberation and an affirmative decision about the ultimate desirability of extending protection. That deliberation and decision ought to rest with the political organ that embodies the broadest representation of the public and its interests, which means that the decision should be legislative, rather than administrative or judicial. Indeed, a basic principle of a reimagined copyright system should be that copyright law will protect particular types of creative products only after an affirmative decision that protection for such works will, on balance, sufficiently advance the public interest. That affirmative decision is essentially a policy choice, and in a copyright system that seeks to embody

---

33   This section draws significantly from R Anthony Reese, 'Copyrightable Subject Matter in the "Next Great Copyright Act"' (2014) 29 *Berkeley Technology Law Journal* 1489.

34   The Berne Convention's illustrative list of works has evolved over time, as have the protected categories enumerated in the US copyright statute. Sam Ricketson and Jane C Ginsburg, *International Copyright and Neighbouring Rights: The Berne Convention and Beyond* (Oxford University Press, 2nd ed, 2006), vol 1, § 8.09, 409; Reese, above n 33, 1492–1496.

the preponderance-of-interests goals identified above, such a choice should be made by the legislature as the most broadly representative lawmaking body.

Deciding whether to protect a particular form of human creativity implicates policy questions that the legislature is best equipped to evaluate. In an instrumentalist system, the fundamental question will be whether protection is needed to encourage greater production or dissemination and whether that need outweighs any costs that protection would impose. In a naturalist system, the fundamental question will be what qualifies as 'authorship' deserving of protection of author's rights.

A legislature is generally better positioned to answer those questions than is a court.[35] A court would consider the question in the context of a live controversy over a particular creation, in which the creator would like to claim copyright in order to stop another party from copying the creation. This very context might lead a court, relying in part on intuitions about those who reap where they have not sown, to incline toward recognising the plaintiff's claimed creation as a product of human creativity within copyright's protection.[36] But, as Benjamin Kaplan noted about copyright litigation generally, 'Our gaze should not be confined to *this* plaintiff and *this* defendant. If the contest is conceived as being thus restricted, a court out of understandable sympathy would be inclined to hold for the plaintiff whenever the defendant was shown to have made any recognizable use of the plaintiff's contribution. That would be a very mistaken attitude.

---

35   This is not to suggest that legislatures necessarily take advantage of their superior institutional capacity to gather the information needed to make these decisions. See e.g. Paul Goldstein and Bernt Hugenholtz, *International Copyright* (Oxford University Press, 2nd ed, 2010) 19 ('While the ideal copyright legislator would, before voting to extend protection to new subject matter or rights, require a showing that the extension is needed as an incentive to continued investment, common law legislatures have in fact regularly, indeed mostly, extended copyright without any empirical showing that authors would produce, and publishers publish, fewer works if the extension were not given'). See also Geiger, above n 17, 105.

36   See Wendy J Gordon, 'On Owning Information: Intellectual Property and the Restitutionary Impulse' (1992) 78 *Virginia Law Review* 149, 151–156. Gordon suggests that a 'common law trend toward granting new intellectual property rights has been fueled' in part by 'an intuition of fairness—a norm often linked to natural rights—that one should not "reap where another has sown"', at 156. As Benjamin Kaplan pointed out, such an intuition on the part of a court may be at best incomplete: '[I]f man has any "natural" rights, not the least must be a right to imitate his fellows, and thus to reap where he has not sown.' Benjamin Kaplan, *An Unhurried View of Copyright* (Columbia University Press, 1967) 2.

There is a further diffused public interest necessarily involved.'[37] That interest, in disputes over whether a particular type of creation is or is not copyrightable subject matter, is the decision of whether, as a *category*, such creations should be protected by copyright, aside from any sympathy for the particular plaintiff in the dispute before the court. And the litigation context tends not to provide the court with the information that would be useful in addressing that larger policy question: whether we need to protect those who produce and distribute this type of creation against unauthorised copying in order to generate the production and dissemination of a socially desirable amount and variety of these creations (or, in a naturalist system, whether the producers of these creations are 'authors' deserving of author's rights).

Not only is the legislature the appropriate site for making the policy choices involved in deciding whether to extend protection to any particular category of creative product, but the legislature also has better tools at its disposal to tailor any protection that it grants. In particular, the legislature can better account for notice and retroactivity concerns in granting protection and has more options with respect to calibrating the form and scope of any protection granted.[38]

For example, calibrating the scope of new protection for a type of authorial creation not previously protected could involve tailoring the exclusive rights and limitations applicable to that type of work, or granting protection for a relatively short term, or offering protection only on the condition of compliance with certain formalities.[39] Or, after examining the issues surrounding a particular type of possible subject matter, the legislature might decide that this type of creative production does not need copyright protection, but that it should receive some more tailored, sui generis form of protection against copying.[40] In considering whether to protect any particular new category of subject matter, the legislature has the power to

---

37 Kaplan, above n 36, at 76.
38 See Reese, above n 33, 1504–1508.
39 To the extent that international copyright treaties do not require a state to protect a particular type of creation, those treaties' obligations to grant a minimum term or not to impose formalities would not apply to any copyright protection granted to that type of creation. See e.g. Goldstein and Hugenholtz, above n 35, 220; Ricketson and Ginsburg, above n 34, 412.
40 See section 1.2.2, below.

decide whether to bring that subject matter fully within the existing copyright regime, or whether to grant some other type of protection, which might, for example, last for a much shorter period of time or confer narrower rights. A court, on the other hand, faced with a claim seeking copyright protection for the same type of subject matter, would likely have a much more difficult time tailoring the scope or form of protection granted. As a result, a judicial decision recognising copyright protection to a form of expression not previously identified as copyrightable may overprotect a type of subject matter that the legislature would have found needed only a more tailored form of protection.

1.1.3. How broadly or narrowly should copyright's subject matter be articulated?

Once we accept that copyright should only protect some *subset* of the entire universe of products of human creativity, and that the legislature should decide which products come within that subset, we must decide how the legislature should articulate that subset in the copyright statute. In other words, what is the proper level of specificity with which a copyright statute should articulate the subject matter eligible for its protection? Perhaps not surprisingly, the best approach seems to lie somewhere between the broadest and most narrow possibilities.

1.1.3.1. Broad articulation

A broad approach might be for the copyright statute to extend protection to all productions of *artistic* creativity. Defining copyright's subject matter in this way should result in more narrow coverage than if copyright protected all products of human creativity. For example, this approach would presumably rule out copyright protection for most inventions thought of as protectable (if at all) by patent law, because even if such inventions are highly creative, they are unlikely to be *artistically* creative.

A statute that took this approach would require the courts and administrative authorities who implement the statute to determine what counts as 'artistic'. Making this determination should not involve judgments about the *quality* of artistic creativity in any particular work. Deciding whether a work is within the subject matter of copyright's protection would simply require determining whether works *of this type* are works of 'artistic' creativity.[41] Once a determination has been made that a particular type of work – for example, photographs – is indeed a form of artistic creativity, all future works of that type would presumably be regarded as within the copyright law's subject matter. To the extent that 'artistic' creativity is viewed as superior to other types of creativity – and the fact that the law is granting copyright protection to artistic creativity and not other types of creativity already indicates a preferential status – it may be a disadvantage of this approach that it commits to judges and bureaucrats the value judgment of whether any particular type of creativity is artistic.

Articulating subject matter in this way would have flexibility: it would likely allow copyright's coverage to expand as views of what constitutes art evolve.[42] For example, if creating a perfume, or a culinary dish, or even a variety of wine, came to be viewed as artistic endeavours, then a copyright statute that protected any work of artistic creativity would presumably apply to those products of artistic creativity without any need to amend the statutory definition of copyrightable subject matter. If the legislature has enacted a rule extending copyright to 'all products of artistic creativity', courts and administrative authorities could simply conclude that a form of human creativity that previously had not been understood as 'artistic' had come to be so understood and had therefore become subject to copyright protection.

Such an approach would not necessarily be in the public interest. The evolution of views on whether a type of creation is artistic *might* mean that society would desire to protect creations of that type by copyright. But just because a particular type of creation is regarded as 'artistic' does not necessarily mean that such artistic creations should get copyright protection.

---

41   As discussed below, *some* evaluation of the creativity embodied in the particular work may be necessary in order to determine whether that work, even if it comes within the subject matter of protection, meets the standards required to obtain protection, since a copyright system that seeks to further the public interest would likely extend protection only to works that embody some minimal authorial creativity.

42   Conversely, this approach might cause copyright's subject matter to contract if a form of expression once viewed as 'artistic" ceased to be viewed as artistic.

The public interest would be better served by requiring deliberation about the desirability of protecting a form of creativity newly regarded as artistic and a specific affirmative decision to extend protection. As discussed in the preceding section, that deliberation and decision ought to rest with the social organ that embodies the broadest representation of the public and its interests. This suggests that the decision should be legislative, rather than administrative or judicial, and that therefore a very broad statutory articulation of copyright's subject matter may not sufficiently delineate which products of human creativity should receive copyright protection.

1.1.3.2. Narrow articulation

At the other end of the spectrum, the public interest in a copyright system that serves the goals identified above is likely not to be well served if copyright law articulates its subject matter with great specificity, particularly if the articulations are tethered to particular technologies. A reimagined copyright law will not work well if it does not protect new technological forms of embodying creativity that are very similar to existing forms of creativity that are already protected. For example, the type of creativity involved in a blog post does not differ substantially from that involved in a newspaper or magazine article. It is difficult to see why a copyright statute that protects periodical articles should not also protect blog posts without requiring the legislature to expressly amend the statute to do so.

Would extremely specific categories of protected subject matter be sufficiently flexible to accommodate new technological developments? They might be. For example, a copyright statute that protected 'newspapers and magazines' *could* be interpreted as extending protection to blog posts once the technology for blogs develops. After all, courts in both Britain and the United States interpreted the statutory term 'book' extremely broadly over the course of the eighteenth and nineteenth centuries,[43] not limiting it to the conventional bound volume but instead interpreting it to include,

---

43   See e.g. *Copyright Act of May 31 1790*, ch 15, § 1, 1 Stat 124, 124 (repealed 1831) (protecting only books, maps and charts). See also *Statute of Anne 1710*, 8 Ann c 19 (England) (protecting only books).

for example, single printed sheets.[44] (The liberal construction had limits, however, as when courts refused to consider product labels as 'books' protected by the statute.)[45] Such an approach might mean that a blog would be deemed to be within a statutory category of 'newspapers and magazines', and therefore within the subject matter of copyright, once the technology for blogs develops.

But such broad interpretation of technologically specific articulations of statutory subject matter is not inevitable. For example, one might doubt whether a copyright statute that protected 'photographs and the negatives thereof' (as the US copyright statute did, beginning in 1865)[46] would extend protection to products of digital photography, which does not, of course, involve negatives as part of its photographic process. The same question might have arisen in Great Britain under the provisions of the *Copyright Act of 1911*, which measured a photograph's term of protection 'from the making of the original negative from which the photograph was ... derived' and deemed the author of the work to be 'the person who was owner of such negative at the time when such negative was made'.[47] Those provisions might well have led to the conclusion that the 1911 Act would not protect a digital photograph, since that photograph would have no 'negative'.

Thus, a copyright statute that articulates protected subject matter using specific terms tethered to particular technologies will raise the risk (though not the certainty) that those terms will be construed too narrowly to include works, enabled by new technologies, that embody the same type of creativity as that embodied in types of works already expressly protected. But particularly in an era of rapid technological development such as ours, subjecting each new technological form

---

44   For examples of interpretations in US courts, see e.g. *Clayton v Stone*, 5 F Cas 999 (CCSDNY 1829) (No 2,872); *Drury v Ewing*, 7 F Cas 1113 (CCSD Ohio 1862) (No 4,095); see also Eaton S Drone, *A Treatise on the Law of Property in Intellectual Productions in Great Britain and the United States* (1879), 142–144. British courts gave the corresponding statutory term a similarly generous construction. See e.g. Pamela Samuelson, *Are Gardens, Synthetic DNA, Yoga Sequences, and Fashions Copyrightable?*, <www.law.berkeley.edu/files/Samuelson_Oct_14_cop_subject_matter.pdf> (unavailable from original source but accessible via archive.org; copy on file with editors) (discussing British judicial interpretations).

45   See e.g. *Scoville v Toland*, 21 F Cas 863 (CCD Ohio 1848) (No 12,553); *Coffeen v Brunton*, 5 F Cas 1184 (CCD Ind 1849) (No 2,946).

46   Act of 3 March 1865, ch 126, § 1, 13 Stat 540, 540 (repealed 1870).

47   *Copyright Act, 1911* (UK), 1 & 2 Geo 5, ch 46, § 21.

in which established types of human creativity can be embodied to uncertainty over the availability of copyright protection seems undesirable.

To return to the example of blog posts, once society has concluded that copyright should protect literary creativity in the form of books, poems, short stories, and periodical articles, it seems sensible to protect blog posts once they come along. (Of course, a blog post might be extremely brief, and the public interest might not be served by protecting extremely short blog posts, just as it might not be desirable to protect extremely short newspaper articles. That concern, though, should be addressed not by excluding blog posts, or newspaper articles, as a *type* of work, from copyright's subject matter, but rather by demanding that any particular blog post or newspaper article embody protectable creativity, as discussed below.)[48]

The authorial creativity involved in creating the new form of literary expression seems extremely similar to that required to create many of the older forms. Given that similarity, the public interest would not be served by a copyright statute that denied protection to extremely similar creative works simply because those works are embodied in new technological forms and instead required the legislature amend the statute to expressly include the newly enabled forms. Where authorial creativity is sufficiently similar to that of existing, protected forms, it makes sense to extend protection automatically to a new form.[49]

1.1.3.3. The Goldilocks articulation

This suggests that the best approach to articulating protectable subject matter is for the copyright statute to grant protection using intermediate-level statutory categories that are not overly tied to particular technologies and that have relatively capacious statutory definitions. For example, if the copyright statute protects 'pictorial works', then copyright protection would likely extend under that term to photographs made either through chemical processing of a light-sensitive carrier that has been exposed to light (as in traditional photography) or through electronic capture by an image sensor (as in

---

48   See section 2.2, below.
49   Of course, the legislature could act to amend the statute to deny protection to that new form if it determined that, despite the similarities, some features peculiar to the form sufficiently differentiate it from the existing protected forms such that the new form does not need or deserve copyright protection.

digital photography). Similarly, protection for 'literary works' would quite easily provide protection for blog posts, even if those do not fit conventional definitions of 'books', 'newspapers', 'magazines' or even 'periodicals'.

1.1.4. Exhaustive or illustrative articulation

The view that the legislature should define copyright's subject matter by statute raises another question beyond the level of specificity that the legislature should use. If a copyright statute articulates its subject matter in the manner just recommended, what should the relationship be between these intermediate-level enumerated categories and the overall subject matter of copyright? A copyright statute that specifies the categories of protectable subject matter could be written in at least two ways, with very different results for what the statute does and does not protect.

In the first approach, which Paul Goldstein and Bernt Hugenholtz refer to as 'exhaustive' categorisation and which Tanya Aplin labels the 'closed list' approach, the list of categories enumerated in the copyright statute as protectable exhaustively identifies the entire universe of subject matter protectable under the law: copyright protects works in those categories and *only* works in those categories. The United Kingdom, Canada, and Austria are all examples of copyright systems with statutes using this approach. For example, in the United Kingdom, the *Copyright, Designs and Patents Act 1988* (CDPA) § 1(1) extends protection to literary, dramatic, musical, and artistic works as well as to sound recordings, films, broadcasts, and the typographical arrangement of published editions.[50] Canada protects 'every original literary, dramatic, musical and artistic work', as well as performer's performances, sound recordings, and communication signals.[51] Austrian law extends protection to 'original intellectual productions in the fields of literature, music, art and cinematography'.[52]

---

[50]   Tanya Aplin, 'Subject Matter' in Estelle Derclaye (ed), *Research Handbook on The Future of EU Copyright* (Edward Elgar, 2009), 49–76.

[51]   *Copyright Act*, RSC 1985, § 5(1) (literary, dramatic, musical, and artistic works); § 15(1) (performer's performances); § 18(1) (sound recordings); § 21(1) (communication signals).

[52]   *Federal Law on Copyright in Works of Literature and Art and on Related Rights* (Austria), BGBl. No 111/1936, Art 1(1); see also Goldstein and Hugenholtz, above n 35, 195.

By contrast, in 'illustrative' categorisation (or an 'open list' approach), the general statement of copyright's subject matter may be followed by a list of more specific categories that are identified as protected, but because the list is not exhaustive, this approach allows copyright 'protection for classes of works falling well outside recognized subject matter categories'.[53] France, as Aplin suggests, offers an excellent example of this approach, protecting 'all works of the mind, whatever their kind, form of expression, merit or purpose', and offering an illustrative list of categories.[54] (It seems unlikely, however, that this statutory language is read literally; Thomas Edison's incandescent lightbulb clearly seems to have been a 'work of the mind', but probably not a copyrightable one.) The Berne Convention also takes this approach, requiring adhering countries to protect 'the rights of authors in their literary and artistic works',[55] explaining that this phrase 'shall *include* every production in the literary, scientific and artistic domain, whatever may be the mode or form of its expression',[56] and then providing a long but only illustrative list of examples.[57]

The United States technically takes the illustrative approach but practically appears to operate under an exhaustive categorisation. The US copyright statute describes the basic subject matter protected under current copyright law as 'works of authorship',[58] but does not affirmatively define that term. Instead, it states that works of authorship 'include' eight specific categories listed in the statute.[59] The use of the word 'include', which the statute defines as being 'illustrative and not limitative'[60] indicates that copyright could be recognised in works that do not fall within any expressly enumerated category, and the statute's legislative history suggests that this may have been the drafters' intent

---

53   Goldstein and Hugenholtz, above n 35, 195.

54   *Intellectual Property Code* (France), Art L112-1.

55   Berne Convention, Art 1.

56   Berne Convention, Art 2 (emphasis supplied).

57   Berne Convention, Art 2. But see Ricketson and Ginsburg, above n 34, at 409 ('[A]n unlisted work's potential status in theory as a "literary or artistic work" for the purposes of article 2(1) has meant very little, if anything, in practice … The only mechanism provided by the Convention to achieve uniformity among Union members on [whether a new category of work is a literary or artistic work] is by a revision conference which amends article 2 so as to include the work in question, or by subsequent multilateral agreements …').

58   17 USC § 102(a).

59   17 USC § 102(a)(1)–(8). The enumerated categories are literary works; musical works; dramatic works; pantomimes and choreographic works; pictorial, graphic, and sculptural works; motion pictures and other audiovisual works; sound recordings; and architectural works.

60   17 USC § 101 ('including').

to some degree.[61] Nevertheless, the US Copyright Office has taken the position that the statute does *not* permit courts or the Copyright Office 'to create new categories of authorship',[62] and I am unaware of any court decision granting copyright protection in the US to a work not found to fall within any of the statutorily enumerated categories.[63]

In comparing the two approaches, Aplin notes that exhaustive categorisation has the advantage of *restraint* that ensures that protection is not extended inappropriately to subject matter that should not be protected. (Aplin also suggests that a closed list offers the advantage of *certainty* of what is and is not protected, though the discussion above regarding the potential for broad construction of a statutory term such as 'book' may undercut the certainty provided even by a closed list.)

By contrast, Aplin identifies the benefits of illustrative categorisation as *flexibility* and *completeness* in protecting subject matter that may not have been expressly contemplated when the law was drafted. (Again, Aplin suggests that the open list offers the advantage of *simplicity* in that new works need not be shoehorned into existing categories, but while it may be possible to tell whether the work is protectable without reference to enumerated categories, to the extent the copyright statute differentiates the rights, remedies, or duration of protection by categories, shoehorning may still be required to determine exactly what copyright protection the work gets.) She notes disadvantages with each approach as well, though indicates that there are ways to minimise them.[64]

---

61   HR Rep No 94-1476 (1976), 51 ('Authors are continually finding new ways of expressing themselves, but it is impossible to foresee the forms that these new expressive methods will take. The bill does not intend either to freeze the scope of copyrightable subject matter at the present stage of communications technology or to allow unlimited expansion into areas completely outside the present congressional intent. Section 102 implies neither that that subject matter is unlimited nor *that new forms of expression within that general area of subject matter would necessarily be unprotected.*') (emphasis added) (as corrected by *Correction of Errors in Printed House Report on S.22*, 122 Cong Record No 143 (daily edition 21 September 1976) at H10727).

62   *Registration of Claims to Copyright*, 77 Fed Reg 37,605, 37,607 (22 June 2012).

63   See generally Reese, above n 33, 1517–1521.

64   Aplin, above n 50, 49–76.

Perhaps the best approach is a long but closed list of numerous categories, each (as noted above) defined broadly and in technologically neutral terms. Formulating a copyright statute in this way can achieve many of the advantages of both the closed list and open list approaches to identifying which types of creations copyright law protects.

Under this approach, extending copyright to additional subject matter – such as perfume, fireworks displays, etc. – that differs *substantially* from the types of creations that have already been enumerated as protected would require legislative deliberation to amend copyright law by adding a new category. This would embody the restraint advantage that Aplin identifies with exhaustive categorisation, by ensuring that a new form of creative expression (such as a digital recording of a scent) or an existing but previously uncopyrightable form (such as a sporting event) would not be protected without an affirmative decision of whether protection would serve the public-interest goals of copyright identified above.

Broad and technologically neutral definitions, though, should help ensure that new technological forms and evolutions of existing types of copyrightable creativity are covered without the need for further legislative action. As discussed in the previous section, forms of creative expression enabled by new technologies would be protected if they are sufficiently similar to existing forms of protected expression to come within an identified category. Under this approach, a copyright law that has protected novels and monographs and newspaper and magazine articles and pamphlets and broadsides as products of 'literary' creativity should have little trouble protecting blog posts. Similarly, protection for photography in the category of works of 'pictorial' creativity should extend seamlessly to digital photographs, and protection for 'sound recordings' or 'phonograms' should cover compact discs and MP3 files as easily as those terms covered 33-1/3 rpm long-playing vinyl records. This approach thus offers at least a significant portion of the flexibility advantage that Aplin identifies with illustrative categorisation, allowing in many (though likely not all) instances protection for new forms of embodying creativity even if those forms were not expressly within the contemplation of the drafters when the copyright statute was adopted.

1.2. Category-based exclusions from copyright

Given the breadth with which copyright protection will be extended even under a closed list of broadly defined categories, a public interest copyright law should also expressly exclude a number of categories of works which should not receive copyright protection.

1.2.1. Edicts of government

A reimagined copyright system should not grant protection to '[e]dicts of government, such as judicial opinions, administrative rulings, legislative enactments, public ordinances, and similar official legal documents'.[65] Copyright control over government edicts has the potential to drive up the cost of and otherwise restrict access to those works. But the obligation of all citizens to obey the law, and the rights of all citizens to participate in their governance, mean that access to these edicts of government should not be restricted by copyright-based claims of exclusivity. In addition, naturalist claims of authorial rights to attribution and integrity do not generally fit well with many of these kinds of works.

While the public interest in maximum access to these edicts of government argues for leaving these works entirely outside the scope of copyright protection, the public also has an interest in ensuring that it has access to accurate and authentic versions of government edicts. Copyright law could provide one method by which government entities can seek to ensure that those who copy and disseminate

---

65   US Copyright Office, *Compendium II: Copyright Office Practices*, § 206.01 (1984) ('Edicts of government, such as judicial opinions, administrative rulings, legislative enactments, public ordinances, and similar official legal documents are not copyrightable for reasons of public policy. This applies to such works whether they are Federal, State, or local as well as to those of foreign governments.'). See also Berne Convention Art 2(4) ('It shall be a matter for legislation in the countries of the Union to determine the protection to be granted to official texts of a legislative, administrative and legal nature, and to official translations of such texts.').

government edicts do so accurately. For example, the government could grant the right to reproduce legal edicts protected by copyright only on the condition that the grantee not alter the text in any way.[66]

But the public interest in accuracy and authenticity can likely be served by more targeted legal provisions, parallel to provisions on fraud and misrepresentation. More targeted provisions could impose penalties on those, for example, who represent to the public that a particular text is an enacted law or a rendered judicial opinion when it is not, or who negligently provide inaccurate versions of government edicts to the public. These more targeted provisions could likely address the public interest in access to accurate and authentic government information while reducing the danger that copyright control will be used to restrict access to such information.

It is not clear that this exclusion should be extended more generally to *any* authorial creation produced by or on behalf of a government entity. For example, one can imagine a government employee, as part of her official duties, creating a poster advertising a national park in the hope of encouraging more people to visit the park. If people find the poster beautiful, they might want to buy prints of it to hang in their homes, or postcards of it to send to friends and family. A government might decide not to grant or assert copyright protection in works produced by government employees or agents, perhaps on the ground that the public has already paid to have those works created by paying the salaries of their creators.[67] But the public interest does not provide as strong a rationale for categorically excluding such works from copyright protection as it provides for excluding edicts of government.

---

66   See e.g. Michael Geist, 'Government of Canada Quietly Changes Its Approach to Crown Copyright' on Michael Geist, *Michael Geist*, (25 November 2013), <www.michaelgeist. ca/2013/11/crown-copyright-change/> (noting that in 2010 Canada had granted permission to reproduce government works for non-commercial purposes as long as the work was reproduced 'in the manner that it is originally published' and without 'any alterations whatsoever'); *Reproduction of Federal Law Order, SI/97-5* (Canada) (allowing anyone, 'without charge or request for permission,' to reproduce federal enactments and judicial and administrative decisions 'provided due diligence is exercised in ensuring the accuracy of the materials reproduced and the reproduction is not represented as an official version'), <laws.justice.gc.ca/eng/regulations/ SI-97-5/FullText.html>.

67   See e.g. 17 USC § 105 ('Copyright protection under this title is not available for any work of the United States Government …'); HR Rep No 94-1476 (1976), 59 (noting the argument that where a work is prepared with the use of government funds, 'the public should not be required to pay a "double subsidy"').

1.2.2. Subject matter protected more appropriately elsewhere

A reimagined copyright system also should not provide protection for subject matter that would be protected more appropriately under another legal regime.[68] In particular, if a particular type of potentially copyrightable subject matter would benefit from a targeted, tailored sui generis regime of protection in order to achieve the public benefit of encouraging the production and dissemination of that type of work while imposing fewer costs (principally in restricted access and reuse) than copyright would impose, then the public as a whole should prefer the sui generis regime rather than copyright protection. In addition, shoehorning into copyright subject matter that only uneasily fits there will require courts to apply copyright doctrines and principles to situations and types of works for which they were not designed and to which they do not easily apply, and doing so may then distort those doctrines and principles in ways that could adversely affect their application to works and uses at the core of copyright protection.

This approach might exclude from protection a number of categories of works that have been the subject of much discussion as to the desirability of sui generis protection. Two of the most prominent are computer programs and industrial design. There is a substantial academic literature on the desirability of a sui generis regime to protect computer software.[69] Indeed, Sam Ricketson and Jane Ginsburg relate that early international efforts were made to create a sui generis system to protect computer programs before a 'heavily pragmatic' move was made to protect them as literary works under copyright law.[70] Industrial design is another product of human creativity that copyright has had difficulty dealing with. Paul

---

68   This principle would largely deny copyright protection to inventions protectable by patent law, because patent protection seems more appropriately tailored to inventions than copyright law. In practice, the articulation of copyrightable subject matter in the manner recommended in Part I.A.3 (this chapter), in conjunction with the articulation of patentable subject matter, should itself eliminate a great deal of the potential overlap, since many patentable inventions will not come within any of the enumerated categories of copyrightable subject matter. In addition, provisions on the scope of copyright protection will help eliminate overlap, if they make clear that copyrightable literary or pictorial representations of an invention do not provide exclusive rights to the invention itself. See e.g. *Baker v Selden*, 101 US 99 (1879); 17 USC § 102(b) (denying protection to any 'idea, procedure, process, system, method of operation, concept, principle, or discovery' embodied in a copyrighted work).

69   See e.g. Pamela Samuelson et al, 'A Manifesto Concerning the Legal Protection of Computer Programs' (1994) 94 *Columbia Law Review* 2308, 2310–2313; and works cited at note 6 therein.

70   Ricketson and Ginsburg, above n 34, §§ 8.92–8.96, 491–494.

Goldstein has described the issue of protectability of industrial design as the most troublesome line in US copyright law.[71] In some places, industrial designs are offered a separate regime of protection that could obviate the need for including them in copyright at all.[72] A third candidate for exclusion on this ground is the design of clothing. While some copyright systems generally protect fashion design[73] and others generally exclude it,[74] both academic investigation[75] and industry-supported legislative proposals[76] suggest that a sui generis system of protection that is less expansive than copyright could be sufficient to meet any public interest in protecting fashion design. If so, fashion design should be excluded from copyright protection.

2. Standards for copyright protection

Defining the subject matter of copyright law provides a threshold definition of which types of human creations are eligible for copyright protection, sorting among types of creativity to determine which ones can and which cannot acquire copyright. But establishing the proper subject matter of copyright should be only one element in identifying what a reimagined copyright system should protect. Not every actual creation that comes within the scope of copyright-eligible subject matter should in fact be protected by copyright. If I stand in front of a crowd and say 'That which does not kill us makes us stronger',[77] a

---

71   Paul Goldstein, *Goldstein on Copyright* (Aspen Publishers, 3rd ed, 2005 and 2015 Supplement) § 2.5.3 at 2:67.

72   Graeme B Dinwoodie and Mark D Janis, *Trade Dress and Design Law* (Aspen Publishers, 2010) 527–566.

73   *Intellectual Property Code* (France), Art L112-2(14) (protecting 'creations of the seasonal industries of dress and articles of fashion').

74   US Copyright Office, *Compendium of US Copyright Office Practices* (3rd ed, 22 December 2014) § 924.3(A) ('[T]he U.S. Copyright Office will not register a claim in clothing or clothing designs.').

75   See e.g. Kal Raustiala and Christopher Sprigman, 'The Piracy Paradox: Innovation and Intellectual Property in Fashion Design' (2006) 92 *Virginia Law Review* 1687; Kal Raustiala and Christopher Sprigman, 'The Piracy Paradox Revisited' (2009) 61 *Stanford Law Review* 1201. But see C Scott Hemphill and Jeannie Suk, 'The Law, Culture, and Economics of Fashion' (2009) 61 *Stanford Law Review* 1147; C Scott Hemphill and Jeannie Suk, 'Remix and Cultural Production' (2009) 61 *Stanford Law Review* 1227.

76   See e.g. *Innovative Design Protection Act*, S 3523, 112th Cong (2012); *Design Piracy Prohibition Act*, HR 2511, 112th Cong (2011); *Innovative Design Protection and Piracy Prevention Act*, S 3728, 111th Cong (2010); *Design Piracy Prohibition Act*, HR 2196, 111th Cong (2009); *Design Piracy Prohibition Act*, S 1957, 110th Cong (2007); *Design Piracy Prohibition Act*, HR 2033, 110th Cong (2007); HR 5055, 109th Cong (2006).

77   See *Peters v West*, 692 F. 3d 629 (7th Cir, 2012).

copyright system based on the goals identified above should probably not award me copyright protection in the nine words that I spoke. Rather, any specific creative work should have to meet certain *standards* in order to qualify for copyright protection. At least four possible standards would help confine copyright protection to instances in which it is likely to further the public interest: independent creation, creativity, fixation and minimum size.

2.1. Independent creation

Copyright laws generally impose a standard of independent creation and deny copyright to works (or elements thereof) that have been copied from someone else's work. Goldstein and Hugenholtz summarise this as a requirement that 'the work distinctively be the product of its author's intellectual efforts and not be copied from some other work or works'.[78] They note that common law systems generally implement this requirement using a standard of originality (the work must originate with the author), while civil law systems demand that a work be 'the author's own intellectual creation'.[79]

The requirement that an author must have created her work herself (and the consequent principle that her copyright protects only those elements of her work that she has not copied) works in harmony with other aspects of a reimagined copyright system. In particular, excluding from copyright protection any material in an author's work that has been copied from another work helps ensure that once a work enters the public domain, it will remain there free for anyone to use, without needing to fear a plausible claim of copyright infringement from a third party who had copied the public domain work (or parts thereof) into her own copyrightable work. In addition, the requirement serves the aim of rewarding authors for their creative efforts by *not* rewarding them for merely copying the creativity of another author.

---

78   Goldstein and Hugenholtz, above n 35, 189.
79   Ibid 193.

2.2. Creativity

The issue of standards raises the recurring question whether copyright should protect only works that embody some creative contribution by their authors or whether it should also protect works that embody only the authors' labour and effort (and perhaps skill) that does not rise to the level of creativity.

A reimagined copyright law could dispense with any standard of creativity (or perhaps even labour) whatsoever, and simply grant protection to any work that falls within the articulated categories protected by the statute so long as the author claiming copyright protection has, as noted in the previous section, created the particular work herself. This would avoid the need for any real evaluation of the content of the work as part of determining its protectability, which would seem administratively simpler. However, the simplicity of such an approach must be weighed against the likelihood that many people could likely mount plausible copyright claims to entirely routine and uncreative works which in many cases would likely amount to little more than unelaborated basic building blocks of authorial expression, such as a short sequence of musical notes, very basic literary phrases or sentences, visual works consisting only of basic geometric shapes, etc. If such copyright claims are plausible in the absence of any standard for protection beyond independent creation, then such an approach would likely lead to overprotection, both because copyright protection is not needed to encourage or reward the production of such works, and because copyright protection for such basic works might hinder the creation and copyrighting of more elaborated works.

For example, if an author holds a plausible copyright in a work that consists merely of a single black stripe running horizontally across a piece of paper, that copyright claim might well inhibit other visual artists who wish to use a horizontal stripe in their works. Even if a later artist wants to use a red stripe, or a black stripe that is thinner or thicker, or more than one black stripe, she might worry that her visual work would be deemed substantially similar to the black stripe, and therefore infringing, and therefore she might not be willing to risk creating her work. The later artist might well ultimately not be liable because the copyright owner might not be able to prove that she in fact copied her stripe from the copyrighted stripe, or that her work is substantially similar to the copyrighted stripe. But the eventual resolution of these issues in infringement litigation would likely provide little solace *ex ante* to the risk-averse later artist, who might instead simply choose to avoid using a horizontal stripe in her work (and might similarly seek to avoid using other basic geometric shapes arguably protected by other copyrights). The public interest would hardly be served by a system in which many authors try to avoid using basic building blocks of their chosen expressive form, even if such a system has the administrative advantage of granting copyright protection without the need for any consideration of whether a work results from authorial creativity or labour.

Some creativity standard thus seems important as a filter for copyright protection. The law, though, should impose a relatively low standard of creativity as the threshold that a work must clear to enter the realm of copyright. Imposing any higher creativity standard would mean that judges or administrators applying the copyright statute would likely have to engage in significant qualitative evaluation of an author's work to determine whether the work is protected. It seems clear that the public would not be well served by such a system. Justice Oliver Wendell Holmes's 1903 observation that '[i]t would be a dangerous undertaking for persons trained only to the law to constitute themselves final judges of the worth of pictorial illustrations outside of the narrowest and most obvious limits'[80] seems equally valid today and equally relevant to other types of creative expression beyond pictorial illustrations. At least some judges may well regard themselves as qualified to make such evaluative judgments, and indeed some judges may well be excellent critics of some forms of copyrightable expression (and indeed some judges may themselves also be authors in some of those forms). But society cannot assume that aesthetic perceptiveness will necessarily be a skill generally shared by those who serve as judges or by agency officials whose primary responsibilities are legal. And society as a whole probably would not benefit from structuring its copyright system in a way that would require staffing courts and agencies (or at least those dealing with copyright issues) only with people who have such skill. Even if it were possible to do so, it is not clear that such specialist judges or officials

---

80   *Bleistein v Donaldson Lithographing Co*, 188 US 239 (1903); see also Diane Leenheer Zimmerman, 'The Story of *Bleistein v Donaldson Lithographing Company*: Originality as a Vehicle for Copyright Inclusivity' in Jane C Ginsburg and Rochelle Cooper Dreyfuss, *Intellectual Property Stories* (Foundation Press, 2006) 77, 96–99.

would necessarily be able to reach uniform, objective qualitative assessments of the extent to which a given work of authorship displays a high degree of authorial creativity. Any required determination of creativity – indeed, any determination of skill and judgment, or even of intellectual labour or effort – will require the judge or agency to make *some* at least somewhat qualitative evaluation of a work seeking copyright protection. But the public interest is better served by minimising the degree of qualitative evaluation needed. As a result, any creativity standard imposed as a requirement for copyright protection should be a relatively low one.

If copyright law imposes only a relatively low standard of creativity, questions of whether a work meets the standard will likely arise mostly with regard to what might be considered marginal works. Most authors' creations that come within copyright's subject matter will easily be judged to have substantially exceeded a low creativity requirement, because most such works will easily be found to embody much more creativity than is required.

While a relatively low creativity requirement will therefore likely filter out of copyright protection relatively few works, it may be precisely at the margins where society will benefit from demanding a modest amount of creativity in order for a work to qualify for protection. Works at the margins will be those that are not obviously and abundantly creative. Such works are more likely to be close to the bone in terms of authorial expression, and may often be just a relatively unarticulated presentation or combination of some of the basic building blocks of their type of expressive form. For example, in terms of graphic works, this might involve a standard size, white business envelope with a thick black stripe running across the width of the upper half of the envelope.[81] In a system designed to achieve the goals outlined above, the argument for protecting such works seems quite weak. Given how little creativity is needed to create these works, copyright protection is likely not needed as an incentive to encourage authors to create and disseminate them (in the instrumentalist view) and the person who creates these works may well not deserve to be

---

81   See e.g. *Magic Marketing v Mailing Services of Pittsburgh*, 634 F Supp 769 (WDPa 1986) (denying claim to copyright in envelope with such a stripe that contained the words 'Priority Message: Contents Require Immediate Attention'); Gorman, Ginsburg, and Reese, above n 25, 85 (reproducing envelopes denied copyright as insufficiently minimally creative).

recognised as an 'author' entitled to protection (in the naturalist view). And in any event, protecting such works does not seem justified given the likely cost of protection. Works that do not even show a very low degree of creativity likely elaborate very little on the basic building blocks of expression, which means that many other authors will likely be using those same building blocks. Allowing a copyright in the uncreative work will present the possibility that the copyright owner could at least bring plausible infringement suits against other, more creative, authors. Society seems better served if every author can use the basic building blocks of copyrightable expressive forms as the raw material to produce her own creative articulations and combinations of those building blocks.

This is not to say that there will not be difficult cases. For example, Kazimir Malevich's 1915 Suprematist painting *Black Square*, a painted black square surrounded by a margin of white, may have marked a dramatic challenge to the conventions of painting at the time, but viewing the final painting as sufficiently creative for copyright protection raises the danger that copyright in the painting might restrict other artists' ability to use as basic a geometric form as the square. But for any standard, there will be instances close to the line where reasonable minds might differ in the determination regarding on which side of the line the work falls. To the extent that copyright needs to impose some standard in order to deny protection to overly minimal works, most of the social benefit in having the standard derives from excluding material that has very little creativity. As a result, society can get that benefit by setting a relatively low creativity standard, and that standard means that the risk of false negatives should principally impact only relatively uncreative works.

A creativity standard, even a relatively low one, seems likely to have the most impact on one particular type of authorial work: collections of factual information.[82] Because facts themselves are generally not protectable by copyright, the only opportunity for creativity in such works is in the collection and presentation of the facts.[83] This usually means that an author must show that she exercised creativity

---

[82]   See Sam Ricketson, 'Common Law Approaches to the Requirement of Originality' in Catherine W Ng, Lionel Bentley and Giuseppina D'Agostino, *The Common Law of Intellectual Property: Essays in Honour of Professor David Vaver* (Hart Publishing, 2010) 233–251.

[83]   See e.g. *Feist Publications Inc v Rural Telephone Service*, 499 US 340 (1991).

in selecting which facts to include, or in arranging those facts in the collection, or both. In many instances, the author will find it difficult to satisfy this creativity standard. Often, for example, the author attempts to present a *comprehensive* collection of the relevant facts, and so engages in no real selection at all, let alone a creative one. And often the facts are arranged in an entirely conventional and uncreative manner, such as alphabetically, chronologically or ordinally. For these collections of information, then, imposing a creativity standard would often mean denying copyright protection. By contrast, most collections of information likely *could* meet a copyright standard that requires only that the collection reflect the author's labour and effort (perhaps even intellectual effort), since in most instances the author will have expended such labour in producing even the non-creative collection. Indeed, some collections of information could likely meet a standard that demands that the author used skill to produce the work, even if skill is more than mere effort but less than creativity.

To the extent that a relatively low creativity standard would have its greatest impact on collections of information and would likely disqualify many of those collections from protection, such collections might generally be more appropriately protected, if at all, by a legal regime other than copyright. As discussed above, the goals of a reimagined copyright system revolve around the production and availability of *creative* works. Collections of factual information that require an investment of labour to produce, but that are not creative, may need some legal protection in order to prevent free-riding copying by third parties that would too greatly undermine the incentive for the initial producer to invest in collecting and organising the information in the first place. That specific problem, though, could be addressed by a legal regime that more directly targets the problem and that tailors the requirements that such collections must meet to be protected, as well as the rights and remedies that a protected product receives.

For example, in the European Union, the Database Directive[84] requires member nations to protect even non-creatively selected or arranged collections of information if the compiler has made a substantial investment in obtaining, verifying or presenting the contents of

---

84   *Directive 96/9/EC of the European Parliament and of the Council of 11 March 1996 on the legal protection of databases* [1996] OJ L 77, 20–28 ('*EC Database Directive*').

the collection.[85] But it provides different rights (the right to prevent extraction or reutilisation of all or a substantial part of the contents of the collection)[86] and limitations,[87] as well as a much shorter nominal term of protection (15 years from when completed, or, if made public during that term, 15 years from when made public).[88] In US law, unfair competition law provides a cause of action for misappropriation where:

> (i) the plaintiff generates or collects information at some cost or expense; (ii) the value of the information is highly time-sensitive; (iii) the defendant's use of the information constitutes free-riding on the plaintiff's costly efforts to generate or collect it; (iv) the defendant's use of the information is in direct competition with a product or service offered by the plaintiff; (v) the ability of other parties to free-ride on the efforts of the plaintiff would so reduce the incentive to produce the product or service that its existence or quality would be substantially threatened.[89]

While many producers of information collections would not likely to be able to bring misappropriation claims because the information they present is not 'highly time-sensitive', the elements of this claim offer a model for how a tailored, non-copyright regime protecting such collections against unfair free riding could be structured, if such protection were deemed necessary.

Protecting collections of information through a tailored, non-copyright regime would be better than having the tail of preventing free riding non-creative collections of information wag the dog of not protecting uncreative expressive works in order to keep basic building blocks of creativity free for all to use. If the most substantial concern about imposing a relatively low creativity standard involves the effects of that standard on non-creative collections of information, those effects would be better addressed by whatever non-copyright protection might be justified for such collections, rather than by lowering the standard to be applied to all works within copyright's subject matter.

---

85   EC Database Directive, Art 7(1).
86   EC Database Directive, Art 7(1).
87   EC Database Directive, Art 9.
88   EC Database Directive, Art 10.
89   *National Basketball Assn v Motorola*, 105 F 3d 841, 853 (2nd Cir, 1997).

2.3. Fixation

Another possible requirement that copyright law might impose for a copyright-eligible creation to obtain protection is that the creation be fixed in some tangible medium in order to be protected.

A fixation requirement helps to preserve the cultural record, and encouraging the creation of that cultural record is a principal purpose of a reimagined copyright law. Once a work is fixed, the likelihood that some embodiment of that work will survive and be available to future audiences increases dramatically (though the survival of at least one embodiment of any work is, of course, in no way guaranteed).[90] Of course, fixation of copyrightable creativity doesn't preserve the cultural record perfectly. For some types of works, a fixation will not convey the full scope of the author's creativity. A film of a stage performance of a play cannot capture the entirety of the live performance, and notation of a choreographic work obviously captures even less of the dance as performed. But a recording of a performed work will still give future audiences, creators, and performers more information about the author's created work then they will have if the work is never fixed in any form.

A fixation requirement also serves to make copyright law more administrable, by providing evidence of the existence and content of the author's creative product. This evidence is obviously crucial when the author of the work claims that a defendant has infringed the work and a court must determine whether the work meets the standards for protection and whether the defendant has indeed infringed on any of the expression in the work.

While the goals of a reimagined copyright system thus support including a requirement that works be fixed in order to be protected, the requirement need not be particularly onerous. It should be technologically neutral so that any form of fixation will qualify. It should perhaps not focus on whether the fixation was made with or without the author's consent – if an audience member tapes a lecturer's impromptu address without permission (and perhaps in defiance of an express prohibition on recording), that should not stop the lecturer

---

90   See e.g. R Anthony Reese, 'What Copyright Owes the Future' (2012) 50 *Houston Law Review* 287, 296–306.

from bringing a claim of copyright infringement and satisfying the fixation requirement by means of the audience member's illicit recording.[91]

While fixation should be a requirement for any particular item of copyright-eligible subject matter to qualify for protection under a reimagined copyright law, the public interest might still be served by granting creators and performers of unfixed works more limited protection, either as part of copyright law or as a separate scheme, against unauthorised fixation of their works. Such protection should be tailored to the particular aims of protecting those who create and perform unfixed works against having their works fixed without their consent.

2.4. Size

Already in the mid-1960s Benjamin Kaplan had given some attention to the question of whether some products of creative expression were too small to be protected by copyright:

> We can, I think, conclude that to make the copyright turnstile revolve, the author should have to deposit more than a penny in the box ... Surely there is danger in trying to fence off small quanta of words or other collocations; these pass quickly into the idiom; to allow them copyright, particularly if aided by a doctrine of 'unconscious' plagiarism, could set up untoward barriers to expression.[92]

More recently, Justin Hughes has written about the problems that may come from recognising copyright protection for quantitatively small amounts of original expression within the scope of copyright.[93] Among other problems, many copyright doctrines are based on a conception of a more substantial 'work' as the basic subject matter of copyright, and may be distorted if they are applied to very small units of expression, which Hughes labels 'microworks'.[94] Protecting a small unit of expression as part of a larger work creates fewer problems

---

91   This would be a departure from, for example, current US law, which requires that a work be fixed 'by or under the authority of the author' in order to qualify for copyright protection. 17 USC § 101 ('fixed').

92   Kaplan, above n 36, 46.

93   Justin Hughes, 'Size Matters (Or Should) in Copyright Law' (2005–2006) 75 *Fordham Law Review* 575.

94   Ibid. See also *Garcia v Google Inc*, 786 F 3d 733, 742–743 (9th Cir, 2015) (en banc).

because, for instance, claims of infringement by copying the small portion of the larger work can be more appropriately handled through considerations of *de minimis*, substantial similarity, *scènes à faire*, and fair use or fair dealing. But if, for example, a single number (such as a price or a parts number) or a phrase of only a few words (or even a short collection of words and other characters that make up a URL) is itself a copyrightable *work*, then copying the number or phrase will be hard to excuse as *de minimis* or insubstantial.

The difficulty, of course, is formulating any absolute rule as to the minimal size necessary for a creative expression to qualify for copyright protection. At the very least, this seems likely to vary a good deal with the type of creation involved. And, as Hughes suggests, it may involve consideration of a number of factors such as independent economic value, artistic viability, separate dissemination, audience perception, and compositional integrity.[95]

A useful approach for dealing with this issue may be to specify that copyright attaches to a creation within the subject matter of protection only when that creation contains an appreciable amount of the creator's original expression. The development of specific tests and principles for applying this quantitative requirement would rest, at least as an initial matter, with administrative and judicial authorities in the application of the requirement to particular instances in which claims to copyright are made in very small units of expression.

In the United States, the Copyright Office interprets the current statute to mean that a work must contain 'at least a minimum amount of creative authorship that is original to the author' in order to be copyrightable.[96] But while courts may have the authority under current law to interpret the statute in this way, the fact that any such requirement is at best implicit seems to have led at least some courts

---

95 Hughes, above n 93, 622–635. See also Paul Goldstein, 'What Is a Copyrighted Work? Why Does It Matter?' (2011) 58 *UCLA Law Review* 1175 (arguing that looking to authorial intent, particularly as reflected in registration records, can often be relied on to counter copyright owners' litigation incentives 'to skew the calibration of his work toward a size more granular than principle, law, or practice might reasonably condone').

96 US Copyright Office, above n 74, (3rd ed) § 309. While this interpretation thus likely plays a role in administrative decisions whether to register claims of copyright, it appears to have played little role in judicial interpretation of the statute.

astray.[97] Making the requirement explicit, even if at a fairly high level of generality, may therefore be an improvement in how copyright law is understood and applied.

As with the creativity requirement, for the vast majority of copyrightable works – books, articles, musical compositions, sound recordings, plays, films, paintings, photographs, sculptures, dances, etc. – where the public would generally want to make copyright relatively easily available, this requirement should pose no hurdle whatsoever to obtaining copyright protection. Indeed, for most copyrightable works, any challenge that the work does not meet the appreciable amount requirement should take a court or administrative agency no more than a couple of sentences to reject. But for claims close to the line, the requirement would serve the public interest by making clear that the law does not recognise an independent copyright in 'microworks' that fall below the threshold of an appreciable amount of original expression and by making it easier to eliminate threatening claims of infringement against those who copy only such small units of expression.

Conclusion

The aims of a copyright system redesigned in the public interest do not dictate a particular definition of copyrightable subject matter or a necessary set of standards for protection. In imagining a copyright law designed from scratch, the law's subject matter and standards for protection would not necessarily look substantially different from some of the current provisions on those issues in various copyright systems, although perhaps no single existing system currently has all of the features recommended in this chapter. The identified goals of a reimagined copyright system argue that the subject matter of copyright should be legislatively articulated in the form of intermediate-level, technologically neutral categories, and that any new categories should be recognised as copyrightable only by legislative decision. In addition, creative productions that can be more appropriately protected by more tailored forms of protection (such as computer programs, industrial design, and non-creative compilations

---

97 See e.g. *CDN Inc v Kapes*, 197 F 3d 1256 (9th Cir, 1999) (holding plaintiff's estimates of prices of collectible coins to be copyrightable works); Hughes, above n 93, 583–600.

of factual information) should be excluded from copyright protection. Once copyright's subject matter has been defined, the public interest would be best served by protecting only works within that subject matter that are independently created, fixed, and minimally creative, and that contain an appreciable amount of authorial expression. To the extent that these identified features do not depart significantly from the way copyright law currently operates, addressing the current challenges to copyright law identified in Chapter 1 will likely require more substantial changes to other aspects of copyright law, many of which are suggested in the other chapters in this volume.

5

Making copyright markets work for creators, consumers and the public interest

Jeremy de Beer

Introduction and overview

Copyright is an important part of marketplace framework policies that support creative industries. Copyright is also increasingly relevant to broader economic and industrial policy. Market-oriented justifications for copyright, therefore, factor heavily in debates about copyright law and policy reform. In this context, discourse often revolves around copyright as a property right, which underpins market transactions.

This chapter endorses market-oriented approaches towards copyright as a means to promote creators' interests, consumers' interests, and the public interest. The conception of copyright as a property right is consistent with the basis of general policymaking in free market economies. Two caveats are, however, important to understand how proprietary rights for creators can and do promote the public interest. First, like all property rights, copyrights are not absolute but appropriately limited by other individual rights and social values. Second, in order to function effectively, copyright entitlements should be structured to facilitate, not frustrate, free market transactions.

This chapter explains why and how copyright's currently layered and fragmented bundles of rights inhibit the public interest in developing efficient copyright markets.

An appropriately limited and structurally simplified bundle of rights, as suggested in this chapter, would increase the efficiency of copyright markets and grow the size of creative industries. More efficient markets will lead to more choices and lower prices for consumers, as well as increased economic opportunities for creators to reach a larger market.

However, such market-oriented approaches may also concentrate power, increase inequality, and marginalise individual creators. This chapter mentions three practical mechanisms to address such concerns: collective bargaining to achieve fairer contracting in creative industries; class action litigation to enforce common rights of individual creators; and certified branding schemes to promote fair trade and equitable consumption of creative content.

The purpose of presenting such mechanisms in this chapter is not to exhaustively debate their merits or resolve doctrinal implementation issues. Rather, these mechanisms merely illustrate the range of options available to mitigate certain adverse impacts that a market-oriented copyright policy might have. This chapter focuses on examples from Canada that other countries, or the international policymaking community, may find informative.

Importantly, regulatory policy mechanisms to achieve fairer market transactions need not be embedded directly into copyright statutes or the common law. Copyright should not be expected to shoulder the entire load of protecting the public interest in creative industries. It can and should be assessed and reformed as part of a broader package of marketplace framework policies. With better integrated framework policies both protecting and regulating copyright, markets can work better for creators, consumers, and the public interest.

A market-oriented policy framework

Some frustration with copyright's current inability to fulfil its putative public interest aims stems from the failures of market-based mechanisms (i.e. transactions based on property rights) to achieve cultural as opposed to economic policy objectives. This critique of copyright is difficult to overcome, as economic and cultural policies are sometimes irreconcilable. Copyright markets cannot be faulted for failing to promote cultural diversity and producing homogenous blockbusters, if that is what consumers demand. Similarly, one should not necessarily expect cultural policy to prioritise economic or industrial outcomes over preserving heritage or promoting the arts.

This chapter does not purport to resolve tensions between copyright's cultural and economic policy objectives. Rather, the chapter focuses on making copyright markets better at what markets are designed for: generating wealth. While there may be reasons to question whether such instrumental aims are always appropriate, this chapter accepts that economic ends are a (if not 'the') dominant justification for copyright. The chapter, therefore, explains why and how markets can better promote the public interest.

The 'public interest' in copyright markets

When juxtaposing the amorphous notions of both 'property rights' and 'the public interest', several difficult issues become apparent. In its current incarnation, copyrights – like other property rights – are justified as in the public interest despite their unabashedly private and individualistic nature. In other words, the privatisation of control over expression is seen to promote public policy goals. This is not inconsistent with the values and beliefs of Western liberal democratic societies.

Yet one risk of conceptualising copyright in furtherance of the public interest is that the discourse devolves into purely utilitarian terms, which are not universally accepted. Rights-based perspectives on both property generally and copyright specifically are sometimes controversial but hardly radical. Whether the protection of an individual's natural rights can be encompassed within a public interest framing of copyright as property remains to be seen, perhaps in other chapters of this volume. In one respect, the essence of the rights-based arguments depends on their recognition as inherent and inalienable on an individual level, not the secondary social benefits that accrue to the public at large. Yet, in another respect, the protection of individual rights generally is a matter of public interest, since the stability of society depends on safeguarding such rights. Thus, rights-based and utilitarian justificatory theories do sometimes align in both theory and practice.

Regardless, the focus of this chapter is economic utilitarian perspectives on copyright. One reason is that to the extent a market-oriented policy framework is flawed – if policies designed to facilitate market-based transactions are not in the public interest – such concerns are not unique to copyright. Problems apply similarly to copyright and many other public policies.

This chapter accepts the dominant economic framework as appropriate for making copyright policy not because it is the status quo in copyright, but because it is the status quo in liberal democratic societies more generally. My reimagining of copyright in the public interest envisions a regime coexisting within, not divorced from, a much broader patchwork of complementary marketplace framework policies. The public interest in copyright policy specifically is, in my view, not entirely separable from the public interest in economic policy generally.

Of course there are other, additional aims that copyright can and should seek to achieve. But among copyright's multiple aims, I believe that facilitating market transactions, growing creative industries, creating employment opportunities and driving economic activity cannot be ignored.

In a sense, market-oriented mechanisms for making copyright policies in the public interest are a variant of both 'preponderance' and 'common interest' theories discussed in Chapter 1 of this volume. That is because the market is essentially a *process* for reaching results believed to be in the public interest. A well-functioning market will generate wealth and enhance overall social welfare by facilitating the flow of legal rights to those who value them most. On this theory, markets determine the ultimate allocation of entitlements more than legal or political institutions.

As a general matter, we in liberal democratic societies tend to accept that since market *processes* are in the public interest, so too are market-driven *outcomes*. Society's acceptance of such outcomes is based partly on the theory that the market is an equal-opportunity institution. Any individual is presumed equally capable of using markets to get ahead. In such circumstances, cloaked behind the Rawlsian 'veil of ignorance' about one's lot in life discussed in Chapter 1, the market is a just institution on which to base copyright (or any other economic) policy.

Yet, the market does not always produce outcomes that, intuitively, seem fair and just to everyone. Sometimes the market seems to fail to further what some people perceive to be the public interest. I accept the public interest is broader than a purely economic paradigm might suggest. There is surely a societal interest in the promotion of markets as a mechanism to generate wealth, but the public interest also comprises things that markets may not do well or at all. For example, markets are notorious for producing inequality. In fact, the unequal distribution of resources is an inevitable feature of free markets. Whether this realisation partly undermines the claim that market-oriented copyright policies promote the public interest is debatable.

I do not claim in this chapter that an unfettered free market is a complete panacea, let alone the *only* solution to copyright's current crisis. Nor do I claim that copyright markets cause no undesirable consequences. Rather, I suggest that we ought not be too quick to dismiss the potential of copyright as a property right within the broader framework of capitalist systems, which are designed to generate wealth by ensuring that objects of property move to their highest value user/use. Some of the frustration we experience around copyright may arise, at least in part, from trying to make a property rights system do everything and anything including welfare provision, cultural policy, industry policy and more.

One option to make copyright work better in the public interest, therefore, is for copyright as a property right to better do what such rights are meant to do, that is, facilitate market transactions to generate wealth, and then address other aspects of perceived public interest problems through a suite of complementary marketplace framework policies.

And I do believe it is possible to mitigate the market's adverse impacts on, for example, individual creators or consumers. Before proposing three specific strategies to protect the creators and consumers who might be marginalised in an unconstrained copyright marketplace, and thereby protect the public interest more generally, the next part of this chapter explains measures to improve the efficiency of copyright markets.

The concept of copyright as a property right

Markets depend on property rights. If property rights are sufficiently exclusive, universal, and transferable, they will form the basis of free markets, and indeed, capitalist economies.[1] In the absence of prohibitive transaction costs, property rights will be transferred to those who value them the most.[2] This, according to basic principles of welfare economics, leads to socially optimal outcomes in the aggregate.[3]

These principles form the backbone of the free market economies in which most of us live. And copyright exists as one of many interconnected marketplace framework policies within our entrenched economic structures. Proposals for copyright reform, therefore, might try to harness the power of the market in ways that amplify positive impacts and mitigate adverse effects. That is an aim of this chapter.

Although exchanges of proprietary copyrights are key to the efficient and effective functioning of creative industries, it is dangerous to invoke the rhetoric of property too literally. Like the 'public interest' admirably described by the editors of this volume in their introductory chapter, the concept of 'property' is malleable. Critical literature on the term describes competing approaches and conflicting interpretations.[4] Property is said by many legal and political philosophers, as well as judges operating in the real world, to be an empty vessel. It means not necessarily the sole and despotic dominion to exclude,[5] nor a static bundle of incidents of ownership,[6] but sometimes, it means many different things.[7] This nominalist perspective on property is not the only one, but it is a powerful one.

---

1   See Richard A Posner, *Economic Analysis of Law* (Aspen Law, 7th ed, 2007) 33; Hernando de Soto, *The Mystery of Capital* (Basic Books, 2000).
2   See Ronald Coase, 'The Problem of Social Cost' (1960) 3 *Journal of Law and Economics* 1.
3   See Adam Smith, *An Inquiry into the Nature and Causes of the Wealth of Nations* (W Strahan, 1776).
4   See, for example, Jeremy Waldron, *The Right to Private Property* (Clarendon Press, 1990); James Harris, *Property and Justice* (Oxford University Press, 2002).
5   William Blackstone, *Commentaries on the laws of England*, (Oxford, 1765–1969), Book II Ch 1.
6   Anthony M Honoré, 'Ownership' in *Making Law Blind* (Clarendon Press, 1987).
7   TC Grey, 'The Disintegration of Property' in J Roland Pennock and JW Chapman (eds), *Property: Nomos XXII: Yearbook of the American Society for Political and Legal Philosophy* 69 (New York University Press, 1980).

Some scholars have taken the supposed disintegration of the concept of property rights as an opportunity to promote a unified theoretical framework applicable to both tangible and intellectual property.[8] I would agree that intellectual property policy is appropriately guided by general principles of property law, but without suggesting that we can directly transpose tangible property rules to solve intellectual property issues, or ignore crucial differences between tangible and ideational resources.

Recognising that the concept of property rights underlying the modern copyright system is itself open to interpretation and redefinition triggers the realisation that we can reimagine copyright too. We need not jettison the principles of property rights that animate copyright in its present form in order to redesign the conceptual and doctrinal features of copyright that make it so dysfunctional in many contexts.

The pragmatic question that shapes this chapter is how far from the existing economic and political structures to stray in reconceptualising copyright. Rather than entirely reimagining copyright outside the framework of liberal capitalist markets – an exercise which does have great value but is not the aim of this particular chapter – the following sections explore how copyright could be designed within the presently dominant political economic paradigm. The objective is to enquire what the structure of copyright should look like if it were to achieve its putative purposes within a market economy.

The structure of copyright's bundle of rights

The current doctrinal structure – under public international laws as well as corresponding domestic laws – of the bundle of copyrights (and/or neighbouring rights) is problematic from a market-oriented perspective. Economic justificatory theories that might support the notion that copyright promotes the public interest (as a wealth-generating market mechanism) depend upon the absence of transaction costs that the structure of copyrights as a fragmented and layered bundle of rights exacerbate rather than ameliorate. If copyright truly promoted the public interest as an effective marketplace framework

---

8   Richard A Epstein, 'The Disintegration of Intellectual Property? A Classic Liberal Response to a Premature Obituary' (2010) 62(2) *Stanford Law Review* 455.

policy, it would not be a fragmented and/or layered bundle of rights, but rather a more coherent, stable, and simple allocation of an exclusive entitlement.

Copyright is not currently structured as a grant of a unitary right, an indivisible whole, but rather of a series of exclusive but limited rights in a work to do specific things. This series, or bundle, of rights may be dealt with as a whole or individually. And just as copyright itself is alienable – it may be assigned or licensed exclusively or non-exclusively – so too may each fragment of the bundle be independently alienable. In this way, a single work may boast multiple 'owners', each independently exercising their rights to exploit their interests in the work. Copyright ownership, by design, may be fragmented.

This leads to numerous challenges in the exploitation of copyright-protected works, including royalty stacking: the layering of multiple payments for permission to use copyright-protected work. In the same work, there are rights of reproduction, performance, distribution, making available and perhaps more. This fragmentation of rights may have made sense in an analogue era, but it is becoming increasingly dysfunctional for digital content. The same single activity (e.g. webcasting) may implicate numerous different rights fragments, with royalties often payable to the same entity (e.g. a composer) through different market channels. This system screams inefficiency, without even considering territorial or temporal issues. Royalty stacking can happen through multiple administrative tariffs, redundant collective licensing structures, or overlapping individual license agreements.

These royalty stacking problems increase uncertainty over the availability of works as potential licensees must identify multiple right holders entitled to participate in revenue streams associated with the exploitation of the work. Similarly, royalty stacking increases transaction costs associated with such exploitation. Royalty stacking also potentially increases the absolute value of wealth transfers to right holders as each holder of an exclusive right is positioned to leverage that exclusivity in an inefficient system.

To this complex framework most copyright laws add further layers of property holders: owners of neighbouring rights. These stakeholders obtain rights not for their contribution to the authoring of creative works, but for contributions to the propagation and dissemination of such works. In an earlier iteration of copyright, these service providers' role in copyright's ecosystem benefited from the sphere of exclusivity afforded the copyright owner, but enjoyed no rights independent of the copyright owner. The appearance of neighbouring rights greatly complicated the copyright industrial ecosystem.

To further complicate matters, neighbouring rights holders may also fragment their bundle of rights. Like copyright, fragments of the neighbouring rights bundle are assignable and licensable on an exclusive or non-exclusive basis. Downstream users and creators now have to negotiate multiple potential claimants, claiming rights in distinct artefacts, to make use of and build on prior works.

The end result is that users and creators dealing with disseminated copies of works often have to transact with multiple right holders exercising numerous classes of rights, with nothing in this structure guaranteeing a common understanding of how to exploit those rights.

Streamlining rights to smooth transactions[9]

One of the main complaints about the current doctrinal structure of copyright is that it adds costs and complicates transactions. Adding costs is not a policy problem per se; if those costs are justified on a principled basis, imposing them simply transfers wealth from one party to another.

Transactional inefficiencies, uncertainties and complications are more serious challenges, however. These can undermine functioning of the market for copyright-protected content, inhibit the introduction of innovative products and services, and cause economic losses to all parties involved. To understand how, we can consider the fundamental economic theories underlying all property rights, including intellectual property rights.

9   Jeremy de Beer, 'Copyright Royalty Stacking' in Michael Geist (ed), *The Copyright Pentalogy: How the Supreme Court of Canada Shook the Foundations of Canadian Copyright Law* (University of Ottawa Press, 2013) 335.

The economic problem with copyright royalty stacking

As introduced earlier in the chapter, Judge Richard Posner, a godfather of law and economics scholarship, points out that property law is most efficient when rights are exclusive, universal and transferable.[10] The last of these features is most relevant to royalty stacking. In an enormously influential and widely cited article, economist Ronald Coase explained how, in a world without transaction costs, rights will be exchanged in markets that efficiently allocate entitlements to those who value them the most.[11] This concept is central to welfare economics, and a primary reason that people believe intellectual property protection is capable of driving economic growth.

Although rarely articulated as such, the Coase theorem underpins the utilitarian concept of intellectual property rights as incentives. Intellectual property provides incentives to invest time, effort and money into intellectual endeavours because rights can be exploited in the market to make profit. Take away market transactions and you are left with a purely psychological theory of incentives or deontological theory of intellectual property protection.

Since Coase's path-breaking article was published in 1960, scholars have sought to better understand the factors that interfere with efficient bargaining. One such factor is the fragmentation and/or layering of rights. Michael Heller identified the problem of property fragmentation in a seminal article published in the Harvard Law Review in 1998.[12] He called this the 'tragedy of the anticommons,' mirroring Garrett Hardin's famous parable of the 'tragedy of the commons' that had been published 40 years earlier.[13] Hardin initially presented private property rights as a solution to the tragic overuse of resources that would occur in a world of open access. Heller did not dispute Hardin's claim, but countered that private property can also be a problem. Too much property is as inefficient as too little.

---

10 Posner, above n 1, 33.
11 Coase, above n 2.
12 Michael A Heller, 'The Tragedy of the Anticommons: Property in Transition from Marx to Markets' (1998) 111(3) *Harvard Law Review* 621.
13 Garrett Hardin, 'The Tragedy of the Commons' (1968) 162 (3859) *Science* 1243.

He and Rebecca Eisenberg applied this insight to intellectual property rights specifically: 'In theory,' they wrote, 'in a world of costless transactions, people could always avoid commons or anticommons tragedies by trading their rights. In practice, however, avoiding tragedy requires overcoming transaction costs … Once an anticommons emerges, collecting rights into usable private property is often brutal and slow.'[14] This phenomenon has also been discussed as a 'thicket, a dense web of overlapping intellectual property rights that a company must hack its way through in order to actually commercialize new technology.'[15] Mark Lemley and Carl Shapiro have also studied the interconnected problems of patent holdups and royalty stacking when a patent covers one important component of a complex product.[16]

Thickets are not just a patent problem; such concerns apply to copyright as well. Daniel Gervais and Alana Maurushat have described, for example, the fragmentation of collectively administered copyright in Canada, explaining how 'the rights contained in section 3 [of Canada's *Copyright Act*] are no longer useful in mapping out the real world'.[17] While their focus is on the practical rather than theoretical problems of fragmentation, they effectively highlight the complexities of copyright licensing transactions.

Scholars such as Epstein are right to analogise tangible and intellectual property, but wrong to suggest that fragmentation is not a problem in either context. While Esptein acknowledges, for example, that 'the key relationship thus asks whether the gains from voluntary fragmentation exceed the added transactions costs of running the system,' he ignores the fact that in copyright the lack of recordation or adequate ownership tracking devices is a major problem.[18] If proposals for copyright registration and tracking requirements,

14   Michael A Heller and Rebecca S Eisenberg, 'Can Patents Deter Innovation? The Anticommons in Biomedical Research' (1998) 280 (5364) *Science* 698. See also Michael A Heller, *The Gridlock Economy: How Too Much Ownership Wrecks Markets, Stops Innovation, and Costs Lives* (Basic Books, 2008).

15   Carl Shapiro, 'Navigating the Patent Thicket: Cross Licences, Patent Pools and Standard Setting' in Adam B Jaffe, Josh Lerner and Scott Stern (eds), *Innovation Policy and the Economy* (MIT Press, 2011) 120.

16   Mark A Lemley and Carl Shapiro, 'Patent Holdup and Royalty Stacking' (2007) 85 *Texas Law Review* 1991.

17   Daniel J Gervais and Alana Maurushat, 'Fragmented Copyright, Fragmented Management: Proposals to Defrag Copyright Management' (2003) 2(1) *Canadian Journal of Law & Technology* 20.

18   Epstein, above n 8, 472.

laid out in other chapters of this book, were to be accepted, the complexity of copyright's fragmented and layered bundles of rights would be of less concern. In the absence of such alternative solutions, however, fragmentation and layering seriously frustrate free market transactions.

The Supreme Court of Canada has also acknowledged that too much copyright protection can cause adverse consequences, ruling in the *Théberge* case: 'In crassly economic terms it would be as inefficient to overcompensate artists and authors for the right of reproduction as it would be self-defeating to undercompensate them.'[19] While the Supreme Court did not elaborate in *Théberge* on the reasons that overcompensation is inefficient (which may be related to transaction costs or other factors), in its more recent jurisprudence it has taken an important step towards a legal interpretation of the *Copyright Act* that reduces royalty stacking.[20]

One argument to counter concerns over transaction costs is that the legislation in most countries contains explicit statutory recognition that right holders may carve up copyrights in any manner they please. Subsection 13(4) of Canada's *Copyright Act*, for example, states clearly:

> The owner of the copyright in any work may assign the right, either wholly or partially, and either generally or subject to limitations relating to territory, medium or sector of the market or other limitations relating to the scope of the assignment, and either for the whole term of the copyright or for any other part thereof, and may grant any interest in the right by licence ...

However, it is important to distinguish particular licensing practices from established legal rights. Contracts may contain a wide variety of unique clauses on payments or permissions enforceable against specific parties, that is, *in personam* rights. But courts need not compound the legal complexity by reinforcing the fragmentation of copyrights *in rem*, enforceable against anyone.

---

19   *Théberge v Galérie d'Art du Petit Champlain Inc*, [2002] 210 DLR (4th) 385, 31 (Supreme Court of Canada).

20   *Entertainment Software Association v Society of Composers, Authors and Music Publishers of Canada*, [2012] 2 SCR 231.

In real property law, the notion that rights should not be fragmented beyond a stable set of fixed entitlements is known as the *numerus clausus* principle. Its origins lie in the civil law system, but the label has also been applied to similar common law concepts.[21] As applied in the well-known common law case of *Keppell v Bailey*, the principle holds that private parties cannot through property transactions or licensing practices create new incidents of ownership.[22] Parties may generally structure contractual relationships however they wish, but cannot by doing so transform the nature of the underlying property rights vis-à-vis third parties or the general public.

Merrill and Smith note that the *numerus clausus* principle applies not only to real property, but is also reflected in other areas of property law, including intellectual property.[23] They remark that the *numerus clausus* is 'an extremely important qualification on the principle of freedom of contract – a principle widely regarded by law and economics scholars as promoting the efficient allocation of resources'.[24] It is particularly useful for limiting adverse effects of excessive fragmentation, that is, an anticommons.[25] While Merrill and Smith's work centres on the limited forms that intellectual property rights in general may take, other scholars have explained how the same principles should prevent fragmentation within intellectual property rights, such as copyrights.[26] The concept has been applied most specifically to digital copyright cases.

The *numerus clausus* serves several important functions required equally, if not more, for intellectual property than for real property. It facilitates transferability of rights, increases certainty of transactions, aids identification of owners, and more. Bruce Ziff points to another rationale for the *numerus clausus* principle: '[I]mpediments to the termination of property rights suggests the need for caution

---

21   Bruce Ziff, 'The Irreversibility of Commodification' (2005) 16(283) *Stellenbosch Law Review* 283.

22   *Keppell v Bailey* (1834) 2 My & K 517.

23   Thomas W Merrill and Henry E Smith, 'Optimal Standardization in the Law of Property: The Numerus Clausus Principle' (2000) 110(1) *Yale Law Journal* 4 [*Merrill and Smith*].

24   Ibid 5.

25   Ibid 6.

26   Christina Mulligan, 'A Numerus Clausus Principle for Intellectual Property' (2012) 80 *Tennessee Law Review* 235; Enrico Baffi, 'The Anticommons and the Problem of the Numerus Clausus of Property Rights' (19 October 2007, unpublished) <papers.ssrn.com/sol3/papers.cfm?abstract_id=1023153>.

in their initial recognition, because doctrinal mistakes cannot easily be corrected.'[27] In other words, once a new right is recognised, it is very difficult to reverse. The one-way ratchet of intellectual property dealings that fragment existing rights or add new ones is a well-documented problem.[28] Policymakers as well as judges should be reluctant to contribute to this phenomenon by recognising new fragments of copyright.

So, based on the *numerus clausus* principle, even if it is true most copyright systems permit owners to structure licensing and administration in creative ways, it does not follow that courts should recognise such arrangements as creating or reinforcing proprietary *in rem* entitlements.

A question remains what more streamlined rights could or should look like if unconstrained by treaty and history. At the very least, copyright's bundle of rights would not be more complicated than it currently is. Far preferably, copyright would be much simpler.

One might imagine, for example, a unitary 'use' right, that is, a basic economic right to exploit a work's value. The right to use a work could take the place of the many more specific incidents of copyright ownership that have been appended to copyright over time, like layers of papier-mâché, to respond to various technological developments or to merely placate special interests. Rather than separate and distinct rights to reproduce, perform, publish or exploit a work in myriad other ways, a pure use right might better suit copyright's function as marketplace framework policy.

Simplifying copyright as such could eliminate many of the uncertainties and controversies surrounding the boundaries between particular rights – reproduction, performance, publication, etc. – which add transaction costs impeding market transactions. Although the price of a licence for the right to use a work would not necessarily be lower

---

27   Bruce Ziff, 'Yet Another Function for the *Numerus Clasus* Principle of Property Rights, and a Useful One at That' (19 March 2012) <papers.ssrn.com/sol3/papers.cfm?abstract_id=2026088>, 1.

28   For example, see Susan Sell, 'The Global IP Upward Ratchet, Anti-Counterfeiting and Piracy Enforcement Efforts: The State of Play' (Research Paper 15, Program on Information Justice and Intellectual Property American University Washington College of Law, Washington, DC, 2010). See also Peter Drahos, 'The Global Ratchet for Intellectual Property Rights: Why It Fails as Policy and What Should Be Done About It' (2003).

than the aggregate of the licences currently required for multiple copyright fragments, these licences would likely be faster and simpler to acquire. As well as reducing royalty stacking, it would eliminate the potential holdout problem that exists where multiple permissions from different copyright owners are required.

While a unitary right would be divisible by licence, such contracts would not create rights *in rem*. Licences might be exclusive or non-exclusive; this need not be prescribed but would be determined by economic conditions and market forces.

Perhaps the most interesting question is not what a use right is defined to be, but whether and how a use right is defined at all. One option is to embed a detailed definition within international treaties and/or national legislation. Instinctively, this is appealing from an economic perspective as it would arguably increase legal certainty and, therefore, reduce transaction costs. On the other hand, a rigidly defined use right might also be so technologically or contextually specific that it creates instabilities as circumstances change over time. A preferable option, perhaps less predictable but not necessarily less efficient over time, would be a right subject to judicial interpretation and application. Judges in many countries have proven capable of providing clear guidance on the scope of copyright, as well as other important matters of economic policy.

Also regarding the scope of a possible unitary use right, there is no necessary reason that the current fair use/dealing provisions or other limitations and exceptions need change. Nor would the principles of exhaustion that govern the boundaries between intellectual and tangible property rights be redrawn. Use may include the first sale of a work to the public.

Fully specifying the contours of such a right in the space of this chapter would be susceptible to premature and unnecessary criticism. My modest aim here is to promote the concept, not the specifics, of simpler, purer rights that are more compatible with the market-based justifications that rightly animate copyright policy.

Inequality as an implication of structural simplification

Structuring copyright as a unitary and indivisible 'use' right may not be easy to implement, given existing legal constraints and vested commercial interests. But, based on sound economic theory, ensuring the copyright's bundle of entitlements stays as streamlined as possible will help to facilitate market transactions and increase the size of creative industries. The simpler (though not necessarily cheaper) it is for businesses to buy and resell copyright-protected content, the faster the market for innovative products and services will develop, and the larger it will grow. This is desirable for consumers, who will have a wider range of choice. This is also desirable for creators, who will have more commercial paths to the market, more competition from intermediaries leading to higher prices, and increased consumer demand for the creative content they sell.

While all stakeholders would benefit from streamlined system of copyright transactions, it is an inherent feature of the market that the benefits are unlikely to be distributed equally. Free markets are not known for their ability to achieve distributive justice. We know from both theory and experience that copyright markets tend to concentrate power and wealth in the hands of intermediaries.

At one time, the most powerful intermediaries tended to be the book publishers, record labels, movie studios, or other entities that mediated between individual creators and the mass market of consumers. More recently, we have witnessed a shift in wealth and market power away from these conventional intermediaries towards the technology companies that provide platforms through which consumers access content. The creative industries' newest power brokers include hardware manufacturers, online retailers and search engines. This shift from old media gatekeepers has been praised for opening up our culture,[29] and criticised for giving a free ride to new information oligopolies.[30]

---

29   Lawrence Lessig, *Free Culture: How Big Media Uses Technology and the Law to Lock Down Culture and Control Creativity* (Penguin Press, 2004).
30   Robert Levine, *Free Ride: How Digital Parasites are Killing the Culture Business, and How the Cultural Business Can Fight Back* (Anchor Books, 2011).

In this tug-of-war between industrial intermediaries, the interests of individual creators as well as individual consumers are easily neglected. Streamlining the rights clearance process in order to make market transactions more efficient admittedly risks exacerbating the inequalities of the current system. Both creators and consumers could become increasingly vulnerable and marginalised, contrary to many people's intuitive sense of distributive justice and therefore 'the public interest'.

Protecting creators, consumers and the public

The final section of this chapter points out three possible ways to mitigate potential distributive injustices of the free market. First, collective bargaining can bolster the contractual negotiating hand of individual creators to reduce power asymmetries in creative industries. Second, class action litigation proceedings can be used to enforce the common interests of those who suffer individually small but aggregately significant economic or other harms. Third, certified branding schemes can be used as a market signal to harness the commercial power of ethical consumers who want to fairly compensate creators.

These protections, notably, may involve marketplace framework policies external to copyright itself. Internal structural reforms to copyright can be extremely valuable when reorienting copyright to better serve the public interest. Within the free market paradigm promoted in this chapter, a recordation system is among the most crucial changes long overdue. Other chapters in this volume mention or deal in depth with the rationale for registration and tracking mechanisms, which I strongly endorse and are fully consistent with the recommendations in this chapter.

The value added by the discussion below is to suggest that promoting the public interest is a job that ought not be left to copyright alone. A public interest oriented copyright system necessarily exists in the context of broader marketplace framework regulation, which provide checks and balances against abuses of market power. Before discussing mechanisms to address creators' rights, it is useful to explain how users' rights fit within a free market framework for copyright policymaking.

Copyright markets and the recognition of users' rights

One of the interesting implications of the conceptual framework adopted for rethinking copyright as a property right in the public interest concerns users' rights. In the natural rights theory justifying creators' rights, it is challenging to find room for, or worry about, the interests of copyright users. While scholars are starting to articulate strong non-economic arguments for limits on authors' rights,[31] support for users' rights is widely believed to depend upon a utilitarian calculus that suggests they cause less harm than good. Reaching that conclusion arguably becomes more difficult the less clear and predictable users' rights are.

There is at first glance some tension between, on one hand, the fair and flexible nature of users' rights originating in principles of equity and, on the other hand, the stable and certain allocation of entitlements that facilitates free market transactions. In this context, user rights that exacerbate uncertainty and create transaction costs ought to be discouraged, or avoided altogether.

On examination, this concern is real, but surmountable. Respecting users' rights within this framework requires understanding 'the public interest' as more than bare utilitarian principles might imply. The public interest in recognising users' rights is to be found in the underlying values these rights promote. A user's right of fair dealing, explains Drassinower, 'is to be understood and deployed not negatively, as a mere exception, but rather positively, as a user right integral to copyright law.'[32]

Although the economic logic and political rhetoric of property has powerful connotations about the supremacy of those rights over other interests, there is nothing extraordinary in recognising that all property rights are somehow limited in time, space, or scope.

---

31 See e.g. Abraham Drassinower, *What's Wrong with Copying?* (Harvard University Press, 2015).

32 Abraham Drassinower, 'Taking User Rights Seriously' in Michael Geist (ed), *In the Public Interest: The Future of Canadian Copyright Law* (Irwin Law, 2005) 462, 467.

Often, property rights yield when confronted by equally or more weighty rights, such as rights of expression or access to information, as examples. Counterbalancing is driven both by individual rights and social values.[33]

Therefore, the analysis in this chapter does not pre-empt the recognition of users' rights on account of the systematic inefficiencies that might be created by doing so. Rather, this chapter's analysis suggests that if copyright's proprietary nature is to be counterbalanced, users' rights cannot be seen merely to serve public interests as well. Users' rights must be understood to represent fundamental rights as or more important than copyrights in certain circumstances.

As an even higher principle, authors' and users' rights are inseparable from each other, and both equally integral to the fabric of an effective marketplace framework policy. The market could not function without appropriate consumer protection mechanisms in place. And consumer protection mechanisms are not merely an inconvenient limit on owner's rights, but rather equally important in setting public policies and negotiating private transactions.

The principle underpinning user rights is manifested not only within copyright limitations and exceptions, but also through market mechanisms external to copyright, including consumer protection laws. Rules that limit the scope of copyright protection by reference to other owners' tangible property rights, through the doctrine of exhaustion, further reinforce users' rights with basic principles of property law.[34]

Fairer contracts through collective bargaining

From an economic perspective, markets depend as much on contracts as they do on property rights. Contracts are the mechanisms through which property rights are transferred to the parties that value them most. Pareto efficient contractual exchanges of rights – trades that leave

---

33   Jeremy Waldron, 'From Authors to Copiers: Individual Rights and Social Values in Intellectual Property' (1992) 68 *Chicago-Kent Law Review* 841.
34   Jeremy de Beer and Robert J Tomkowicz, 'Exhaustion of Intellectual Property Rights in Canada' (2009) 25 *Canadian Intellectual Property Review* 3.

at least one party better off without making anyone worse off[35] – are what the current copyright system is designed to promote. However, Pareto optimal transactions do not necessarily (and frequently do not) increase either equality or overall social welfare.[36]

If the public interest is defined within a theoretical framework modelled on Rawls' theory of justice, as discussed in the introduction to this volume, then equality is a major concern that the free market alone cannot solve. Limiting the accumulation of wealth and power by intermediaries in creative industries may require putting regulatory limits on their freedom to contract or finding other ways to adjust the balance of negotiating power. Existing approaches within copyright are theoretically and practically inadequate.[37]

There are two ways in which the freedom of contract may be constrained or contractual bargaining power recalibrated: by embedding limitations on contracts within copyright itself, or by leveraging framework mechanisms from areas other than copyright. A comparison and consideration of both mechanisms suggests that more generally applicable approaches are preferable.

One example of a limitation, internal to copyright, that exists in some jurisdictions concerns creator's rights of reversion. In Canada, for example, copyright in works reverts back to an author's estate 25 years after the author's death. (Technically, the law is that grants or licences become void at that time, but the practical effect is the same.)[38] The author's right of reversion in Canada traces to the similar provision in the laws of the United Kingdom, from which Canadian law derives. It is similar in principle to author's termination rights in the United States.

Reversionary rights are putatively designed to provide protection for authors against bad deals. However, they are ineffective in most circumstances at doing so. First, rights revert not to authors but rather to their estates or heirs, a result that might seem nice for those heirs

---

35   Vilfredo Pareto, *Manual of Political Economy* (Ann S Schwier trans, Augustus M Kelley, 1972).

36   Amartya Sen, *Markets and Freedoms: Achievements and Limitations of the Market Mechanism in Promoting Individual Freedoms* (1993) 45(4) *Oxford Economic Papers* 518.

37   See generally Giuseppina D'Agostino, *Copyright, Contracts, Creators: New Media, New Rules* (Edward Elgar, 2010).

38   *Copyright Act*, RSC 1985, c C-42, s 14(1).

but lacks any justification related to instrumental or natural property rights. Second, the practical impact of reversionary rights is to create confusion and uncertainty in the marketplace for no good reason.

From the perspective of law and economics adopted in this chapter, the problems outweigh the benefits.[39] That conclusion is not surprising since, according to general property theory, rights of termination and reversion are undoubtedly a form of restraint on alienation not normally encouraged in the design of efficient property rights systems. Many British Commonwealth countries have repealed the equivalent provisions in their laws, and repeal has been recommended in Canada too.[40]

The purpose of discussing reversion rights here is not to conduct an exhaustive analysis of that particular mechanism for protecting authors' rights vis-à-vis intermediaries. Rather, it exemplifies the problem that arises when policymakers expect a single market-oriented instrument to do many things at once. If copyright is designed as a property right in order to promote efficient market transactions, then burdening the rights with the complex possibility of termination or reversion is unwise. In practice, this ostensible creator-protection mechanism fails to protect anyone, but instead risks frustrating the market completely.

A better approach is to invoke protections that are effectively used elsewhere in the legal system to address inequities caused by the concentration of market power. One example is collective bargaining by parties who are vulnerable to exploitation.

Bargaining collectively for better contractual terms is a strategy that has been used effectively, for example, by visual artists in Canada. A legislative framework modelled on general principles of labour law exists in Canada to protect artists against exploitation.[41] It clearly states the policy purposes of recognising the cultural, social, economic and political importance of artists, and establishes a framework to ensure freedom of artists' expression, association and organisation to negotiate and protect artists' interests.

---

39   Kate Darling, *Occupy Copyright: A Law & Economics Analysis of U.S. Author Termination Rights* (1 March 2014) Social Science Review Network <ssrn.com/abstract=2422672>.
40   Bob Tarantino, 'Long Time Coming: Copyright Reversionary Interests in Canada' (2013) 375 *Développements récents en droit de la propriété intellectuelle* 1.
41   *Status of the Artist Act*, SC 1992, c 33.

A description of ongoing negotiations between visual artists and an art gallery helps demonstrate the potential of the collective bargaining mechanism. In Canada, two organisations certified by the governing labour tribunal[42] to represent visual artists negotiated with the National Gallery of Canada over minimum exhibition fees to be paid by the gallery for exhibiting artworks. While an argument was made that this negotiation process could conflict with the Copyright Board of Canada's royalty-setting procedures involving users and collective societies, the Supreme Court of Canada held there was no such conflict.[43] Legally, the negotiation of these minimum royalty rates does not bind collective societies. The labour law procedures, rather, protect the interests of artists who have not assigned their rights to a collective society.

Practically, the collective bargaining mechanisms available through labour laws complement the collective management mechanisms available through copyright laws. Artists have more choice in administering their rights, which competition should lead to more efficiencies in and better terms with intermediary collective societies. The negotiation mechanisms of labour law also help to establish fairer industry practices that should become benchmarks against which licences from collective societies can be measured.

Currently, in Canada, the power of organisations to bargain on behalf of authors is confined to negotiations with federally governed entities. This limitation is a corollary of Canadian federalism, which allocates responsibility for most labour law issues to the provincial level. This chapter does not address whether a similar approach would be desirable or feasible at the interprovincial or international level. Rather, it raises the example of collective bargaining as a way in which author's rights can be protected in the public interest other than via paternalistic approaches within copyright law, such as termination and reversion rights.

There is no doubt that collective bargaining procedures constrain the free market by empowering creators and limiting the control of creative industry intermediaries. From a purely libertarian perspective,

---

42   At the time, a specialised tribunal called the Status of the Artists Tribunal, but now the same Canada Industrial Relations Board that handles other federal labour matters.

43   *Canadian Artists' Representation v National Gallery of Canada* [2014] SCC 42 (14 May 2014).

this may not be ideal. However, a market-oriented copyright system can be structured to facilitate transactions while at the same time other framework policies help to promote fair and equitable treatment of persons who might otherwise be marginalised by uninhibited free market transactions.

Class proceedings to enforce common interests

As the discussion of collective bargaining demonstrates, individual creators may be disempowered by free market approaches to copyright policy. While this outcome is not inconsistent with the theory or practice of welfare-maximising liberal economic policy generally, it can create distributive inequalities that sit uneasily with many people's sense of justice. A series of cases brought through the Canadian courts as class proceedings shows how individual copyright owners have been able to assert their rights and reclaim a degree of market power.

In one important case, *Robertson v Thomson Corp*, freelance authors were able to stop the reproduction in electronic databases of contributions they had made to newspapers.[44] The newspaper publisher had digitised decades' worth of content, and was selling licences to access databases containing works authored by its own employees as well as freelance writers.

The precedent established in the *Robertson* case helped to empower freelance authors. Although, admittedly, that particular decision failed to change dominant industry practices (newspaper publishers are now more explicit in the assignment or license agreements they obtain from authors), it did provide important recognition of authors' rights as well as financial compensation. The case also inspired other copyright owners to take action protecting their rights. Also in Canada, lawyers brought class proceedings against the operators of legal databases that reproduced and sold access to court pleadings drafted by lawyers, which are copyright-protected works. After a lengthy process of litigation and negotiation, the dispute was settled.[45]

---

44 *Robertson v Thomson Corp* [2006] 2 SCR 363 (Supreme Court of Canada).
45 *Waldman v Thomson Reuters Canada Limited* [2016] ONCA 2622 (28 April 2016).

Arguably, these kinds of cases are only feasible as class proceedings. It would be extremely difficult for any individual freelancer to commence, let alone complete, litigation against a publisher seeking to enforce her copyrights in a small number of articles. The value of each alleged copyright infringement would not be significant enough to warrant the cost and complexity of a lawsuit.

Class action procedures, however, grant one plaintiff standing to represent a larger group of similarly situated would-be plaintiffs. In order to be certified by a court as a class proceeding, there must be a cause of action that involves common issues, among an identifiable class of two or more persons, represented by a suitable plaintiff or defendant, for which a class proceeding is the preferable procedure to resolve.[46]

Enabling access to justice is one of the key purposes of class proceedings. Judicial economy is another. A third reason for class actions is behaviour modification and the deterrence of wrongdoing.[47] All of these purposes are well aligned with the goal of addressing power imbalances that can be created by copyright markets. Class proceedings can help to mitigate some of the potential inequities that might result from further streamlining market transactions.

The purpose of class proceedings is somewhat similar to the rationale for the original collecting societies that emerged around the turn of the 20th century: protecting and administering the rights of authors more efficiently through collective action than is possible individually. Class proceedings actually have numerous advantages over collecting societies, including more flexible procedural mechanisms and more effective remedial powers. It is not surprising, therefore, that class proceedings are becoming increasingly common mechanisms for protecting individual creator's rights.

Class proceedings have also helped protect authors against creative industry intermediaries other than publishers. In the case of *Northey v Sony Music*, individual songwriters and music publishers brought

---

46 See, for example, *Class Proceedings Act,* SO 1992, Ch 6, s 5.
47 *Hollick v Toronto* [2001] 3 SCR 158 (Supreme Court of Canada).

an action against the major record labels for failing to pay proper royalties.[48] The judicially approved settlement required record labels to distribute almost $50 million they had failed to pay over many years.

Canada is not the only place where class proceedings are being used to protect the rights of individual creators. In the United States, musicians have sued over the refusal of satellite radio companies to pay royalties on certain old songs.[49] Several class actions have been brought against digital music providers, such as Spotify.

The Google Books case in the United States, *Author's Guild v Google Inc*, is a hybrid example of class proceedings brought to protect both the rights of individual authors and powerful publishing companies against an equally or even more powerful technology company.[50] Whether one agrees with the plaintiffs or defendant, the case demonstrates how power asymmetries in the copyright industry are being adjusted by procedural mechanisms outside of copyright itself.

Bringing disputes into a judicial forum where both parties are equal before the courts is, presumably, preferable to leaving one or the other party vulnerable to the power structures of the free market. The supervisory jurisdiction, procedural flexibilities, and remedial powers of the courts should in principle lead to fairer outcomes (including perhaps fairer negotiated settlements) than would have resulted in the absence of a class proceeding.

Finally, the power of class proceedings have been leveraged by consumers to protect users' rights in the creative industries. When one of the major record labels several years ago included surreptitious digital rights management software on compact discs, violating consumers' privacy rights and causing security vulnerabilities, a class

---

48   See *Craig Northey v Sony Music Entertainment Canada Inc et al* [2011] ONSC CV 08000360651 (27 March 2011); media coverage in Christine Dobby, 'Judge approves settlement in music royalties class action' *Financial Post* (Toronto) 30 May 2011; and settlement at <harrisonpensa. com/expertise/class-actions/list-of-cases/pending-lists-new>.

49   'The Turtles v Sirius Conformed and filed Complaint' (1 August 2013) <www.scribd.com/ doc/157678779/The-Turtles-v-Sirius-Comformed-and-Filed-Complaint-3>; see also 'The United States against Pandora' (17 April 2014) <www.scribd.com/doc/218883012/Pandora-Complaint-Filed>; See also 'Sirius XM Radio' (11 September 2013) <www.hollywoodreporter.com/sites/ default/files/custom/Documents/ESQ/bc520981.pdf>.

50   Jeremy de Beer, 'New Forms of Governance for Digital Orphans' in Mira Burri and Thomas Cottier (eds), *Trade Governance in the Digital Age* (Cambridge University Press, 2010), 344.

action lawsuit was used to enforce users' rights.[51] Most recently, class proceedings were successfully brought against the music publishing company that claims to own and collect royalties for the song, 'Happy Birthday'.[52] The lawsuit, which would have been uneconomical as an individual action, sought to stop dubious copyright claims and thus protect the public domain.

This subsection of the chapter has shown that, to the extent streamlining market transactions leads to the concentration of wealth and market power in the hands of intermediaries, class proceedings can be a useful mechanism to remedy power imbalances. Policymakers need not expect procedures internal to copyright, such as collective administration schemes, to shoulder the entire load. Class proceedings can enhance creators' access to justice, and help to modify the behaviour of intermediaries who might otherwise abuse market power.

Certification schemes to harness public support

The final mechanism for addressing inequities in copyright markets discussed in this chapter is the adoption of certification schemes. Following several years of groundwork, proposals for 'fair trade' branding strategies in the music industry have begun to gain traction. Through certification and branding schemes, creators can harness the power of the market to protect their interests. If consumers demand, and are willing to pay for, creative works that fairly remunerate authors, market intermediaries will be pressured to adjust their practices to satisfy consumer demand.

While the idea of a 'fair trade music' system has only recently received widespread attention,[53] the idea took several years to come to fruition. First developed in 2009, the concept was based on the belief that consumers want creators to be treated fairly:

---

51   Jeremy de Beer, 'How Restrictive Terms and Technologies Backfired on Sony BMG' (2006) 6(12) *Internet & E-Commerce Law in Canada* 93.

52   *Rupa Marya v Warner/Chappell Music Inc*, Docket 2:13cv04460 (United States District Court Central District of California).

53   International Council of Creators of Music (CIAM), *Creators Call for Fairer Digital Revenues Distribution Model, Inspired by the Fair Trade Movement* (24 October 2014) CISAC <cisac.org/ CisacPortal/consultArticle.do?id=1871>.

> Fair Trade Music's vision is a global music business in which market-based mechanisms facilitate more respect for the rights of creators, consumers and the communities to which they all belong. The idea is to certify the actions of influential parties in the music business as being compliant with a set of core values – dignity, equity, respect, and transparency – that define fair practice. Parties whose practices espouse these values can leverage certification into a powerful branding strategy that turns associated goodwill into a competitive advantage in the music market. The result will be socially responsible commercial success.[54]

The initial proposal for a five-step certification process was based on the successful experiences in other fields, ranging from agriculture to textiles.[55]

In the years since the idea was proposed, some modest but important steps were independently taken towards implementation. A local group of musicians in Portland, Oregon established 'Fair Trade Music PDX',[56] certifying live music venues that meet certain criteria. Facebook and Twitter were used to promote the concept.[57] The concept of 'fair trade copyright' also attracted scholarly attention, although proposing a donation system instead of a profit-driven branding scheme.[58] More momentum began building when the Songwriters Association of Canada (SAC) publicly disclosed the idea in 2013.[59]

The contours of a fair trade music initiative are still evolving. But the core principles of inclusiveness, fairness, and transparency remain true to the initial vision. Details of the concept and clarifications

---

54   Jeremy de Beer and S Javed, 'Changing Tune: A Proposal for Fair Trade Music' (October 2009, unpublished). See also Helienne Linvall, 'Could sites such as Muzu and Spotify help musicians get their fair share?', *The Guardian* (online), 23 April 2009 <www.theguardian.com/music/musicblog/2009/apr/23/downloads-spotify-muzu-fair-trade>.

55   See Graeme Auld, *Constructing Private Governance: The Rise and Evolution of Forest, Coffee, and Fisheries Certification* (Yale University Press, 2014); Daniel Jaffee, *Brewing Justice: Fair Trade Coffee, Sustainability and Survival* (University of California Press, 2007); Gavin Fridell, *Fair Trade Coffee: The Prospects and Pitfalls of Market-Driven Social Justice* (University of Toronto Press, 2007).

56   Fair Trade Music <www.fairtrademusicpdx.org>.

57   Fair Trade Music (23 November 2014) Facebook <www.facebook.com/Fair.Trade.Music> and Fair Trade Music (23 November 2014) Twitter <@Fairtrademusic>.

58   Lital Helman, 'Fair Trade Copyright' (2013) 36(2) *Journal of Law & the Arts* 157.

59   Songwriters Association of Canada, *Announcing the 'Fair Trade Music' Initiative* (4 June 2013) <www.songwriters.ca/news/337/130604fairtrademusic.aspx>; Songwriters Association of Canada, *Fair Trade Music: Letting the Light Shine In* (22 October 2013) <www.songwriters.ca/news/344/131022fairtrademusic.aspx>.

of misunderstanding have been usefully fleshed out in the academic literature by industry proponents.[60] This should help those who are thinking critically about policy reform take the idea of fair trade music more seriously.

The main advantages of deploying the fair trade certification concept in the creative industries related to its independence from government and consistency with market-oriented approaches. Just after the turn of the 21st century, in the heyday of Napster and before Apple's iTunes music store, copyright policy debates were heavily influenced by proposals for alternative compensation schemes. Such schemes would essentially be expanded versions of private copying levies, with fees being paid by internet service providers, hardware manufacturers, or other intermediaries.[61] Most (though not all) proposals were for statutory, non-exclusive remuneration rights granted in exchange for immunity from liability for peer-to-peer file sharing.

A key reason alternative compensation schemes have not been adopted is the almost insurmountable difficulty of building the consensus necessary for such dramatic law reform. One virtue of a fair trade certification scheme is that it requires no legislative reforms at all. Success depends not on governments' political will but on creators' and consumers' ability to insist on fair and equitable behaviour by industry intermediaries. While nobody would equate music creators with poor farmers in developing countries, this is not the point of the initiative. The point is to provide ethical consumers with a signal so that they can make informed choices in the marketplace. What those signals are, and whether the market embraces them, depend entirely on what consumers want, not any prescriptive policy direction on what consumers *should* want.

The idea of certified fair trade music (or other cultural works) harnesses rather than hinders the power of the market to promote public interests. Because it is entirely consistent with the general market-oriented framework that theoretically and doctrinally underpins copyright,

---

60   Eddie Schwartz, 'Coda: fair trade music: letting the light shine in' in Susy Frankel and Daniel Gervais (eds), *The Evolution and Equilibrium of Copyright in the Digital Age* (Cambridge University Press, 2014), 312.
61   For discussion and analysis of various proposals, see Jeremy de Beer, 'The Role of Levies in Canada's Digital Music Market' (2005) 4(3) *Canadian Journal of Law & Technology* 153.

it is likely to succeed. This demonstrates yet another way in which to mitigate what might otherwise be inequitable impacts of streamlining copyright structures to grow the size of creative industries overall.

Conclusion

This chapter has demonstrated that existing copyright policy is soundly premised on facilitating exchanges of proprietary rights in the free market. The layered and fragmented doctrinal structure of copyright, however, is often too complex to promote efficient market transactions. Well-established economic theory and practice indicates that simplifying and streamlining copyright in order to reduce royalty stacking would grow the size of the creative industries. This would lead to more innovation through market competition, more choice for consumers, more paths to market for creators, and more wealth generated through copyright assignments and licensing.

Free market mechanisms to grow the creative industries may, however, exacerbate inequalities through the uneven distribution of economic benefits among creators, intermediaries, and consumers. There is a risk that streamlining copyright markets will further concentrate wealth and power in the hands of creative industry intermediaries, including traditional publishers and producers as well as digital retailers and service providers.

Rather than relying entirely on doctrinal reforms internal to copyright to protect the public interest in ensuring the fair and equitable allocation of economic benefits, this chapter proposes several external marketplace framework mechanisms to complement copyright policy. Such mechanisms include collective bargaining, class proceedings, and certification schemes. The conclusion to be drawn from a discussion of these ideas is not that any one is a panacea for the public interest. Rather, this chapter has shown that a market-oriented approach to copyright, in the context of broader market regulatory frameworks and liberal economic policymaking generally, can work for creators, consumers, and the public interest.

6

Reimagining copyright's duration

Rebecca Giblin[1]

Introduction

This collection's foundational chapter revisited the vexed historical rationales for the grant of copyright. That uneasy juxtaposition of instrumentalist and naturalist motivations is perhaps most evident during debates about the duration of those rights. If we granted copyrights purely on instrumentalist grounds, we would grant the minimum we determined necessary to incentivise a socially optimal amount of creation. If we were driven exclusively by naturalist considerations, those rights would be perpetual.[2] Instead, we are motivated by a combination of these desires. We want to incentivise creation of cultural and informational works in order to spread

1   Faculty of Law, Monash University. A Research Accelerator Grant from Monash University substantially supported the development of this work (and the project) over 2013–2014. I am also grateful to the Centre d'Études Internationales de la Propriété Intellectuelle at the Université de Strasbourg which hosted our project workshop in 2014, and to each of the project participants for the valuable suggestions and feedback they provided during that process. Some of this work was completed while I was in residence as a Senior Visiting Scholar at Berkeley Law School. Thanks also to Professor Jane C Ginsburg, who rigorously critiqued an earlier version of this paper.
2   Indeed, perpetual copyright was 'nearly adopted as the ideal standard' in the preliminary negotiations to the original iteration of the Berne Convention. Sam Ricketson, 'The Copyright Term' (1992) 23 *International Review of Intellectual Property & Competition Law* 753, 755, citing Sam Ricketson, *The Berne Convention for the Protection of Literary and Artistic works: 1886–1986* (Kluwer, 1987) at 41–42. Ricketson argues that recognition of the interests of the public is a key reason why natural rights theories 'have … never triumphed in their pristine form'. Sam Ricketson, 'The Copyright Term' (1992) 23 *International Review of Intellectual Property*

knowledge and culture, and we want to recognise the personality and labour authors pour into their works and reward them for those endeavours (or at least ensure that the fruits of their labours aren't reaped by those who had nothing to do with the sowing). As this chapter will show however, current approaches to copyright terms – which international treaties lock us into indefinitely – are demonstrably counterproductive to both aims.

In 1906, author Samuel Clemens (known better as Mark Twain) testified to Congress in favour of extending copyright terms from the existing period of 42 years to a term of the author's life plus 50. His claim was based not on the value of those books, but their *lack* of value: he argued that the commercial value of almost every book is extracted after its first few years, and doubted there were 20 Americans per century whose works were worth publishing beyond the existing copyright term. When copyrights expire, he argued, those few valuable books continue to be published, and the valueless continue not to be; the only difference is that the profits are diverted to publishers instead of authors or their heirs. In those circumstances Clemens argued there was no downside to giving lengthy copyrights to every work. That would enable authors to reap the benefits of those few that proved to be of lasting value, and the rest would be lost to obscurity regardless.[3]

This idea that there's no downside in granting ever-longer terms may help explain the prodigious term extensions world legislatures have so casually locked us into over the last few generations. But while Clemens' reasoning may have been sound a century ago, when high costs of production and dissemination made investment in obscure or unpopular works unfeasible, it no longer holds good. This paper demonstrates that current inordinate terms of protection are poorly justified by any of the dominant rationales trotted out in support of them, and result in real harms for authors and the broader public. It then shows how, if unconstrained by international treaty obligations and existing ways of doing things, we might retain incentives for creation, direct a bigger share to creators, and increase the social benefits that flow from access to cultural and informational works.

& *Competition Law* 753, at 755. Even countries which once offered perpetual protection, such as Mexico, Guatemala and Portugal, have now reined it back. Sam Ricketson, 'The Copyright Term' (1992) 23 *International Review of Intellectual Property & Competition Law* 753, at 755 n 7.

3   James Boyle and Jennifer Jenkins, *Intellectual Property: Law & the Information Society* (CreateSpace Independent Publishing Platform, 1st ed, 2014) 284–288.

1. Justifications for current terms

Current approaches to duration

Since copyright's inception, terms have ratcheted steadily upwards. In 1710, the Statute of Anne awarded rights for 14 years, reverting to authors for 14 more if they were still living after the initial term.[4] Within a century, France had granted post-mortem rights ('pma' for *post mortem auctoris*) for up to 10 years after the death of the author.[5] Those pma rights crept steadily upwards, with the Berlin Act of the Berne Convention recommending minimum terms of life plus 50 in 1908, and the Brussels Revision making them mandatory 40 years after that.[6] Then in 1965 Germany unexpectedly (and with remarkably little debate) increased terms to 70 years pma.[7] When the European Union harmonised copyright law in the 1993 Directive, all member states became obliged to match the German term, which was then the longest in Europe.[8] In 1998, the US increased its durations to match the Europeans and, since then, has enthusiastically exported those extended terms still further through bi- and plurilateral trade agreements.[9] The combined result of these various international instruments is that most countries now protect works for life plus 50 or 70 years; terms for other subject matter such as films and sound recordings have increased in parallel, and now commonly endure for

---

4   *Act for the Encouragement of Learning* (Statute of Anne), 8 Ann, c 19 (1709/1710), section c11 (Great Britain).

5   Gillian Davies, *Copyright and the Public Interest* (Sweet & Maxwell, 2nd ed, 2002), 136–137.

6   From the time of the Berlin revision in 1908, a term of 50 years pma had been recommended, but it did not become a mandatory minimum until the Brussels Act of 1948. See Ricketson, 'The Copyright Term', above n 2, 777–778.

7   Gillian Davies, above n 5, 201.

8   See *Council Directive 93/98/EEC of 29 October 1993 harmonizing the term of protection of copyright and certain related rights* [1993] OJ L 290/9, recital 11 (emphasising the importance of harmonisation as justification for the increase to 70 years pma protection).

9   See e.g. *Australia–United States Free Trade Agreement*, signed 18 May 2004 [2005] (entered into force 1 January 2005), Art 17.4. A leaked draft of the Trans-Pacific Partnership dated 16 May 2014 showed that a range of proposed minimum terms for works ranging from 50 to 100 years pma. An earlier draft dated 3 August 2013 showed that countries including the US and Australia were proposing a term of 70 years pma protection. See <wikileaks.org/tpp/>.

50, 70 or even 95 years.[10] These terms are typically awarded as a 'lump sum' at the time of creation, and few jurisdictions seek to protect authors' interests by limiting the alienability of those rights.[11]

We might expect that, before locking in such lengthy minimums via difficult-to-alter international instruments, policymakers would have given careful consideration to whether these constantly expanded terms would achieve their intended outcomes. That didn't happen. As Ricketson has chronicled, the development of international norms governing duration has been 'notable for an almost complete absence of debate of the policy and theoretical issues involved'.[12]

To fill the gap, this chapter evaluates the justifiability of existing copyright terms. As explored within the foundational chapter, the aims of copyright are many, varied and subject to fierce dispute. In the duration context however, we can identify four that are dominantly used to justify existing terms:

1. To incentivise initial cultural production;

2. To incentivise further cultural production by producing rewards that will subsidise investment in new works;

3. To incentivise *ongoing* investment in existing works (i.e. to ensure their preservation and continued availability); and

4. To recognise and reward authors for their creative contributions.

Do these rationales, in combination, justify existing mandated minimum terms?

Justification #1: That current approaches to duration are necessary to incentivise sufficient initial cultural production

Incentivising its initial creation is one obvious reason for granting monopoly rights over the fruits of creative endeavour. As the foundational chapter explained, this rationale motivates not only

---

10   In Europe, film copyrights potentially last even longer still, since they expire 70 years after the death of the last survivor of the director, screenwriter, or composer. See *Directive 2006/116/EC of the European Parliament and the Council of 12 December 2006 on the term of protection of copyright and certain related rights* [2006] OJ L 372/12, Art 2.

11   For discussion of some jurisdictions that do limit creators' abilities to trade their rights, see Hugenholtz et al, 'The recasting of copyright and related rights for the knowledge economy' (Research Paper No 2012-38, Institute for Information Law, 2012) 165.

12   Ricketson, 'The Copyright Term', above n 2, 777.

policymakers from instrumentalist traditions, but traditionally naturalist ones as well.[13] The idea that monopoly rights are necessary to incentivise cultural production is at the core of the traditional economics approach to copyright.[14] The expensive part of an informational 'good' is its initial creation; once created, it has characteristics of a public good, being non-rivalrous in consumption and minimally excludable.[15] Economic incentive theory posits that, if a right holder has no right to impose monopoly rents, free-riding competitors driving the price to marginal cost would heighten their risk of being unable to recover their costs of initial creation.[16] If competitors could simply come along and produce the same content without having to compensate authors, the original producer would be undercut. This suggests that some grant of monopoly rights is necessary to encourage the desired cultural production. (Of course, this is obviously not always the case, a point I'll return to later.)

Significantly, existing minimum terms go far beyond incentive levels. To understand how far, it is necessary to consider two key concepts: the 'time value of money', and cultural depreciation. The time value of money recognises that, the further away in time a benefit will be received, the less it is currently worth. A dollar received today is worth a little bit more than a dollar received tomorrow, and a lot more than a dollar received a hundred years down the track. This means that, in determining the present value of future earnings, we need to discount them with reference to the applicable interest rate. In a brief to the US Supreme Court ('the Eldred Brief') a group of prominent economists, including five Nobel laureates, conducted some simple modelling to demonstrate how the time value of money affects incentives for

---

13   See R Giblin and K Weatherall, 'If we redesigned copyright from scratch, what might it look like?, this volume.

14   See e.g. Neil Weinstock Netanel, 'Copyright and a Democratic Civil Society' (1996) 106 *Yale Law Journal* 283, 307; Stephen G Breyer, 'The Uneasy Case for Copyright: A study of copyright in books, photocopies, and computer programs' (1970) 84 *Harvard Law Review* 281; William M Landes and Richard A Posner, 'An Economic Analysis of Copyright Law' (1989) 18(2) *Journal of Legal Studies* 325.

15   Anne Barron, 'Copyright infringement, "free-riding" and the lifeworld', in Lionel Bently, Jennifer Davis and Jane C Ginsburg (eds), *Copyright and Piracy: An Interdisciplinary Critique* (Cambridge University Press, 2010) 93, 94.

16   Landes and Posner, above n 14, 327.

creation. Assuming a real interest rate (net of inflation) of 7 per cent, they showed that a dollar today is worth $0.93 if received in a year, just $0.0045 in 80 years and a mere $0.0012 in 100.[17]

Works today are commonly covered by copyright for a hundred years or more. But given the time value of money, *at the time of creation* the value of those later years of protection is infinitesimal. Indeed, this model shows that the total present value of royalties received in the 80th to 100th years of protection is just 0.33 per cent more than the combined royalties for the first to 80th years.[18] In other words, even if a work will still be generating a consistent stream of royalties in a century (an assumption I'll return to shortly), the dollars that will be obtained in those later years are still worth virtually nothing at the time of creation.[19] Of course, as the time of copyright expiry draws near, the *present* value of term extension becomes much higher. But in considering the scope of rights necessary to incentivise initial production and investment, it is the value of those rights at the time of a work's *creation* that is relevant.

So the first important point is that the time value of money reduces incentives over time even if a work is still generating a consistent stream of royalties. The second point to understand is that *very few works actually do so.* 'Cultural depreciation' refers to works' loss of market value over time. Cultural depreciation rates are important in determining the necessary incentives because, as the empirical evidence shows, the vast majority of a work's commercial value is generally extracted shortly after creation.[20] In most music genres, for example, revenues are typically a tiny fraction of their starting point within half-a-dozen years of release; in the case of books, the

---

17   Economists Brief in *Eldred v Ashcroft*, 537 US 186, 4–7 (2003).
18   This modelling was conducted by a team of economists (including five Nobel laureates) and is based on the conservative assumption that revenues would remain stable over time. This is unlikely, given that most copyrighted works tend to lose value over time, so in fact the present value of later years is likely to be even lower than the model reflects. See Economists Brief in *Eldred v Ashcroft*, 537 US 186, 4–5 (2003).
19   See Landes and Posner, above n 14, 326, 363; Economists Brief in *Eldred v Ashcroft*, above n 17, 7–8. But cf Stan J Liebowitz and Stephen E Margolis, 'Seventeen Famous Economists Weigh in on Copyright: The Role of Theory, Empirics and Network Effects' 18(2) (2005) *Harvard Journal of Law and Technology* 435 (questioning the assumptions in the brief).
20   See, for example, detailed empirical analysis in William M Landes and Richard A Posner, 'Indefinitely Renewable Copyright' (2003) 70 *University of Chicago Law Review* 471, 501–507.

number of copies sold tends to drop sharply within a year.[21] This isn't the case for every work, of course, or even every sub-class. Classical music compositions are likely to have more enduring appeal than this week's 'Top 40' hits, for example, and beloved novels such as *Pride and Prejudice* or *To Kill a Mockingbird* appreciate in the decades after their release rather than the other way around. As a rule however, most works have limited commercial lifespans. This can be illustrated by historical copyright renewal rates. Before 1976, US law granted a relatively short fixed term which could be renewed for a further period upon payment of a nominal fee.[22] Prior to the introduction of automatic renewals in 1992, renewal rates ranged from 3 per cent in 1914 to 22 per cent in 1991, suggesting that even after a relatively short period, the vast majority of works had virtually no value to the owners of the rights.[23] Those data also demonstrate that cultural depreciation rates differ across classes: far more films and music had their copyrights renewed, for example, than did technical documents, suggesting their value tends to be more enduring.[24] But still, the commercial value of almost all works depreciates over time.

On the basis of the time value of money alone, Landes and Posner observe that the prospect of income that will be received 25 years in the future will have little impact on present decisions, and that the potential for royalties in a century's time would do nothing to incentivise most authors.[25] Pollock has developed a more comprehensive model factoring in not just the time value of money, but rates of cultural depreciation, the mathematical supply function for creative works, and the welfare associated with new works.[26] Assuming a discount rate of 6 per cent and cultural depreciation of 5 per cent, his model estimates optimal

---

21   See e.g. HM Treasury, *Gowers Review of Intellectual Property* (December 2006), <www. gov.uk/government/uploads/system/uploads/attachment_data/file/228849/0118404830.pdf>, 52–53; Hugenholtz et al, above n 11, 113. It has been estimated that more than 95 per cent of copyrighted back catalogue recordings are not currently released, further demonstrating their lack of current commercial value. See Hugenholtz et al, at 114.

22   The fees over time are set out in Landes and Posner, above n 20, n 10.

23   See Barbara A Ringer, 'Renewal of Copyright', in Copyright Society of the USA (ed) 1 *Studies on Copyright: Arthur Fisher Memorial Edition* 503, 616–620; Landes and Posner, above n 20, 499–500.

24   William F Patry, *How to fix copyright* (Oxford University Press, 2011) 106.

25   Landes and Posner, above n 14, 361–362.

26   Rufus Pollock, 'Forever Minus A Day? Calculating Optimal Copyright Term', (2009) 6(1) *Review of Economic Research on Copyright Issues* 35; available at <papers.ssrn.com/sol3/papers. cfm?abstract_id=1436186>, 3.

copyright terms to be around 15 years.[27] These economic models (and the dearth of empirical evidence to show that recent term extensions have resulted in an increase in cultural production)[28] strongly suggest that existing minimum terms far exceed what can be justified as necessary to incentivise the initial production of works.[29]

Since current terms go beyond what is necessary to incentivise initial cultural production, they are justifiable only to the extent to which they satisfy other goals. What does the evidence have to say about that?

Justification #2: That current approaches to duration are necessary to incentivise new cultural production by subsidising investment in other works

Above-incentive terms impose additional costs on the creation of some new works by making it more expensive for subsequent authors to build upon them.[30] But do they also result in greater investment in the creation and distribution of *other* cultural works? Longer terms are sometimes justified by claims that the windfall rewards resulting from above-inventive copyrights subsidise investment in new works, thus bringing about more new creation overall. The idea is that a right

---

27　Pollock, above n 26, 21. Boldrin and Levine have also developed an economic model based on the idea that, as the elasticity of total monopoly revenue increases, the scope of copyright should decline with the size of the market, and reached the conclusion that optimal terms are likely seven years or less. See Michele Boldrin and David K Levine, 'Growth and Intellectual Property', (Working Paper 12769, National Bureau of Economic Research, December 2006) <www.nber.org/papers/w12769.pdf>.

28　One study linked recent 20-year term extensions in a number of OECD countries to increases in the number of movies produced. However, the study was never peer-reviewed or published. See IPL Png and Qiu-hong Wang, 'Copyright Duration and the Supply of Creative Work' (2006), available at <www.ssrn.com/abstract=932161>. A subsequent non-peer-reviewed paper by the same authors incorporated that research with other work they had conducted, and 'found no statistically robust evidence that copyright term extension was associated with higher movie production'. See IPL Png and Qiu-hong Wang, 'Copyright Law and the Supply of Creative Work: Evidence from the Movies' (2009) <www.comp.nus.edu.sg/~ipng/research/copyrt.pdf> (unavailable from original source but accessible via archive.org; copy on file with editors).

29　See e.g. William Cornish, 'Intellectual Property' in (1994) 13 *Yearbook of European Law* 485, 489–490, explaining that these terms cannot be justified on utilitarian grounds: 'it cannot be that an extension of the right from fifty to seventy years *post mortem auctoris* is required as an economic incentive to those who create and those who exploit works. They make their decisions by reference to much shorter time scales than these. It is only considerations of moral entitlement which can possibly justify even the present minimum term in the Berne Convention …'.

30　See e.g. Mark A Lemley, 'Property, Intellectual Property, and Free Riding' (2005) 83 *Texas Law Review* 1031, 1058 (recognising that 'intellectual property rights interfere with the ability of other creators to work, and therefore create dynamic inefficiencies').

holder reaping profits from some successful works is more likely to reinvest them in unproven ones. If that's so, it might offset the negative impacts current terms have on future creativity.

To establish the net benefit of such reinvestment, it's necessary to distinguish between investments that would not have been made without those windfall profits, and those that would have gone ahead regardless. If the investment would have proceeded anyway, it cannot be attributed to the above-incentive grant of rights. In the Eldred Brief, those laureate economists also explained the circumstances in which rational producers might be expected to invest in new projects:

> In general, a profit-maximising producer should fund the set of projects that have an expected return equal to or greater than their cost of capital. If a producer lacks the cash on hand to fund a profitable project, the producer can secure additional funding from financial institutions or investors. If the producer has resources remaining, after funding all the projects whose expected returns are higher than the cost of capital, this remainder should be invested elsewhere, not in sub-par projects that happen to be available to the firm.[31]

That is, rational producers will only fund projects which they expect to be profitable, and in those cases will do so as long as the expected return exceeds the cost of capital – regardless of whether that money comes from cash at hand or other sources. This suggests that a great deal of the investment paid for by above-incentive rewards would occur even in their absence. 'If a producer pursues the same set of projects in any event, then its incentives will not be improved from the mere fact of a windfall from consumers.'[32]

The analysis changes, however, where a producer has no access to capital markets. Consider the individual artist or small publisher who is unable to obtain a loan or other source of funding. In such cases the profits generated from older projects may well be the only source of funding for new ones, and thus indeed lead to investment in creations which would not otherwise have occurred.[33]

---

31 Economists Brief in *Eldred v Ashcroft*, 537 US 186, 9 (2003).
32 Economists Brief in *Eldred v Ashcroft*, 537 US 186, 9 (internal note omitted) (2003).
33 Economists Brief in *Eldred v Ashcroft*, 537 US 186, 9 (2003).

Overall, this analysis suggests that the grant of additional incentives translates poorly into new productions that would not otherwise have been funded. In many cases the 'reinvestment' will result in works which would have been produced in any event. There is little justification for making blanket awards of above-incentive terms in the mere *hope* the resulting windfall will be reinvested in new creation.

Justification #3: That current approaches to duration are necessary to incentivise copyright owners to continue to invest in existing works

Another key rationale for terms that exceed what's necessary to incentivise initial production is that they are necessary to incentivise copyright owners to *continue* to invest in existing works. This justification was relied upon heavily by supporters of the retroactive 20 year term extension enacted in the US in 1998.[34] One of the most explicit references came from the then Register of Copyrights, Marybeth Peters, who testified to Congress that a 'lack of copyright protection … restrains dissemination of the work, since publishers and other users cannot risk investing in the work unless assured of exclusive rights'.[35] This reasoning suggests that, although the public has paid to incentivise the creation of the work, it must keep paying and paying again to persuade the right holder to *continue* to make it available.

In evaluating this justification it is necessary to consider two distinct kinds of investment: investments in continuing to make the *original* work available, and investment in works *deriving* from the original – such as audiobooks, films or plays from a novel.

---

34   Mark A Lemley, 'Ex ante versus ex post justifications for intellectual property' (2004) 71 *University of Chicago Law Review* 129, 133–134, citing Orrin G Hatch and Thomas R Lee, '"To Promote the Progress of Science": The Copyright Clause and Congress's Power to Extend Copyrights' (2002) 16 *Harvard Journal of Law & Technology* 1, 3; Orrin G Hatch, 'Toward a Principled Approach to Copyright Legislation at the Turn of the Millennium' (1998) 59 *University of Pittsburgh Law Review* 719, 736–737; Brief of Amicus Curiae American Intellectual Property Law Association in Support of Respondent, *Eldred v Ashcroft*, No 01-618, 16–17 (S Ct filed 5 August 2002) (available on Westlaw at 2002 WL 1822117); Brief of Amici Curiae of the Nashville Songwriters Association International (NSAI) in Support of Respondent, *Eldred v Ashcroft*, No 01-618, 14 (S Ct filed 2 August 2002) (available on Westlaw at 2002 WL 1808587); Robert A Gorman and Jane C Ginsburg, *Copyright: Cases and Materials* (Foundation, 6th ed, 2002) 347.

35   *Copyright Term Extension Act*: Hearing on HR 989 Before the Subcommittee On Courts and Intellectual Property of the House Committee on the Judiciary, 104th Congress (Statement of Marybeth Peters, Register of Copyrights and Associate Librarian for Copyright Services, Library of Congress).

Are existing terms necessary to incentivise copyright owners to continue to make original works available?

This argument assumes that nobody will invest in making existing works available if they have to compete with others providing the same content. The best empirical evidence in support of this claim is a study into the effects of US copyright law pre-1920, when it did not recognise copyright in foreign books. The study found evidence that publishers were hesitant to risk the heavy financial investments associated with typesetting and printing unless they had some guarantee of exclusivity.[36]

By contrast, a number of more recent and extensive empirical studies have found that works restricted by copyright are actually subject to less investment and narrower dissemination than their counterparts in the public domain. For example, research conducted in 2005 on behalf of the National Recording Preservation Board at the Library of Congress examined the exploitation of sound recordings created in the first 75 years of that medium's availability. Under US law, sound recordings pre-dating 1972 can be protected by a patchwork of state and common law until 2067, with the consequence 'that there are almost no pre-1972 US sound recordings in the public domain across the United States.'[37] One of the key rationales for granting that lengthy term was to give owners an incentive to invest in making those older recordings available to the public.[38] In a number of other jurisdictions however, those recordings have fallen into the public domain. This gives rise to a natural experiment: if it is true that works will be under-exploited in the absence of copyright, those older recordings should have been made more available by their owners, who are not only likely to have the best access to master copies, but greater incentives to produce them thanks to their ongoing monopoly rights. However,

---

36   See Paul J Heald, 'Property Rights and the Efficient Exploitation of Copyrighted Works: An Empirical Analysis of Public Domain and Copyrighted Fiction Bestsellers' (2008) 92 *Minnesota Law Review* 1031, 1035, citing B Zorina Khan, 'Does Copyright Piracy Pay? The Effects of US International Copyright Laws on the Market for Books, 1790–1920' (Working Paper No 10271, National Bureau of Econ Research, 2004) 21, 21–24.

37   See Eva E Subotnik and June M Besek, 'Constitutional Obstacles? Reconsidering Copyright Protection for Pre-1972 Sound Recordings' (2014) 37 *Columbia Journal of Law & the Arts* 327, 330–331.

38   Tim Brooks, *Survey of Reissues of U.S. Recordings* (August 2005) <www.clir.org/pubs/reports/reports/pub133/pub133.pdf> v: 'One consideration by Congress in extending copyright protection to owners for such a long period was to give those owners an incentive to reissue, and thereby preserve, older recordings.'

the study found that, on average, just 14 per cent of sound recordings published between 1890 and 1964 had been re-released by right holders on compact disc. Non-right holders re-released 22 per cent of those recordings without the benefit of any monopoly rights – over 50 per cent more than those that did.[39]

Similar findings were reached in Heald's major study into the impact of copyright protection on the price and availability of books over time. Once again, US law provided ideal conditions for the experiment: books published between 1913 and 1932 had fallen progressively into the public domain from 1988 until 1997, but then a 20-year retroactive term extension ensured that books published from 1923 to 1932 would continue to be restricted by copyright until at least 2018. If the under-investment theory were correct, the data should show that the works in the public domain were being neglected by comparison to the works that were still subject to copyright. But once again the opposite proved true. Between 1988 and 2001, the public domain books were in print at the same rate as copyrighted books, and after 2001 they became available at a rate which was 'significantly higher'.[40] By 2006, 98 per cent of the public domain sample was in print, compared to just 74 per cent of the copyrighted works.[41] Public domain books also averaged significantly more editions – 6.3 compared to 3.2 – and were available to the public at significantly lower cost.[42] Only a small part of this discrepancy is explainable by the lower costs of digital distribution: there were still 5.2 editions of public domain titles available when ebook editions were excluded.[43] Heald hypothesised that under-exploitation of works in the absence of copyright protection was likely only to be a problem where the costs of reproduction and distribution are high.[44] There is less risk of 'ruinous competition' in the case of works that are easily and cheaply reproducible. In the digital world, this includes not only books, but also movies, music, photographs, software, music and more.

---

39   Tim Brooks, *Survey of Reissues of U.S. Recordings* (August 2005) <www.clir.org/pubs/reports/reports/pub133/pub133.pdf> 7–8. Note that some reissuers may have claimed copyright in the 'remastered' recordings; other producers claim copyright in the accompanying artwork.
40   Paul J Heald, 'Property Rights and the Efficient Exploitation of Copyrighted Works: An Empirical Analysis of Public Domain and Copyrighted Fiction Bestsellers' (2007) 92 *Minnesota Law Review* 1031, 1040.
41   Ibid.
42   Ibid 1048–1050.
43   Ibid 1043.
44   Ibid 1050.

In a separate, subsequent study, Heald discovered that copyright seems to actually have a negative, rather than positive, impact on the availability of books. Using a random sample of 2,266 new editions of books available for sale on Amazon, and controlling for factors such as duplicates and multiple editions of the same title, the availability of copyrighted works was found to drop sharply shortly after release, before increasing dramatically upon entry to the public domain.[45] When the figures are adjusted for the number of total books published in each decade, the trend became starker still.[46] The lack of availability of print copies is not being filled by the ebook market either: though 94 per cent of public domain 'bestsellers' were available in electronic formats, the same was true of just 27 per cent of copyrighted books.[47]

The orphan works problem further illustrates how poor a job the blanket grant of long terms does of encouraging the continued availability of existing works. Countless millions of works are sterilised (in that their DNA cannot become part of future creation) or lost altogether because their owners cannot be traced.[48] Very often, this is caused by works having commercial life spans shorter than their terms of protection.[49] The range of orphaned works in cultural collections is enormous, 'spanning published books, commercial photographs, journals, newspapers, television shows, films, sound recordings, plays and music compositions, as well as email messages, home videos, private letters, community pamphlets, postcards, government publications and other non-commercial ephemera.'[50] Some 90 per cent of the photographs held by UK museums are orphans, as are about 13 per cent of in-copyright books;[51] some EU archives

---

45   Paul J Heald, 'How Copyright Keeps Works Disappeared' (2014) 11(4) *Journal of Empirical Legal Studies* 840–841.

46   Ibid 842–843.

47   Ibid 852–853.

48   Ian Hargreaves, *Digital Opportunity: A Review of Intellectual Property and Growth* (Department for Business, Innovation & Skills, 18 May 2011), 38.

49   See e.g. Ellen Franziska Schultze, 'Orphan works and other orphan material under national, regional and international law: analysis, proposals and solutions' (2012) *European Intellectual Property Review* 313, 213. Orphaning is also partly caused by the lack of formalities in copyright: see Dev Gangjee's fuller discussion of this in 'Copyright formalities: A return to registration?', this volume.

50   Australian Digital Alliance and Australian Libraries Copyright Committee, Submission No 586 to Australian Law Reform Commission, *Copyright & the Digital Economy*, November 2012, 52.

51   See Anna Vuopala, 'Assessment of the Orphan works issue and Costs for Rights Clearance' (May 2010) *European Commission*, 5.

claim orphaning rates around 40 per cent.[52] Hargreaves decries this state of affairs as 'cultural negligence': '[a]s long as [it] … continues, archives in old formats (for instance celluloid film and audio tape) continue to decay, and further delay to digitisation means some will be lost for good'.[53] The phenomenon is by no means limited to old works. A recent project to preserve New Zealand's early video game heritage, for example, was unable to track down the owners of key pieces of software coded in the 1980s.[54] There are people who wish to invest in preserving and disseminating these works; preventing them from so doing imposes all cost and no benefit on society. Even where adequate library exceptions exist, libraries have limited preservation resources. By the time such works finally enter the public domain, perhaps more than a century from now, many of them will be irretrievable from physically deteriorated and technologically obsolete containers.

Many other works are not technically orphans but are lost to society nonetheless because of what might be described as 'parental neglect'. Copyrighted works are often so little valued that their owners don't bother investing in making them available, despite having monopoly rights to do so. Unlike in Twain's day, when high costs of production and dissemination meant that less popular works simply could not be kept available, many of these works could be rapidly and cheaply made available online for others to learn from and build on. Under current arrangements though, they are lost to society because their copyrights last longer than the owner's interest in them.

The available evidence suggests that current terms do little to entice copyright owners to make their works available on an ongoing basis. In fact, the empirical evidence suggests they may have a negative impact on availability by making it more difficult for others to do so. A blanket grant of long terms in the mere *hope* they will lead to greater availability is poor policy. If we really are motivated to grant exclusive rights in exchange for continuing availability, those should go to those who *do* invest in those works, not those who *could* but don't.

---

52   Hargreaves, above n 48, 38.
53   Ibid.
54   See Susan Corbett, *The law – is it an ass?* (1 April 2014), Play It Again Project <playitagainproject.org/the-law-is-it-an-ass/>.

*Are existing terms justified as necessary to incentivise investment
in derivative works?*

This one is easy, and can be answered by taking a quick look around
our environment – derivatives of public domain works are everywhere.
There have been countless reimaginings of *Alice in Wonderland*, for
example, since it entered the public domain, including films, TV shows,
illustrated and annotated editions, comic books, drawings, sculptures,
and paintings. (Do an online image search for 'Alice in Wonderland
art' to get an idea of the breadth of the inspiration drawn from that
work.) Several of the film versions were made by Disney, a firm which
famously built its empire on the retelling of stories from the public
domain. Indeed, Walt Disney was so dedicated to using public domain
works that he reputedly delayed making the first *Alice* film until he
was completely sure the rights had lapsed.[55] Disney has released
dozens of major works based on public domain stories, including,
notably, *Snow White and the Seven Dwarfs* (its first feature length
animated film), Kipling's *The Jungle Book* (released just a year after
the story's copyright expired), and recent hits *Frozen* and *Maleficent*
(reimaginings of classic fairy tales by Hans Christian Andersen and the
Brothers Grimm).[56] Kipling himself drew extensively on other works
in creating his story, and was drawn upon in turn by others (such as
Edgar Rice Burroughs in writing *Tarzan of the Apes*).[57] These anecdotal
observations are confirmed by empirical work, finding, for example,
that public domain works are exploited more than their copyrighted
brethren in the case of audiobook recordings.[58]

The current explosion of creativity exploring the Sherlock Holmes
universe further demonstrates enormous willingness to invest in
creating derivative works from material in the public domain, even
where that means competing with others who are doing the same.

---

55   Amicus Brief of Peter Decherney, *Golan v Holder*, 609 F 3d 1076, 17–18 (US 2012).

56   For a list of 50 Disney films created from stories in the public domain, see Derek Khanna,
50 Disney Movies Based On The Public Domain (2 March 2014) Forbes <www.forbes.com/sites/
derekkhanna/2014/02/03/50-disney-movies-based-on-the-public-domain/>.

57   Kembrew McLeod and Rudolf Kuenzli (eds), *Cutting Across Media: Appropriation Art,
Interventionist Collage, and Copyright Law* (Duke University Press, 2011) 256.

58   This study found that more than twice as many public domain books were available as
recordings than protected books (33 per cent compared to 16 per cent). See Christopher
Buccafusco and Paul J Heald, 'Do bad things happen when works enter the public domain?
Empirical tests of copyright term extension' (2013) 28 *Berkeley Technology Law Journal* 1, 22.
Even when only commercial recordings are taken into account, public domain works were still
more available to the public than their protected counterparts. See page 29.

The grant of exclusive rights in these derivative works is more than ample to encourage their production. The grant of above-incentive rights in the original cannot be justified as necessary to achieve it.

Justification #4: That current approaches to duration are necessary to recognise and reward creators

This final justification is one of the most important (and perhaps the least understood).

As the opening chapter demonstrated, we are not only motivated by a desire to incentivise creation; we also want to *reward* creators with a bigger share of the social surplus of their creations in recognition of their contributions of personality and labour.[59] Such motivations explain why even historically utilitarian copyright traditions often incorporate features such as moral rights, reversion, artists' resale and performers' rights.[60] In Ricketson's words, 'There is a strong moral argument ... that as authors confer benefits on society through their creative activity – the provision of learning, instruction and entertainment – this contribution should be duly rewarded.'[61] Recognising and rewarding authors is fundamental to the function and legitimacy of any copyright system. Thus, even if creators would be willing to create works for relatively small incentives (or none at all), that does not mean that's where the grant of rights should end.

The power and importance of rewards rationales can be seen in how persistently authors' interests have been used to justify broader and longer terms of protection. For example, rhetoric accompanying the 1998 US term extension focused on the desirability of '[a]uthors [being] able to pass along to their children and grandchildren the financial benefits of their works'.[62] The theme echoes Clemens'

---

59   Canvassing the possible reasons for this intuition, see Stephen Breyer, 'The Uneasy Case for Copyright: A Study of Copyright in Books, Photocopies, and Computer Programs' (1970) 84 *Harvard Law Review* 281, 284–291.

60   Even the US Supreme Court, against a backdrop of constitutionally mandated utilitarianism, has sometimes showed echoes of such thinking in the jurisprudence, once observing that 'sacrificial days devoted to ... creative activities deserve rewards commensurate with the services rendered'. See *Mazer v Stein*, 347 US 201, at 219 (though note that the Court's ultimate decision relied heavily on utilitarian justifications).

61   Ricketson, 'The Copyright Term', above n 2, 757.

62   Committee Reports, 105th Congress, 2nd Session, House Report 105–452, 105 H Rpt 452; *Copyright Term Extension Act* <homepages.law.asu.edu/~dkarjala/OpposingCopyrightExtension/legmats/H.R.105-452(1998).html>.

entreaty to Congress of a century before. Such arguments are highly effective because they appeal to our inclinations to reward authors for their creative contributions. In practice however, relatively few of copyright's rewards find their way to those creators. Indeed, such a huge proportion of the benefits of increased protection are captured by other cogs in the cultural production machine that authors are sometimes viewed as a mere 'stalking horse' masking the economic interests of others.[63] In the case of the US term extension for example, the beneficiary of the unbargained-for windfall from the US term extension was the right holder at the time it was granted; very little of it accrued to the original author or their family if it had previously been transferred.[64]

Teasing out the reasons for creators' poor economic outcomes requires revisiting that key tenet of economic incentive theory – that works will be created only if the fixed costs of production can be recovered, which is why we need to grant exclusive rights in the first place. This section canvasses the reasons why that rule does not always hold good in the context of creative labour, and how those realities might contribute to poor outcomes for creators.

As hinted at above, there are a great many intrinsic and extrinsic motivations for engaging in creative activities other than securing exclusive rights. Creative production might be triggered by external subsidies or prizes, assignments set by teachers, for the prestige associated with doing so, or because the creator is driven to do so by a problem she needs to solve, a story she needs to tell. Tushnet has written about the ways in which 'the desire to create can be excessive, beyond rationality, and free from the need for economic incentive'.[65] When authors explain why they write, they 'invoke notions of compulsion, overflowing desire, and other excesses' far more commonly than the urge to make money.[66] In many cases, those

---

63   See e.g. Peter Jaszi, 'Toward a Theory of Copyright: The Metamorphoses of "Authorship"' (1991) 40(2) *Duke Law Journal* 455, 471.

64   See *Copyright Extension Act* of 1995, S 483, 104th Congress, 1st Session (1995). The only exception was that the *Extension Act* did amend the *Copyright Act* to give authors and their heirs a termination right at the end of the original 75 years from first publication, but only if they hadn't exercised their prior termination right at the end of 56 years from first publication. See 17 USC § 304, (c) and (d).

65   Rebecca Tushnet, 'Economies of Desire: Fair use and Marketplace Assumptions' (2009) 51 *William & Mary Law Review* 513, 515.

66   Ibid 523.

reasons 'are not the products of conscious choice or rational weighing of utilities'.[67] This is not to say that a desire to make a living is not also a powerful motivator,[68] but it does help explain why a great deal of creation occurs independently of economic motivations (or, at least, would occur even if those fixed costs of production could not be recovered).

Non-economic motivations may have translated poorly to outputs when high costs of production and dissemination meant the production of cultural works (inevitably) required significant financial investment. Today, however, many cultural artefacts can be made and disseminated for unprecedentedly little outlay, and there is evidence of widespread cultural production occurring independently of copyright's incentives.[69] Millions of individuals contribute product reviews, Wikipedia edits, and internet movie database entries without any expectation of financial reward. Others supply an extraordinary amount of original music and video to online platforms (Soundcloud has over 40 million registered contributors), produce free and open source software, dedicate their photographs to the public domain, and record audio versions of public domain novels to share online. As Boyle muses, that there seems to be some 'innate human love of creation that continually drives us to create new things even when homo economicus would be at home in bed, mumbling about public goods problems'.[70]

There are other reasons too why creators may be inclined to create for smaller economic incentives than we would anticipate from rational economic actors. For one thing, creative labour can be more satisfying and enjoyable than other forms of work, and that can lead to individuals being willing to supply it at lower wages than they

---

67   Ibid 524.

68   See e.g. TJ Stiles, 'Among the digital Luddites' 38 *Columbia Journal of Law & the Arts* 293.

69   See e.g. Mark A Lemley, 'IP in a world without scarcity' 90 *NYU Law Review* 460, 492. Regarding the phenomenon of commons-based production, see Yochai Benkler, 'Coase's Penguin, or, Linux and the Nature of the Firm' (2002) 112(3) *Yale Law Journal* 369; see also Michael J Madison, Brett M Frischmann and Katherine J Strandburg, 'Constructing Commons in the Cultural Environment' (2010) 95 *Cornell Law Review* 657.

70   James Boyle, 'The Second Enclosure Movement' (2003) 66-SPG *Law & Contemporary Problems* 33, 45–46.

would otherwise work for.[71] That's why the Screen Actors' Guild has to prohibit members from taking work that doesn't comply with union minimums. As Johnson explains, 'the only way actors can overcome the temptation to work for below scale is to enter into a group pledge to punish one another for doing so'.[72]

The desirability of artistic work is further highlighted by the fact that, though salaries in creative industries tend to be relatively low, there is nonetheless a considerable oversupply of artistic labour (defined as individuals wishful of engaging in arts work but who are un- or under-employed).[73] Some creative production may also be explained as a consequence of over-optimism, with individuals overestimating their chances of emulating those who enjoy high-profile success.[74]

Creators' keenness to practice their crafts can lead them to accept lower prices for their works than they would if motivated exclusively by their economic interests.[75] As Towse explains, '[f]irms in the creative industries are able to "free-ride" on the willingness of artists to create and the structure of artists' labour markets, characterised by short term working practices and oversupply, mak[ing] it hard for artists to appropriate rewards'.[76] It also tends to put creators in relatively poor bargaining positions in their dealings with investors and intermediaries, which can lead them to transfer a great deal of the rewards of their creative labours to others.[77] Rational firms don't limit themselves to securing the minimum they need to justify their investment – they take everything they can get. For example, since at least 1919, the standard language in contracts between US music publishers and songwriters has commonly required the benefit

---

71   See e.g. discussion in Ruth Towse, *Creativity, Incentive and Reward* (Edward Elgar, 2001) at 53–58; see also Throsby and Thompson, 1994 (cited in Towse at 57) (results of an extensive survey study of Australian artists demonstrating that artists often worked in non-arts jobs, but only to the extent necessary to support their artistic occupation).

72   Eric E Johnson, 'Intellectual Property and the Incentive Fallacy' (2012) 39 *Florida State University Law Review* 623, 668–669.

73   See e.g. Towse, above n 71, 58.

74   See e.g. Towse, above n 71, 58; Christopher Buccafusco and Christopher Jon Sprigman, 'The Creativity Effect' (2011) 78 *University of Chicago Law Review* 31.

75   Tushnet, above n 65, 545.

76   Ruth Towse, 'Copyright and Cultural Policy for the Creative Industries', in Ove Granstrand (ed), *Economics, Law and Intellectual Property* (Kluwer, 2003), 427.

77   Towse, above n 76, particularly 429; Tushnet, above n 65, 545.

of any and all future term extensions to vest in the intermediary.[78] Even influential and famous composers have sometimes been forced by their publishers into sharing authorship credit and royalties.[79] And Hollywood contracts often require artists to sign over their rights not just within the realm of planet earth, but throughout the universe at large.[80] Thus, if a lucrative extraterrestrial market emerges, the bulk of its benefits will automatically be channelled away from creators. In the music industry, the 'vast majority' of musicians make little from their copyrights and performers rights, with the lion's share going instead to intermediaries and a small minority of stars in more powerful bargaining positions.[81]

Given these realities, current terms are a poor tool for benefiting creators. The Gowers report observed that, '[i]f the purpose of extension is to increase revenue to artists, given the low number of recordings still making money 50 years after release, it seems that a more sensible starting point would be to review the contractual arrangements for the percentages artists receive'.[82] Ricketson has also suggested that reform may better focus on formulating 'appropriate safeguards for the licensing and assignment of their rights'.[83] Some countries already have statutory limits to protect authors against too-broad transfers.[84] In many jurisdictions however, creators often have little choice than to assign their economic interests in their works as a condition of investment or distribution.[85] Given that current arrangements see so much of the benefit of above-incentive rewards diverted to intermediaries and investors, they are poorly justified as being for the benefit of creators.[86]

---

78   William F Patry, 'The Copyright Term Extension Act of 1995: Or How Publishers Managed to Steal the Bread from Authors' (1996) 14 *Cardozo Arts & Entertainment Law Journal* 661, 675–676.
79   Ibid 665.
80   See e.g. Dionne Searcey and James R Hagerty, 'Lawyerese Goes Galactic as Contracts Try to Master the Universe' *The Wall Street Journal* (online) 29 October 2014, <online.wsj.com/articles/SB125658217507308619>; Done Deal Professional, *Work for Hire Agreement #1* (31 January 2001) <www.donedealpro.com/members/details.aspx?object_id=275&content_type=1&section_id=13>.
81   Towse, above n 71, 126.
82   HM Treasury, above n 21, 51.
83   Ricketson, 'The Copyright Term', above n 2, 784.
84   See e.g. discussion in Hugenholtz et al, above n 11, 165.
85   Ricketson, 'The Copyright Term', above n 2, 757.
86   See e.g. Silke von Lewinski, 'EC Proposal for a Council Directive Harmonizing the Term of Protection of Copyright and Certain Related Rights' (1992) 23 *International Review of Intellectual Property and Competition Law* 785, 788–789.

2. Reconceptualisation

The above analysis shows that the public is getting a poor return on its generous grant of above-incentive rights. Current terms are neither optimised to maximise continued investment in existing works nor to recognise and reward creators, and they cause knowledge and culture to languish underused, or even vanish altogether. If we were starting from scratch, unconstrained by international treaty obligations, existing business models and questions of political feasibility, how might we rethink our approach to duration – and do a better job?

Before getting to that question, it's necessary to make explicit – a better job of *what*? What are my assumptions about what copyright policies should seek to achieve? There are tremendous possibilities for economic and social gains if we were to be more creative and explicit about copyright's aims. However, this chapter's rethinking is based on the assumption that we primarily wish to achieve the same aims that were identified above as justifying current duration policy. This is intended to enable a direct comparison of how much more effective copyright policy could be if it were freed from current proscriptions. Thus, I assume that we're primarily motivated to:

1. incentivise initial cultural production;
2. incentivise further cultural production by producing rewards that will subsidise investment in new works;
3. incentivise *ongoing* investment in existing works (i.e., to ensure their preservation and continued availability); and
4. recognise and reward authors for their creative contributions.

So what might an alternative look like?

The foundational chapter set out a number of conceptual frameworks that might assist in determining where the public interest lies, including with reference to all individuals' interests, the preponderance of those interests, or moral validity (assuming of course that moral validity is capable of determination). Here I adopt the framework of Ho's 'representative individual', which usefully frees the mind from self-interest and vested interests, while desirably encouraging consideration of all aspects of the cultural production and access equation. The question then, is this: how would a person who had an equal chance of being anyone in society design duration policy to help achieve these aims?[87]

My starting point is to recognise that the twin desires of *incentivising* and *rewarding* creation need to be satisfied in different ways. Incentivising the creation of cultural and informational works may be achieved by granting *just enough* monopoly rights to give creators and investors a reasonable prospect of recouping their capital and some sufficient return on their investments. The grant of incentive-level rights is justified on the grounds that they are necessary for those works to be created. Rewarding creation requires securing to authors an additional share of the value of their creations above and beyond the incentive price. Here, the justification is that, even if they did not *need* it to create those works, they *deserve* it for having done so.

Having said that, even reward rationales don't justify granting creators the whole value arising from their creations. Even in the current paradigm some parts of all works are always reserved to the public, including the ideas within them, *de minimis* or non-substantial takings, and tolerated or excepted uses. That's because society is not motivated to incentivise or reward creation as an end in and of itself. Instead, we incentivise initial cultural production and ongoing investment in existing works to encourage the dissemination of knowledge and culture, and we reward authors (at least in part) out of gratitude for the benefits that flow from that access.[88] Thus, some share of those benefits must be reserved to society as a whole. In considering where to divide the pie, the representative individual would be well advised to heed Lemley's warning that the full internalisation of a work's positive externalities may not only invite rent-seeking but could actually reduce them as well.[89]

The following sketch describes one possible way in which our representative individual might better achieve the four identified aims. It imagines a four-stage system of rights which would maintain incentives, increase rewards for creators, and simultaneously unlock

---

87   See Giblin and Weatherall, above n 13.

88   Brett M Frischmann and Mark A Lemley, 'Spillovers' (2007) 107 *Columbia Law Review* 257, 258–261.

89   See generally Mark A Lemley, 'Property, Intellectual Property, and Free Riding' (2005) 83 *Texas Law Review* 1031.

a great deal of currently neglected value for the public. Since the very point of the exercise is unconstrained 'blue sky' thinking, it includes elements that would clearly be prohibited under Berne and other international instruments or simply politically unfeasible. The aim is to start the conversation about how we might do a better job if we were permitted to do so – and to raise awareness about what current treaty obligations force us to lose.

The incentive stage: A fixed initial term of exclusive rights

My reimagined approach begins with the grant of a fixed initial term of exclusive rights intended to incentivise initial production of the work ('incentive rights'). These would be calculated at the approximate value needed to incentivise the creation of the work plus any initial investments necessary to get it to the market. While it would be impractical to determine this on a case-by-case basis, we could broadly classify different classes of works with little difficulty.[90] Software, for example, would likely have a shorter term than films. Optimal figures would need to be approximated by economic modelling taking into account the complete contours of the law, particularly the scope of rights and exceptions. However, existing economic modelling suggests that, even for the most expensive works, it would be relatively short: given the time value of money and cultural depreciation, the potential to earn money from a work after the first 25 years would do little or nothing to persuade a rational investor to make the work in the first place.[91] For the sake of illustration, the following explanation proceeds on the assumption of a 25-year initial term for all types of works.

As under the current system, the initial grant of incentive rights would not be subject to any formalities. Consistent with the approach favoured by Gangjee in the succeeding chapter, this gives artists an opportunity to assess which works are most valuable and reduce their overall costs of registration. This is important given the incredible number of works that can be quickly generated using existing technologies: a photographer who takes tens of thousands of pictures

---

90   Ricketson, 'The Copyright Term', above n 2, 770–771.
91   See e.g. Landes and Posner, above n 20, 476 ('[T]he incremental incentive to create new works as a function of a longer term is likely to be very small (given discounting and depreciation) beyond a term of twenty-five years or so').

every year will need some time to establish the ones in which she has an ongoing personal or economic interest. It is also desirable to ensure individual artists are not disadvantaged relative to commercial producers. As Elkin-Koren has explained, authors may initially create without any profit motive, but still seek to share in the rewards in the event that their creations achieve popularity.[92] An upfront registration requirement may prevent them from doing so; it may also enable corporate players to co-opt the fruits of their labours.[93] As demonstrated by the use of the GPL (GNU General Public License) for open source software, copyright can be a useful tool for preventing corporations from free riding on unpaid creative labour.[94]

The reward stage: Rolling creator-rights

After the initial fixed period, copyright in the work would expire. Then would commence a second stage of rights. Here the reward rationale comes into play, and the overall regime starts departing sharply from the status quo.

After the expiry of the initial incentive-value rights, creators would be entitled to assert their continuing interests over works by registering for a 'creator-right'. Creator-rights would give their owners slightly less comprehensive rights than the initial grant of rights. As noted above, even in the current paradigm some parts of all works are always in the public domain. When a work moves from the incentive stage to the reward stage, some additional uses could join that list. They might include enhanced rights to engage in non-commercial transformative uses and a broader range of unremunerated educational uses.[95] Key national cultural institutions might gain greater rights to engage in preservation activities; given the cheapness and ubiquity of storage and transmission, systems might even require deposit of copies to guarantee future preservation and access.

---

92   Niva Elkin-Koren, 'Can formalities save the public domain? Reconsidering formalities for the 2010s' (2013) 28(3) *Berkeley Technology Law Journal* 1537, 1553.
93   Ibid 1555–1556.
94   Ibid 1556.
95   In order to exercise their rights, authors, preservation societies and members of the public would have to have a right to bypass any technological protection measures that had been applied when the works were protected by copyright.

An increased range of uses might also be permitted-but-paid:[96] subject to compulsory licences that require payment of equitable remuneration. This could facilitate the creation of social welfare-enhancing initiatives such as digital public libraries. This could enable us to remunerate authors on a per-loan basis similar to some existing public lending right arrangements while simultaneously increasing access for the public. The use of such mechanisms could also help facilitate the emergence of new distribution platforms and make it easier for artists to find audiences. Compulsory-type licences could also help facilitate uses of works which had a great many creative contributors, as is often the case with films.

For uses falling outside the more expansive exceptions and compulsory licences, creators would be entitled to make fresh bargains with intermediaries and investors, and have veto rights over undesired uses. Thus in many cases the author would retain the right to exclude. This is not inconsistent with the broader 'access to culture' aims outlined above; it is simply part of the evolving balance between improving access to culture while recognising the creator's continuing interest in her works. Alongside this system of rights there would need to be an appropriately tailored moral rights regime existing independently of registration in order to protect artists' non-economic rights.

Careful thought would need to be given to drawing the boundaries of the scheme, and particularly to the kinds of creators who would be eligible for these rewards. Existing legal systems already draw that line in different places; such differences could no doubt be accommodated in this new system as well. Regardless of where the boundary falls however, creator-rights would vest only in those who made creative contributions. They would not benefit mere investors, and, vitally, they would not be transferable until shortly before the expiry of the previous term of rights. This arrangement would impose little in the way of fresh burdens – an artist receiving a creator-right could assign it in its entirety each term if she wished to do so – but it *would* position creators to reap more of the fruits of their labours. It

---

96   Jane Ginsburg authored this catchy descriptor: see Jane C Ginsburg, 'Fair Use for Free, or Permitted-but-Paid?' (Working Paper No 481, The Center for Law and Economic Studies Columbia University School of Law, 2 June 2014).

would also open up new opportunities for investment by individuals or firms who believe they could do a better job of exploiting them than those who previously held the rights.

Unlike incentive rights, creator-rights would arise only upon registration. (In the current paradigm, of course, this would be prohibited under Berne.) That threshold requirement would make it simple for prospective users to determine whether works have entered the public domain and reduce the tracing costs involved in getting in touch with the creator to negotiate licences for those that have not. By requiring contact details to be kept up to date, orphan works could be virtually eliminated. Gangjee more deeply explores the potential of formalities to fix the deficiencies of current approaches, including those caused by too-long terms of protection, in the following chapter. By imposing a proactive obligation on authors to register their continuing interests in works, the system would dramatically reduce the losses of knowledge and culture that occur by granting lengthy blanket terms irrespective of whether the author or owner has any continuing interest in their work. While it may sometimes be difficult to identify who made what creative contribution, and apportion the rewards, those are the same difficulties we already confront in determining ownership. In any event, they could be significantly ameliorated by the development of policies, guidelines and precedents as the system became established.

This is a system of rolling rights: after each period of rights draws to a close, a further registration would cause a new creator-right to vest afresh in the author. Granting creator-rights for a period equal to each full incentive-based term ensures there will be enough protection to encourage even the most lavish new investments. That leads to the question: how many renewals might there be? As explained above, though the rationale of rewarding and recognising creators dictates that they should receive a greater share of the rewards of their work, it does not justify infinite protection. Sooner or later the rights must expire for good – but when? It is easy to make the case the creator should be entitled to continuing rights over her lifetime, but less clear that it should be transferable to heirs after death. While the idea that copyright terms should allow authors to provide for their dependants has 'almost assumed the status of an article of faith', significant changes in social conditions since the 19th century reduce the power of the rationale,[97] as do systems which reserve for others the benefits ostensibly intended for descendants.[98] However, as outlined above, enabling authors to provide for their descendants has a powerful moral appeal. As long as protection is granted on an opt-in basis rather than as default, post-mortem protection would ensure fairness in outlying cases while causing little harm elsewhere.[99] Empirical evidence could be gathered to help determine when creator-rights should ultimately expire. It might be however that in the case of works involving a limited number of authors, creator-rights could be renewed for life plus a generation; larger ensemble works might last until the demise of the last registered creator. This would be unlikely to comply with the Berne minimum of author's life plus 50 years (and almost certainly be shorter than the life-plus-70 terms that trade agreements have locked in to an increasing number of domestic laws).

The transition stage: Between expiry and registration

Artists could be encouraged to preregister their works so they can be alerted when the initial expiry of rights draws near. However, even with strong awareness about how the system works, some creators would inevitably fail to register works: perhaps because they do not realise that they still hold value, or simply because they forget to do so. To avoid that, there could be a transition stage after the previous expiry of rights during which time creators would be permitted to retroactively register their continuing interests.

Use of works in the transitional stage should be encouraged by preserving those who engage in them from obligations to pay for past use. That's because they would have an important signalling function informing artists about continuing interest and value in their works. New industries would no doubt spring up to identify works which were proving to have continuing value in the period after the initial lapse of rights, and to assist creators in registering their continuing interests in works.

The transition stage would end upon registration (with the works then being protected by creators-rights) or lapse of time.

---

97 Ricketson, 'The Copyright Term', above n 2, 761.
98 von Lewinski, above n 86, 789.
99 Ricketson, 'The Copyright Term', above n 2, 762–763.

The public domain

The final stage is entry into the public domain. This could occur upon donation by the creator, after failure to register by the closure of the transition window, upon lapse of creator-rights (i.e. non-renewal) or at the point of ultimate expiry, where no further renewals are permitted. As noted above, appropriately tailored moral rights would be a necessary complement to protect authors' non-economic interests. Though thinking about their shape is outside the scope of this chapter, the need for them would be particularly important given that authors who chose not to register continuing interests might well outlive their economic rights.

Illustrations

The following case studies illustrate how the above-described system might work in practice:

1. A global digital public library obtains a blanket licence over all books of 25 years and older. Where their authors have registered for creator-rights, the library pays them equitable remuneration each time one of them is borrowed by a user until such time as they enter the public domain.

2. An author writes a book, and gains a 25-year copyright. Assume a film studio exclusively licenses the film adaptation rights, and makes the book into a film five years later. The film is protected for its own 25-year term. When the book reaches the end of the copyright period (20 years after the film is made), the author registers her interests and receives a creator-right in her book. That enables her to negotiate with others to make new derivative works including further film adaptations (or perhaps even reach a deal with the original studio not to agree to grant a licence elsewhere for the term of the creator-right). When the copyright on the film expires, the author of the book may register a creator-right over that as well, in recognition of her creative contribution to the work.[100] She would share in the proceeds of the film's exploitation with its other creative contributors.

---

100 This is similar to a French rule which treats book authors as the co-author of their film adaptations. See Article L 113-7 of the *Intellectual Property Code* (France).

3. A number of 25-year-old computer games have fallen out of copyright and not been registered. Shortly after, a revival of interest in that era results in people beginning to convert those games to currently playable formats. An investor tracks down the original programmers and asks them to register their creator-rights and grant a licence to enable the investor to commercially exploit the works. Those who previously converted the games have no liability for doing so, but can no longer commercially exploit them. Some right holders cannot be traced; when they don't act within the registration window, their games officially enter the public domain.

4. A band records a song, and assigns the copyrights in music and lyrics to their record label. After the initial term of protection lapses, the band members register creator-rights. Anyone can continue to use the sound recording, subject to equitable remuneration being paid to the creators. A producer wants to put it in a movie soundtrack, negotiates a licence to do so, and the proceeds are shared among the creators.

5. A band records several albums but none of the creative contributors register for creator-rights. After the works enter the public domain, another musician samples some of their tracks and includes that material in her own release without requiring any licence to do so.

6. An artist produces various culturally important photographs, posters and political cartoons, and, when the copyrights expire, registers her creator-right over each of them. Non-profit cultural institutions are freely able to make copies for preservation purposes, but commercial users are obliged to negotiate a licence.

Benefits of this reimagined approach to duration

This reimagining of duration would have a number of benefits over the existing system.

First, it would secure to creators a larger slice of the pie, regardless of their relative lack of bargaining power or legal nous. This might include the session musicians who contribute instrumentals or vocals at live or recorded performances, typically in exchange for a flat-fee rather than a right to a royalty.[101] It could also benefit those who make creative contributions as part of large ensembles, giving some ongoing financial interest in their films (in contrast to the current system, which typically sees investors ending up with the bulk of the rights).[102] By better securing the rewards of copyright to creators themselves, this reimagined system would also enjoy greater legitimacy than existing approaches. For reasons explained by Weatherall later in this collection, that could in and of itself do a great deal to promote effective enforcement of rights.[103]

Another crucial advantage of the proposed approach is that it would facilitate the emergence of new distribution platforms. This is important, because distribution, visibility and access to their outputs are vital to creators. As author Heidi Bond explains:

> Distribution is an issue – it doesn't matter how many people have potential access to your book; if it's not in a distribution channel that is, in fact, accessed by people, it doesn't exist. Access to distribution channels – and the decreasing number of those channels – is a serious issue. Visibility is an issue.[104]

Thus, the attractiveness of new distribution mechanisms depends on the size of the audience they reach. The 'network effect' is the value that one user of a network has to others. The more users there are, the more valuable the network becomes. The catch is that those users will come only if the service is offering the content they want. Accordingly, new distribution platforms often live or die depending on whether they can secure the rights to existing popular artists and material. In many fields, rights are highly concentrated among a handful of intermediaries. That gives those right holders considerable power to shape emerging new platforms in ways that align with

---

101 See e.g. *What About Royalties? A Sound Guide for Musicians* (November 2006) Venture Navigator <www.venturenavigator.co.uk/content/royalties_guide_for_musicians> (unavailable from original source but accessible via archive.org; copy on file with editors) ('Often session musicians and backing vocalists are asked to sign a standard consent from (drafted by the Musicians Union and Equity respectively). This waives their rights to be paid each time their performance on a recording is used. Instead they get a one-off payment for the session.'); Brecknell, *What singers and musicians need to know* <www.jamesbrecknell.com/what-singers-and-musicians-need-to-know.html> ('To avoid ambiguity, and in accordance with standard industry practice, my session musicians will be asked to sign a waiver of rights in the creative work.').

102 See e.g. Ricketson, 'The Copyright Term', above n 2, 768–769.

103 Kimberlee Weatherall develops this point in 'A reimagined approach to copyright enforcement from a regulator's perspective', this volume.

104 Email from Heidi Bond to Cyberprofs mailing list, 17 May 2014.

their interests. Consider the example of online music streaming. It's extremely difficult to attract listeners to such a service without securing the rights to popular music, which makes it necessary for new providers to do deals with existing major labels. Not surprisingly, such deals end up being negotiated to suit the record companies, and not the artists (who typically neither control the rights nor have a spot at the negotiating table). Thus the majors took a stake in Spotify as a condition of access to their catalogues, and pay only a small fraction of the royalties they receive from the service to artists.[105] A recent industry study found that the after-tax payments of French music subscription services were split 73 per cent to major labels, 16 per cent to writers and publishers, and just 11 per cent to performing artists.[106]

Since artists are often poorly placed to negotiate a better deal (for the reasons already discussed), the current system perpetuates the status quo, with creators obliged to sign over their rights in order to get the visibility and access that are so often the keys to success. By putting works back up for grabs after 25 years, the proposed system would reduce the concentration of rights and facilitate the emergence of new platforms that could offer creators a better deal.

My reimagining has some commonalities with the idea of the 'paid public domain' (known in France as a *domaine public payant*, and Germany as *Urhebernachfolgevergütung*). As first mooted by Victor Hugo in 1878, the concept would have seen works become the property of the nation immediately upon the author's death, subject to a fee being paid for their exploitation in perpetuity. Revenue would go to direct heirs during their lifetimes, then to a general fund

---

105 See e.g. Stuart Dredge, 'Billy Bragg: labels not Spotify deserve streaming music payouts scrutiny', *The Guardian* (online), 7 November 2013 <www.theguardian.com/technology/2013/nov/07/billy-bragg-spotify-artist-payouts>; David Byrne, 'The internet will suck all creative content out of the world' *The Guardian* (online), 12 October 2013 <www.theguardian.com/music/2013/oct/11/david-byrne-internet-content-world>; Stuart Dredge, 'Thom Yorke calls Spotify "the last desperate fart of a dying corpse"' *The Guardian* (online) 7 October 2013 <www.theguardian.com/technology/2013/oct/07/spotify-thom-yorke-dying-corpse>. Generally, see also Eddie Schwartz, 'Code: fair trade music: letting the light shine in' in Susy Frankel and Daniel Gervais (eds), *The Evolution and Equilibrium of Copyright in the Digital Age* (Cambridge University Press, 2014).

106 The report is published at SNEP, *Le Marche De La Musique Enregistree-Bilan 2014* (3 February 2015) <www.snepmusique.com/actualites-du-snep/bilan-de-lannee-2014>, see English-language précis at Tim Ingham, *Major Labels Keep 73% of Spotify Premium Payouts – Report* (3 February 2015) Music Business Worldwide <www.musicbusinessworldwide.com/artists-get-7-of-streaming-cash-labels-take-46/>.

to support emerging authors.[107] Variations on the concept have since been adopted in a number of countries: some require payments to be made in perpetuity while others are limited in time; some attract remuneration for commercial uses only; fees can be flat percentages of revenue, lump sums, or determined by an independent body; some apply only to certain classes of works. Rights may belong to the state, authors' societies or unions. Some require prior permission, while others allow any use upon payment of a fee.[108] The author-right scheme envisaged in this work achieves many of the social and cultural advantages sought by paid public domain schemes while minimising their detriments. By operating on an opt-in basis instead of capturing every work by default, it would enable the public to obtain the full benefit of works that are worth less to authors than the nominal cost of registration. Combined with ongoing renewal requirements, it would enliven rather than stultify the public domain. Further, by allocating the rewards to specific authors rather than a general pool for reallocation, it avoids criticisms that have been made of some paid public domains: that they give the state too much control over culture[109] or that the revenues are 'just another tax'.[110]

---

107 David Falkayn, *A Guide to the Life, Times and Works of Victor Hugo* (University Press of the Pacific, 2001) 29. The proposal was made to a worldwide audience in a speech opening the 1878 International Literary Congress in Paris. The Congress ultimately passed a resolution recommending the adoption of a *domaine public payant*. Ricketson, *The Berne Convention For the Protection of Literary and Artistic Works: 1886–1986*, above n 2, 47.

108 For details of these nations and the outlines of their schemes see generally: United Nations Educational, Scientific and Cultural Organization – World Intellectual Property Organisation, *Committee of Non-Governmental Experts on the 'Domaine Public Payant – Analysis of the Replies to the Survey of Existing Provisions for the Application of the System of 'Domaine Public Payant'* in National Legislation*, UNESCO/WIPO/DPP/CE/I/2 (10 March 1982) <unesdoc.unesco.org/images/0004/000480/048044eb.pdf>; Peter Schonning, 'Survey of the term of protection of authors' rights: Toward More Universal Protection of Intangible Cultural Property' (2000; 11(4) *Entertainment Law Review* 59; Séverine Dusollier, 'Scoping Study on Copyright and Related Rights and the Public Domain', Committee on Development and Intellectual Property (CDIP), 4 March 2011, 39–40; Cathryn A Berryman, 'Toward More Universal Protection of Intangible Cultural Property' (1993–1994) 1 *Journal of Intellectual Property* 293. See also Ryszard Markiewicz and Janusz Barta, 'The new Polish Copyright Act – standards and particularities' (1995) 26(3) *International Review of Intellectual Property and Competition Law* 337, 342 (describing the 1994 introduction of a paying public domain into Polish law, which required 5–8 per cent of gross income from the sale of copies of expired works to be paid into a 'creativity promoting' fund).

109 That was the reason for the German proposal being derailed in 1965. See Davies, above n 5, 201. For a fuller history of this proposal see Paul Katzenberger, 'Die Diskussion um das "domaine public payant" in Deutschland' in *Festschrift für Georg Roeber* zum 10 Dezember 1981, Schriftenreihe der UFITA – Edition 63, Freiburg 1982, 193–230.

110 Dusollier, above n 108, 40; Carlos Mouchet, 'Problems of the "Domaine Public Payant"' (1983–1984) 8(2) *Columbia VLA Art & Law* 137.

Conclusions

This reimagined system doesn't just envisage giving creators a bigger slice of the cultural pie – it seeks to make the pie itself bigger. The online registry would actively facilitate markets between creators and exploiters. By increasing the opportunities for both commercial and non-commercial exploitation, reducing tracing and other transaction costs, and unlocking the value of works in which the creator has no further interest, the system would likely increase both revenue and consumer surplus. At the same time, the social welfare costs of granting rights in excess of what is necessary to incentivise production would be reduced by carving out certain socially valuable uses from the scope of the creator-right. That, combined with greater use of compulsory licenses, would facilitate the development of a broader range of initiatives for preserving and sharing our cultural heritage, including via digital public libraries, music repositories, film archives and more. Overall, the proposed system would maintain incentives while substantially improving access and securing a greater share of revenues to creators.

Despite its advantages however, this reimagined system would be impossible to implement. That is not because of technical limitations: the widespread ability to cheaply compile, store, communicate and access information, and the low transaction costs now involved in tracking usage and transferring funds, would make such a system perfectly feasible right now (at least in countries with developed communications infrastructure, which are also the biggest producers and users of copyrighted works).

It's impossible because we are welded to inexorable copyright terms via international treaties that make it 'virtually impossible to deal with term on a logical basis'.[111] Various elements of this proposal would fall foul of existing international obligations: by being shorter than mandated minimums, by requiring formalities, and by introducing carve-outs that could violate the three-step test.

---

111 Whitford Committee, *Report of the Committee to Consider the Law on Copyright and Designs* (March 1977) The Whitford Committee Report [41].

It would technically be possible to adapt elements of this proposal into an authors' reversion scheme which would still do a better job than our existing approach (by at least securing more of copyright's above-incentive rewards to creators) while being compliant with international law. However, such a compromise would do little to reduce the extraordinary societal loss that arises from the automatic locking away of our cultural heritage regardless of authors' continued interest in their works. And even this far-from-optimal solution would be politically infeasible in practice. Despite growing evidence that existing terms are actively counterproductive to what we want to achieve, there is persistent political pressure to extend them still further.[112] The powerful intermediaries who benefit most from existing frameworks and engage in constant rent-seeking to expand the rights of *owners* would fight ferociously against any proposal to allocate more rights to *authors*.

In recognition of this intractable practical problem, Landes and Posner have proposed a system of 'indefinitely renewable' copyright.[113] It would permit those right holders who indicate continued interest in their works to renew them *ad infinitum*. They argue that this would reduce the rent-seeking which occurs when still-valuable works near their expiry of protection, and at least cause those unwanted or less valued works to enter the public domain.[114] Such a system would do little to incentivise the production of additional works (for the reasons discussed at the beginning of this paper). And it would do little to recognise or reward the author's creative contributions, since the benefits would go to those who owned the works at the time of renewal. In fact, it would perpetuate the problem of copyright's rewards being co-opted by entrepreneurs or investors rather than creators or their heirs. But the proposal is nonetheless attractive, despite being unjustifiable on any recognised rationale for protection, because it would at least unlock a great deal of the culture that is cumulatively valuable to society despite being of no further interest to its owners. This kind of deal is perhaps the best we could hope for given current legal and political realities.

---

112 Buccafusco and Heald, above n 58, 10–11.
113 Landes and Posner, above n 20, 471.
114 Ibid 517–518.

It is not the point of this project to propose such compromises. This chapter unabashedly proposes an ideal. Copyright could do a much better job if freed it from existing constraints. We could design terms to simultaneously incentivise ongoing creation, increase social welfare, give creators a fair go, improve the preservation and dissemination of our cultural heritage and eliminate orphan works. Currently neglected value could be unlocked. We could make the pie bigger. If we better understood our motivations for granting copyright protection, and acted on them by disaggregating incentives and rewards, authors and the public alike could strike a far better deal. But although the ideas proposed for achieving these aims are not revolutionary, current frameworks simply won't admit them.

7

Copyright formalities: A return to registration?

Dev S Gangjee[1]

Introduction

Among the regimes constituting the field of intellectual property (IP) law, copyright stands apart. Unlike patent, trademark or (with some qualifications) design protection,[2] the recognition and enforcement of proprietary interests is automatic, arising upon creation. It is not conditioned upon the fulfilment of formalities.[3] This relative informality of copyright is celebrated as a virtue, as well as a necessary by-product of underlying normative commitments. However the ease with which proprietary rights are generated, their profusion and the ensuing difficulty of keeping track of them have led to calls for the (re)introduction of formalities, to bring some much-needed clarity to copyright entitlements.[4]

1   Faculty of Law, University of Oxford. I am profoundly grateful to the editors and my fellow contributors for comments during the workshop in Strasbourg (2014), which initiated this project, as well as to Jane Ginsburg for insightful suggestions and gentle rebuke.
2   While designs are protected via various registration-based regimes, they are also accommodated under copyright, unfair competition and unregistered designs systems. For a comprehensive review of national laws, see WIPO Secretariat, *Summary of Replies to the Questionnaires (Parts I and II) on Industrial Design Law and Practice (SCT/18/7 and SCT/18/8 Rev.)*, WIPO/Strad/INF/2 Rev.2 (19 June 2009).
3   S Dusollier, *Scoping Study on Copyright and Related Rights and the Public Domain*, WIPO Committee on Development and Intellectual Property, CDIP/7/INF/2 (4 Mar 2011), Annex 32.
4   The arguments of proponents and opponents are considered in Section 3 below.

Most other contemporary IP regimes continue to prescribe mandatory formalities – pre-eminently, registration[5] – as does real property, in the form of land registration. What's more, copyright was not always an outlier in this regard. Until the late 19th and early 20th centuries, formalities such as the registration of ownership, periodic renewal requirements, recording the transfer of ownership, signalling notice of protected status and the deposit of protected subject matter featured prominently in national copyright regimes.[6] The question taken up in this chapter is whether it would be in the public interest to adopt mandatory formalities once again and, if so, which ones.

The reintroduction of formalities is particularly suited to a thought experiment. A blank canvas seems necessary because the writing is otherwise on the wall, in the form of article 5(2) of the Berne Convention: 'The enjoyment and the exercise of these [Convention and national law] rights shall not be subject to any formality'.[7] This prohibition was subsequently reinforced, via its incorporation into the TRIPS Agreement and the WIPO Copyright Treaty.[8] While a Berne Union member remains free to impose formalities on its own nationals or works produced within that jurisdiction under article 5(3), works produced by non-domestic authors or initially published elsewhere cannot be subjected to formalities affecting the enjoyment (recognition) or exercise of copyright. Consequently, the vast majority of countries

---

5   B Sherman and L Bently, *The Making of Modern Intellectual Property Law: The British Experience 1760–1911* (Cambridge University Press, 1999) (For the definitive history of the emergence of registration systems in Britain and their significance in making intangible subject matter more 'manageable' as the object of property rights); C Dent, 'Registers of Artefacts of Creation – From the Late Medieval Period to the 19th Century' (2014) 3 *Laws* 239.

6   S van Gompel, *Formalities in Copyright Law: An Analysis of their History, Rationales and Possible Future* (Wolters Kluwer, 2011) (history of formalities in the UK, Continental Europe and the US); D Lipszyc, 'Historical Appearances and Disappearances of Formalities: From Berne to National Laws' in L Bently, U Suthersanen and P Torremans, *Global Copyright: Three Hundred Years from the Statute of Anne, from 1709 to Cyberspace* (Edward Elgar, 2010) 367 (history across Latin America).

7   *Berne Convention for the Protection of Literary and Artistic Works*, opened for signature 9 September 1886 (amended in 1914, 1928, 1948, 1967, 1971, and 1979) 1161 UNTS 3 ('Berne Convention'), 35.

8   See respectively Art 9(1) of TRIPS (*Marrakesh Agreement Establishing the World Trade Organization*, opened for signature 15 April 1994, 1867 UNTS 3 (entered into force 1 January 1995), annex IC (*Agreement on Trade-Related Aspects of Intellectual Property Right*)) and Art 1(4) of the WIPO Copyright Treaty (*World Intellectual Property Organization Copyright Treaty*, opened for signature 20 December 1996, 36 ILM 65, entered into force 6 March 2002).

do not impose mandatory formalities on their own nationals either.[9] The Berne prohibition ensured that copyright moved from being an opt-in system to one of largely automatic protection.

Contemporary debates are therefore preoccupied with the scope of the Berne prohibition and the room to manoeuvre around it.[10] By contrast, this chapter takes advantage of its counterfactual remit. Assuming we could have formalities today, would we want them? Its starting premise is a world without article 5(2) but having retained all the historical lessons around formalities. This speculative 'escape from history' is narrowly crafted, because of the obvious dangers of an abstract, functional or otherwise decontextualised approach to such a topic.[11] The other drawback of a counterfactual approach is the difficulty in establishing causation – change *this* aspect of copyright to achieve *that* desired outcome – when there are so many moving parts. As we will see below, formalities proposals resonate with issues ranging from protectable subject matter to the duration of copyright protection. This chapter is therefore very much intended to be read alongside the other contributions in this volume.

Such a thought experiment is nevertheless valuable because the question of 'who owns what' looms large over copyright. Molly Van Houweling describes the problem as having three dimensions:

> proliferation (how many works are subject to copyright ownership), distribution (how many different people own copyrights), and fragmentation (how many, what type, and what size of separately-owned rights exist within each copyright bundle). As proliferation, distribution, and fragmentation increase, copyright becomes more atomistic.[12]

---

9   S van Gompel, *'Les formalités sont mortes, vive les formalités!* Copyright Formalities and the Reasons for their Decline in Nineteenth Century Europe' in R Deazley, M Kretschmer and L Bently (eds), *Privilege and Property: Essays on the History of Copyright* (OpenBook Publishers, 2010), 157 n1.

10   For the scope of the Berne Convention prohibition, see S Ricketson and J Ginsburg, *International Copyright and Neighbouring Rights: The Berne Convention and Beyond,* (Oxford University Press, 2nd ed, 2006) 325. On the room to manoeuvre, see the contributions to the Symposium Issue 'Reform(aliz)ing Copyright for the Internet Age' (2013) 28 *Berkeley Technology Law Journal.*

11   On the dangers of universal theoretical models which ignore historical context, see P Knapp, 'Can Social Theory Escape from History? Views of History in Social Science' (1984) 23(1) *History and Theory* 34.

12   MS Van Houweling, 'Author Autonomy and Atomism in Copyright Law' (2010) 96 *Virginia Law Review* 549, 553.

This fragmented patchwork of entitlements in turn generates greater search and transaction costs, especially since the legal and technological context within which copyright operates has undergone a paradigm shift.

> In the past, a short term of copyright coupled with formalities and the natural restraints that arose in the hard copy world—significant costs in production and distribution— limited the public's innocent exposure to copyright infringement. With a functionally perpetual copyright duration, no formalities, and instant global distribution, matters have greatly changed.[13]

The principal problem that formalities address is that of inadequate information. Van Houweling illustrates this with the discovery of an old photograph, which qualifies as protectable subject matter:

> It could be in the public domain because [it didn't satisfy previously-applicable mandatory formalities or because] its copyright has expired; or it could be under copyright, held by an unknown copyright holder. Without more information (or an applicable limitation like fair use), the only safe assumption is that all of those activities that implicate the exclusive rights granted by copyright … are prohibited.[14]

Given the growing appetite for the reuse of content online, the lack of adequate information inhibits rights clearance efforts while also impeding the reuse of material that might already be in the public domain and freely available for repurposing. This in turn encourages either caution (to the point where rights clearance costs entirely prevents projects) or rampant infringement.

Such high information costs and the attendant ambiguity are all the more puzzling when we live in an information society. Technological developments directly address one of the primary motivations for article 5(2), which responded to the difficulties experienced by creators confronted with a daunting array of jurisdiction-specific formalities. However the 'pragmatic arguments that inspired the abolition of formalities from national and international copyright law have also largely evaporated in the digital age. Nowadays, registration and deposit can be organized much more efficiently and made applicable

---

13   W Patry, *How to Fix Copyright* (Oxford University Press, 2011) 204.
14   MS Van Houweling, 'Land Recording and Copyright Reform' (2013) 28 *Berkeley Technology Law Journal* 1497, 1498.

to virtually any type of work'.[15] Revisiting the question of formalities is neither regressive nor backwards looking. According to Maria Pallante, the US Register of Copyrights, to 'address twenty-first century challenges we need twenty-first century solutions ... the question is not whether the rules of the nineteenth and early twentieth centuries should be reintroduced, but rather, whether new rules might serve the policy objectives of the digital age'.[16]

Against this backdrop, this chapter specifically considers whether mandatory or strongly incentivised registration would serve the public interest better than automatic copyright. To that end, section 2 defines formalities, and introduces the most common types historically associated with copyright law. The rationales for formalities are then mapped on to distinct public interest outcomes. Section 3 reviews the arguments both for and against the reintroduction of formalities. The concerns underlying article 5(2) of Berne would have to be addressed by any reform efforts. Bearing these in mind, section 4 contains the principal substantive contribution of this chapter. It outlines what a mandatory copyright registration system at the national level might look like. It draws inductively upon existing studies of voluntary copyright registration, and other IP and land registration systems. Section 5 concludes that, given the option, it would be irrational to continue to operate as we presently do.

1. Formalities and the public interest

1.1. What are formalities?

Broadly understood, formalities 'refer to the procedural mechanisms which are required for acquiring a valid copyright, such as registration, notice, deposit, or renewal procedures'.[17] They are conditions *independent of those substantive requirements* relating to the creation of the work, such as the originality or fixation

---

15   van Gompel, above n 5, 263.

16   MA Pallante, 'The Curious Case of Copyright Formalities' (2013) 28 *Berkeley Technology Law Journal* 1415, 1416.

17   C Sprigman, 'Reform(aliz)ing Copyright' (2004) 57 *Stanford Law Review* 485, 487.

requirements.[18] Land law scholars further emphasise the distinction between substance and form, so that 'in law, a formality is a requirement that matters of substance must be put into a particular form (in order to have a specified legal effect)' with sanctions for non-compliance.[19]

Thus the article 5(2) prohibition encompasses 'everything which must be complied with in order to ensure that the rights of the author with regard to his work may come into existence' as well as prerequisites before the right can be exercised.[20] However the prohibition is copyright-specific and does not extend to generally applicable rules of evidence and procedure. Finally, formalities have varied across jurisdictions, historical periods and categories of works. While there was a notice requirement for engravings, prints and photographs in some situations, there was an additional deposit requirement for literary works in others.[21]

1.2. Types of formalities

Certain copyright formalities have largely dropped away from contemporary debates. Examples would be a 'local manufacturing or working' requirement, which called for printing within a jurisdiction and favoured local labour interests,[22] as well as opt-out formalities, whereby the right holder needs to expressly claim rights over certain uses of a work (e.g. producing translations) by way of a notice.[23] The ones considered below remain relevant and have direct parallels with the other IP regimes, namely:

---

18   Mihály Ficsor, *Guide to the Copyright and Related Rights Treaties Administered by WIPO and Glossary of Copyright and Related Terms* (WIPO, 2003), [BC-5.7].
19   P Critchley, 'Taking Formalities Seriously' in S Bright and J Dewar (eds), *Land Law: Themes and Perspectives* (Oxford University Press, 1998) 507, 508.
20   J Ginsburg, 'The US Experience with Copyright Formalities: A Love-Hate Relationship' (2010) 33 *Columbia Journal of Law and the Arts* 311, 315–316.
21   van Gompel, above n 5, Ch 3.
22   Ginsburg, above n 19, 313. Ginsburg revisits opt-out formalities in the context of mass digitisation projects, arguing that a presumption to authorise digitisation and dissemination, unless the author actively opts out, would be incompatible with the Berne Convention. See JC Ginsburg, 'Berne-Forbidden Formalities and Mass Digitization' (2016) 96 *Boston University Law Review* 101.
23   Exemplified by Art 10*bis*(1) of the Berne Convention, which permits the reproduction of articles on current events in the press or contained in broadcasts, unless rights over this content are expressly reserved. See M Senftleben, 'How to Overcome the Normal Exploitation Obstacle: Opt-Out Formalities, Embargo Periods, and the International Three-Step Test' (2014) (1) *Berkeley Technology Law Journal Commentaries* 1.

1.2.1. Registration

Registration is a requirement common to patent, trademark and industrial design protection regimes, where the object of protection is identified within a publicly accessible register.[24] The application also contains information regarding ownership and the priority date for protection. For copyright registries, additional details relate to the category of work (literary, musical, artistic etc.); its title; the date and place of publication; and details related to the payment of fees.[25] For some IP regimes, public registration[26] is unavoidable, being intrinsically linked to their normative foundations. Patent protection for example represents a bargain between the inventor and the public. New and useful technical information is disclosed within a publicly accessible register, in return for the grant of proprietary rights.[27] For such systems, the question of *what* is protected has additional significance, but the question of *who* (i.e. ownership) has importance across all fields of proprietary entitlements. Property law:

> is centrally concerned with coordinating multiple rights in the same asset and managing the information burden that property rights place on third parties ... Since property rights are enforceable in rem against third parties, anyone wishing to acquire or deal with a resource incurs information costs in discovering and measuring any private property rights that may be held in the resource.[28]

Registration facilitates both publicity and – when coupled with rigorous examination – trustworthiness.[29]

In turn, accessible ownership information improves the security of title and facilitates the transfer of proprietary interests (or licensing, in the case of IP) which makes for a more efficient marketplace. Registration

---

24 van Gompel, n 5, [2.1.1].

25 WIPO, *Summary of the Responses to the Questionnaire for Survey on Copyright Registration and Deposit Systems*, (WIPO, 2010) Part A - 8.

26 Public here has two connotations: both publicly managed, i.e. operated by the state, as well as publicly accessible, so the information is widely available.

27 R Burrell, 'Trade Mark Bureaucracies', in GB Dinwoodie and M Janis (eds), *Trade Mark Law and Theory: A Handbook of Contemporary Research* (Edward Elgar, 2008) 95, 96–97 (Querying whether trademark registration is therefore essential, given the incomplete and imperfect information associated with the register).

28 P O'Connor, 'The Extension of Land Registration Principles to New Property Rights in Environmental Goods' in M Dixon, *Modern Studies in Property Law, Vol 5* (Hart, 2009) 363, 364.

29 M Ilmari Niemi 'The Public Trustworthiness of Land Registers in the Nordic Countries' in E Cooke (ed), *Modern Studies in Property Law, Vol 1* (Hart, 2000) 329, 329.

simplifies proof, reduces risk and streamlines transactions.[30] To facilitate the comprehensiveness of ownership records, registration is therefore either mandatory[31] or optional but incentivised via the provision of evidentiary or remedial advantages.[32] This logic broadly applies to IP registration with some qualifications, as section 4 elaborates below.

1.2.2. Renewal

Once an IP registration is obtained, it requires renewal after a specified period in order to prolong protection up to the maximum term available. Trademark protection is available indefinitely, but requires periodic renewal every 10 years.[33] To avail of the maximum 20-year term in patent law, maintenance fees must be paid, varying from an annual maintenance fee to one payable every three or four years.[34] Historically, many copyright registration systems had a renewal requirement and the US is notable for having retained both mandatory registration and renewal until relatively recently.[35] Under the *Copyright Act of 1909*, after an initial 28-year period of registered protection from the date of first publication, a second statutory term of 28 years was available upon applying for renewal. Without renewal, the work would enter the public domain.[36] As a potential policy lever, the renewal process discourages the (re-)registration of commercially insignificant works.[37] Research reviewing renewal data as a proxy for the author's desire to maintain protection concludes that less than 15 per cent of all US registered copyrights were being renewed after the initial term of protection across the 20th century.[38] Renewal of copyright registration historically served a filtering function, with works which are no longer renewed passing into the public domain.[39]

---

30 P O'Connor, 'Registration of Title in England and Australia: A Theoretical and Comparative Analysis' in E Cooke (ed), *Modern Studies in Property Law, Vol 2* (Hart, 2003) 81, 84.

31 For a review of the UK's transition to a mandatory, constitutive registration system i.e. title *by* registration, see E Cooke, *The New Law of Land Registration* (Hart, 2003).

32 For an overview of US land registration principles, see Van Houweling, above n 13.

33 WIPO Secretariat, *Summary of Replies to the Questionnaire on Trade Mark Law and Practice (SCT/11/6)*, WIPO/STrad/INF/1 Rev (25 January 2010), 182–190.

34 WIPO, *Intellectual Property Handbook: Policy, Law and Use* (WIPO Publication No. 489(E), 2nd ed, 2004), [2.82].

35 The history of US formalities is reviewed in Ginsburg, above n 19, 322–331; van Gompel, above n 5, Ch 3.

36 S 23 of the *Copyright Act of 1909*; 17 USC § 24 (1947).

37 WM Landes and RA Posner, 'Indefinitely Renewable Copyright' (2003) 70 *University of Chicago Law Review* 471 (Advocating sufficiently high fees to encourage such weeding out).

38 Sprigman, above n 16, 519–521.

39 *Kahle v Gonzales*, 487 F3d 697, 699 (9th Cir, 2007).

1.2.3. Recordation

Recordation or recordal requires that information about transfers, or the creation of related property interests (such as charges) be made publicly available. The 'key to an effective recording system is its completeness, and ideally all links in a chain of title should be placed on record'.[40] Recordation complements a mandatory registration system that provides the initial information identifying the copyrighted work, first ownership and the commencement of the copyright term. Alternatively this information could be submitted alongside that relating to the transfer of ownership.[41] According to Pallante:

> [the] recordation system is extremely important because it has the potential to connect registration information … to the ongoing chain of commerce for a particular work (which could span decades). It provides information regarding who has acquired what exclusive rights and whether and how copyright ownership has changed hands.[42]

Recordal has significant effects – it generally constitutes notice to the world at large of the facts recorded, and the transferee receives priority over (i) subsequent conflicting transfers or interests, (ii) as well as (potentially) against prior but unrecorded interests, so long as there was no actual notice of their existence.[43] Recordation must usually occur within a specified time window to be effective.[44]

1.2.4. Notice

Notices are used in IP regimes to signal the protected status of subject matter – the familiar ® or ™ symbols associated with trademark law, or the © symbol in association with the first owner's name and year of publication are fairly ubiquitous. In general the adoption of

---

40 A Latman, *The Recordation of Copyright Assignments and Licenses* (US Copyright Office, Study No 19, 1998) 124–125.

41 JC Ginsburg, '"With Untired Spirits and Formal Constancy": Berne Compatibility of Formal Declaratory Measures to Enhance Copyright Title-Searching' (2013) 28(3) *Berkeley Technology Law Journal* 1583.

42 Statement of Maria A Pallante, Register of Copyrights and Director of the United States Copyright Office, 'Oversight of the U.S. Copyright Office', Hearing Before the Subcommittee on Courts, Intellectual Property, and the Internet, Committee on the Judiciary United States House of Representatives (18 September 2014).

43 For the effects of 'race', 'notice' and 'race-notice' regimes, see A Green et al, *Improving Copyright Information Management: An Investigation of Options and Areas for Further Research* (Stanford Law School, Law and Policy Lab 2014) 20.

44 van Gompel, above n 5, [2.1.3].

such notices is entirely voluntary,[45] with legal rules sanctioning only their misleading use.[46] However legal consequences are possible, as US history illustrates. The Copyright Acts of 1790, 1802 and the 1831–1905 Acts all required the record of registration to be published – initially in newspapers and subsequently in a specified location on the work (the title page).[47] Failure to comply initially resulted in exclusion from protection and subsequently publication without notice shifted the work into the public domain. This requirement has been diluted over time: and today the only significant consequence is that the defence of innocent infringement may be available where a published work lacks a copyright notice.[48] The interesting aspect of the US copyright notice requirement is that from 1909 it became detached from the registration requirement and operated as a standalone formality. Therefore, a standalone notice requirement coupled with an effective recordation register – both being obligatory – might ensure that up-to-date ownership as well as term information was provided to the public.

1.2.5. Deposit

Depositing one or more copies of the work for which protection is desired has been a feature of copyright legislation since at least the Statute of Anne:

> Those who printed books were obliged to deposit nine copies with the Stationers Company for distribution to the Royal Library, six Universities, Sion College in London and the Faculty of Advocates in Edinburgh; failure to do so made not only the printer but the 'proprietor' and bookseller liable to a fine ... The obligation was collateral in the sense that deposit was not an express condition of protection under the Statute.[49]

---

45   A notable counter-example is the obligatory requirement to signal protected geographical indication status in the EU. See D Gangjee, 'Proving Provenance: Geographical Indication Certification and its Ambiguities' (2017) *World Development* (forthcoming).

46   van Gompel, above n 5, [2.1.5].

47   For a very convenient history in tabular form, see Ginsburg, n 19, 326–327.

48   A Reid, 'Claiming the Copyright' (2016) 34 *Yale Law and Policy Review* 425 (advocating a return to an effective notice requirement as a means of claiming copyright, by proposing an 'innocent infringer' defence in the absence of such claiming).

49   W Cornish, 'The Statute of Anne 1709–10: Its Historical Setting' in L Bently, U Suthersanen and P Torremans, *Global Copyright: Three Hundred Years from the Statute of Anne, from 1709 to Cyberspace* (Edward Elgar, 2010) 14, 23.

Here the public interest lay in increasing collections in public libraries and developing cultural repositories. A WIPO survey indicates that a deposit requirement has been widely adopted.[50] However over time, it has become detached from the question of copyright subsistence. The penalty for non-compliance is usually a fine and not the forfeiture of copyright.[51]

The WIPO survey also documents the various functions served by a deposit requirement:[52]

- Proof of both publication and (potentially) the date of creation
- Proof of ownership
- Supporting research and development by making publications available
- Preservation of cultural heritage (archiving) along with the publication of a national bibliography
- Statistical information generated from deposited works.

Beyond these functions, deposit also assists in the process of identifying the intangible object of protection. In the absence of representative registration, a deposit of the physical embodiment of the work – the actual book itself – was the exemplar of the intangible subject matter.[53]

The formalities identified above can be further classified in terms of their legal nature and effects. Stef van Gompel has developed a helpful taxonomy,[54] differentiating between mandatory and voluntary formalities while going on to consider further divisions based on legal effects: (i) 'constitutive', operating as necessary preconditions for protection; (ii) 'maintenance' focused, such as renewal; and (iii) 'declaratory', which are required for giving effect to rights previously recognised. We might also distinguish between the 'old-style' formalities discussed above and 'new-style' formalities, which embrace digital technology to facilitate ownership tracing.[55]

---

50   WIPO, *Summary of the Responses to the Questionnaire for Survey on Copyright Registration and Deposit Systems*, (WIPO, 2010), Part B - 1.

51   Ibid.

52   Ibid 2.

53   See Section 4, below.

54   van Gompel, above n 5, [2.2]–[2.2.4].

55   van Gompel, 'Copyright Formalities in the Internet Age: Filters of Protection or Facilitators of Licensing' (2013) 28(3) *Berkeley Technology Law Journal* 1425, 1435.

This would include private sector digital repositories of rights management information and metadata associated with digital works, which have both benefits and drawbacks.[56] Alternatively, Christopher Sprigman has described new-style formalities as Berne-compliant 'nudges' to provide ownership information, by offering attractive remedial options for doing so.[57]

1.3. Correlating formalities with public interest(s)

The public interest features frequently in copyright (and broader IP) doctrine and debates, either to advance proposals for reform or to serve as the baseline against which to assess new developments.[58] At its core, the grant of private proprietary rights over intangibles is conventionally understood to promote the public interest, based on consequential reasoning.[59] However the very appeal of this term – its capaciousness – is also its weakness. It has been considered vague, is difficult to measure, has been used inconsistently by different writers and many of its concepts are considered indistinguishable from morality.[60] Another major concern, which is nicely illustrated in the copyright context, is the difficulty in identifying a homogenous collective interest. What happens when the interests of authors/ creators and the general public, or that of creators and those who invest in or distribute creative works diverge? Or if one of these groups claims to speak in the name of all?

However neither of these concerns is insurmountable. Drawing on the public interest(s) as a reference point for rethinking copyright remains compelling for three reasons.[61] First, alongside equally resonant terms like justice and freedom, the public interest functions as a normative

---

56   See Section 4, below.
57   CJ Sprigman, 'Berne's Vanishing Ban on Formalities' (2013) 28(3) *Berkeley Technology Law Journal* 1565, 1566–1567.
58   S Siy, 'Two Halves of the Copyright Bargain: Defining the Public Interest in Copyright' 31 *Cardozo Arts & Entertainment Law Journal* 683; PA Jaszi, 'Goodbye to All That – A Reluctant (and Perhaps Premature) Adieu to Constitutionally-Grounded Discourse of Public Interest in Copyright Law' (1997) 29 *Vanderbilt Journal of Transnational Law* 595; *Washington Declaration on Intellectual Property and the Public Interest* (2011).
59   R Merges, *Justifying Intellectual Property* (Harvard University Press, 2011) 3.
60   See B Bozeman, *Public Values and Public Interest: Counterbalancing Economic Individualism* (Georgetown University Press, 2007) 83–99.
61   See Rebecca Giblin and Kimberlee Weatherall, 'If we redesigned copyright from scratch, what might it look like?', this volume.

ideal, creating the space to debate the political morality of legislative measures. It can also be particularised, having specific meanings within a defined context – here, copyright law in the early 21st century, with its attendant international constraints, encoded assumptions regarding creation and distribution as well as economic and technological context. Second, it is the antidote to pure self-interest or divisive group politics. It encourages a broader understanding of social relations and provides the language for resisting the marketisation of state functions, a utopian vision of markets and a preference for private ordering.[62] Following on from this, it aligns with pluralistic copyright theorising which acknowledges norms in addition to those identified by a consequentialist approach which prioritises economic efficiency to maximise public welfare.[63] The third reason builds on the second. As a normative counterweight to reductive economic individualism, the public interest 'may be presumed to be what [people] would choose if they saw clearly, thought rationally, acted disinterestedly and benevolently'.[64] So a copyright system designed in the public interest would result, as discussed by Giblin and Weatherall in their introduction, if people chose from behind the 'veil of ignorance'[65] while also having in mind both market as well as non-market values (e.g. facilitating democratic deliberation) when making this choice.

With this in mind, what purposes do formalities serve and how does this align with the public interest? A helpful first move is to disaggregate the category of formalities. While formalities serve an array of distinct goals, two are prominent in contemporary debates.[66] The first is the provision of reliable information regarding the ownership of copyright works.[67] Thus registration, notice and recordation all serve to ensure

---

62   LD Brown and LR Jacobs, *The Private Abuse of the Public Interest: Market Myths and Policy Muddles* (University of Chicago Press, 2008) 2.

63   The literature is reviewed in O Bracha and T Syed, 'Beyond Efficiency: Consequence-Sensitive Theories of Copyright' (2014) 29 *Berkley Technology Law Journal* 229.

64   W Lippmann, cited in Bozeman, above n 59, 83. Bozeman, at 17, provides an alternative conception emphasising the inter-generational, social dimension: 'An ideal public interest refers to those outcomes best serving the long-run survival and well-being of a social collective construed as a "public"'.

65   See Rebecca Giblin and Kim Weatherall, 'If we redesigned copyright from scratch, what might it look like?', this volume.

66   As reflected in the choice of title: 'Filters of Protection of Facilitators of Licensing'. See van Gompel, above n 54.

67   Ibid 1443. See also Pamela Samuelson et al, 'The Copyright Principles Project: Directions for Reform' (2010) 25 *Berkeley Technology Law Journal* 1175, 1186 (pointing out that current incentives for registration in the US have not guaranteed an informative register).

that owners are easier to trace, which facilitates rights clearance transactions. Assuming that we are not challenging the entire edifice of copyright and a regime of author-protective proprietary rights is considered appropriate, the provision of better quality information regarding ownership is clearly in the public interest. The benefits were previously summarised in section 2.2(a), when considering the rationale for land registration systems. In contemporary copyright scholarship new-style formalities, such as incentivising the provision of publicly accessible rights management information, are thought to have similar potential.[68]

The second major goal is the enhancement of the public domain, also referred to as the filtering function of formalities.[69] For works which are protected, accessible information about subsistence would enable accurate predictions about when they will enter the public domain, removing much of the present ambiguity. More importantly, constitutive formalities act as an entry level barrier into copyright protection, by requiring positive acts on the part of those seeking protection. Non-compliance with formalities is likely to result in more works entering the public domain.[70] A burgeoning public domain that is regularly replenished has several advantages, which are considered to be in the public interest.[71] It facilitates a vibrant cultural commons, which is considered the wellspring for future creative endeavours;[72] it makes a viable public sphere possible, as envisaged by Jürgen Habermas, with the capacity to critique the state since political discourse can draw on the matrix of cultural production;[73] and – despite no IP protection – generates considerable economic value.[74]

---

68   van Gompel, above n 54, 1443.
69   WIPO, *Copyright Registration and Documentation Systems*, WIPO: <www.wipo.int/copyright/en/activities/copyright_registration/> ('Registration can also help to delimit the public domain, and consequently facilitate access to creative content for which no authorization from the right owner is needed'); BA Greenberg, 'More Than Just a Formality: Instant Authorship and Copyright's Opt-Out Future in the Digital Age' (2012) 59 *UCLA Law Review* 1028, 1043–1044; Ginsburg, above n 19, 312–313; Sprigman, above n 16, 487.
70   van Gompel, above n 54, 1433.
71   G Davies, 'The Public Interest in the Public Domain' in C Waelde and H MacQueen, *Intellectual Property: The Many Faces of the Public Domain* (Edward Elgar, 2007) 86.
72   J Boyle, *The Public Domain: Enclosing the Commons of the Mind* (Yale University Press, 2008).
73   M Rose, 'Nine-tenths of the Law: The English Copyright Debate and the Rhetoric of the Public Domain', 66 *Law & Contemporary Problems*, 75.
74   Dussolier, above n 2, 19–20; K Erickson et al, *Copyright and the Value of the Public Domain* (UK IPO, 2015).

However the counterpoint to this is that the public interest in supporting authors/creators could be deprioritised in a system which adopts constitutive formalities. Thus 'formalities predicate to the existence or enforcement of copyright can serve to shield large copyright owners who routinely comply with formalities from the infringement claims of smaller copyright owners, particularly individual authors, who may lack the information or resources systematically to register and deposit their works'.[75] Here the balancing of competing public interests, via appropriate institutional design choices, is essential. Having mapped the main categories of formalities and identified the public interests at stake, it is possible to assess more detailed arguments for and against their adoption.

2. Arguments for and against formalities

Today the reintroduction or adaptation of formalities is under serious consideration. Formalities have found favourable mention in policy documents addressing copyright's more serious deficiencies.[76] The problem of orphan works is also helping to focus minds on their potential. Orphan work is 'a term used to describe the situation where the owner of a copyrighted work cannot be identified and located by someone who wishes to make use of the work in a manner that requires permission of the copyright owner'.[77] Tracing difficulties vary across categories of works. A study for the European Commission estimates that 13 per cent of in-copyright books, 90 per cent of photographs in museum collections and 129,000 films in film archives are orphaned.[78] Where authors are unidentifiable or cannot be traced, the risk of litigation is enough to deter libraries, archives, publishers and filmmakers from making use of the work.

---

75 Ginsburg, above n 19, 313.
76 UK IPO, © *The Way Ahead: A Strategy for Copyright in the Digital Age* (2009), [108]–[109]; Samuelson et al, above n 66, Part III, Recommendations 1 and 2; Report of the Comité des Sages, *The New Renaissance* (Brussels, 10 January 2011) 5, 18–19, 20–21; Australian Law Reform Commission, 'Copyright and the Digital Economy' (Discussion Paper 79, May 2013), 265.
77 US Copyright Office, *Report on Orphan Works: A Report of the Register of Copyrights* (2006) 15. To similar effect, see Art 2 of *Directive 2012/28/EU of the European Parliament and of the Council of 25 October 2012 on Certain Permitted Uses of Orphan Works*, [2012] OJ L 299, 5.
78 A Vuopala, *Assessment of the Orphan Works Issue and Costs for Rights Clearance* (European Commission, DG Information Society and Media Unit E4: Access to Information, May 2010) 4–5.

Even attempting to trace right holders is time-consuming and expensive. The BBC's Archive Trial reported that checking 1,000 hours of the most straightforward content – factual programming – for rights clearance cost them 6,500 person hours. Extrapolating from available figures on clearance and the associated costs, the UK Intellectual Property Office has estimated that it would take between £6.6 billion and £8.4 billion to fully search and clear the content of the BBC archives and the British Library.[79] The orphan works problem is a direct consequence of 'informal' copyright and the insufficiency of ownership information.[80] The result is stalled digitisation projects, endemic uncertainty and the regrettable under-utilisation of considerable cultural resources.

These difficulties have given rise to a body of scholarship exploring the benefits of technologically upgraded and sensitively adapted variants of historic formalities. With the notable exception of van Gompel's detailed historical and comparative work, the majority of these scholars draw on US experiences with formalities, which remained central to copyright protection until 1976, before diminishing in 1989.[81] A high-altitude survey of arguments in support of formalities would look something like this: a copyright register reduces search and tracing costs. Yet historical experience suggests registration was an unacceptable burden for authors, especially those seeking international copyright protection. The subsequent abandonment of formalities resulted in an inefficient and opaque property regime, more 'mud' than 'crystals' when it comes to defining entitlements. Present day digital technologies have made the Library of Alexandria dream of universally accessible knowledge appear tantalisingly within reach. Digital technology, in the form of cheap, effective e-filing and digital deposits, coupled with vastly improved search capabilities,

---

79 UK IPO Consultation, *Copyright Works: Seeking the Lost* (UK IPO, 2014) 65–70.
80 DR Hansen, 'Orphan Works: Causes of the Problem' (White Paper No 3, Berkeley Digital Library Copyright Project, 2012) 11.
81 See Landes and Posner, above n 36; Sprigman, above n 16; J Gibson, 'Once and Future Copyright' (2005) 81 *Notre Dame Law Review* 167; D Fagundes, 'Crystals in the Public Domain' (2009) 50 *Boston College Law Review* 139; Samuelson et al, above n 66; Patry, above n 12, 203–209; van Gompel, above n 5. Digitally enhanced formalities also feature in the work of Lawrence Lessig: see e.g. *The Future of Ideas: The Fate of the Commons in a Connected World* (Random House, 2001) 251–252 and *Remix: Making Art and Commerce Thrive in the Hybrid Economy* (Bloomsbury, 2008) 260–265.

also means that formalities need not be cumbersome or expensive.[82] Non-compliance also need not deprive an author of copyright. Instead a pause button might be pressed: via a moratorium on infringement claims until registration, or limits on the scope of available remedies. Formalities would therefore help channel more works into the public domain as well as facilitate rights clearance, through the provision of accurate, periodically refreshed information. Registration would additionally generate reliable 'big data' on the culture industries, while digital deposits would function as a cultural repository.

There is, however, another side to this story, since formalities were abandoned for good reasons. The first objection relates to the incompatibility of formalities with the underlying conceptual and normative commitments of copyright regimes in *droit d'auteur* systems. Central to this argument is a natural rights-based justification – whether Lockean or Hegelian – which privileges the act of creation itself.[83] As Ginsburg puts it, if 'copyright is born with the work, then no further state action should be necessary to confer the right; the sole relevant act is the work's creation'.[84] Mandatory formalities fashioned to achieve instrumental outcomes, such as the public availability of better quality information, should not be permitted to trump these natural rights foundations.

This objection has been thoroughly investigated by van Gompel and his conclusion is both nuanced and convincing. Towards the end of the 19th century:

> there was a growing consensus that the existence of copyright should not be subject to formalities and that failure to comply with formalities should never be the occasion of a loss of copyright … At the same time, it was acknowledged that the protection of literary and artistic works was not unconditional, but should always be established in accordance with the public interest and societal order.[85]

---

82 For interesting insights into bureaucratic registration systems as a form of technology, see Dent, above n 4.

83 Daniel Gervais and Dashiell Renaud, 'The Future of United States Copyright Formalities: Why We Should Prioritize Recordation, and How To Do It' (2013) 28(3) *Berkeley Technology Law Journal* 1459, 1463.

84 JC Ginsburg, 'A Tale of Two Copyrights: Literary Property in Revolutionary France and America' (1990) 64 *Tulane Law Review* 991, 994.

85 van Gompel, above n 5, [3.3.2.1].

While natural rights foundations were in tension with constitutive formalities relating to the *existence or acquisition* of proprietary rights, the *exercise* of these rights could be regulated in the public interest. Meanwhile the Berne prohibition was based on practical difficulties faced by authors seeking to secure copyright protection abroad and did not arise from epistemological or justificatory divergences.[86]

Turning to these practical impediments, the first relates to the difficulties in satisfying formalities requirements and the second relates to the harsh consequences for not complying with them. For the former, historic experience indicates:

> the failure [might not] be attributable to the author (for example, if the formality could also be legally complied with by the publisher), if a formality was not fulfilled because of the intricacy and costs involved (for instance, if the facilities where the formality must be completed were located too far away) or if it concerned mere technical failures (for example, innocent mistakes or late submissions of applications). In the nineteenth century, it was not uncommon for authors to lose protection as a result of any of these practicalities.[87]

For the latter, Ginsburg suggests that the US experience is more of a cautionary tale than an inspirational template. Disproportionate penalties for non-compliance are manifestly unfair, since:

> not all those who fail to fulfil these obligations do so because they do not care about their works. Some lose track; some are ignorant of the obligation, particularly if they reside in foreign countries which do not impose formalities; some may find the fees prohibitive.[88]

A third concern is that formalities – and registration in particular – will favour commercial copyright owners as well as repeat players. It has been argued that the US regime, which incentivises formalities, 'privileges the interests of repeat, sophisticated rights holders, often at the expense of smaller, less sophisticated creators'.[89] Nina Elkin-Koren points out that the hypothetical calculus underpinning formalities – estimating whether a work is sufficiently valuable to protect – is seriously flawed, since creators may not be able to assess the value

---

86 van Gompel, above n 8, 158.
87 Ibid 185.
88 Ginsburg, above n 19, 342.
89 J Tehranian, 'The Emperor Has No Copyright: Registration, Cultural Hierarchy, and the Myth of Copyright Militancy' (2009) 24 *Berkeley Technology Law Journal* 1399, 1399.

of their works *ex ante*. The regime might be biased towards repeat players in the content industry and disadvantage individual creators.[90] The resulting danger is that individuals who may occasionally wish to exercise their copyright will lose out. It 'seems unfair for someone to capture sensational news on a photo, post it online to share it with friends, and then see her photo being (commercially) exploited by various kinds of news services'.[91]

These are legitimate concerns that should be reflected in the design of any reform proposals. However recent empirical research on voluntary US copyright registration suggests that there is a roughly even split between individuals and firms in terms of overall registrations (51.9 per cent by firms and 48.1 per cent by individuals). Variations emerge along the lines of categories of works.

> Nearly two thirds of Sound Recording, Text, and Visual Material are registered by firms. Dramatic Work, Music, and Sound Recording and Music are predominately registered by individuals. The remainder, Sound Recording and Text, are relatively evenly split between individuals and firms. These percentages are consistent with notions of how accessible markets are to individuals.[92]

Current practice therefore suggests that individuals are willing to register for certain categories of works.

The fourth concern follows directly on from the narrowness of a system focusing on commercially motivated repeat players, at the cost of user-generated content and social production. The paradigm for vast swathes of cultural creation and distribution has shifted. Apart from lowering transaction costs, a digital network 'brings about more fundamental changes, transforming the way we create, disseminate, and consume cultural works'.[93] Individuals are both authors and users of existing works since '[w]orks in digital format can be easily mixed and matched, cut and pasted, or edited and remixed. The ease of changing and adapting enables users to appropriate cultural icons to express new meanings and to aggregate existing works into new

---

90 Nina Elkin-Koren, 'Can Formalities Save the Public Domain' (2013) 28(3) *Berkeley Technology Law Journal* 1537, 1543.

91 van Gompel, above n 54, 1442.

92 D Oliar, N Pattison, K Ross Powell, 'Copyright Registrations: Who, What, When, Where and Why' (2014) 92 *Texas Law Review* 2211, 2226.

93 Elkin-Koren, above n 89, 1545.

content'.[94] Should bloggers or online parodists be forced down the path of formalities? And how should collaboratively produced works such as Wikipedia be incorporated into any system of formalities?[95]

Finally, in a mandatory formalities regime which discourages individual, non-professional creators, who ultimately harvests the benefits of creative labour in a digital ecosystem? One suggested answer is online intermediaries, who would like their content 'inputs to be "free" (in both cost and repurposing senses) while they need their outputs to be appropriable if they want to receive a return on investment for their innovations'.[96] Alternatively, if the expectation is that everyone can opt-in to formalities, by setting the qualification thresholds low enough, we are then faced with the problem of scale. There will simply be too many works to keep up with formalities and for many creative professionals who make use of the internet, registering each tweet or photograph will quickly add up, making even reasonably priced registration prohibitively expensive.[97] However Ginsburg suggests a response to this in the form of a combination of an annual registration account into which a discounted annual blanket fee could be paid, which covers one year's output for a specified type of work.[98]

The fifth concern is that we should we careful what we wish for. A perfect and accessible record of ownership would encourage rights clearance as a default position. We would be channelled towards obtaining licences for uses which might be *de minimis* or otherwise permitted under copyright exceptions or limitations.[99] There is some evidence to support this from current automated systems like Google's Content ID, most conspicuously used by YouTube. Once a digital

---

94 Ibid.

95 The question is raised by Elkin-Koren, above n 89, 1545. However such large scale, multi-author and constantly evolving collaborative works are also difficult to accommodate within the present copyright regime: see D Simone, 'Copyright or Copyleft? Wikipedia as a Turning Point for Authorship' (2014) 25 *Kings Law Journal* 102.

96 MS O'Connor, 'Creators, Innovators and Appropriation Mechanisms' (2015) 22 *George Mason Law Review* 973, 974. However this unevenness of bargaining power is problematic under the present copyright arrangements as well. For a sophisticated critique of contemporary network capitalism and attempts to exploit immaterial labour in the context of free and open source software, see A Barron, 'Free Software Production as Critical Social Practice' (2013) 42 *Economy and Society* 597.

97 Greenberg, above n 68, 1046–1056.

98 Ginsburg, above n 19, 346.

99 Elkin-Koren, above n 89, 1561.

sample of the protected work has been electronically deposited, it is used as the template against which to check for copies, via automated search algorithms, when new work is submitted. If a match is found, the 'registered' copyright owner can choose to mute audio that matches their music, block a whole video from being viewed, monetise the video by running ads against it or track the video's viewership statistics.[100] Without prior human review and involvement, the system is susceptible to false positives and accidental matches. It also lacks the ability to qualitatively assess the amount of a work that has been used, making the automated response potentially disproportionate to any unauthorised use.[101]

There is an additional reason to query whether better quality information will reduce transaction costs. Tracing costs are only a part of the problem. 'Acquiring a license also involves the cost of locating the owners, contacting them, negotiating a license, and paying a license fee'.[102] While the introduction of formalities cannot directly address these costs, recent developments such as the UK's Copyright Hub have the potential to do so.[103] The Hub was first envisioned as a Digital Copyright Exchange in the Hargreaves Review[104] and further developed in collaboration with representatives from UK creative industries (music, publishing, audiovisual, images) as well as two affected sectors (educational institutions and archives/libraries/museums).[105] One of the envisaged outcomes for this industry-backed Hub is to establish a marketplace for rights and provide streamlined licensing solutions. It will cater for high-volume, low-value transactions with otherwise low processing costs, such as shops that want to play music or documentary filmmakers who want to use an archive clip. A related purpose of the Hub is to develop and distribute open technologies for the benefit of copyright licensing industries in general. The Hub was officially launched in July 2015 and its operations will no doubt be closely followed.

---

100 See 'How Content ID works' at <support.google.com/youtube/answer/2797370?hl=en-GB>.
101 B Boroughf, 'The Next Great YouTube: Improving Content ID to Foster Creativity, Cooperation, and Fair Compensation' (2015) 25 *Albany Law Journal of Science and Technology* 95.
102 Elkin-Koren, above n 89, 1545.
103 See <www.copyrightdoneright.org/> and <www.copyrighthub.org/>.
104 I Hargreaves, *Digital Opportunity: A Review of Intellectual Property and Growth* (Independent Report for the UK IPO, May 2011).
105 R Hooper and R Lynch, *Copyright Works: Streamlining Copyright Licensing for the Digital Age* (Independent Report for the UK IPO, July 2012).

While this section has set out a compendium of the major concerns, there will inevitably be others.[106] The challenge is to address them in any proposed reforms to formalities, by drawing on these teachings when determining the point of time in the life cycle of a work at which formalities become necessary, by making them as convenient and as efficient as possible in both design as well as implementation and by proportionately tempering the consequences of non-compliance.

3. Reconsidering registration

With a better sense of the categories of copyright formalities, their functions and the reasons for abandoning them, it is time to re-evaluate registration – arguably the defining formality of modern intellectual property law. If we could impose some degree of mandatory registration for both national authors and foreigners, would it make sense to do so today? This requires us to confront a series of questions relating to the nature of a copyright register and its effects, which would be applicable to both mandatory and voluntary registers so the exercise is not entirely hypothetical. There is a growing interest in making existing voluntary registration systems work better.[107] What follows is necessarily selective, but addresses some of the fundamentals.

3.1. Registration infrastructure: e-filing

Any copyright registration system needs to be easy to use, economical and efficient in terms of processing information. Electronic registration is the obvious solution. Here the European Union Intellectual Property Office (EUIPO, formerly known as OHIM)[108] is an acknowledged leader. The success of its unitary trademark and designs registries, both in terms of application volumes and processing speeds, is attributed to the significant financial investment in e-business and e-filing systems which entered a new phase in 2002. The move towards a paperless

---

106 See generally Elkin-Koren, above n 89, who considers the significant role of digital mega-platforms as well as private initiatives as alternative information providers; see also Greenberg, above n 68, who raises an interesting epistemological issue: Will a registration system perpetuate a 'high art v low art' hierarchy of aesthetics? Paintings might be registrable via digital deposit but what about performance art?

107 The WIPO Survey (see WIPO, *Summary of the Responses to the Questionnaire for Survey on Copyright Registration and Deposit Systems*, (WIPO, 2010)) arose in response to this interest.

108 See <euipo.europa.eu/ohimportal/en/>.

system included 'electronic filing ... electronic communication and e-payment, online banking services and tools for examining and tracking the progress of registration online'.[109] They range from online options for renewal, recording changes in ownership and filing notices of opposition to pre-application tools like the Goods and Services Builder, helping an applicant to determine which goods and services they would need to apply for.[110] These investments have been well received: in trademarks for example, 98 per cent of applications in 2014 were submitted via e-filing.[111]

By contrast, WIPO's 2011 Survey revealed that of the 48 respondents having copyright registration systems, less than half (46 per cent) had search facilities, 84 per cent had no publicly accessible online search facilities and only 21 per cent provided for digital storage of registered works,[112] and while access to registered works is granted, it is often a long, costly and bureaucratic process. Present day copyright registries seem to prioritise the evidentiary advantages of registration for the applicant/copyright holder,[113] instead of functioning as an informative resource for the public. However there are some exceptions. The US Copyright Registry's eCO Registration System, launched in 2008, allows for the electronic registration of 'basic claims', which include 'literary works, visual arts works, performing arts works, sound recordings, motion pictures, single serial issues, groups of serial issues and groups of newspaper/newsletter issues'.[114] The entire process can be completed electronically, from filing the application to securely paying the fees (including the option of advance deposit accounts for frequent users) and submitting an electronic deposit of the work in prescribed file formats.[115] Fees are comparatively modest at the time

---

109 OHIM, *Strategic Plan 2011/2015* (2011) 13.

110 See <euipo.europa.eu/ohimportal/en/online-services>.

111 OHIM, *Annual Report 2014*, 14.

112 Victor Vazquez, 'Second Survey on Voluntary Registration and Deposit Systems' (14 October 2011, Geneva), <www.wipo.int/export/sites/www/meetings/en/2011/wipo_cr_doc_ge_11/pdf/vazquez.pdf>.

113 This would include a rebuttable presumption of authorship, ownership, or the date of creation as found on the register. See the WIPO Survey: WIPO, *Summary of the Responses to the Questionnaire for Survey on Copyright Registration and Deposit Systems*, (WIPO, 2010), 5.

114 See <copyright.gov/eco/>.

115 For an overview of the registration process, see US Copyright Office, *Compendium of US Copyright Office Practice* (3rd ed, 22 Dec 2014) Chapter 200.

of writing, with an online Single Application (one author, one work) being $35 and an online Standard Application (for all other filings) costing $55. Paper based registrations cost $85.[116]

While eCO is primarily geared towards the registration of claims, the US Copyright Registry has electronic records of registration, renewals and recordation from 1978 onwards, which are electronically searchable via the online records catalogue.[117] The Digitisation and Public Access Project, currently underway, is converting the vast card catalogue backlog into electronic formats and will provide web access to the pre-1978 Copyright records when complete.[118] Based on a request by member states from Latin America, WIPO has also developed the GDA (Gestión de Derecho de Autor) system to assist copyright offices in automating the administration and management of copyright registration data.[119] The system is built using open source software and designed for use by optional, publicly managed copyright registries. By this stage there is certainly operational experience when it comes to establishing electronic registries[120] as well as digitising prior registration records.

Apart from existing public registries, '[p]rivate copyright registration and documentation systems around the world arguably constitute the largest pool of information concerning copyright and related rights'.[121] Michael Carroll identifies three groups of such entities: (1) registries administered by organisations that either own rights under copyright or related rights, or act as transactional agents for right holders – for example, Collective Management Organisations (CMOs);[122] (2) third party registries or copyright documentation services that do not solely rely upon input from right holders to gather information about works and their owners (e.g. YouTube's ContentID registry);

---

116 See <copyright.gov/about/fees.html>.

117 See <www.copyright.gov/records/>.

118 See <www.copyright.gov/digitization/>.

119 See <www.wipo.int/copyright/en/initiatives/gda.html>.

120 WIPO provides e-filing for its international registration regimes under the Patent Cooperation Treaty, the Madrid System for the International Registration of Trade Marks and the Hague System for the International Registration of Designs. See <www.wipo.int/services/en/>.

121 M Ricolfi et al, *Survey of Private Copyright Documentation Systems and Practices* (WIPO, 2011) 4.

122 CB Graber, 'Is There Potential for Collective Rights Management at the Global Level? Perspectives of a New Global Constitutionalism in the Creative Sector' in D Gervais and S Frankel (eds), *The Evolution and Equilibrium of Copyright in the Digital Age* (Cambridge University Press, 2014) 241, 244.

and (3) organisations that compete in parallel with public registration systems to provide right holders with copyright documentation services, such as notice (e.g. watermarking), registration, or deposit.[123] These systems – more specifically (1) and (3) – are of interest for two reasons.

First, with comprehensiveness in mind, a publicly managed copyright registration system should be connected to these private registries to increase the coverage of records. However at present, 'the majority of copyright registering bodies are not interconnected to other copyright data systems provided either by public or private entities'.[124] Many public registries have not yet made the transition to electronic systems, while for those that have done so compatibility and interoperability with private registries remains a major issue. Compatibility is also a major issue between entities such as CMOs, based on research conducted for WIPO by François Nuttall, a Senior Consultant for the International Confederation of Societies of Authors and Composers (CISAC).[125] CISAC is one of the largest umbrella organisations of authors' societies. As of January 2015, it represented 230 authors' societies (CMOs) across 120 countries, primarily in the fields of music, audiovisual productions, drama, literature and the visual arts.[126]

Reviewing the gradual integration of individual members' records, Nuttall documents the adoption of technical standards for identifying authors, right holders, works and data relevant to transactions such as licensing arrangements. In a title-based property register, where ownership records are linked to the name of the protected work, accurately identifying both the owner and the work is crucially important – and hard. A key requirement is the need to disambiguate parties or works that have the same name (there are 139 artists whose

---

123 Carroll's conclusion is that – within the constraints of Art 5(2) of the Berne Convention – the way forward involves better integration between public and private registration systems while also regulating private registries, increasing transparency in their operations and facilitating interoperable technological solutions. MW Carroll, 'A Realist Approach to Copyright Law's Formalities' (2013) 28(3) *Berkeley Technology Law Journal* 1511.

124 WIPO, *Summary of the Responses to the Questionnaire for Survey on Copyright Registration and Deposit Systems*, (WIPO, 2010) 2.

125 FX Nuttall, *Private Copyright Documentation Systems and Practices: Collective Management Organisations' Databases (Preliminary Version)* (WIPO, 2011).

126 See <www.cisac.org/Our-Members>.

name includes 'Michael Jackson'),[127] or where the name is expressed differently, such as with linguistic variances, not to mention the inevitable spelling mistakes. For ownership and remuneration tracing, the response is to assign a unique Party Identifier to the owner, as part of the metadata associated with a work. Options include the Interested Party Identifier (IPI) system used by CISAC, or the International Standard Name Identifier (ISNI), which is a draft ISO standard (ISO 27729).[128] Again, the experience gained via private registration systems could inform the design of public copyright registries.

The second reason why private registries are of interest is that they operate almost entirely digitally.[129] They allow a range of digital file formats to be deposited; use bar codes or other unique identifiers such as a permanent URL to identify registered works; and – in bypassing the examination stage (on which more below) – permit rapid or even real-time registration.[130] Private registries have also experimented with applicant identity verification, identifying the work (using digital fingerprints and hash-codes) and recording the time of creation (using a trusted time stamp on upload).[131] Initiatives to create a trustworthy environment for transactions, by clearly linking an author with her work, are also being developed in the context of Creative Commons registries such as Registered Commons.[132] Those wishing to use CC-licensed materials need to be able to rely on the licence and proof of ownership is integral to this. This corpus of experience can be drawn upon when implementing national copyright registration systems.

---

127 Nuttall contrasts it with only one IPI # 0002961801. See the presentation by F Nutall, 'Private Copyright Documentation Systems and Practices: Collective Management Organisations' Databases' (Conference on Copyright Documentation and Infrastructure, WIPO, Geneva Oct 2011).

128 Nuttall, *Private Copyright Documentation Systems and Practices: Collective Management Organisations' Databases (Preliminary Version)* (WIPO, 2011), 9–10. As an illustration, an ISNI is made up of 16 decimal digits, the last one being a check character; e.g. ISNI 1422 4586 3573 0476. ISNIs are attached to the public identities of parties involved in creative processes. It operates as an open layer, above proprietary Party identification systems such as IPI.

129 The most prominent are Safe Creative, Registered Commons, Copyright Deposit, and Numly. They are described in Annex I of Nuttall (*Private Copyright Documentation Systems and Practices: Collective Management Organisations' Databases (Preliminary Version)* (WIPO, 2011)).

130 M Ricolfi et al, *Survey of Private Copyright Documentation Systems and Practices* (WIPO, 2011) 4–5.

131 Ibid, 11–13.

132 R Alton-Scheidl, J Benso and M Springer, 'The Value of Registering Creative Works' in MD de Rosnay and JC De Martin, *The Digital Public Domain: Foundations for an Open Culture* (Open Book Publishers, 2012) 189.

Finally, turning to the question of institutional support for electronic registration, Lawrence Lessig has proposed publicly regulated private registrars, along the lines of the present domain name system.[133] The global top-level domain name system provides a reference point since it consists of a central coordinating agency, the Internet Corporation for Assigned Names and Numbers (ICANN) which accredits the registrars actually registering top-level domain names.[134] Given enormous numbers of potentially registrable works, the notion of parallel entry points into the registration system is appealing.

Copyright registrars could be allowed to compete via value-added services, while the copyright office would set out qualifying conditions for registrars to be recognised, monitor compliance, specify the minimum information required for each application, produce lists of acceptable verification methods and indicate technical specifications for the storage and transmission of data to ensure compatibility. However the ICANN experience suggests that it is important to have a public entity closely involved, for at least one very pragmatic reason: private registrars disappear (e.g. through bankruptcy). ICANN has developed a two-stage response to this. First, all registrars are required to 'escrow' their customers' domain name registration data, by forwarding it to a third party for safe keeping.[135] Second, it created a De-Accredited Registrar Transition Procedure, under which a 'gaining registrar' is the recipient of a bulk transfer of domain names.[136] This preserves ownership records and allows parties to use or transfer domains. Anecdotal evidence suggests that the 'longevity' of private copyright registrars is a genuine concern, especially given the extended duration of copyright term.[137] Therefore while a hybrid public-private registrar network continues to be attractive, the OHIM and eCO examples considered above suggest that efficient public registrars are also viable prospects.

---

133 L Lessig, *Free Culture: How Big Media Uses Technology and the Law to Lock Down Culture and Control Creativity* (Penguin Press, 2004), 287–291.

134 An overview of the registrar accreditation process can be found at <www.icann.org/resources/pages/accreditation-2012-02-25-en>.

135 See *ICANN Registrar Accreditation Agreement* (2013), [3.6], <www.icann.org/resources/pages/approved-with-specs-2013-09-17-en>.

136 Available at <www.icann.org/en/system/files/files/dartp-11jul13-en.pdf>.

137 See *Choosing a Copyright Registration Service* at <www.copyrightaid.co.uk/advice/copyright_registration>; M Ricolfi et al, *Survey of Private Copyright Documentation Systems and Practices* (WIPO, 2011), 35 n 85.

3.2. Legal effects and the timing question

The evidence suggests there is potential for relatively fast, accessible and affordable electronic copyright registration systems. But should registration be mandatory? While patents and trademarks are supported by mandatory registration these regimes have historically belonged to the domain of industrial property with its attendant commercial logic.[138] Section 3 identified concerns associated with the reintroduction of formalities. Registration-based systems tend to favour commercial parties and repeat players, but individuals are responsible for a great deal of creative output. Consider the blogger seeing her work reproduced, without authorisation, by a commercially motivated third party, or the photographer whose digital photograph is showcased on someone else's ecommerce site, without attribution or remuneration.

There are two potential responses – either alternatives or cumulative – to this concern. The first would be to continue granting copyright automatically upon creation, allowing an initial period of formality-free protection but requiring mandatory registration in order to benefit from the remainder of the copyright term. As an example, US copyright law previously recognised an initial period of 28 years of automatic protection, although both registration and deposit were necessary before commencing with infringement proceedings even during this initial period.[139] Mandating registration prior to litigation ensures that ownership information and the date of creation or publication are placed on public record. Otherwise it is difficult to determine whether a work has crossed the initial duration threshold (say 28 years) of automatic protection.[140] This would grant the photographer or blogger automatic protection for a reasonable period, sufficient to allow them to assess the commercial significance of the work *ex post* creation.[141] They would retain the option to subsequently register the work and

---

138 For the historic differences between literary and artistic property on the one hand and industrial property on the other; see WIPO, *Introduction to Intellectual Property – Theory and Practice* (Kluwer Law International, 1997) 3; J Hughes, 'A Short History of "Intellectual Property" in Relation to Copyright' (2012) 33 *Cardozo Law Review* 1293.

139 *Copyright Act of 1909*, ch 320, § 12, 35 Stat 1075, 1078 (repealed 1976).

140 However if protection for the initial period was conditioned upon a notice requirement, then registration could be entirely done away with for the initial period, including for the purposes of litigation.

141 On the average viable commercial lifespan for works, see R Giblin, 'Rethinking copyright's duration', this volume.

enjoy extended protection. For those who did not opt for registration, a work could either fall into the public domain at one (extreme) end of the spectrum or the rights and remedies available might become restricted for unregistered works, which is explored below.

The second option would be to require registration at or around the time of publication of the work, as an obligatory requirement. Failing to do so would result in thinner protection being granted; a form of copyright-lite or Copyright 2.0.[142] This two-tier copyright regime could be given effect by limiting the remedies available. Sprigman has proposed that the consequence of failing to comply with formalities would be to allow the work to be used under a compulsory licence, for a low royalty fee. More specifically, 'owners of unregistered works would continue to recover actual damages as measured by the reasonable value of a license, but they would be ineligible to receive either disgorgement or preliminary or permanent injunctive relief'.[143] Copyright would effectively shift from a property to a liability-based regime for unregistered works, by limiting remedies to actual damages calculated based on the value of a licence negotiated *ex ante*. The Copyright Principles Project proceeds along similar lines. Protection for unregistered works might be thin, being restricted to exact or near-exact copying, with other uses being deemed fair use. Additionally, remedies for infringing unregistered works would not include statutory damages or attorney's fees. Registered works would enjoy correspondingly broader rights and remedies.[144] A combination of these two options is also possible – an initial period of automatic protection would be followed by a period of attenuated protection for unregistered works. What this demonstrates is that a suitably nuanced registration-based system could accommodate the concerns of the blogger, the amateur photographer or user/creators more generally.

---

142 Proposed by M Ricolfi, 'Consume and Share: Making Copyright Fit for the Digital Agenda' in C Geiger (ed), *Constructing European Intellectual Property Law: Achievements and New Perspectives* (Edward Elgar, 2013) 314 (arguing that, for cultural works, as production and distribution functions become more distributed, the pathway from creators to the public gets shorter and copyright should be correspondingly attenuated to the right to attribution, in the absence of a notice).

143 Sprigman, above n 56, 1567. See also Sprigman, above n 16.

144 Samuelson et al, above n 66, 1200–1201.

There are two additional considerations which argue against imposing excessive penalties for non-registration. To begin with, there is the unfairness for those who inadvertently do not register, or lack the knowledge, means or capacity to do so. Additionally, exclusion from copyright protection might lead to a corresponding expansion of the scope of unfair competition law to accommodate such situations.[145] In the past, utilitarian works, or those resulting from the sweat of the brow,[146] or those closer to ideas rather than expression such as TV formats[147] have been rehoused within unfair competition prevention regimes, where one of the central claims relates to the prevention of misappropriation of valuable intangibles. Unfair competition determinations are case-specific and lack many of the structural checks and balances of copyright law. Inadvertently encouraging its expansion into the domain of copyright is undesirable.

3.3. Representative registration?

Should the intangible object protected by copyright be identified by representative registration, described as 'the process whereby the creation was represented in pictorial or written terms rather than via a copy or a model'?[148] The specification, claims, abstract and drawings of a patent or the graphical representation of a trademark reflect this approach to identifying the intangible objects of protection. This question is worth raising, if only to dismiss, because it serves as a reminder that a mandatory public copyright register would operate very differently from a patent, design or trademark register in terms of defining the scope of the intangible property and the boundaries of the work.

---

145 See R Callmann, 'Copyright and Unfair Competition' (1940) 2 *Louisiana Law Review* 648 (characterising the recognition of property in factual yet time sensitive 'hot news' as one such development).

146 T Scassa, 'Originality and Utilitarian Works: The Uneasy Relationship between Copyright Law and Unfair Competition' (2003–2004) *University of Ottawa Law & Technology Journal* 55.

147 L Logan, 'The Emperor's New Clothes? The Way Forward: TV Format Protection under Unfair Competition Law in the United States, United Kingdom and France' (2009) *Entertainment Law Review* 37 (Part 1) and 87 (Part 2).

148 Sherman and Bently, above n 4, 72.

Copyright registration has historically prioritised the ownership question ('who owns what') rather than the one of the scope ('what intangible expression is being claimed').[149] Characterising copyright as pre-modern, Sherman and Bently observe:

> The difference between patents and copyright created by the different modes of identification was further enhanced by the fact that even if the law had chosen to use registration as a means of identifying the copyright work, this was said to have been excluded by the nature of the work protected. While it was possible to reduce the intangible property embodied in a machine to paper, it was said to have been impossible to capture the essence of literary and artistic works: 'who can give a specification for the making of an "Inferno"? If anyone undertakes to do so, it will not be a Dante, but a Dennis'.[150]

Therefore one powerful argument against representative registration was 'the belief that it was not possible to reduce the subject matter of copyright law beyond the material form in which it existed'.[151] This argument was reinforced by the deposit requirement.

Stef van Gompel also identifies a historical trajectory, relating to the scope of protection, which counteracted any initiatives towards representative registration. In the early decades of copyright, thin protection against literal copying obviated the need for identifying the protected expression. 'The privileges and stationers' copyright protected these [registered] works against unauthorized reprinting, importation and distribution, but rarely against adaptation, translation or public performance. Thus, the two systems did not protect works *qua abstractum*, but the printed matter as such'.[152] During the latter part of the 19th century, the scope of protection was considerably extended, to protect works:

---

149 For a recent attempt to address the scope question through formalities, see PS Menell, 'Economic Analysis of Copyright Notice: Tracing and Scope in the Digital Age' (2016) 96 *Boston University Law Review* 967.

150 Sherman and Bently, above n 4, 154.

151 Ibid 183.

152 van Gompel, above n 5, [2.3.2.1]. As a counter-example, papal privileges extended protection to adaptations, translations and extensions of protected works. JC Ginsburg, 'Proto-Property in Literary and Artistic Works: 16th Century Papal Printing Privileges' (2013) 36 *Columbia Journal of Law and the Arts* 345, 358–361.

qua abstractum, by focusing the protection on the personal and unique form of expression of the author's thoughts or ideas. This gave even more prominence to the intangible character of copyright and eventually led to the recognition of protection for the multiple ways in which a work could be exploited.[153]

This led to difficulties delimiting the work: with copyright defined in 'formalities seemed less indispensable for copyright protection. Rather than defining *ex ante* the essence and boundaries of the intangible property via formalities, it was left to the courts to demarcate the nature and limits of literary and artistic works ex post'.[154] It might be summarised thus: with thin protection against literal copying, defining the scope of protected expression was unnecessary; with more expansive protection, identifying it *ex ante* during registration was not practicable. The consequence is that copyright registration systems have prioritised the identification of owners with works, as designated by titles (e.g. book or song titles) and/or deposits of the physical (and now digital) embodiments of the works themselves.

Following through on its implications, Jeanne Fromer describes the process by which this impacts upon the scope of the monopoly being claimed: patent claims articulate boundaries, giving public notice of the extent of the patentee's rights, 'usually by listing [the] necessary and sufficient characteristics' of protected embodiments.[155] Copyright, on the other hand 'implicitly adopted a system of central claiming by exemplar, requiring the articulation only of a prototypical member of the set of protected works … Copyright protection then extends beyond the exemplar to substantially similar works, a set of works to be enumerated only down the road in case-by-case infringement litigation'.[156] With technology increasingly facilitating digital deposit, it seems likely that the 'central claiming by exemplar' approach to the scope of copyright will be reinforced by registration. Somewhat counterintuitively, better technology could ensure that copyright remains 'pre-modern' in this regard.

---

153 van Gompel, above n 5, [3.3.2.3].
154 Ibid.
155 JC Fromer, 'Claiming Intellectual Property' (2009) 76 *University of Chicago Law Review* 719, 721.
156 Ibid.

3.4. Comprehensive coverage or work-specific?

The subject matter coverage of copyright registers requires an engagement with the debate over whether copyright systems are 'open' or 'closed'; whether the categories of subject matter should be confined to an expressly enumerated list or open-ended.[157] Conventionally, the UK has been a prime example of the 'closed list' approach, whereby eight and only eight categories of works are entitled to protection. By contrast, under article L112-1 of its Intellectual Property Code, France protects 'the rights of authors in all works of the mind, whatever their kind, form of expression, merit or purpose'. Article L-112-2 proceeds to illustrate works of the mind that largely corresponds to the literary and artistic works found within article 2 of the Berne Convention – books and other writings; lectures; dramatic works; works of choreography; musical works; cinematographic works and so on.[158]

The challenge would be to accommodate an open-ended approach to subject matter within registration systems that have historically worked with narrower categories of specific works. To take one example, in jurisdictions which do not have a fixation or recording requirement, certain categories of works are protected (e.g. perfume)[159] in the absence of an established convention for representing such subject matter. From the historical record it appears that registration systems and associated bureaucratic practices accreted around specific categories of subject matter – for instance, literary works and the Stationers Company Register,[160] and the registers of CMOs.[161] The subject matter categories will therefore continue to remain relevant for bureaucratic processing, as is illustrated by the US response to the WIPO survey: 'All copyright works can be registered, but the Register of Copyrights has specified certain administrative classes into which works are placed for purposes of deposit and registration with the Copyright

---

157 On this divide, see R Anthony Reese, 'What should copyright protect?', this volume.

158 T Aplin, 'Subject Matter' in E Derclaye (ed), *Research Handbook on the Future of EU Copyright* (Edward Elgar, 2009) 54–58.

159 See generally C Cronin, 'Genius in a Bottle: Perfume, Copyright, and Human Perception' (2008–2009) *Journal of the Copyright Society USA* 427.

160 For details, see Ch 2 of C Blagden, *The Stationers Company: A History, 1403–1959* (Stanford University Press, 1960).

161 CMOs originated with early initiatives by groups of authors sharing a common in interest in a certain type of subject matter, as the basis for collectivizing. See D Gervais (ed), *Collective Management of Copyright and Related Rights* (Kluwer Law International, 2nd ed, 2010).

Office'.[162] Therefore US registration practice requires applications to be channelled according to the more flexible 'Type of Work' and the administrative classification of a 'Class of Work', determined by the application form used.[163] Despite bureaucratic registration processes working with pre-existing categories increasingly sophisticated search engine algorithms could add nuance, for example if subject matter categories are included as an optional keyword instead of forming the basis of a closed classification system.[164] Alternatively, European trademark law provides a model: open-ended categories of signs are accommodated in the EUIPO database by providing a catch-all 'Other' heading in addition to discrete categories such as Word, Figurative, 3D and Colour marks.[165]

3.5. Examination

The briefest possible summary here might be: substantive examination is possible but undesirable. Substantive examination would evaluate *ex ante* subsistence criteria, such as qualifying as a recognised type of work, clearing an originality threshold and potentially satisfying a fixation requirement: such examination is conducted by the US.[166] From the preceding analysis, it is evident that substantive examination would be in tension with (i) the speed, cost and ease of registration; as well as (ii) Fromer's characterisation of the scope of copyright resting on central claiming by exemplar. Courts would invariably refine the scope of the protected work during any infringement proceedings. To take a simple example, the fact that an examiner concludes a book is original will not preclude a court from later determining that

---

162 *WIPO Registration Questionnaire – Response of the United States* (30 June 2010).

163 Oliar et al, above n 91, 2221–2222.

164 As appears to be the case when searching through US copyright records at <www.copyright.gov/records/>.

165 See <euipo.europa.eu/eSearch/#advanced/trademarks>.

166 See Ch 600: 'Examination Practices in the US Copyright Office', *Compendium of US Copyright Office Practices* (3rd ed, 2014). Cf TG Field, 'Originality: Does the Copyright Office Hide the Ball?' (2009) 37 *AIPLA Quarterly Journal* 425, 426 (registration is usually *pro forma* although there are very occasional originality-based objections).

elements of it are in the public domain. A further reason for being sceptical is that the originality threshold is seen as modest in most jurisdictions,[167] so examination may not filter out undeserving works.

4. A modest model

In the spirit of this volume, it is time to let go of the side of the pool and float a proposal. What might a 'mandatory' registration-based copyright system look like – one which would aspire to be effective in terms of its informational content while simultaneously accommodating individual, possibly non-professional creators?

How:

- To begin with, it would inevitably be digital and facilitate e-filing, responding to historic perceptions of formalities as an onerous imposition, by drawing on today's comparable electronic registers to ensure relatively quick and inexpensive registration.

- This registration system could be managed either by a national (public) registrar – the national Copyright Office or equivalent – or, inspired by the domain name system, by a constellation of private registrars operating under the oversight of a public regulator. Some public involvement is unavoidable given the potential for private registrars to fail or withdraw. Countries would be left free to adopt either model, while public entities would also be engaged in the international coordination of copyright registration.

- In terms of e-filing registration requirements, experiments are already underway to generate unique identification codes for both works and owners, which would improve the quality of information contained in the register. There would be a clear choice in favour of digital deposits of entire works (where possible)

---

167 This has led to proposals to calibrate the degree of protection afforded in accordance with the degree of originality of the underlying work. See G Parchomovsky and A Stein, 'Originality' (2009) 95 *Virginia Law Review* 1506. See also, E Lavik and S van Gompel 'On the Prospects of Raising the Originality Requirement in Copyright Law: Perspectives from the Humanities' (2013) 60 *Journal of the Copyright Society of the USA* 387; J Miller, 'Hoisting Originality' (2009) 31 *Cardozo Law Review* 451.

and representative registration is unlikely. Registration systems could draw on techniques already in use (such as OHIM's 'Other' classification) to process an indicative, yet open-ended, list of the most common types of works.

- At the time of registration, there would be no substantive examination of originality.

Why:

- Registration would continue to confer evidentiary advantages, such as proof of publication, fixation (reinforced by deposit), and a rebuttable presumption that the applicant is the right holder (author or first owner). It would also give constructive notice to the public and defeat a defence of innocent infringement.

- The purpose of registration would be to improve the quality and availability of ownership information so the consequences of non-registration would be fashioned accordingly. During Phase One – a period of 10 years from creation – copyright would subsist and registration would only be a necessary precondition for infringement proceedings. Registration would permit proceedings to be brought for infringing conduct taking place even prior to registration. However this retrospective effect would be limited to injunctive relief and damages based on the actual loss suffered by the claimant. The recovery of costs/fees, gains-based damages and statutory damages (as applicable) would only be available for infringing acts which take place after registration. At the end of this period, Phase Two would commence for the duration of the copyright term. Registration would be a necessary precondition for infringement and it would only have prospective effects, opening up the full suite of remedies for infringement only taking place after registration.

- A strongly incentivised recordal system would encourage up-to-date ownership information. This would facilitate a market for licences and clearly be in the interests of copyright owners.

- For Phase One, defendants who were genuinely unable to identify or locate the copyright holder because they were not registered could avail of an 'innocent infringer' defence.

- Across both Phases, moral rights such as the right to attribution (where possible) or integrity would remain available regardless of registration status.

While registration at the time of creation is not mandatory, infringement becomes the point at which ownership information must be placed within a publicly accessible register. The system described above attempts to retain meaningful rights and remedies for creators while also balancing this against the interests of those who have infringed because they lack the necessary information for rights clearance. What this model has not addressed is the question of international copyright protection, which is greatly facilitated by the absence of formalities. Here too there are options. The proposed model would continue to recognise proprietary interests in Phase One, giving creators ample time to decide on whether to pursue registration. International recognition might in turn adopt some of the key features of WIPO's Madrid System for the International Registration of Marks. A single centralised application in one language and one set of fees is the gateway to a bundle of distinct but more conveniently managed national registrations.[168] Readers may disagree with some of the details, but the model outlined here demonstrates that a contemporary registration system at the national level could strike a balance between the competing interests involved.

Conclusion

The copyright formalities debate helps to make all that is familiar strange once again. In recognising rights automatically, on the basis of creation, copyright law is an outlier. There are tremendous information costs associated with the opacity of the entitlements it generates. Liberated from the strictures of article 5(2) of the Berne Convention and equipped with the lessons learned from historic formalities, it is possible to fashion a more sensible yet sensitive system which responds to these critiques. This chapter demonstrates that a return to copyright registration is worthy of consideration, since the pragmatic concerns which engendered article 5(2) may no longer exist.

This chapter has argued that we ought to change the law and adopt mandatory registration if we could. In addition, its analysis is helpful in two further ways. First, optional copyright registration is the focus of renewed policy interest, as informed by recent empirical research

---

168 See <www.wipo.int/madrid/en/>.

exploring the operation of existing public and private registries. In comparison to the other registration-based IP systems, voluntary copyright registration is still taking tentative steps but there are valuable lessons to be learned, as documented in section 4, above.

Second, the formalities debate – and the registration option in particular – could act as a baseline when evaluating contemporary reform proposals. There is so much we could be asking of those making a claim to copyright protection, which we refrain from asking, in stark contrast to most other areas of IP law. Yet when it comes to proposed solutions for the orphan works problem, some options are extremely onerous on users and downstream creators, effectively (and inequitably) imposing on them all the burdens we have chosen to spare the initial creators. Consider for example the UK 'solution' introduced in 2014,[169] which requires anyone desiring to make use of an apparent orphan work to (1) search the Orphan Works register, (2) conduct a 'diligent search' to establish that the owner cannot be identified, or if identified cannot be located,[170] (3) and if the work *is* an orphan work, apply to the UK IP Office for a licence (paying both an application fee, and the determined licence fee), giving details of the search conducted. After all of this, the applicant may (if the IPO is satisfied a sufficient search has occurred, and that it is not against the public interest) obtain a non-exclusive licence authorising use of the orphan work(s), which applies only within the UK, and can last only up to seven years.[171] Note the extent of *ex ante* obligations imposed on the user:[172] we have

---

169 *The Copyright and Rights in Performances (Certain Permitted Uses of Orphan Works) Regulations 2014* (UK) No 2861; *The Copyright and Rights in Performances (Licensing of Orphan Works) Regulations 2014* (UK) No 2863.

170 Guidance for what constitutes a diligent search for different kinds of copyright material has been produced by the UK IPO: see <www.gov.uk/government/publications/orphan-works-diligent-search-guidance-for-applicants>.

171 Cultural heritage institutions (CHIs), which include archives, libraries, museums, educational establishments and public service broadcasters, may conduct a diligent search and, if satisfied a work is an orphan work, make it accessible to the public, and copy it for the purposes of digitisation, preservation, cataloguing or indexing. Note that this exception covers literary, cinematographic and audiovisual works and sound recordings. It does not include standalone artistic works like photographs, maps, plans and drawings.

172 Cf other proposals for addressing Orphan Works which are *ex post:* in the sense that use can occur without applying for a licence, with limitations on remedies in the event that a copyright owner comes forward after use commences. For a review and discussion of ex ante versus ex post systems, see Marcella Favale et al, 'Copyright, and the Regulation of Orphan Works: A comparative review of seven jurisdictions and a rights clearance simulation' (CREATe Working Paper No 2013/7, July 2013), available at <zenodo.org/record/8377/files/CREATe-Working-Paper-2013-07.pdf>.

essentially flipped the formalities burden onto downstream creative activity and cultural reuses. The formalities debate – the fact that we could have notice, registration and recordation but have chosen not to, for reasons which favour right holders at the cost of others with a legitimate interest in copyright protected works – should also be borne in mind when considering proposals to regulate and reform CMOs. Drawing back even further, the formalities debate serves as a reminder that the world we inhabit wasn't always this way, we do have choices and reimagining what copyright might be is the first step in any project to reform it.

8

Calibrating copyright for creators and consumers: Promoting distributive justice and Ubuntu

Caroline B Ncube

Introduction

Current copyright law fails to adequately incentivise the creation of books in certain markets and languages. After examining some of the reasons for that failure, this chapter considers ways in which a reimagined copyright law might do a better job of creating the literature, particularly children's literature, which is so sorely lacking in disadvantaged communities around the world. It does so by envisaging a copyright law that furthers the public interest by applying principles of distributive justice, and with reference to the African concept of 'Ubuntu', a metanorm in favour of 'humaneness, social justice and fairness'.[1]

---

1   *S v Makwanyane* [1995] 3 SA 391 (Constitutional Court), [236]. Also see Moeketsi Letseka 'Ubuntu and justice as Fairness' (2014) 5(9) *Mediterranean Journal of Social Sciences* 544, 549.

The problem – neglected languages and neglected markets

Shortages of literature occur in neglected languages across both the developed and developing worlds. In the developing world, South Africa provides a good example of such shortages. The last census, conducted in 2011, found that the population stood at 51,770,560.[2] 13.5 per cent of the population's first or home language was Afrikaans, while 9.6 per cent spoke English, 74.9 per cent spoke African languages,[3] 0.5 per cent used sign language and 1.6 per cent spoke 'other' languages.[4] The most widely spoken African language was IsiZulu, spoken by 22.7 per cent of the population. (This explains the use of the phrase 'neglected languages' rather than 'minority languages' – some neglected languages are actually spoken by the majority of a given state's population.)

Despite the large number of individuals speaking African languages, existing and potential consumers of literary works struggle to access literary texts in languages other than English and Afrikaans.

The situation is particularly dire when it comes to local general trade publishing. In 2012 only 24 new children's fiction titles were published in African languages, and those were probably 'readers for use in classrooms'.[5] If this is indeed the case, then to all intents and purposes there were no general trade fiction publications for children in African languages in 2012. In contrast, 61 and 299 new titles were produced in children's fiction in English and Afrikaans respectively.[6] No children's non-fiction titles were produced in African languages, while 43 and 67 new titles were produced in English and Afrikaans respectively.[7] In 2013, only 15 new children's titles were produced locally in African languages, again primarily as classroom readers.[8] This is a decrease from 2012, which is unexplained by the report.

---

2   Statistics SA (2011) *Census 2011: Key Results – The South Africa I Know, The Home I Understand*, 3.
3   IsiNdebele, IsiXhosa, IsiZulu, Sepedi, Sesotho, Setswana, SiSwati, Tshivenda and Xitsonga.
4   Statistics SA, above n 2, 6.
5   Publishers' Association of South Africa (PASA), *Annual Book Publishing Industry Survey 2012* (2013) 61.
6   PASA (2013), above n 5, 61.
7   PASA (2013), above n 5, 61.
8   PASA, *Annual Book Publishing Industry Survey 2013* (2014), 26.

34 and 174 new titles were produced in children's fiction in English and Afrikaans respectively, with the decrease in English titles being attributed to the 'availability of imported English fiction titles'.[9] As in 2012, no children's non-fiction titles were produced in African languages, while 231 and 161 new titles were produced in English and Afrikaans respectively.[10] There was an exponential growth in children's non-fiction titles in both English and Afrikaans while African language titles remained non-existent.

The situation is somewhat brighter when it comes to school text books. The Publishers' Association of South Africa (PASA) reports that in 2012 a total of 2,303 new schoolbooks were published, largely stimulated by the new national curricula implemented that year.[11] Of these '604 were English titles, 388 Afrikaans titles and 1,311 African language titles. [Isi]Zulu accounted for 277 of the African language titles and [Isi]Xhosa 199.'[12] In 2013, there was further growth driven by the new curricula as it continued to be incrementally implemented. In total, 4,527 new school books were published, of which '1,734 were English titles, 1,078 Afrikaans titles and 1,699 African language titles. [Isi]Zulu accounted for 235 of the African language titles and [Isi]Xhosa 295'.[13] These statistics substantiate Shaver's assertion that African language textbooks are plentiful because they constitute 56.9 per cent and 37.5 per cent of schoolbooks produced locally in 2012 and 2013 respectively.

Being school books, the books were purchased mostly by schools; books in government schools are paid for from government funds. In percentage terms, in 2012 'English language books accounted for 68.1 per cent of all schoolbook turnover, followed by African languages contributing 19.8 per cent and Afrikaans schoolbooks 12.0 per cent'.[14] In 2013, 'English language books accounted for 74.8 per cent of all schoolbook turnover, followed by Afrikaans contributing 12.7 per cent and African languages schoolbooks 12.4 per cent'.[15] African language books' turnover decreased by

---

9   PASA (2014), above n 8, 26.
10   PASA (2014), above n 8, 26.
11   PASA (2013), above n 5,114.
12   PASA (2013), above n 5, 114.
13   PASA (2013), above n 5, 55.
14   PASA (2013), above n 5, 123.
15   PASA (2014), above n 8, 61.

7.4 per cent. It is not clear from the annual reports what caused this decrease. However, it would be accurate to say that English and Afrikaans publications generate the most revenue.

Works in African languages include those that have been originally written in them and those that have been translated from another language. The proportion of children's literature which is translated into an African language, rather than being initially authored in that language, is difficult to ascertain. However some research has found translated works to be more prevalent than natively African works.[16]

The above statistics show that there is very limited production and distribution of children's literature in African languages in both the educational and general trade categories. The following section considers the factors which affect authors and translators of such texts, in a bid to explain the low levels of production.

Possible explanations for the lack of books in neglected languages

In the case of South African languages, certain kinds of text-based material, such as textbooks, religious titles and newspapers, are abundant. This is attributable to the 'relative efficiency of production models based on alternative incentive systems'. That is, they are produced because of government procurement policies, evangelism and 'high-volume sales of time-sensitive content and advertising revenue'.[17] Where those factors are absent however, production tends not to occur, leaving other authors with few or no avenues to publish their works.

An oft-cited reason for the limited literature in African languages is that there are only a few authors who choose to write in African languages. Various reasons are cited for this, such as colonial and current national language policies that favour literature in dominant

---

16   Viv Edwards and Jacob Marriote Ngwaru, 'African language publishing for children in South Africa: Challenges for translators' (2011) 14(5) *International Journal of Bilingual Education and Bilingualism* 590, 593.
17   Ibid.

languages.[18] Another reason is societal attitudes that consider African languages to be inferior to other languages, which may be partially caused by colonial and current educational policies and practices.[19] Several publishing industry related constraints have been highlighted consistently in the literature.[20] These include government procurement policies, poor distribution systems and 'lack of inter-African book trade'.[21] Another key constraint is the perceived lack of a market or readership for works in African languages.[22] I label this constraint as a perception, rather than as a fact, because it has been persuasively challenged. Ngulube asks:

> when we talk of the lack of a reading culture being inimical to publishing especially in the indigenous languages, what epistemologies are we using to come to such a conclusion? Are we not running the danger of reinforcing the already entrenched stereotypes that Africans do not read ... The suitability of materials may be one of the major reasons for creating an unfavourable reading environment. Again, we may ask: is the reading environment rooted in local realities? Are the books suitable for the readers? Do we know our readers? Or do we paint them all with one brush that sees things in terms of illiteracy and literacy? By means of whose language is literacy provided, and by using what methods?[23]

---

18   Enna Sukutai Gudhlanga and Godwin Makaudze, 'Writing and publishing in indigenous languages is a mere waste of time: A critical appraisal of the challenges faced by writers and publishers of Shona literature in Zimbabwe' (PRAESA Occasional Papers No 26), 4–5.

19   Gudhlanga and Makaudze, above n 18, 8; Bernard Naledzani Rasila and MJ Mudau, 'Challenges of writing and publishing in indigenous languages and impact on rural development' (2013) *Journal of Education, Psychology and Social Sciences* 1339.

20   For a literature survey see Hans Zell, *Publishing, Books & Reading in Sub-Saharan Africa: A Critical Bibliography* (Hans Zell Publishing, 2nd ed, 2008).

21   Peter Lor, 'Preserving, developing and promoting indigenous languages: Things South African librarians can do' (2012) 45 *Innovation* 28, 31. Also see Solani Ngobeni, 'Scholarly Publishing in South Africa' in Solani Ngobeni (ed), *Scholarly Publishing in Africa: Opportunities & Impediments* (Africa Institute of South Africa, 2010) 69, 78.

22   Cynthia Daphne Ntuli, *From oral performance to picture book: A perspective on Zulum children's literature* (Doctor of Literature and Philosophy, University of South Africa, 2011) 1.

23   Patrick Ngulube, 'Revitalising and preserving endangered indigenous languages in South Africa through writing and publishing' (2012) 78(1) *South African Journal of Libraries & Information Science* 11, 17–18.

Valid or not, the perception of a limited market for literature in African languages makes publishers reluctant to publish and promote this literature. Therefore, they focus mostly on publishing for the educational sector, which has a guaranteed market courtesy of government procurement.[24]

Self-publishing has recently become more popular but it has not taken real root among African language authors in South Africa.[25] This hints at the existence of 'entrepreneurial barriers [which] include psychological barriers, barriers in relation to the business environment, barriers relating to external ability and barriers in relation to the influence of demographics'.[26]

Translators face additional challenges. From a copyright perspective, licences will be required to authorise the translation before it can occur. Professional and publishing concerns 'include the high level of specialism required for working with children's literature and issues around standardisation'.[27] Variations in the same languages as they are spoken in different parts of the country also create the need for highly nuanced translation practices.[28]

Under-production in the field also means that authors who are offered publication contracts may receive disadvantageous terms. Authors may not be in a position to bargain equally with third parties due to limited legal or technical knowledge, information asymmetries and resource constraints.

It is unsurprising that under-production of creative and informational works occurs where potential markets are resource-poor and profit margins thin or non-existent. Copyright encourages investment in informational and creative works by entitling investors to charge a monopoly price that exceeds the marginal cost of production, thus enabling them to recoup their initial fixed costs of investment.

---

24   Jana Moller, 'The state of multilingual publishing in South Africa' *E-rea* 2013 <erea.revues.org/3507>.

25   Aphiwe Ngcai, 'Challenges in writing and publishing in indigenous languages' Academic and Non-fiction Authors Association of South Africa (ANFASA), April 2013 <www.anfasa.org.za/Newsletter/jit_default_1117.Newsletter_April_2013.html> (site discontinued).

26   Joel Baloyi 'Demystifying the Role of Copyright as a Tool for Economic Development in Africa: Tackling the Harsh Effects of the Transferability Principle in Copyright Law' (2014) 17(1) *Potchefstroom Electronic Law Journal/Potchefstroomse Elektroniese Regsblad* 85, 91.

27   Edwards and Ngwaru, above n 16, 593.

28   Edwards and Ngwaru, above n 16, 596–597.

Thus, where a market cannot or will not pay the monopoly price necessary to justify investment, it may result in unmet demand. That is, the inability of some markets to pay that monopoly price means that works to satisfy their needs simply not be created. This imposes a great deal of deadweight loss upon society in the form of benefits forsaken by those who could have afforded at least the marginal cost of production, but who are unable to afford monopoly pricing.

In such cases the traditional copyright structure fails to achieve its primary utilitarian goal of encouraging the production of creative and informational works. How might it be reimagined to do a better job of encouraging the creation and distribution of works in currently neglected languages?

What should a reimagined law be seeking to achieve? The public interest, Ubuntu and distributive justice

In assisting the reimagination exercise, this book project utilises the unifying principle of 'the public interest'. The concept of the public interest serves as 'a rhetorical device', 'a statement of current policy' and as 'a normative standard'.[29] Most of the discontent around its usefulness is a result of its frequent use as a rhetorical device without much thought being given to its normative content.[30] Many scholars have lamented the lack of clarity about the definition of the public interest, and therefore question its value.[31] As noted in Chapter 1, the public interest is an amorphous concept that has been appropriated by different agendas over time. It has been identified with a number of different constituencies. For example, Tang notes that the public interest in copyright is multidimensional and consists of authorship

---

29   Geoffrey Edwards, *Defining the Public Interest* (PhD thesis, Griffith University, 2007) 1.

30   Isabella Alexander, *Copyright Law and the Public Interest in the Nineteenth Century* (Hart Publishing, 2010) 16.

31   RC Box, 'Redescribing the public interest', (2007) 44 (4) *The Social Science Journal* 585, 586; V Held, *The Public Interest and Individual Interests* (Basic Books, 1970) 1; HJ Storing, 'Review: The Crucial Link: Public Administration, Responsibility, and the Public Interest' (1964) 24 (1) *Public Administration Review* 39–46; CJ Friedrich (ed), *Nomos V: The Public Interest. Yearbook of the American Society for Political and Legal Philosophy* (Atherton Press, 1962); Schubert *The Public Interest: A Critique of the Theory of a Political Concept* (The Free Press, 1960) 224; F Sorauf, 'The Public Interest Reconsidered' (1957) 19 *Journal of Politics* 616.

and access public interest.[32] Granting authors economic monopolies and protecting their moral rights would be in the public interest because it would 'promote creativity and learning and provide a framework for investment by the creative industries' (authorship public interest).[33] Granting user access to copyright-protected works through devices such as exceptions and limitations would also be in the public interest as it facilitates access to educational information, culture and entertainment (access public interest).

It could be argued that copyright law is truly in the public interest when it balances these two types of interests appropriately. However, this argument would raise at least three concerns. First, pigeonholing the stakeholders into the two listed categories would be overlooking the highly nuanced positions and interests of each stakeholder.[34] Indeed, Tang is at pains to highlight the contours of these interests throughout her text. Secondly, once stakeholders are categorised in this manner, the arguments for the public interest tend to conflate the public interest with one set of stakeholders. This is problematic because, as argued in Chapter 1, the public interest 'must comprehend a range of goals.' Thirdly, by resorting to the much-used metaphor of balance, it raises the vexing question of what measure one is to use to gauge such balance.[35] Therefore, other conceptualisations of the public interest have to be sought. It is necessary to seek to define the concept because, despite the difficulties in doing so, it retains an allure due to its evocation of 'justice and fairness for the common good.'[36]

As noted in Chapter 1, Held articulated a threefold categorisation of theories that may be used to elucidate the public interest concept, namely preponderance, common interest and unitary theories.[37] This chapter adopts the first of these, the preponderance theories. These theories posit that an outcome or policy position will be in

---

32 Guan H Tang, *Copyright and the Public Interest in China* (Edward Elgar, 2011) 50.

33 Ibid.

34 Teresa Scassa, 'Interests in the Balance' in Michael Geist (ed), *In the Public Interest: The Future of Canadian Copyright Law* (Irwin Law Publishers, 2005) 41–65, 41.

35 Carys J Craig, 'The Evolution of Originality in Canadian Copyright Law: Authorship, Reward and the Public Interest' (2005) 2(2) *University of Ottawa Law and Technology Journal* 425, 441.

36 Caroline B Ncube, 'Fair is as fair does: Contractual normative regulation of copyright user contracts in South Africa' in G Dinwoodie (ed), *Intellectual Property and General Legal Principles: Is IP a Lex Specialis?* (Edward Elgar, 2015) 49, 55–56; Gillian Davies, *Copyright and the Public Interest* (PhD thesis, Aberystwyth University, 1997) 1.

37 Held, above n 31, 42–46.

the public interest where it serves majority of interests. Arriving at such a majoritarian position will require a settled and fair process in which participants engage impartially in good faith. As Lippman wrote, 'the public interest may be presumed to be what men would choose if they saw clearly, thought rationally, acted disinterestedly and benevolently.'[38] Similarly, Down notes that:

> the concept of public interest is closely related to the universal consensus necessary for the operation of a democratic society. This consists of an impartial agreement amongst people concerning two main areas: the basic rules of conduct and decision-making that should be followed in the society; and general principles regarding the fundamental social policies that the government ought to carry out.[39]

These preponderance theories have been critiqued for their perceived 'artificiality' which resulted from their undemocratic 'assumptions about ... aggregated individual interests and the arbitrary rejection of other subjective legitimate preferences'.[40]

However, if the national legislative or administrative process through which the majoritarian position is reached is fair, then democratic demands are adequately met.[41] Another difficulty with this conception is that the literature leaves it unsettled how the majority will be determined. In this work I will rely on majority of numbers, rather than weight of political strength or any other measure.

The normative content of the public interest will be directed by each state's socioeconomic context and its national priorities. Such a process and its outcome is an inevitable outcome of Rousseau's conceptualisation of the social contract[42] or Down's social consensus.

---

38   W Lippman, *The Public Philosophy* (Hamish Hamilton, 1955) 44, quoted in J Morison and G Anthony 'The Place of Public Interest' in G Anthony et al (eds), *Values in Global Administrative Law* (Hart Publishing, 2011) 215, 217

39   Anthony Downs, 'The Public Interest: Its Meaning in a Democracy' (1962) 29(1) *Social Research* 1, 5.

40   Morison and Anthony, above n 38, 218. Also see William Fisher, 'Theories of IP' in Stephen Munzer (ed), *New Essays in the Legal and Political Theory of Property* (Cambridge University Press 2001) 168.

41   Caroline B Ncube, 'Harnessing Intellectual Property for Development: Some Thoughts on an Appropriate Theoretical Framework' (2013) 16(4) *Potchefstroom Electronic Law Journal/ Potchefstroomse Elektroniese Regsblad* 375; Anupam Chander and Madhavi Sunder, 'Is Nozick kicking Rawl's ass? Intellectual property and social justice' (2007) 40 *UC Davis Law Review* 563, 577.

42   Jean-Jacques Rousseau, *The Social Contract* (1762).

As stated in the introduction, this chapter reimagines a copyright law that would seek and achieve distributive justice. Such a law would stimulate the production of literature in neglected languages in order to improve education and cultural participation; creating necessary and appropriate mechanisms for the remuneration of authors to spur and reward such production; and ensuring access to those works in order to facilitate their beneficial educational or cultural use.

In Sub-Saharan Africa these ideals of the public interest find expression in the metanorm[43] or concept of Ubuntu,[44] which exists in Botswana, Lesotho, Malawi, Mozambique, Namibia, South Africa, Swaziland, Zambia and Zimbabwe.[45] In Zimbabwe and South Africa, it was critical in the transition to democracy.[46] The South African Interim Constitution of 1993 expressly mentioned Ubuntu and, although it does not appear in the final Constitution of 1996, it has received judicial endorsement through a number of Constitutional Court (CC) judgments. It is applicable to all areas of law[47] and has found application in constitutional, criminal, delictual, contractual and defamation matters.[48] Therefore, it is an accepted part of the legal canon.

Ubuntu's meaning is somewhat elusive,[49] but it generally denotes 'humaneness, social justice and fairness'.[50] It is based on an appreciation of each individual's duty and right to participate in the communal endeavour. It focuses simultaneously on individuality and interdependence. One's individuality is constituted through one's relationships with others, expressed in the Nguni languages as 'umuntu ngumuntu ngabantu' ('a person is a person through others').[51] It also

---

43   Thomas W Bennet, 'Ubuntu: An African Equity' (2011) *Potchefstroom Electronic Law Journal/Potchefstroomse Elektroniese Regsblad* 30, 35.
44   Letseka above n 1, 547.
45   Ibid.
46   Christian BN Gade, 'The Historical Development of the Written Discourses on Ubuntu', (2011) 30(3) *South African Journal of Philos*ophy 303, 309–315; S Samkange and TM Samkange. *Hunhuism or Ubuntuism: A Zimbabwe Indigenous Political Philosophy* (Graham Publishing, 1980).
47   Chuma Himonga, Max Taylor and Anne Pope, 'Reflections on judicial views of Ubuntu' (2013) 16(5) *Potchefstroom Electronic Law Journal/Potchefstroomse Elektroniese Regsblad* 370, 376.
48   Ibid 396–405; Bennet, above n 43, 32–46.
49   Bennett, above n 43, 30–31.
50   *S v Makwanyane*, above n 1, [236]. Also see Letseka, above n 1, 549.
51   Letseka, above n 1, 548; Desmond M Tutu, *No future without forgiveness* (Doubleday, 1999) 36. Also see *MEC for Education: KwaZulu-Natal v Pillay* [2008] 1 SA 474 (Constitutional Court) [53].

loosely translates to 'I am because you are'[52] or 'I am because we are'.[53] Ubuntu encompasses notions of both restorative[54] and distributive[55] justice. Most pertinent to this discussion, is its potential to 'illuminate the always thorny problem revealed when individual interests collide with public interests'.[56] In such cases, it adopts a preponderance perspective and seeks a communally beneficial outcome.

This alignment of preponderance public interest theories with the Ubuntu metanorm creates a lens through which to view ground-up copyright reform that has resonance with both western and African philosophies. That resonance is important because the focal point of this chapter's reimagination exercise is Africa. Intellectual property (IP) laws and principles have failed to gain traction in Africa because they are based upon western ideas of an individual's rights to intangible property that fail to factor in widespread communitarian perspectives. Highlighting the distributive justice aspects of Ubuntu goes some way in better relating copyright to African philosophy and thus garners some 'cultural legitimacy'[57] for it. Similar arguments have been made in relation to human rights in Africa.[58]

In the IP context, cultural legitimacy concerns have been raised with respect to the protection of traditional knowledge, which remains a challenge for conventional IP protection.[59] This is because, in its communities of origin, traditional knowledge is created by, maintained and exploited for the benefit of the collective, rather than for the

---

52   As translated by Jacob Lief and Andrea Thompson, *I Am Because You Are: How the Spirit of Ubuntu Inspired an Unlikely Friendship and Transformed a Community* (Rodale Inc, 2015).

53   As used in Fred L Hord and Jonathan Scott Lee, *I Am Because We Are: Readings in Black Philosophy* (University of Massachusetts Press, 1995).

54   Bennett, above n 43, 35; Himonga, Taylor and Pope, above n 47, 396–405.

55   DJ Louw, 'The African concept of ubuntu and restorative justice' in D Sullivan and L Tifft (eds), *Handbook of Restorative Justice* (Routledge, 2008) 161,165; O Schachter, 'Human dignity as a normative concept' (1983) 77 *American Journal of International Law* 848, 851.

56   Himonga, Taylor and Pope, above n 47, 422.

57   A term used by Chuma Himonga in making a case for relating Ubuntu to human rights in order to legitimate it, in Chuma Himonga, 'The right to health in African Cultural Context: The role of Ubuntu in the realization of the right to health with special reference to South Africa' (2013) 57 *Journal of African Law* 165–195, 165.

58   Ibid; Josiah AM Cobbah, 'African Values and the Human Rights Debate: An African Perspective' (1987) 9(3) *Human Rights Quarterly* 309.

59   JT Cross, 'Property rights and traditional knowledge' (2010) 13(4) *Potchefstroom Electronic Law Journal/Potchefstroomse Elektroniese Regsblad* 12.

individual.[60] They have been the foundation for calls for a *sui generis* system of protection for traditional knowledge or for more carefully considered IP protection. These claims can be extended to copyright protection in general. If part of copyright's aim is to stimulate the production and dissemination of cultural works, should it not have cultural legitimacy? This chapter proceeds on the assumption that this legitimacy could be derived from copyright's service of the public interest via a focus on distributive justice and close alignment with the Ubuntu metanorm.

In reimagining copyright, it's important to note that the interests of a preponderance of persons will vary in relation to the type of work at issue. For example, there may be a national policy to promote literacy and a constitutional obligation for the state to provide access to a basic education.[61] Such imperatives may mean that the public interest in relation to copyright-protected works, which are used in educational contexts, is different from that which pertains to other copyright-protected works that are not central to the acquisition of a basic education and literacy.

This following section considers some ways in which a copyright law might further the interests of a preponderance of individuals in accordance with principles of Ubuntu and distributive justice. That is, it considers how the law might better:

1. Stimulate the production of literature in neglected languages in order to improve education and cultural participation;

2. Remunerate authors to spur and reward such production; and

3. Ensure access to those works in order to facilitate their beneficial educational or cultural use.

---

60   Dijms Milius, 'Justifying Intellectual Property in Traditional Knowledge' (2009) 2 *Intellectual Property Quarterly* 185, 190.
61   For example, see Enynna S Nwauche, 'The public interest in Namibian copyright law' (2009) 1 *Namibia Law Journal* 43, 66; L Arendse, 'The Obligation To Provide Free Basic Education In South Africa: An International Law Perspective' (2011) 14(6) *Potchefstroom Electronic Law Journal/Potchefstroomse Elektroniese Regsblad* 97; Shireen Motala, 'Educational Access In South Africa' (2011) *Journal of Educational Studies Special Issue Social Justice* 84.

Reimagining copyright

This section suggests a number of different ways in which the existing law might be amended to better further the interests of a preponderance of individuals and the public interest aims outlined above. These span the acquisition of rights; their duration and content; exceptions and limitations; assignment; licences and remedies. The proposals aim to do a better job of identifying the public interest aims identified above, by promoting the creation of new works in African languages, facilitating translations of existing works into those languages, helping authors get a better deal and improving access.

Currently translating works is hampered by the need to obtain licences and its attendant difficulties. There are at least four ways of ameliorating this, namely providing for:

1. constitutive copyright registration;
2. a two-tier copyright system;
3. a limited translation right for copyright-protected works; and
4. introducing local language limitations.

The following pages consider each of these possibilities in turn.

Constitutive registration

Requiring constitutive registration provides authors with the option of opting out of the copyright system and in so doing would ensure that more public domain works are available, which can then be translated without the need to obtain licences. An additional benefit of registration would be the enhancement of legal certainty due to the availability of information about which works are protected.[62] Such information would then be available to enable potential licensees to seek out copyright holders in order to obtain licences.[63]

---

62 Niva Elkin-Koren, 'Can formalities save the public domain? Reconsidering formalities for the 2010s' (2013) 28 *Berkeley Technology Law Journal* 1537, 1541.
63 Ibid; Christopher Sprigman, 'Reform(aliz)ing Copyright' (2004) 57 *Stanford Law Reform* 485, 501.

Any such registration system ought to be implemented both on and offline. Sole reliance on an online system would be inappropriate for a developing country where internet access remains unaffordable for some. Simple registration systems can be achieved as shown by Kenya's voluntary copyright registration system that entail the completion of a simple administrative form, payment of a small fee and the deposit of a copy of the work.[64]

Taking such an approach would better serve the public interest by treating works differently based on commerciality (see section below on tiers) or creative motivation. So for example, a work created for religious ends, such as a papal decree, would be protected differently from a movie or other work created for entertainment purposes and motivated by profit-making. Some creators of works are not motivated by copyright or commercial concerns but find that copyright law automatically foists an economic monopoly upon them. As noted by Tushnet:

> Creativity is messy in ways that copyright law and theory have often ignored to their detriment. Creators speak of compulsion, joy, and other emotions and impulses that have little to do with monetary incentives.[65]

Copyright law's current approach of granting all authors the same rights is the result of its undue focus on the author's creative output, rather than the reason why she created the work in the first place.[66] Heymann notes that, considering this focus on the product, it is odd that copyright law is often justified in relation to the motivation of the creator.[67] The utilitarian justification for copyright posits that people create because of the incentives provided by the exclusivity afforded them by copyright law. However, reality forces one to accept that creators are not always motivated by such incentives. Examples of such creators include those who are religiously motivated to disseminate certain information; those who write for business and personal communication purposes; those who author model legal codes; those

---

64 Section 8 of the *Kenya Copyright Act 2001*; Kenya Copyright Board (KECOBO) (2014) *Requirements for Registration of a Copyright Work and Application for Anti-Piracy Security Device.*
65 Rebecca Tushnet, 'Economies of Desire: Fair Use and Marketplace Assumptions' (2009) 51 *William & Mary Law Review* 513, 546.
66 Laura A Heymann, 'A Tale of (At Least) Two Authors: Focusing Copyright Law on Process Over Product' (2009) 34(4) *The Journal of Corporation Law* 1009, 1009.
67 Ibid.

who take amateur and home photos and videos to archive memories and those who create merely to express their creative talent.[68] Granting the same rights to this diverse body of authors creates a 'uniformity cost'[69] in that creators or authors are saddled with more rights than they want or less than they need.

Those copyright holders who wish to permit others to use their works currently have to take positive action to enable this to happen. This is palatable for commercially driven copyright holders. Indeed, their aim is to be in a position to negotiate and license the use of their protected works. But it presents a barrier to copyright holders who do not set out to commercially exploit their works in this manner but who simply want to disseminate their works and perhaps to also allow others to use them in further creative efforts. To achieve this goal, they have to license users of their works, even where they do not wish to levy licence fees. They could choose not to do this and simply 'put their work out there' for use by whoever wanted to and then desist from suing these users for infringement. This would work for some users, but the risk-averse user is likely to avoid using the work at all, due to the risk of being sued for infringement. Such a scenario thwarts the intention of the creator of the work. The way out of this quandary is for such creators to openly license their works upfront so that any potential user who is willing to abide by the licence terms, may use the work without seeking out the right holder or entering into negotiations with her. Copyright holders who wish to take this approach have to draft the requisite licences which requires some copyright law knowledge or the retention of attorneys, invariably at significant expense. These attendant knowledge and expense difficulties may cause some copyright holders to decide not to license their works in this manner and thus leave society bereft of the benefits of their works.

Non-profit organisations such as Creative Commons have stepped into the gap by providing copyright holders with a simple online mechanism to source such open licences. While these licences work well the law can be criticised for foisting rights upon persons who neither want nor need them thereby forcing them to take action to

---

68   Ibid 1010; Jessica Litman, 'The Public Domain' (1990) 39 *Emory Law Journal* 965, 974.
69   See Michael W Carroll, 'One for All: The Problem of Uniformity Cost in Intellectual Property Law' (2006) 55 *American University Law Review,* 845.

exercise their licensing rights in order to enable use of the copyright-protected works that is not catered for by existing exceptions and limitations. An open licence does not divest a copyright holder of her rights. Rather it short-circuits what might otherwise be a lengthy and complicated licence negotiation and conclusion process by allowing the right holder to license works upfront and present them to users on a 'take it or leave it' basis.

The necessity for open licences is the consequence of copyright laws that do not take cognisance of creator's motivations or intentions. It would be better to create a copyright system that gives economic monopolies, through registration and renewal, to those who want or need them. That would protect authors' interests, while at the same time opening up access to a greater range of works.

A two-tier copyright system

Another possible option might be to create a two-tier copyright system structured to facilitate the entry of works into the public domain earlier than current copyright law allows. Such a system would not grant the same rights in the same way to all creators. The model suggested in this chapter would allow creators, informed by their personal motivation and commercial aspirations, to select a tier under which to protect their work. The proposed tiers are set out below.

Tier 1 works would get copyright protection for a non-renewable prescribed duration of 10–14 years.[70] Tier 2 works would obtain initial protection for one year which would be renewable for a prescribed maximum term upon the payment of renewal fees, provided that the work meets a set revenue threshold.[71] If the system imposes relatively high registration and renewal fees, it is likely that a significant number of copyright holders would not renew their copyright.[72] Only those works which achieve significant commercial success are likely to have their copyright renewed. The system could be further nuanced to set revenue thresholds that must be met by works to render them eligible for renewal. This would enable blockbusters, such a hit Nollywood

---

70   Martin Skaldany, 'Unchaining Richelieu's Monster: A Tiered Revenue-Based Copyright Regime' (2012) 16:1 *Stanford Technology Law Review* 131, 141.
71   Ibid 142.
72   Richard A Posner and William M Landes, 'Indefinitely Renewable Copyright' (2003) 70 *University of Chicago Law Review* 471, 517–518.

or Bollywood films, to secure and maintain copyright for maximum prescribed term of copyright. Some proposals for copyright reform have suggested an indefinite term of copyright,[73] but such an approach would not serve the aims of distributive justice. The determination of an appropriate maximum term would have to be determined either through a new international agreement or nationally. Socially valuable works such as documentaries or literary works in neglected languages may not attain sufficient commercial success to pass the renewal threshold. To promote the production and dissemination of such works, it is proposed that provision be made for the waiver of renewal fees, upon application by the copyright holder. Criterion for determining the social value of a work could include its contribution to the cultural and educational needs of neglected markets.

The benefits of implementing this proposal would be manifold. First, many non-commercial works could be dedicated to the public domain by an author's choice to not seek protection. Secondly, those non-commercial works which would be protected under tier 1 would enter the public domain much quicker than is the case under current copyright law. Thirdly, commercial works that are protected in tier 2 would also enter the public domain in a relatively shorter time than is currently the case due to the revenue thresholds that must be met to sustain protection. A work would only continue to meet these thresholds if consumers continued to spend money to access the work. In that sense, the consumer would be the 'final arbiter' of which works are protected. Fourth, this proposal would eliminate orphan works as only those works which are registered would secure copyright protection, opening up still more works for public use.

Translation rights, limitations and compulsory licences

Under current copyright law, a copyright holder has exclusivity over translations of the protected works for the full term of copyright protection. The Berne Appendix and the Universal Copyright Convention[74] contain substantively equivalent provisions on

---

73   Skaldany, above n 70.
74   *Universal Copyright Convention*, United Nations Educational, Scientific and Cultural Organization, Art V.

compulsory licences for translation and reproduction.[75] This section focuses on the Berne Convention, which has more currency due to its entrenchment in the TRIPS Agreement[76] and the WIPO Copyright Treaty.[77]

The Berne Appendix provides for a non-exclusive and non-transferable compulsory licensing scheme which developing countries can use to enable or facilitate the production of neglected works. These licences can only be issued in relation to 'printed or analogous forms of reproduction.'[78] While there has been some controversy as to the meaning of this phrase and whether it includes digital works, the more pervasive view is that it does.[79] These compulsory licences are available only for (i) translation 'into a language of general use in the country'[80] for 'teaching, scholarship or research purposes'[81] and/or (ii) 'reproduction for use in connection with systematic instructional activities'.[82] These uses are very restrictive and exclude the translation of texts for other purposes such as cultural enrichment or literacy enhancing initiatives that fall outside formal education. For instance, a local library or community centre may run read-a-thons or holiday reading programs which would benefit from the availability of books in local languages. Translation compulsory licences are of particular interest to this chapter, which seeks to find ways of stimulating the

---

75   Alberto J Cerda Silva, 'Beyond the Unrealistic Solution for Development Provided by the Appendix of the Berne Convention on Copyright' (PIJIP Research Paper no 2012-08, American University Washington College of Law, 2012), 7.

76   Art 9.1 of the TRIPS Agreement (*Marrakesh Agreement Establishing the World Trade Organization*, opened for signature 15 April 1994, 1867 UNTS 3 (entered into force 1 January 1995), annex IC (*Agreement on Trade-Related Aspects of Intellectual Property Rights*)) obligates Contracting Parties to comply with Articles 1 to 21 and the Appendix of the Berne Convention (*Berne Convention for the Protection of Literary and Artistic Works*, opened for signature 9 September 1886 (amended in 1914, 1928, 1948, 1967, 1971, and 1979) 25 UST 1341, 828 UNTS 221, entered into force 5 December 1887). However it excludes provisions on moral rights.

77   Art 1(4) of the WIPO Copyright Treaty (*World Intellectual Property Organization Copyright Treaty*, opened for signature 20 December 1996, 36 ILM 65, entered into force 6 March 2002) obligates Contracting Parties to comply with Articles 1 to 21 and the Appendix of the Berne Convention.

78   Berne Convention, Appendix, Arts II (1), II (2)(a), and III.7.

79   Silva, above n 75, 27–31.

80   Berne Convention, Art II (3)(a).

81   Berne Convention, Art II (3)(5).

82   Silva, above n 75, 8.

production of children's literature in African languages. The scope of the translation compulsory licences is very ambiguous, because of the uncertainty of the meaning of the phrase 'a language in general use'.[83]

The licences are to be granted by a competent authority in the relevant state if certain conditions are met and subject to the payment of fair compensation to the copyright holder.[84] The conditions applicable to the issuance of translation licences include waiting periods of three years,[85] which may be reduced to one year in the following two scenarios:

i.   if the language the work is being translated into is 'not in general use in one or more developed countries which are members of the Union';[86] or

ii. developed country member states of the Union have given their unanimous consent and duly notified this consent to the Director-General of WIPO. In addition the relevant language must be in general use in the consenting countries. However such consent cannot be given where the language in question is English, French or Spanish.[87]

Further, there are additional applicable grace periods of six or nine months which must be waited out before a translation licence is issued.[88] The grace period is six months when the full three-year waiting period is obtained, and nine months when a shortened waiting period of one year is obtained. The purpose of these grace periods is to afford the copyright holder an opportunity to translate the work. If the right holder translates the work during the grace period, a compulsory licence will not be issued.[89] There are waiting periods that are applicable only to reproduction licences,[90] which shall not be enunciated here because of the chapter's focus on translation licences.

---

83   Silva, above n 75, 24, n117 citing WIPO Diplomatic Conference for the Revision of the Berne Convention Paris, July 5–24, 1971, General Report of Paris Conference § 34, which defined this phrase to mean that 'a language could be one of general use in a given geographic region of the country, an ethnic group, and even a language generally use[d] for particular purposes'.
84   Berne Convention, Art IV (6).
85   Berne Convention, Art II (2)(a)–(b).
86   Berne Convention, Art II (3)(a).
87   Berne Convention, Art II (3)(b).
88   Berne Convention, Art II (4)(a).
89   Berne Convention, Art II (4)(b).
90   Berne Convention, Art III (4)–(5).

As noted by Štrba these grace periods serve to 'shield' copyright holders after they have failed to provide, or licence someone else to produce, a translation in a manner that is not provided for in patent law compulsory licence provisions.[91]

Finally, there are further conditions that are applicable to both translation and reproduction licences.[92] One of these is the provision of proof by the applicant that:

a. he was denied a licence by the right holder or
b. that the original work in question is an orphan work and despite a diligent search he was unable to identify the copyright holder.[93]

Operationalisation of the compulsory licensing regime provided for in the Berne Appendix is two-staged. The first stage is the filing of notifications with the Director-General of WIPO together with the requisite renewal notice after the passage of the prescribed period. The second stage is the enactment of domestic statutory provisions in copyright legislation as supplemented by the necessary implementing regulations. Some developing countries that have domesticated the Appendix's compulsory licence provisions have failed to operationalise the licensing regime due to their omission of promulgating implementing regulations.[94]

The merits of the Berne Appendix's regime of compulsory licences for translation and reproduction have been canvassed at length by several scholars.[95] It is clear from this scholarship that the Berne Appendix is inadequate as it is 'an obsolete, inappropriate, bureaucratic, and extremely limited attempt to provide an air valve for developing countries'.[96] The main reasons for the 'market failure'[97] of the

---

91 SI Štrba, *International Copyright Law and Access to Education in Developing Countries: Exploring Multilateral Legal and Quasi-Legal Solutions* (Brill, 2012), 93.

92 Berne Convention, Art IV (1)–(6).

93 Berne Convention, Art IV (1).

94 Štrba, above n 91, 100.

95 For example see Štrba, above n 91, 89–109; Salah Basalamah 'Compulsory Licensing For Translation: An Instrument Of Development?' (2000) 40 *IDEA – The Journal of Law and Technology* 503; Silva, above n 75, 25; and Ruth L Okediji 'Sustainable access to copyright digital information works in developing countries' in Keith E Maskus and Jerome H Reichman (eds), *International Public Goods and Transfer of Technology Under a Globalized Intellectual Property Regime* (Cambridge University Press, 2008) 143–187.

96 Silva, above n 75, 11.

97 Okediji, above n 95, 162.

Appendix are the myriad of complex conditions and lengthy waiting periods which often frustrate developing nations who wish to use the Appendix for their citizenry's benefit.

To illustrate these difficulties, it is useful to work out an example in a country (X) that has acceded to the Berne Appendix as follows. A book on natural sciences has been published in English in X by Y publishers. Y denies local publisher Z a licence to translate the work into a local language for teaching in primary schools. Country X would be unable to grant a compulsory licence to Z until the full three-year waiting period has lapsed because it is unlikely that unanimous consent could be obtained from all developed country member states of the Berne Convention. In addition, X would have to wait for the lapse of an additional six months' grace period before issuing the licence to Z. A total of three and a half years is an inordinately lengthy period of time and in some fields this would render the knowledge held in the book in question obsolete. In such instances a translation delayed is, in fact, a translation denied.

Finally, Z would have to pay fair compensation to Y, as determined by the relevant national authority. In resource-poor nations, there may very well be few, if any, local publishers or other entities that are able to pay such compensation, especially if the target market cannot sustain highly priced translated texts so that the translators are unable to recoup their expenses through profit.

In order to facilitate the grant of compulsory licences under the Berne Appendix, countries have to enact specific regulations and set up an elaborate administrative system to implement these provisions. This requires expertise and resources which are already spread quite thinly in most countries, so the cost to the state is high. In addition, fair compensation has to be paid to the copyright holder, so there is also a cost to the translating entity. Where the translated books are sold to readers or consumers, there is also a cost to individuals. Where translation initiatives are state driven, for example by an education department, there will be an indirect cost to society through its funding of the national fiscus via taxes. On the other hand, the benefits do not appear to be commensurate because of the very restrictive scope of the conditions under which compulsory licences may be granted.

Consequently, only a few developing countries have filed notifications under the Berne Appendix, many of whom have failed to renew these notifications.[98] In some cases, developing countries have introduced provisions for compulsory licences in their domestic copyright legislation, without bothering to file a notification. In other instances, developing countries have crafted their own national legislative solutions that are not informed by the Berne Appendix at all, an approach that Silva has characterised as 'idiosyncratic'.[99]

Some suggestions have been made to overcome the inadequacies of the Berne Appendix. These range from amending the Appendix to crafting a new international instrument to replace it.[100] Since this chapter is in search of national solutions, it will not engage with international reforms of this nature. Rather, it suggests the reduction of the term of the translation right, the introduction of local language limitations and compulsory licences under national law.

Reducing the duration of the translation right

Eliminating this right or reducing its scope and duration would facilitate translations of existing works and may be an appropriate amendment to a copyright law seeking to further the interests of a preponderance of individuals. India's *1914 Copyright Act* provided for a translation right of 10 years' duration for works first published in India.[101] If the author published a translation or authorised another person to do so, within those 10 years, the term of the translation right would be extended to the full duration of the relevant copyright in respect of that particular language into which the work had been translated.[102] The work could still be translated into other languages, if an authorised translation into those languages was not produced in the 10 years. Translation of the work after the expiry of 10 years would be deemed to be non-infringing. Prior to this statutory provision Indian courts had held that translation of works was non-

---

98   Štrba, above n 91, 100.

99   Silva, above n 75, 3, 11. See Silva, above n 75, 18–24 and Štrba, above n 91, 100–109 for a description of these approaches.

100 See Silva, above n 75, 40–52 for detailed proposals on the content of such a new instrument.

101 Lionel Bently, 'Copyright, Translations, and Relations between Britain and India in the Nineteenth and Early Twentieth Centuries' (2007) 82(3) *Chicago-Kent Law Review* 1181, 1181.

102 Ibid.

infringing[103] and its legislature had mooted the idea of a translation right of three years' duration.[104] Translation of the work after the three-year translation right term would be deemed non-infringing.[105]

However, pressure from British publishers and then the position taken at Berne (resulting in the Berne Appendix), left India with no choice but to limit the translation right only in respect of Indian works or works first published in India. The 1914 provision was therefore a 'symbolic gesture' by India of its desire to 'limit the translation right for all works, wherever they were published.'[106] It also showed 'a genuine attempt to improve dissemination of learning in India, by maximizing the translation of *Indian* works within India'.[107] Had India implemented its proposal for a three-year translation right in relation to all works, it would have provided a useful model for other developing countries to consider.[108] Nonetheless, its 1914 provision evidences hope of what can be achieved in the absence of legal and political constraints.

Local language limitations

The purpose of this chapter is to imagine what an ideal copyright law might look like. With that in mind, it proposes the enactment of 'local language limitations' that would enable permission-free translations to help address the problem of neglected languages and markets.[109] The limitations would apply to all works and provide that text-based works in specific, local, neglected languages that have been translated or adapted from works in more readily available languages be deemed to be non-infringing. This would create room to translate or adapt works into neglected languages, in circumstances where copyright owners have declined to do so, without fear of infringement proceedings. This provision ought to be coupled with copyright eligibility exclusions

103 Ibid 1205, citing *Munshi Shaik Abdurruhma'n v Mirza' Mahomed* (1890) 14 ILR (Bombay) 586 and *Macmillan v Shamsul Ulama M Zaka Shira'zi* (1895) 19 ILR (Bombay) 557.
104 Ibid 1226, citing the 1885 Copyright Bill.
105 Ibid, 1885 Copyright Bill, Clause 8.
106 Bently, above n 101, 1237.
107 Ibid.
108 Rochelle C Dreyfuss, 'Creative Lawmaking: A Comment On Lionel Bently, Copyright, Translations, and Relations Between Britain and India in the Nineteenth and Early Twentieth Centuries' (2007) 82(3) *Chicago-Kent Law Review* 1243–1250, 1243.
109 Lea Shaver, 'Local Language Limitations: Copyright and the Commons' (2014), unpublished paper on file with the author.

for the resultant translated works, which will enable the creation of a commons. For instance, unauthorised translated works which are deemed non-infringing under local language limitations would be excluded from protection and thus form part of the commons. This would facilitate further translation into other local languages, which would be beneficial in South Africa which has nine official African languages, other than Afrikaans.

Compulsory licences

Since the *1914 Copyright Act*, India has significantly changed its translation rights regime with the enactment of the *1957 Copyright Act*. This Act also provides for the bifurcated treatment of Indian[110] and other works. Section 31A of the *1957 Copyright Act* provides for compulsory licences to publish or translate unpublished 'Indian works', authored by a person who is 'dead or unknown or cannot be traced, or the owner of the copyright in such work cannot be found'. Prior to filing a compulsory licence application, the would-be translator is required to publish his proposal in an English language and the Indian language into which the work is to be translated.[111]

Section 32(1) provides the right to apply for compulsory licences to translate any literary or dramatic works into any language, seven years after the first publication of the work. Where the work is an Indian work and the translation is required for teaching,[112] scholarship or research,[113] the waiting period is reduced to three years.[114] If the language of translation is 'not in general use in any developed country' the waiting period is further reduced to one year. These provisions are inspired by the Berne Appendix[115] and are consequently blighted by

---

110 *1957 Copyright Act* (India), section 31 defines 'Indian work' as including:
   (i) an artistic work, the author of which is a citizen of India; and
   (ii) a cinematograph film or a sound recording made or manufactured in India.
111 *1957 Copyright Act* (India), section 31A(2).
112 Section 32's explanatory note defines teaching as including 'instructional activity at all levels in educational institutions, including Schools, Colleges, Universities and tutorial institutions' and 'all other types of organised educational activity'; *1957 Copyright Act* (India), section 32.
113 Ibid: Section 32's explanatory note defines research as being exclusive of 'industrial research, or purposes of research by bodies corporate (not being bodies corporate owned or controlled by Government) or other associations or body of persons for commercial purposes'.
114 *1957 Copyright Act* (India), section 32(1A).
115 Berne Convention, Art II (2)(a)–(b) and Art II (3)(a).

the interpretative difficulties that apply to their source, which have been highlighted above. A copyright law which furthers the interests of a preponderance of individuals would facilitate the making of translations in appropriate cases, not stymie them with bureaucracy.

In addition to the above proposals, principles of distributive justice and Ubuntu would suggest that more needs to be done to protect the interests of authors. The following pages consider possible ways of doing so.

Author reforms: Non-assignable copyright, standard licences and pro-author interpretative rules, or assignable copyrights plus reversion?

As explained above, authors in disadvantaged contexts are often not in a position to bargain equally with third parties due to financial and other constraints. There are a number of ways in which the current copyright law might be amended to ameliorate this problem.

One way of doing so might be to limit the transfer or assignment of copyrights, perhaps by allowing licensing only.[116] This would ensure that the creator always retains a proprietary interest in the work in issue. In order to prevent further difficulties that maybe created by the need to negotiate and conclude licensing contracts, a responsive copyright law would be supported by the provision of standard form contracts. This would be necessary because reliance on contracts would place creators at a disadvantage due to their probable lack of knowledge of copyright and other relevant laws. Another answer to this vulnerability would be the government's provision of technical assistance with the drafting of contractual clauses, where the parties wish to depart from standard clauses.

The downside of providing for non-assignable copyright is that it deprives creators of an opportunity to sell their works even in circumstances where it would be beneficial for them to do so. To avoid such a situation, it would be more prudent to simply enact a provision

---

116   Baloyi, above n 26, 131.

that would set aside inequitable contracts. This of course then raises the question of the determination of inequity. If it is left unregulated by legislation, it will be necessary for courts to rule on inequity. This means that a disgruntled creator would have to find resources to mount the required litigation, which in disadvantaged contexts will often be beyond her reach. Copyright legislation could prevent or limit the need to seek recourse from courts through provisions setting out the types of terms that would be deemed unfair or inequitable. Consumer protection legislation employs this approach through its black and grey lists. Black lists prohibit specified clauses and render them *void ab initio*, and grey lists create a rebuttable presumption that other clauses are unfair, unreasonable or unjust.[117] This model could easily be adapted to suit the creator-intermediary or creator-publisher context. Alternatively, reliance can be placed on consumer protection legislation in terms of which the creator would be treated as a consumer of an intermediary or publisher's services.

It may also be prudent to include a pro-author default rule[118] in the copyright legislation. The gist of this provision would be that all intended exploitation of a work must be expressly enumerated in an author-publisher contract and that where there is any ambiguity in contractual terms, the ambiguous term should be interpreted in favour of the author.

The alternative to non-assignable copyright is assignable copyright coupled with reversionary rights.[119] Such provisions would allow copyrights that had been assigned to a third party to revert to the creator of the work after a certain period of time. This would afford the creator a second opportunity to exploit the work economically. Such a second opportunity could be valuable where, perhaps due to a lack of resources, legal knowledge, or bargaining powers, creators have assigned their copyrights to third parties on terms that are not favourable. This is a malaise that affects creators everywhere but is exacerbated by the socioeconomic conditions in developing countries. It is hoped that by the time copyright reverts to the creator he would

---

117 Ncube, above n 36, 66; Tjakie Naudé, 'The use of black and grey lists in unfair contract terms legislation in comparative perspective' (2007) 124 *South African Law Journal* 128.
118 Giuseppina D'Agostino, *Copyright, Contracts, Creators: New Media, New Rules* (Edward Elgar, 2010) 261–267.
119 D'Agostino, above n 118, 263.

have acquired some resources and sufficient legal and industry knowledge to enable him to better exploit the work on his own account.

Past iterations of imperial copyright law, including section 5 of South Africa's *1911 Copyright Act*, included a reversionary right.[120] In South Africa this right is still applicable to works made before 11 September 1965 by authors and composers who died between 25 to 50 years ago.[121] It was relied upon by the heirs of Solomon Linda (the composer of *imbube,* a song made famous by Disney's *Lion King*) who secured a settlement of their litigation against Disney and are reported to be now earning royalties on his work.[122] Although there are 'competing narratives', this incident is viewed as a triumph of copyright protection of authors by some.[123] Linda died destitute and his heirs found themselves in the same situation a generation later, while the song continued to earn royalties. The use of the reversionary right to secure equitable treatment for them has been much celebrated. Recognising the value of the reversionary right, the Copyright Review Commission recommended that efforts must be made 'to collect royalties on behalf of heirs of other South African composers to whom section 5 of the 1911 Act applies'.[124]

Conclusion

This chapter argues that the public interest is not served by a one-size-fits-all approach and that, if copyright were designed to further the interests of a preponderance of individuals, it would be better calibrated to satisfy both creators and users. It suggests that, in order to achieve this, more consideration be given to ways in which authors' and users' shares of the copyright bargain can both be increased.

---

120 Tana Pistorius, 'The Imperial Copyright Act 1911's role in Shaping South African law' in Uma Suthersanen and Ysode Genfreau (eds), *A Shifting Empire 100 years of the Copyright Act of 1911* (Edward Elgar, 2013) 204, 216.

121 Ibid.

122 Ibid 216–217; For an account by the heirs' lawyer see Owen Dean, *Awakening the Lion* (Tafelberg, 2013).

123 Colin Darch, 'The Political Economy of Traditional Knowledge, Trademarks and Copyright in South Africa' in *The Sage Handbook of Intellectual Property* 263, 272. For a competing narrative see Håvard Ovesen and Adam Haupt, 'Vindicating capital: Heroes and villains in *A Lion's Trail*' (2011) 61 *Ilha do Desterro* 73.

124 Copyright Review Commission Report (2012), 14 [3.1.7].

This might involve making copyright non-assignable, encouraging greater use of standard copyright licences, pro-author interpretation rules, or coupling assignable copyright with rights of reversion. In relation to stimulating the production of original neglected works or translations of existing works into neglected languages, it suggests that consideration be given to constitutive registration of copyright, a two-tier copyright system, the reduction of the duration of the translation right and the greater use of compulsory licences coupled with local language limitations.

The above suggestions are proffered as individual proposals and not as components of a complete copyright system. For the most part, it would be possible to combine them into a composite system. However, some proposals are mutually exclusive. For example authors' protections pertaining to non-assignment copyright coupled with standard licences and a pro-author interpretation rule cannot be combined with the proposal for assignable copyright with reversionary rights.

9

A reimagined approach to copyright enforcement from a regulator's perspective

Kimberlee Weatherall

Introduction

In a copyright system designed in the public interest, what would enforcement and dispute resolution look like? Since we appear to be in the midst of a knock-down-drag-out fight over copyright enforcement which has persisted for over two decades, this qualifies as a hard question. It is inconceivable however that anyone who set out, with a blank slate, to design mechanisms for copyright enforcement in the public interest would come up with anything like our present system. Copyright enforcement is plagued with inconsistency and injustice affecting both creators and (accused and proven) infringers. At least in some parts of the world, we are caught up in a deterrence death spiral that is failing to achieve basic copyright goals.

This chapter explores some ideas for breaking away from current unproductive thinking on enforcement, drawing on regulatory theory and research in psychology. At its heart lies a thought experiment: what if we created a public copyright regulator, tasked with using a fixed pool of public resources to attempt to secure widespread observance of copyright principles? How would such a regulator approach their task, and what tools would they need? The public copyright regulator is not a proposal but an intuition pump:[1] thinking through how such a regulator might choose their priorities gives us some clues about how we might choose our own in the real world. Perhaps the insights of regulatory theory can help us break out of a cycle of deterrence failure and escalation, and move towards a positive vision where enforcement contributes to both creators' and society's goals.

Let us be clear at the outset: the ideal copyright enforcement matrix depends significantly on the rest of copyright law. Imagine if copyright were a very narrow set of rights: say, if it consisted of limited duration, proprietary rights to exclude commercial activities that substitute for a copyright owner's own exploitation, granted only following registration and after meeting substantive thresholds, where licensing is easy, there are protections for user rights built in and individual creators secure a significant share of the returns. In such a copyright system, 'enforcement' might be largely confined to actions brought against commercial operators whose actions deprive creators of a livelihood. In that alternative universe, our chief concerns in enforcement design might be to ensure broad access to systems of justice equipped and ready to ensure that copyright's highly targeted rights are fully and frequently upheld. That, of course, is not (and will likely never be) our copyright world, as the accumulated chapters in this volume amply demonstrate (and it may not even be the copyright world we want, as again these chapters suggest). This chapter therefore assumes something like our current copyright: long, broad rights covering a wide range of subject matters with potential infringers ranging from the individual at home to the commercial counterfeiter and all kinds of public and private intermediaries in between. And in that world – ours or something very like it – we could use some new ways of thinking.

---

1   Daniel Dennett, *Intuition Pumps and Other Tools for Thinking* (WW Norton & Company, 2013).

1. The deterrence death spiral

1.1. The costly pursuit of deterrence and its problems

Modern copyright treaties and rules often put deterrence or similar concepts at the forefront of the enforcement calculus,[2] and the rhetoric of public debate frequently links deterrence to ever-more-draconian penalties. As a result, we have seen 'the punitive provisions of copyright laws … on a mindless upward curve, defying both gravity and any relationship to need or purpose'.[3] In no sensible world would a US law professor be able to calculate his (hypothetical) liability for an ordinary day's activities at US$12 million;[4] nor would the theoretical 2012 maximum damages bill for an iPod full of infringing content be US$8 billion.[5] And draconian punishments are not wholly hypothetical. US decisions have rendered certain unfortunates into scapegoats to appease the angry gods of general deterrence,[6] awarding civil damages which dwarf any conceivable measure of harm or potential criminal fine.[7] A UK student spent two years fighting extradition to the US and a threatened 10-year jail term over a website he created as a teen.[8]

---

2   Many treaties require contracting states to provide 'remedies which constitute a deterrent to further infringements': see e.g. *Marrakesh Agreement Establishing the World Trade Organization,* opened for signature 15 April 1994, 1867 UNTS 3 (entered into force 1 January 1995), annex 1C (*Agreement on Trade-Related Aspects of Intellectual Property Rights*) ('TRIPS'), Art 41.1; *World Intellectual Property Organization Copyright Treaty,* opened for signature 20 December 1996, 36 ILM 65 (entered into force 6 March 2002) ('WIPO Copyright Treaty') Art 14.2. Cf the European IP Enforcement Directive which uses different language, requiring that 'measures, procedures and remedies shall … be effective, proportionate and *dissuasive'* (emphasis added): *Directive 2004/48/EC of the European Parliament and of the Council of 29 April 2004 on the Enforcement of Intellectual Property Rights* [2004] OJ L 195/16 Art 3.2.

3   William Patry, *How to Fix Copyright* (Oxford University Press, 2011), 194. Copyright is not the only field seeing a shift towards a more punitive style of regulation: Robert Baldwin, 'The New Punitive Regulation' (2004) 67 *Modern Law Review* 351, 352–360.

4   John Tehranian, 'Infringement Nation: Copyright Reform and the Law/Norm Gap' (2007) (3) *Utah Law Review* 537, 543–547.

5   'The $8 Billion iPod' on *TEDBlog* (20 March 2012) <blog.ted.com/2012/03/20/the-numbers-behind-the-copyright-math/>.

6   General deterrence is aimed at deterring members of the general public, cf specific deterrence which is aimed at deterring the particular individual apprehended or punished.

7   High damages awards have been awarded in the US in *Capitol Records Inc v Thomas-Rasset* 692 F 3d 899 (8th Cir, 2012) (US$222,000 for 24 songs made available on peer-to-peer networks); *Sony BMG Music Entertainment v Tenenbaum* 719 F 3d 67 (1st Cir, 2013) (US$675,000 for 30 songs on peer-to-peer networks).

8   Adam Gabbat and Owen Bowcott, 'Richard O'Dwyer's two-year extradition ordeal ends in New York', *The Guardian* (online), 8 December 2012 <www.theguardian.com/uk/2012/dec/06/richard-o-dwyer-avoids-us-extradition>.

Today's global copyright law and order auction has spawned an unrelenting parade of new proposals to end infringement which appear at a rate which cannot be absorbed by democratic processes. From criminalisation of non-commercial activity and anti-circumvention rules, to notice-and-takedown, graduated response, website blocking and 'follow the money' approaches, advocates have moved onward and upward before the public policy processes of discussion and consensus-building for the last idea are complete. Older mechanisms are branded inadequate, but not gracefully retired.[9]

The public and private cost of this pursuit of deterrence is unquantified,[10] but almost certainly high in some countries. In theory, society should devote resources to enforcement up to the point where the marginal benefits of fighting infringement (preferably, increased incentives and hence more creativity) equal the marginal cost of enforcement activities. No society in the world knows if it meets this benchmark. To some extent it cannot be calculated, since some of the benefits of enforcement are non-monetary: for example, the benefits from enforcement of authors' moral rights. But even leaving those issues to one side, there has been little attempt to examine the impact of enforcement initiatives on creative income. And even back-of-the-envelope calculations of the resources consumed in the quest for more perfect copyright compliance are challenging.[11] Expenditure borne by the taxpayer would include:[12]

---

9   Australia in 2006 introduced a legislative scheme to allow the police to issue on-the-spot fines for infringement: *Copyright Amendment Act 2006* (Cth) Schedule 1. The scheme remains on the books unimplemented. In 2010, the UK introduced a legislative framework for graduated response – that is, the application of escalating measures against internet access customers identified as infringing. Four years later, after exhaustive policy processes, no scheme is in effect and attention has shifted to industry negotiations: *Digital Economy Act 2010* (UK).

10   A recent National Research Council study identified, as the first research question on enforcement, 'How much money do governments, copyright owners, and intermediaries spend on copyright enforcement?': Stephen Merrill and William Raduchel, *Copyright in the Digital Era: Building Evidence for Policy* (National Research Council, 2013), 3.

11   For a discussion and some efforts to this end, see Joe Karaganis, 'Rethinking Piracy' in Joe Karaganis (ed), *Media Piracy in Emerging Economies* (Social Science Research Council, 2011) 1, 19–20.

12   Ian Hargreaves, *Digital Opportunity: A Review of Intellectual Property and Growth* (UK Intellectual Property Office, 2011), 81. I note that not all of these costs are entirely borne by the taxpayer: in some cases, copyright owners will pay fees that defray or cover some of these costs. In that case, those costs become part of the private spend recognised immediately below.

- Bureaucratic and policymaker costs: staff time within government departments and coordinating bureaucracies (e.g. the US intellectual property (IP) enforcement czar), spent on activities such as administering enforcement schemes, and analysing and consulting on proposals;
- Direct policing costs: customs, police and prosecutor time and resources (including warehousing of seized materials);[13]
- General civil and criminal court staff and resources, including in some countries the establishment and operational costs of specialised courts;
- Costs incurred by trade negotiators, specialised embassy staff, and seconded officials (time and travel) negotiating the expanding web of IP enforcement treaties, consulting with stakeholders, and reporting to and attending meetings of IP working groups;
- Costs of dedicated enforcement and related research programs of the OECD, WIPO, WTO, and assorted IP Offices;
- Costs of public education campaigns.

Then there is the accumulated private spending on enforcement, including:

- Investigation costs associated with civil proceedings and police processes;
- The cost of enforcement proceedings;
- Operational costs of specialist organisations like the Motion Picture Association of America (MPAA), Recording Industry Association of America (RIAA), etc.;
- Spending on lobbying and policy processes (both by right holders and by third parties responding); and
- Spending by intermediaries such as online service providers and payment service providers on notice-and-takedown, graduated response, website blocking and other enforcement activities.[14]

---

13   Or organisations such as the French online enforcement body HADOPI, with estimated costs in the tens of millions: Rebecca Giblin, 'Evaluating Graduated Response' (2014) 37(2) *Columbia Journal of Law and the Arts* 147, 155.

14   Industry Canada suggested that sending a single notification of alleged infringement cost large ISPs C$11.73 ($32.78 for small ISPs) (2006); UK government estimates were that the *Digital Economy*

The total sum currently borne by society is likely to exceed that which would be considered optimal, both because it is spread across multiple parties, and owing to the disconnect between the parties receiving direct benefits (copyright owners) and parties whose resources are used to create that benefit (third parties and the public). The fact that spending is spread across a range of actors reduces our ability to consider holistically the effectiveness of the enforcement matrix. There is therefore an additional risk that, even if the overall resource allocation is excessive, there is nevertheless underspending in some areas (e.g. providing accessible mechanisms for enforcement by smaller creative operations) and overspending in others (e.g. trade negotiations that fail to provide tangible benefits). As for the disconnect, copyright owners have few incentives to be sparing in their demands on the public purse. In these circumstances the total spend is likely to exceed the resources a copyright owner would devote if they had to justify them against measurable results. We can defend expenditure of public resources by reference to the societal benefits of both copyright and public respect for law, but we should be aware of the risk of excessive spending, and apply caution when calls for new resources are made.

I return below to questions regarding how to respond to these disconnects. First, however, we need to ask: is deterrence the right framework for thinking about enforcement?

1.2. The research on deterrence

Research in a range of fields suggests that foregrounding deterrence and trying to achieve it through draconian penalties reflects a misunderstanding of the reasons people comply with law.

Gary Becker's classic insight is that a rational actor will adjust their behaviour in response to the expected, rather than the maximum legal sanction: that is, the legal penalty discounted to reflect the probability of being punished.[15] We can increase the expected sanction either by raising the penalty, or increasing the likelihood of being prosecuted.

Act three strikes scheme would cost £290–500 million: Ian Brown and Christopher Marsden, *Regulating Code: Good Governance and Better Regulation in the Information Age* (MIT Press, 2013), 83.

15   Gary Becker, 'Crime and Punishment: An Economic Approach' (1968) 76 *Journal of Political Economics* 169; similar ideas trace back at least as early as Jeremy Bentham, *The Rationale of Punishment* (R. Heward, 1830).

Becker's insights, however, applied to *rational* actors, while research in cognitive psychology underlines that human behaviour is not purely rational. Thus the empirical evidence suggests that increasing prosecution rates has greater impact;[16] that perceived risk must reach a high threshold before it will have any effect,[17] and that perceived risk is often lower than actual risk, making it even harder to achieve deterrence.[18] It seems too that social influence has a significant impact on legal compliance: individuals' perceptions of each other's values, beliefs, and behaviour affect conduct:[19] in an environment where disobedience to a legal rule seems widespread, individuals are likely to infer both that the risk of getting caught is low, and that, even if caught, they will incur little stigma or reputational cost. The combined effect is to make disobedience more likely (think about the level of compliance with road rules in Delhi).

Another challenge in relying on higher penalties to effect deterrence is that in order to be dissuaded from a course of action by *law*, one must have some knowledge of the law and the potential penalty, and an ability to take it into account in framing one's activities.[20] It must also be possible to comply with the law without disproportionate difficulty.

Finally, in circumstances where the application of sanctions is unlikely, securing compliance with law means influencing what people do in circumstances where there is little or no threat of immediate punishment.[21] Psychologists have conducted research probing why people choose to comply with law. At least two intertwined elements

---

16 Dennis Nagin, Dennis, 'Deterrence: A Review of the Evidence by a Criminologist for Economists' (2013) 5 *Annual Review of Economics* 83; Bentham, above n 15, also identifies *delay* between wrong and penalty as a further factor.

17 H Laurence Ross, *Deterring the Drinking Driver: Legal Policy and Social Control* (Lexington Books, 1982), 105. See also Baldwin, above n 3, 373 referring to general 'risk underestimation or under-deterrence'.

18 Paul H Robinson and John M Darley, 'The Utility of Desert' (1997) 91(2) Northwestern University Law Review 453, 460–463. This is subject to an availability heuristic: people overestimate the likelihood of risks that have recently eventuated: Amos Tversky and Daniel Kahneman, 'Availability: A heuristic for judging frequency and probability' (1973) 5(2) Cognitive Psychology 207.

19 Dan Kahan, 'Social Influence, Social Meaning, and Deterrence' (1997) 83(2) *Virginia Law Review* 349.

20 Paul Robinson and John Darley, 'Does Criminal Law Deter? A Behavioural Science Investigation' (2004) 24(2) *Oxford Journal of Legal Studies* 173.

21 Tom Tyler, 'Compliance with Intellectual Property Laws: A Psychological Perspective' (1997) 29 *NYU Journal of International Law and Politics* 219, 224. '[A] law-abiding society is one in which people are motivated not by fears, but rather by a desire to act in socially appropriate and ethical ways ... To have a law-abiding society, we must have a polity in which social values

impact on the likelihood of voluntary compliance with legal rules.[22] First, it is easier to ensure observance of a law that is consistent with commonplace morality – that is, individuals' feelings about what is right and wrong. Second, people are more likely to comply with laws they consider legitimate:[23] that is, laws that are fair and which they believe were enacted through legitimate processes.[24]

In sum, raising the expected sanction in order to deter infringement of the law is harder in the real world than we would expect in theory. On the other hand, compliance is influenced by other factors unrelated to deterrence: ease of compliance with the law, and whether the law is perceived to be consistent with societal or community standards, and legitimate based on the processes by which it has been made.

Consider how these insights apply to the challenge of enforcing copyright today. Technology has made infringement easy, which, if we are concerned with deterrence, suggests that we need to raise the expected sanction. Increasing the likelihood of prosecution so as to have an appreciable impact on deterrence is hard because, with very widespread infringement, even large absolute numbers of prosecutions will affect a small proportion of infringers. It will be particularly difficult for smaller creators to rely on deterrence, given their limited resources to pursue infringement: a focus on deterrence may therefore advantage certain kinds of (well-organised, large) copyright owners. The perception, fostered by copyright owners, that infringement is widespread likely lowers the perceived risk of experiencing any sanction. It may be equally difficult to raise penalties, since sanctions are already high, and radically disproportionate penalties (especially

---

lead them to feel responsible for following rules, irrespective of the likelihood of being caught and punished for rule breaking': Tom Tyler and John Darley, 'Building a Law-Abiding Society' (2000) 28 *Hofstra Law Review* 707.

22   Tyler, above n 21. Other researchers raise additional factors but support the importance of moral consistency and legitimacy. Winter and May, for example, divide compliance influences into three categories: normative factors (Tyler's morality and legitimacy); social factors (stemming from a desire to be respected and approved, and avoid negative publicity, shame, guilt and disapproval) and calculated factors (factors such as the cost of compliance, likelihood of detection and likely penalties): Søren Winter and Peter May, 'Motivation for Compliance with Environmental Regulations' (2001) *Journal of Policy Analysis and Management* 675.

23   Tyler, above n 21, 224–225; 232.

24   Patry, above n 3, 186–187.

when out of kilter with sanctions in other areas of law) risk being undermined by the exercise of prosecutorial or judicial discretion.[25] In sum, deterrence is, at best, challenging to achieve.

The ease of complying with copyright varies significantly between countries, and between kinds of copyright content. For consumers, 'compliance' means buying legitimate copies, which may or may not be possible depending on whether and how copyright owners have chosen to make material available: as Ncube discusses in this volume, access at affordable prices is highly restricted in many countries.[26] Where licensing is required, the ease of compliance depends on the ability of a prospective licensee to identify copyright owners, the willingness of copyright owners to license, and, where large numbers of works are involved, mechanisms for collective licensing. Licensing is hard, as both Gangjee's and de Beer's chapters point out, owing to copyright's long duration, fragmented ownership, and the absence of registration. This constrains or delays the creation of legitimate content distribution services, and so has feedback effects on ease of compliance for consumers.

And copyright has an image problem.[27] Although the broad idea that people deserve rewards from their own creative efforts may be consistent with many people's views of right and wrong, the complex, technical rules of copyright law accreted through decades of industry-to-industry negotiations and lobbying only poorly reflect that principle. Nor is copyright widely perceived as a law that rewards creators, as contributions to this volume emphasise: in the current caricature, flesh and blood creators mostly scrape together a living (at best) while intermediaries (record companies, movie studios, technology companies) reap the profits. In less developed countries, copyright is likely seen as a law that benefits the richer developed world at the expense of everyone else.[28] And even aside from a general decline in trust for government,[29] at least in those countries where

---

25   Mark Lemley and R Anthony Reese, 'Reducing Digital Copyright Infringement Without Restricting Innovation' (2004) 56 *Stanford Law Review* 1345, 1405; Paul Robinson and John Darley, 'The Role of Deterrence in the Formulation of Criminal Law Rules: At Its Worst When Doing Its Best' (2003) 91 *Georgetown Law Review* 949.

26   For stark figures illustrating that this is often not done, see Karaganis, above n 11.

27   Jane Ginsburg, 'How Copyright Got a Bad Name for Itself' (2002) 26(1) *Columbia Journal of Law and the Arts* 61.

28   Karaganis, above n 11.

29   Tyler, above n 21.

changes to the law have come about through trade agreements, copyright suffers from the perception that it is designed, domestically and at an international level, by big corporations against the interests of the broader population.[30] This has been recognised by WIPO Chief Francis Gurry, who has argued that:[31]

> [what] we have to do is challenge society to share responsibility for a fundamental question of cultural policy: How are you going to finance cultural production in the digital environment and in the twenty-first century? Because it can't be free. How are we going to do that? That is the question that we should ask society as a whole to share, and for which to share the responsibility.

Current copyright law does not clearly map to this goal. So an important element of a truly persuasive case is some redesign of copyright law in the public interest,[32] including some redesign to try to ensure more protection for actual creators (rather than just intermediaries).[33] If we are going to persuade people to observe copyright restrictions and respect the rights of creators, it does need to be a law that people can believe in, or at least accept as a necessary tool to pursue a worthy and important social end.

But for now, a single-minded focus on deterrence is a pathway to a policy death spiral.[34] Most enforcement innovations are likely to fail, because infringement is easy, deterrence is not achieved, and other psychological motivators for compliance are absent. This leads to lobbying for even more draconian responses. The impetus for political action is built by creating a perception of widespread disregard of copyright which, perversely, may encourage non-compliance by normalising infringing behaviour. Higher penalties have negative feedback effects: both the spectacle of lobbying and the resulting ever-more-outrageously draconian copyright law will be presented by opponents as proof of copyright's lack of justice and legitimacy.

---

30   Ginsburg, above n 27.
31   Francis Gurry, 'Copyright in the Digital Environment: Restoring the Balance: 24th Annual Horace S Manges Lecture, April 6, 2011' (2012) 35(1) *Columbia Journal of Law and the Arts* 1, 7.
32   In the real world – the world outside this workshop and outside this book – we can head some way in this direction with some recognition of user and public interests: for example, the adoption of fair use defences; the removal of some of the most ridiculous rules.
33   For a discussion, see Senftleben and Geiger in this volume.
34   Not every country has gone down this route, but some appear to be caught in such a cycle: the US, Australia and the UK arguably among them.

The dynamics of this deterrence death spiral can be ruinous for infringers and intermediaries caught up in it. But they are also a problem for creators and creative industries.[35] Imagine yourself in the shoes of the beleaguered right holder. Current systems provide limited justice; enforcement feels like a very long and losing battle against the Hydra, where no sooner is one infringer banished to oblivion but several more rise in its place. You confront an unattractive set of expensive enforcement options that incur negative publicity. Actions against uncontroversially bad actors building businesses through unconstrained infringement lead to limited, temporary successes. A copyright owner who pursues ordinary people engages in a war against fans; one who pursues intermediaries looks like an anti-technology and anti-innovation dinosaur.

We need refreshed thinking in this space based on a broader set of principles beyond deterrence. What this might mean I examine further below. But first, I should address one vision of IP enforcement: perfect enforcement through technology.

1.3. A perfect technology of copyright justice?

One abiding question is whether, in some future technological world, we could short-circuit even the need to persuade people to respect copyright, by moving towards frictionless copyright management. This is the vision conjured up memorably in the concept of the 'Celestial Jukebox' popularised by Paul Goldstein in the mid-1990s.[36] Goldstein imagined:

> a technology-packed satellite orbiting thousands of miles above earth, awaiting a subscriber's order – like a nickel in the old jukebox, and the punch of a button – to connect him to a vast storehouse of entertainment and information through a home or office receiver combining the powers of a television, radio, CD and DVD player, telephone, fax, and personal computer.[37]

---

35   This paper is not concerned with explaining why copyright interests continue to push an enforcement agenda that seems so self-destructive: see Karaganis, above n 11; Peter Drahos, 'Securing the future of intellectual property: intellectual property owners and their nodally coordinated enforcement pyramid' (2004) 36(1) *Case Western Reserve Journal of International Law* 53.

36   Paul Goldstein, *Copyright's highway: From Gutenberg to the celestial jukebox* (Hill and Wang, 1994).

37   Ibid 187. See also Janelle Brown, *The Jukebox Manifesto*, Salon, (14 November 2000) <www.salon.com/2000/11/13/jukebox/>.

Although the technology of Goldstein's vision has dated, the shift towards streamed content and subscription services in some parts of the world potentially exceeds even the promises of Goldstein's vision. Goldstein posited that the Celestial Jukebox would not only provide access to a cornucopia of content, but would enable creators to understand their markets. Every transaction would reveal consumer preferences, and creators could channel investments ever more precisely to meet demand.[38] Present day systems like Pandora, Spotify or Netflix not only fulfil these visions, but use revealed preferences as input for tailored individual recommendations – informing consumers as well as copyright owners.[39] And while Goldstein's vision focused on consumer access, there are also agonisingly slow steps towards 'one click' or one-stop-shop licensing at the 'wholesale' level of copyright, embodied in technologies like Google's ContentID, which identifies use of copyright content on YouTube and offers removal or licensing options, or the United Kingdom's Copyright Hub, intended to simplify low-value licensing. In a world of frictionless copyright transactions, the role for enforcement is, in theory, much reduced, especially if the Jukebox is supported by technology that limits access to those with the right credentials.

Nevertheless, technology remains something of a wildcard for copyright and our societal goals. The perfect technology of justice remains elusive:[40] the 'answer to the machine' has not yet been found in the machine.[41] Comprehensive digital rights management through trusted computing, an obsession of the 1990s and the other side of the Jukebox 'coin', has been eschewed by many: not least because it would require a level of centralised control over other people's devices that is Orwellian, anti-innovation, and technically challenging. The emphasis today seems to be towards technology as a means, not

---

38 Goldstein, above n 36, 188. Another set of approaches built on 'frictionless' copyright are arguably proposals around the greater use of copyright levies: for example, levies on internet access to compensate copyright owners for filesharing, or levies on blank media to compensate for private copying. See, for example, William Fisher, *Promises to Keep* (Stanford University Press, 2004).

39 Joshua Gans, *Are music artists exiting the music business?*, Digitopoly (31 May 2014) <www.digitopoly.org/2014/05/31/are-music-artists-exiting-the-music-business/>.

40 Lawrence Lessig, 'The Zones of Cyberspace' (1996) 48(5) *Stanford Law Review* 1403 ('Law as code is a start to the perfect technology of justice').

41 Charles Clark, 'The Answer to the Machine is in the Machine' in P Bernt Hugenholtz (ed), *The Future of Copyright in a Digital Environment* (Kluwer Law International, 1996), 139.

for control of content in the hands of consumers, so much as for either blocking access (for example, through website or geo-blocking) or to detect infringers through sharper online surveillance.

There are serious questions too whether a frictionless copyright world is a desirable societal goal from a creator's perspective. First, it is not obvious that such a vision works beyond content like music. Music may lend itself to the all-you-can-eat model (although some musical artists and fans would disagree), but what about books? Or visual art? And if investment is perfectly informed by data analysis would the result be infinite diversity, or the triumph of the bland? There are also questions about who benefits:[42] artists have raised concerns about returns from subscription services like Spotify.[43] If the Celestial Jukebox is a vertically integrated monopoly or oligopoly, would independent creators be excluded, or what would they have to give up in order to be included?

There are also problems from a user perspective. The model would likely involve perfect price discrimination: that is, charging consumers different prices for the same content, where the price variation cannot be explained by variations in costs. Perfect price discrimination is controversial: it involves significant wealth transfer from consumers to creators/distributors but also perhaps facilitates access for the disadvantaged.[44] And finally, in a perfectly controlled world, questions arise about how we ensure activities presently enabled by copyright exceptions.[45]

In sum, at least for now, technology is either not an answer, or not the answer that we want, although technology can of course provide partial answers to specific issues and is doing so successfully.

---

42   See generally Greg Lastowka, 'Walled Gardens and the Stationers' Company 2.0' (Working Paper, 21 January 2013), available at <ssrn.com/abstract=2204465>.

43   Rebecca Giblin, 'Reimagining copyright's duration', Chapter 6 in this volume.

44   Fisher, above n 38, 164–169.

45   See generally Dan Burk and Julie Cohen, 'Fair Use Infrastructure for Rights Management Systems' (2001) 15 *Harvard Journal of Law and Technology* 41.

2. A thought experiment: Introducing the public copyright regulator

This volume is built on the idea that a thought experiment can help us to see beyond current problems. And so to break out of the deterrence death spiral and deal with enforcement holistically, I imagine how a hypothetical public regulator of copyright might approach their task, drawing some inspiration from Ho's Representative Individual discussed in Chapter 1.

Imagine you are appointed as the first public copyright regulator, tasked with promoting widespread observance of copyright norms. You will be provided with a fixed level of resources (ample, but not infinite). Your task will be to survey the infringement landscape and tools available to address it, prioritise enforcement activities, and devise mechanisms for addressing infringement effectively and efficiently. You will have overall responsibility for copyright enforcement across the board. You will also design the regulatory tools, the powers and remedies you will need, and policies to guide use of those tools. What powers would you consider essential, and what principles would guide your decision-making? What goals would you adopt, and how would you prioritise in allocating your resources?

Adopting the perspective of the hypothetical public copyright regulator is a tool for reimagining copyright enforcement in the public interest. Such a regulator should focus on the societal rather than the private interest in copyright and in enforcement of rights. Her primary aim should be to maximise the societal benefits of copyright: that is, to promote the interests of all individuals in society in the aggregate, creators, consumers and others.[46] My assumption is that the chief goals of copyright are to provide incentives for the production and dissemination of a diverse range of creative works, in order to ensure (1) fair returns for creators, enabling at least some creators to make a living from their work; (2) access to creative and informational works for the broader society; and (3) broad opportunities for participation in the cultural life of the community, enjoyment of the arts and sharing

---

46   For a discussion of the concept of the public interest, including the 'aggregate' approach, see Chapter 1 in this volume.

in scientific advancement and its benefits.[47] A focus on diversity and on enabling creators to make a living implies a concern particularly with individual creators.

An obvious objection to my thought experiment is that copyright is not susceptible to public management and enforcement. Copyright, a critic might say, creates proprietary interests, and it is the task of copyright owners to enforce their property rights, if necessary by suing infringers in the civil courts for copyright infringement. But this is a caricature of copyright as it really exists in most countries.

In common with a wide range of property rights, we already treat respect for copyright as a matter of public interest by creating criminal sanctions for breach. Further, copyright today has many regulatory aspects:[48] various countries have piecemeal public systems for mediating certain disputes and making adjustments to IP rights for assorted public purposes.[49] Administrative tribunals exercise oversight over copyright licensing[50] and create exceptions;[51] public officials make numerous enforcement decisions.[52] Further, current enforcement initiatives focus on making parties *other* than the copyright owner (including non-infringing parties) spend resources on enforcement: this can only be justified by a belief that there is some public interest in the enforcement of copyright beyond the pure private interest of right holders: otherwise, we would expect that right holders would

47   To adopt the language of article 27 of the Universal Declaration of Human Rights.
48   Joe Liu, 'Regulatory Copyright' (2004) 83(1) *North Carolina Law Review* 87; Kimberlee Weatherall, 'Of copyright bureaucracies and incoherence: Stepping back from Australia's recent copyright reforms' (2007) 31(3) *Melbourne University Law Review* 967; Thomas Streeter, 'Broadcast Copyright and the Bureaucratization of Property' (1992) 10 *Cardozo Arts and Entertainment Law Journal* 567; Shuba Ghosh, 'When Property is Something Else: Understanding Intellectual Property through the Lens of Regulatory Justice' in Axel Gosseries, Alain Strowel and Alain Marciano (eds), *Intellectual Property and Theories of Justice* (Palgrave Macmillan, 2008).
49   Examples include Ofcom's role in the (stalled) three strikes system established by the *Digital Economy Act 2010* (UK); the public bureaucracy established to administer a 'three strikes' system for penalising infringing users in France; the US Register of Copyrights process for creating new exceptions to anti-circumvention law; Australia and New Zealand's Copyright Tribunals; competition authority oversight of collecting societies in Australia and the US: for an overview of some of the Australian processes see generally Weatherall, above n 48; in the US see Liu, above n 48.
50   Australian Copyright Tribunal; UK Copyright Tribunal; New Zealand Copyright Tribunal; Copyright Board of Canada.
51   For example, the role assigned to the US Register of Copyrights in creating exceptions to the prohibition on circumvention of copyright technological protection measures under 17 USC § 1201.
52   Both customs officers and police officers must make decisions whether to pursue enforcement when informed of infringement by copyright owners.

have to pay intermediaries to get involved. In short, no natural pattern for the mix of private and public involvement in enforcement would be violated in establishing a copyright regulator.[53]

In early drafts of this chapter I contemplated imagining enforcement of copyright, for the purposes of this experiment, as an exclusively public function, depriving authors and intermediaries of standing to bring proceedings. There were three difficulties with imagining copyright as a purely public right. First, as Gangjee has pointed out in his chapter, the more abstract our thought experiment, the less we can learn from it when we 'return' to thinking about copyright as it is today. Second, it would be unprecedented to treat a proprietary right thus, and even beyond property there are relatively few legal rules we treat as exclusively matters for public vindication: murder and manslaughter can be the subject of civil proceedings for wrongful death. Third, such an approach would remove from the thought experiment the interesting and difficult questions we face around how to manage the interface between public and private enforcement initiatives.

Instead, therefore, I have chosen to imagine a public copyright regulator who has the usual tools of the state to enforce the law. These include police powers: the power to initiate both criminal proceedings with a view to criminal convictions, fines and possibly imprisonment; powers via customs procedures to prevent entry of infringing goods into the jurisdiction. They also include powers to commence civil proceedings for infringement seeking civil remedies including injunctions and damages (with a view to obtaining rulings on important issues, or on behalf of copyright owners who suffer harm); powers to require alternative dispute resolution or seek enforceable undertakings from private parties in lieu of court proceedings; and the power to provide authoritative information around copyright and undertake public

---

53   The mix of private and public enforcement can vary significantly, both across areas of law, and within areas of law but across jurisdictions. Cf the extended literature in the field of corporate law illustrating the different mixes of private and public enforcement in corporate law: e.g. Howell E Jackson and Stavros Giantinis, 'Markets as Regulators: A Survey' (2007) 80 *Southern California Law Review* 1239; John C Coffee Jr, 'The Law and the Market: The Impact of Enforcement' (2007) 156 *University of Pennsylvania Law Review* 229, 256; Eloise Scotford and Rachael Walsh, 'The Symbiosis of Property and English Environmental Law - Property Rights in a Public Law Context' (2013) 76(6) *Modern Law Review* 1010.

education campaigns. Comparable regulators would include the US Federal Trade Commission, the UK's Ofcom, or Australia's Australian Competition and Consumer Commission (ACCC).

In my thought experiment, copyright owners would still be entitled to bring actions for copyright infringement seeking to recover damages. The public regulator would have the power to intervene in such private litigation, for the limited purpose of making submissions on questions of public interest which might arise and which might not otherwise be aired in an adversarial litigation system.

Obviously this is a thought experiment, or intuition pump, not a proposal. Not only does my simplified thought experiment violate principles regarding the separation of powers which are fundamental in at least some countries, but my hypothetical is clearly idealised. In the real world, a public copyright regulator would risk being captured, or focusing in a narrow and single-minded way on copyright enforcement at the cost of broader societal goals. My hypothetical regulator takes a broad view of the public interest rather than assessing her performance by reference only to enforcement- or infringement-related Key Performance Indicators (KPIs). Few actual regulators would refuse the expansion of their powers, but mine binds herself, Odysseus-like, removing the temptation to overuse regulatory power by precommitting to limited and tailored powers. In other words, she is superhuman. Superhumans are useful in a thought experiment: trying to find one and appoint her is quite a different matter.

3. What would the public copyright regulator do?

The next stage of the thought experiment is to consider when and how the public copyright regulator would use her powers. The discussion necessarily proceeds at a high level of generality, but even so, significant differences may be observed between thinking this way, and how enforcement works currently.

3.1. Principles guiding when the regulator uses her powers: Copyright's quid pro quo

If society's goals for copyright are, as discussed above and in Chapter 1, both to promote creativity and to ensure access and participation, this implies a quid pro quo: creators are granted rights *in return* for societal benefits, and the public copyright regulator is entitled to enforce both sides of the bargain.

This means that the enforcement orientation of a public copyright regulator differs from that of the private copyright owner. An emphasis on copyright's quid pro quo suggests not only that compulsory licences will sometimes be appropriate, but also that, both in considering the allocation of resources towards enforcement, and what remedies to seek,[54] she could justifiably take into account the absence or degree of public access to the relevant content. The regulator ought to (with some qualifications considered below) prioritise spending of enforcement resources on material made readily available to the public (whether in the private market, or through reasonably priced access in public institutions like libraries), and refuse to spend public resources where materials are not available, or negotiate for better access as a precondition of devoting public resources to enforcement. Note that this approach has a beneficial feedback effect: to the extent that infringement is exacerbated by a lack of (reasonably priced) legal alternatives, then a regulator who improves access simultaneously helps reduce infringement.

This reasoning would need to be qualified in situations where copyright content is in draft form and/or will be available imminently: subject to comments below regarding delayed release windows, a creator *planning* to exploit their material ought, in general, to be the first one to release material publicly and gain the benefits of a well-timed, well-promoted first release. Distinct considerations might apply to certain kinds of content, such as the products of indigenous peoples' creativity which may be governed by very different rules. Questions might also arise regarding moral rights: a creator's right to

---

54   I am clearly not the first person to think of this: see e.g. Pamela Samuelson, 'The Copyright Principles Project: Directions for Reform' (2010) 25 *Berkeley Technology Law Journal* 1175, 1223–1226 (suggesting availability should be relevant to court decisions to grant or refuse injunctions).

be recognised and to exercise some control over the presentation of their work may also require a different approach: a point to which I return below.

My argument that enforcement and remedies can legitimately be conditioned on access might be criticised for re-writing copyright law as a 'use it or lose it' system inconsistent with its history and with the recognition of authors' natural rights. Within the bounds at least of this thought experiment, I do not resile from that position: perhaps copyright *should* be 'use it or lose it', subject to the exceptions mentioned above. Regardless of how it might be used in the real world, copyright is neither designed nor intended to provide a default privacy law or a mechanism for private censorship.[55] In any event, we are talking about the expenditure of public enforcement resources: nothing in this analysis would prevent a copyright owner from bearing the full costs of enforcing their own copyright.[56] Demanding some level of access in return for enforcement of copyright is not a demand that copyright owners subsidise the public, rather, it is a refusal to subsidise creators in the absence of clear societal benefit.

Harder questions arise if copyright content is available, but on unreasonable terms: for example, it is unaffordable to 90 per cent of the population.[57] I would propose however that a public copyright regulator spending public resources is entitled to take into account broader issues of equity and distributive justice, and treat such material as functionally unavailable. This could be justified as a matter of basic democratic principles external to copyright. It could also be justified by reasoning internal to copyright: if we want to encourage creativity in the long term, then ensuring broad access to culture is more likely to encourage participation in creation from the broadest

---

55   Some people use copyright to enforce privacy or commercial confidentiality in unpublished material. The focus here, however, is on *copyright* in the public interest: privacy interests ought to be managed by the law of privacy or commercial confidentiality; they cannot be appropriately addressed through copyright. Reliance on copyright leads to anomalies. For example, copyright can protect privacy in emails or in unpublished letters, but does not confer property rights on the subject of an (intimate) photograph or film.

56   Subject to cases where a compulsory licence would be appropriate: i.e. in circumstances where the public interest in use of copyright material overrides the copyright owners' rights to allow use, and where payment is appropriate. Different countries have different rules governing when compulsory licences are available, and the limiting principle at an international level would be the three-step test.

57   Karaganis, above n 11.

possible proportion of the population. Remember that creators themselves are not always from the wealthiest parts of the community, and themselves require access to a full cultural storehouse to feed their own creativity.

Further, and bearing in mind the discussion earlier, remember that the regulator must take into account (a) the need for regulatory tools of persuasion as well as coercion and (b) evidence emphasising the importance of the law being seen as both consistent with morality and legitimate. Building a persuasive case for copyright is going to be much more difficult where it serves only the wealthy elite. The issues obviously become more difficult where the disparity in access is less stark: what if material is available to 50 per cent of the population? At what point is it the responsibility of the State to step in to subsidise access? Nevertheless, the principle is clear: equitable access is a valid consideration for a public copyright regulator in determining the distribution of enforcement resources.

What if material is *going* to be made available, but at a later date than elsewhere? Do copyright's goals require timely public access to content? There is no single principled answer to this question. On the one hand, to the extent that we are concerned about copyright incentives, there are arguments in favour of release 'windows' chosen by copyright owners to maximise their returns. On the other hand, a public copyright regulator could legitimately question whether they should devote their limited resources to sheltering copyright owners from the impact of disruptive technological innovation and globalisation, when at least part of the solution lies in their own hands via global release dates.[58] The regulator's response would likely depend on the nature of the material. She might offer incentives for earlier release (for example, providing targeted enforcement around the release date). But in cases where copyright content is an input to other businesses – for example, if local businesses were denied or charged highly disadvantageous prices for software necessary for international competitiveness – then the position becomes much starker, and there might be a public interest case for refusing to lift a finger.

---

58   Patry, above n 3, 186. To the extent that delays in release are due to State action (e.g. censorship processes) this reasoning would not apply.

Another objection will doubtless have occurred to the reader by this point. I seem to be proposing that a public copyright regulator sit in judgment over copyright owners' decisions regarding timing, pricing, and means of distribution. Surely the market best decides how to distribute the rewards of creativity, and by creating proprietary rights in content, copyright allows consumers, through the market, rather than patrons, or the State, to determine which creators succeed, and their level of reward? As de Beer points out, our assumption has been that some matters are best dealt with by rules outside copyright.

I acknowledge that emphasising copyright's quid pro quo reduces copyright owners' control; the assumption in this chapter is that we grant rights of control for societal benefit, not the natural rights of the creator. But again, there are a number of responses. First, I am assuming that a copyright owner could still delay or limit access to their content and/or charge very high prices, *provided* they are prepared to bear the full costs and risks of this strategy. Second, the expenditure of public resources on enforcement can be characterised as a subsidy to copyright owners that supports pricing and distribution strategies that would not otherwise be possible: we are not in fact operating in a 'pure' market in any event. Third, I am not arguing that the regulator should sit in judgment on *content*: if we accept that a goal of copyright is the production of *diverse* content, then there should be no expectation that enforcement investment of a regulator would depend on content being 'worthy'.

3.2. What remedies would a public copyright seek, and when?

Having established the kinds of cases in which a public copyright regulator would exercise their powers, the next question is, what remedies or enforcement approaches would they use? In thinking through this issue from a regulator's perspective, we can benefit from considering regulatory theory.

Regulatory theory explores ways to direct limited resources to further the substantive goals of the law and promote widespread compliance. This literature suggests that a regulator ought not always meet infringement with legal action (civil or criminal). While having the ability to escalate enforcement action to serious penalties is a tool regulators can use, such penalties should not be a regular occurrence.

Unlike much of our debate in copyright, regulatory theory does not foreground a simple model of deterrence linked to draconian penalties, but builds in a role for the tools of persuasion.

According to responsive regulation theories, regulators' tools for securing compliance can be conceptualised as a pyramid. At the wide base are the soft tools of persuasion: guidelines, educational strategies, and engagement of regulated parties in a dialogue. The presumption is that the regulator should start with these tools, which are less costly and coercive and can therefore be more broadly employed, and can, where an actor is inclined to be law-abiding, secure voluntary compliance. When such methods fail, then the regulator should deploy progressively more coercive tools: industry co-regulatory schemes; civil proceedings seeking court orders for damages and/ or injunctions. Irrational actors who cannot be persuaded any other way may need to be 'incapacitated' (i.e. prevented from doing harm), whether that means imprisonment, loss of a licence or closure of a business. Generally, the regulator adopts a 'tit for tat' approach which assumes people wish to act virtuously until events prove otherwise.[59] Persuasion and deterrence are linked in an overall strategic approach in which the regulator is a 'benign big gun', one who 'speaks softly but carries a big stick'. This variegated stance stands in marked contrast to a mentality which assumes all infringers are bad people who are deterred only by threat of punishment.

The later regulatory literature elaborating on this basic model recognises that enforcement in the real world is complex. It can be wasteful, for example, to always start at the base of the enforcement pyramid. In some circumstances it may be more efficient to target certain kinds of actors: commercial counterfeiters do not deserve a 'softly softly' approach. In addition, 'smart regulation' proponents note the potential for moving 'across' regulatory techniques rather than just 'up' the pyramid. For example, *ex ante* controls (like screening) or non-state controls (norms, markets) may be more effective.[60] It may be possible

---

59   To a copyright reader, this may *sound* like graduated response, but don't be too sure: as discussed below, current graduated response schemes are more like a caricature rather than a faithful embodiment of responsive regulation approaches.

60   Neil Gunningham and Peter Grabosky, *Smart Regulation* (Clarendon Press, 1998), Chapter 6; see also Richard Johnstone, 'Putting the Regulated Back into Regulation' (1999) 26 *Journal of Law and Society* 378, 383.

to change the environment, or 'architecture',[61] to make compliance easier and non-compliance harder. This takes us back to the question of technology: in the copyright field, it could involve attempts to make infringement physically difficult or impossible, through digital rights management or other intermediary-based techniques, such as website blocking or notice-and-takedown. As discussed above, these kinds of techniques raise issues around accountability, transparency, and the potential impact on innovation; nevertheless, they illustrate that escalation is not the only approach.

Another qualification is that big sticks are not always good, and bigger sticks are not always better. Consistent with the earlier discussion, moral intuitions and the legitimacy of regulation matter. This means that fairness and proportionality, and not just whether an infringer is compliant or recalcitrant, are important when assessing penalties: the rule of law is discredited if large actors who cause serious societal harm (but comply when caught) are punished significantly less than individuals who cause little harm.[62]

Further, empirical research suggests that attempting to characterise illegal behaviour as immoral where this view is not widely shared can backfire, leading to resistance rather than compliance. In one case study by Christine Parker, an Australian regulator sought to require firms accused of cartel behaviour to acknowledge their wrongdoing, and publicised the criminal nature of the behaviour. Regulated firms responded by lobbying for restraints on the regulator.[63] We have seen similar dynamics emerge when right holders have attempted to paint downloading copyright material as a criminal act akin to stealing a handbag: such attempts have led to parody rather than a change in culture.

One objection to using regulatory theory in the context of copyright enforcement is that theories like responsive regulation were developed in the context of industry regulation and assume a relationship between regulator and regulated of some longevity, involving repeat interactions, in which the regulator can try different approaches and in which the regulated parties get to know the regulator's attitudes

---

61   Lawrence Lessig, *Code and other laws of cyberspace* (Basic Books, 2000).

62   Karen Yeung, *Securing compliance: A principled approach* (Hart Publishing, 2004) 168–170.

63   Christine Parker, 'The "Compliance" Trap: The Moral Message in Responsive Regulatory Enforcement' (2006) 40(3) *Law & Society Review* 591.

and approaches. There is some truth to this objection, but I do not think it fatal. First, there are many contexts for copyright 'dealings' which do fit the classic regulation model: think, for example, about large users of copyright material (educational institutions, media organisations, internet intermediaries) and large copyright rights organisations. Second, it is by no means clear that regulators in general do have ongoing relationships with the objects of regulation (Australia's corporate regulator would have little contact with the vast majority of registered companies in Australia).

Certainly the copyright enforcement environment is complex, with many different kinds of infringement, ranging from the market counterfeiter (and their online equivalent), through to legitimate businesses and institutions through to a range of different individuals. The creator and copyright owner landscape is also complex, ranging from individual and small creatives (who may be operating in niche or popular contexts) through to larger creators and intermediaries engaged in production/publication and distribution.

Despite this complexity, the literature on regulatory theory provides useful insights when it comes to how *remedies* might work better in copyright. It is not at all clear that copyright as currently written benefits from these various insights. While regulatory theory recommends a strategic and varied approach, in which different cases are treated differently, and the most serious penalties are reserved for the most serious and recalcitrant offenders, current copyright infringement and remedial rules are drawn broadly and treat unlike cases alike.[64] Good faith or attitude on the part of the infringer is mostly disregarded in analysing infringement.[65] Penalties and remedies in copyright present, not as a pyramid, but a great, fat cone, with no clear apex. Our hypothetical public copyright regulator should undertake some sharpening.

---

64 For example, criminal copyright laws in developed countries treat single and isolated infringements in a commercial context as criminal, regardless of the impact on copyright owners' interests. US copyright law subjects non-commercial infringement to the same punitive statutory damages awards as would be available against a commercial counterfeiter.

65 Many jurisdictions do recognise defences for 'innocent infringers'. Such defences, however, are often limited to actors who neither knew, *nor had the opportunity to know* that their conduct involved infringement. Thus a good faith actor who was merely ignorant is not necessarily excused. Innocent infringer defences also tend to limit monetary, but not other remedies.

There is no lack of ideas for constructing a fiercely pointy enforcement apex for the most harmful and recalcitrant infringers. In many countries, serious, commercial, deliberate infringement of copyright attracts criminal penalties,[66] including imprisonment.[67] These ought to be 'apex' punishments, rarely applied: criminal liability has a special impact, imposing stigma that can lead to long-term limitations on the life choices of a person, or the prospects of a business.[68]

Internationally, however, there has been a push, particularly by the US, to treat single commercial infringements of copyright as criminal acts.[69] Such laws are sometimes justified on the basis that they are necessary to ensure proceedings do not fail on technical issues of proof. On this view, while the *law* may be drafted broadly, a prosecutor or regulator can *apply* the law in 'pyramid fashion'. There are problems with this argument, however. The availability of serious penalties for ordinary commonplace behaviour not harmful to copyright owners creates inconveniences for legitimate businesses, and brings the law into disrepute. Opponents love to satirise the absurdity of extreme copyright. Second, to the extent that the provision of serious penalties serves the rhetorical purpose of conveying the seriousness of infringement, that message given is muddied by over-extensive provisions. A public copyright regulator who takes seriously the research around regulation and compliance with law will take different approaches for different kinds of infringers, and will want to ensure that their enforcement system has 'teeth', without breeding disrespect for the law through an excessively punitive approach. Assuming they do, as suggested, wish to precommit to limited use of remedies,

---

66 Required by TRIPS, Art 61.

67 Required by ACTA (*Anti-Counterfeiting Trade Agreement*, opened for signature 1 May 2011 [2011] ATNIF 22 (not yet in force)) but not by TRIPS; examples include UK (*Copyright, Designs and Patents Act 1988* (UK), s 107), Australia (*Copyright Act 1968* (Cth) ss 132AC-132AM), and US (17 United States Code § 506(a) and 18 United States Code § 2319(b)).

68 Douglas Husak, *Overcriminalisation: The Limits of the Criminal Law* (Oxford University Press, 2008).

69 The argument that single or small-scale commercial infringements ought to be treated as criminal was central to the US' dispute with China in the WTO: Panel Report, *China—Measures Affecting the Protection and Enforcement of Intellectual Property Rights—Report of the Panel*, WTO Doc WT/DS362/R (26 January 2009). The US has also pushed to include such provisions in recent trade agreements, including, most recently, Art 18.77.1 of the *Trans-Pacific Partnership Agreement between the Government of Australia and the Governments of: Brunei Darussalam, Canada, Chile, Japan, Malaysia, Mexico, New Zealand, Peru, Singapore, United States of America and Vietnam* ('TPP'), signed 4 February 2016 [2016] ATNIF 2 (not yet in force).

criminal liability in particular should be available only in extreme cases: of commercial, market-substituting uses or deliberate, sustained undermining of creators' markets.

In both the legislative design and application of remedies, therefore, the public copyright regulator would 'triage' infringement complaints. There are some obvious bright lines that might be drawn: commercial v non-commercial; acts which cause substantial harm v acts which do not; substitution for the copyright owner's exploitation v unauthorised use in the context of non-competing activities. There surely are cases which should only *ever* be disputed in a civil context: infringement by public/non-commercial institutions, and arguably, infringement that does not involve market substitution for the original product.

In the regulatory theory, too, 'incapacitation' is an apex remedy: one that ought not be a commonplace occurrence. A range of incapacitating remedies are included in many copyright laws: permanent seizure and destruction of infringing articles,[70] seizure of implements used to infringe, and confiscation of proceeds of crime and assets traceable to the proceeds of crime.[71] Again, regulatory theory would suggest that remedies of these kinds ought to be sparingly used and explicitly confined to serious cases. It is also possible that such remedies, which go beyond compensation for harm and stray into the realm of punishment, ought to be either confined to proceedings brought by the regulator or only sought in private proceedings with the leave of the regulator.

3.3. How would the regulator allocate resources?

Another key set of questions for the public copyright regulator is how they would allocate their resources across the range of enforcement activities. An idealised public copyright regulator would have a budget, and would undertake both a prospective cost/benefit analysis of enforcement initiatives and *ex post* review to assess the value for money of past initiatives.

---

70   TRIPS, Art 61; ACTA, Art 25.
71   ACTA, Art 25.

She faces some interesting conundrums. She could consider, for example, which provides better value: customs or police? If she can cover, say, a fixed number of full-time equivalent salaries for officers to act on copyright enforcement, what proportion of her human resources should be devoted to stopping pirated goods at the border, and what proportion to police addressing a broader range of copyright crime? What proportion devoted to enforcement online, and how much to physical infringement? Is it possible to make an informed assessment regarding the relative harm caused by the different forms of infringement? Or, assuming she has set a budget to address widespread online infringement of popular content, how could those resources best be allocated: to blocking gateway websites? To identifying infringing consumers and taking steps to educate them? To more general education campaigns?

While I would not argue that these various mechanisms for securing compliance with copyright are substitutable, I *would* suggest that they should be considered together and that a public copyright regulator would want to assess their relative effectiveness and allocate resources accordingly. One of the most valuable things a regulator could do would be to perform a dispassionate analysis of the relative benefits of different enforcement mechanisms: perhaps seeking input from a broad range of copyright owners and creators as to *their* enforcement priorities to inform that analysis.

The very existence of a regulatory *pyramid* suggests that some proportion of resources ought to be devoted the soft tools of persuasion as an integral part of an overall enforcement strategy: seeking to encourage compliance both by making it easier, and by increasing awareness and understanding of the law. Governments, such as the Australian government, have often discussed the *need* for copyright owners to address access questions to encourage compliance, without seeing the promotion of that access as part of their role. Seeing these questions through the lens of regulatory theory, however, suggests that in fact, promoting copyright's quid pro quo is part of the role of the State, and integral to successful enforcement.

Controversially, integrating persuasive techniques might well include attempting to target educative efforts on infringers who might be convinced to comply – for example, by having online service providers send infringement notices to BitTorrenting users. The astute reader will immediately see that this suggestion looks like a watered down version of graduated response. But a public copyright regulator will inevitably have limited resources – which means that not every identified infringement is going to lead to a notice.[72] She will also want her notices to be effective. One way to do so is to make the message concrete, rather than abstract. A targeted form of infringement-and-education notice might therefore be based around targeted campaigns relating to particular (legitimately available) content and around particular economically important points in time, like release dates.

Regulatory theory also recognises that regulators may need to focus resources based on an assessment of the risks that certain persons, firms, or behaviour pose to their overall objectives.[73] Some forms of non-compliance are cheaper and more efficient to address than others.[74] This could mean targeting behaviour that creates the most havoc for copyright owners; or focusing on actions that offer the best chance for the highest risk reductions for a given level of expenditure. Some care must be taken however in applying these latter principles, because economic efficiency, and the economic magnitude of harm, are not the only considerations relevant to copyright enforcement. Many of the chapters in this volume emphasise the need to promote the interests of individual creators. The discussion above has added its own note to this chorus: ensuring that copyright is more clearly linked to its goals, and genuinely promotes the interests of creators is likely to contribute to the overall legitimacy of copyright, and hence to the persuasive factors that will assist in encouraging compliance. Consistent with this reasoning, another goal of the public copyright regulator ought to be to ensure that some proportion of the resources devoted to enforcement benefit individual creators, perhaps by devoting some proportion of the resources allocated to bringing test cases or civil proceedings to cases brought on behalf of, or cases that are important to, such creators (for example, by clarifying legal questions important to such creators).

---

72   Giblin, above n 13.
73   See generally Robert Baldwin and Julia Black, 'Really Responsive Regulation' (2008) 71 *Modern Law Review* 59, 65–68 (describing risk-based approaches), and sources cited therein.
74   Ibid 66–67.

3.4. How would the work of a public regulator interact with technology and technological intermediaries?

A final question of interest is how the public copyright regulator ought to operate in the digital environment. Technology is the scene of many of the great ongoing battles in copyright enforcement. Beyond cases where the intermediary is a wrongdoer (for example, they set out to induce infringement or build a business based on infringement), intermediary liability is sometimes justified on the basis that it offers more efficient enforcement than taking action against individual infringers. Conversely, intermediary liability is *criticised* for shifting enforcement costs from copyright owners to third party businesses and to their customers, some of whom are innocent. Since intermediary liability involves using the intermediary as a 'tool' to get to ultimate infringers, the question arises: is this a tool that a public copyright regulator would seek to use, and if so, how?

A public copyright regulator ought, for all the obvious reasons, to be very slow to start dictating technological design, and as a general principle, ought not to get distracted by the goal of 'solving' infringement through 'the machine'. As Brown and Marsden noted some time ago, a focus on trying to solve the issue of infringement this way has 'distracted attention from business innovation for more than a decade'.[75] Nevertheless, a copyright regulator who wants creators to receive benefits from their creativity cannot remain entirely agnostic about technology and the direction of its development, since clearly technology can develop in ways that are more, or less, supportive of creators' interests, and more or less supportive of other societal interests in copyright. Is there action a public regulator should take to encourage the development of technology in ways supportive of the goals of copyright?

For example, to what extent should the copyright regulator back copyright owner attempts to manage enforcement through technology, for example, by prohibiting the circulation of circumvention technology? It is clear that such technologies *can* play a useful role in copyright enforcement.[76] From the perspective of regulatory

---

75   Brown and Marsden, above n 14, 86.
76   Samuelson et al, above n 54.

theory, such technology, by making it more difficult to infringe, may encourage observance of copyright principles – especially if coupled with moves to make compliance easier by making material accessible at a reasonable cost. On the other hand, a regulator concerned with other *societal* benefits of copyright – including access and, importantly, participation in cultural life and the arts – would wish to encourage development of 'smarter' measures which do not prevent legitimate activity including valuable forms of reuse. On this basis, it would be legitimate to take into account the impact of any technological measures adopted by a copyright owner on public access in determining enforcement priorities. To the extent that a copyright owner chooses to implement technological measures and *fails* to take account of legitimate uses, they have freely chosen technology over copyright, and could, perhaps, be held to that choice.

To what extent should digital intermediaries be required to enforce copyright, or develop internal technologies to help enforce copyright? At present, both copyright exceptions, and principles of primary and secondary liability already play a role in encouraging service providers to participate in deploying reasonable measures and discouraging widespread infringement. In the US, it is notable that the desire of technological intermediaries to make out a defence of fair use has led, in cases like *HathiTrust*[77] and in the context of the Google Book project,[78] to technological design that seeks to protect owner interests. And, as Samuelson et al note, 'safe harbors are an important legal device that can be used both to limit liability in appropriate ways and to encourage those providers to help reduce widespread infringement'.[79] There is therefore attraction to Samuelson et al's proposal to provide a safe harbour for intermediaries who deploy reasonable, effective, and commercially available measures to minimise infringement.

---

77   *Authors' Guild v HathiTrust*, 755 F 3d 87 (2nd Cir, 2014).
78   *Authors Guild Inc v Google Inc*, 804 F 3d 202 (2nd Cir, 2015).
79   Ibid. See also Eric Goldman, 'Want to end the litigation epidemic? Create lawsuit-free zones', *Forbes.com* (online), 10 April 2013, <www.forbes.com/sites/ericgoldman/2013/04/10/want-to-end-the-litigation-epidemic-create-lawsuit-free-zones/>. Goldman argues that safe harbours provide useful 'lawsuit-free zones,' thus avoiding 'the individual and social costs of adjudicating disputes, including the settlements payments to get rid of nuisance and otherwise meritless lawsuits. Plus, lawsuit-free zones stimulate business investments by providing more legal certainty to entrepreneurs, which should translate into more jobs. So finding ways to dial down litigation might be the best "jobs stimulus" effort our legislators could undertake.'

How far would we take the idea that efficient enforcement through technology is something a public copyright regulator would seek to promote? Pushing the idea further might involve a regulator paying or subsidising intermediaries to act: an idea that is less outrageous than it sounds, given the extent of public funding that has been applied to promote recent enforcement initiatives. A public copyright regulator might well wish to have at least some involvement in private enforcement developments. Industry schemes for managing copyright infringement online have come to particular prominence in recent times: in 2014, the US Copyright Alert system commenced operations, sending escalating notices to customers detected engaging in online copyright infringement, based on a Memorandum of Understanding between a number of large internet access providers and copyright owners. Similar industry schemes have been considered in both the UK and Australia.[80]

This raises the important question of how far we ought travel down the path of 'governance' rather than 'regulation'. 'Governance' is an umbrella term for the idea that private parties have a role in the tasks traditionally seen as the role of 'regulation'.[81] Governance includes 'privatized regulation through cooperative standard-setting, licensing of compliant implementations, joint ventures, and other collaborative activities by market participants.'[82] We have seen a growing emphasis on this idea in copyright too, with recent treaties including terms encouraging 'voluntary arrangements' particularly for online enforcement of copyright. Governance-based approaches have certain efficiencies, but they raise difficult questions about both accountability and transparency. The assumption in this chapter is that a public copyright regulator ought actively to exercise oversight over private efforts.

Given the scale of online copyright infringement, and limited public resources, I would expect that a public copyright regulator would be generally favourable towards these kinds of scheme, with two provisos. First, the copyright regulator would want to be sure that procedural

---

80   For detailed analysis of the scheme, see Ann-Marie Bridy, 'Graduated Response American-Style: "Six Strikes" measured against Five Norms' (2012) 23 *Fordham Intellectual Property, Media and Entertainment Law Journal* 1.

81   Julie E Cohen, 'What Privacy is For' (2013) 126 *Harvard Law Review* 1904, 1928.

82   Ibid.

fairness or due process was being observed, even in private schemes.[83] This might be achieved, for example, by requiring regulator approval of schemes before they come into effect. Second, a copyright regulator concerned with ensuring diversity in creation would look for ways to ensure that voluntary deals of this kind did not lock out smaller or independent creators:[84] even if that meant, perhaps, subsidising participation by smaller creators.

Conclusions: What can we learn from the thought experiment?

A number of ideas have emerged from the discussion above that are worth gathering together:

- The goal of a public copyright regulator would be, not to simply enforce copyright, nor even simply to reduce infringement, but to maximise the overall societal goals of copyright, including, but not limited to, ensuring appropriate incentives;

- Pursuit, and indeed *enforcement* of both these goals means that both in deciding *whether* to enforce copyright in a given situation, and what *remedies* to seek, a public copyright regulator would take into account whether members of the public can access the material, on reasonable terms, from a legitimate source. The regulator could legitimately decide not to enforce copyright in content not made available on reasonable terms;

- The copyright regulator ought to approach (many) infringers at least in the first instance on the assumption that they are law-abiding types who want to do the right thing – this implies a persuasion-based approach rather than an immediately punitive or deterrence-based approach;

- Over-deterrence and over-criminalisation are likely to breed disrespect for the law. Criminal provisions and other highly punitive mechanisms ought to be confined to serious cases;

---

83   See further Bridy, above n 80.
84   Cf Giblin, above n 13.

- Enforcement measures ought to be assessed holistically, directly compared for their effectiveness in promoting the full range of copyright goals, and allocated resources according to their effectiveness.

There are numerous infringement and enforcement scenarios we could analyse in depth, to consider how a public copyright regulator would analyse the situation and apply her regulatory tools. We have not considered here how she would deal with moral rights disputes; how she would handle disputes involving arguable fair use, or how best to oversee the potentially monopolistic behaviour of collecting societies insofar as they are engaged in enforcement and may impact on the persuasive force of copyright law. There simply isn't space, in one short paper, to think through every scenario.

Nevertheless, the discussion above has certain raised some possibilities that could be considered in real world copyright reform: the possibility that criminal liability and incapacitating remedies ought to be confined in legislation to serious cases; the possibility that other remedies could be assessed and even limited by reference to the degree of access the public have to copyright material; perhaps the possibility that resources for new enforcement initiatives ought to be allocated from an existing budget according to their proven or projected effectiveness.

Something as widespread as current copyright infringement is more than misbehaviour. It is, in part, resistance: resistance to the rules of copyright; resistance to the frequent threats of existential annihilation (or at least disconnection from the internet) for copyright infringers. We need copyright enforcement, because copyright rights without enforcement are a nullity. But we need a more positive vision of what enforcement could be, and how it could operate to promote the goals of the copyright system. I hope that my thought experiment has proved it has value, in that it offers a different way of thinking through enforcement issues – in particular, shifting our attention away from the deterrence death spiral and into more positive ways of thinking about building legal compliance and a more positive vision of copyright and how we can promote the societal goals of copyright.

10

A collection of impossible ideas

Rebecca Giblin and Kimberlee Weatherall[1]

This is a collection of impossible ideas

As flagged in the introduction, this book's contributions exhibit rich divergence: they identify the aims of copyright differently, offer a variety of conceptions of the 'public interest', and sometimes fundamentally disagree with one another. We do not, in this book, offer one coherent vision for a future, redesigned, ideal copyright law. We are reimagin*ing* copyright law – and much more debate is needed, from a larger variety of stakeholders, before solutions might be found. But nonetheless, these collected chapters combine to provide some salient themes and lessons which recur throughout the book.

This concluding chapter is not intended to merely summarise the collected chapters: each is a complex and standalone set of ideas, and each deserves its own reading. Instead, the questions we want to explore in this final instalment speak to a bigger picture. First, what are those common threads or ideas for a reconception of copyright in the public interest: when our authors took a step back, what were some of their core reimaginings? Second, how achievable are those

---

1   In writing this chapter the authors benefited from discussions with a range of experts, including in particular Professor Sam Ricketson (University of Melbourne), Professor Tim Stephens (University of Sydney), and Professor Chester Brown (University of Sydney). We thank them for their assistance; any errors are of course our own.

ideas on the spectrum from attainable to pipedream? And finally, where to from here? Is this collection is merely an ode to what 'could have been', or, impossible or not, do the ideas here still have a role to play in the current debates racking international and national copyright systems?

Emerging themes and ideas

Designing copyright 'in the public interest' means giving *more* to authors

The first common theme that emerges strongly from these collected chapters is that, when invited to think about the design of copyright in the public interest, most of our contributors evinced a concern that current copyright rules do a poor job of protecting the interests of individual authors and creators. Many chapters are informed by a desire for a system that would better recognise authors' ongoing interests in their works and better reward them for their creative labour. These motivations are reflected in a wide range of suggestions: incorporation of a more nuanced understanding of the variegated goals of different kinds of artists (Senftleben); facilitation of ongoing author involvement in the exploitation of their creative works in order to better secure to them the fruits of their labours (Senftleben, Giblin); promoting opportunities for authors to write in their own languages (Ncube); or facilitating collective bargaining (de Beer). These chapters don't write out other important players such as producers and publishers from copyright either. Unfragmented ownership along the lines of de Beer's suggestions might demand a different industry structure but would not suggest an absence of intermediaries; Giblin's proposals on term and Gangjee's proposals regarding registration would explicitly protect and encourage the distinct contributions and investments of producers as well as those of creators.

In other words, when this book talks about *the public interest* in copyright, it is never as a proxy for user interests or consumer interests. Quite the contrary: whether contributors reimagined copyright via a conception built upon a preponderance of interests, or from the perspective of a representative individual sitting behind a veil of ignorance, they recognised the importance of supporting creativity, and ensuring a rich and productive cultural life, and have made suggestions for better accommodating various competing interests. The ideas in these chapters are not a menu of ways to destroy rights. They are ideas for unlocking some of the value *for creators and society as a whole* that are blocked under current system, and for making the pie bigger for all.

An increased role for reciprocity

Reciprocity is a second key thread that runs through this collection. Many of the contributing authors have argued that, if copyright is to serve the public interest, it is going to require some measure of reciprocity. This understanding of copyright implies both rights *and* duties or responsibilities for everyone: users, creators and others. As Gangjee puts it in his chapter, '[t]here is so much we could be asking of those making a claim to copyright protection, which we refrain from asking, [and this is] in stark contrast to most other areas of IP [intellectual property] law'.

Copyright has rarely been thought of this way: the international legal framework is very clear about the obligations of users and the public generally in relation to copyright – chief among these being a duty not to infringe.[2] It was not until the *Marrakesh Treaty to Facilitate Access to Published Works for Persons who are Blind, Visually Impaired or Otherwise Print Disabled* was settled in 2013 that significant internationally mandated minimums for access were recognised,[3] and even these are expressed as exceptions rather than as reciprocal obligations of copyright owners.[4] Nonetheless, one of copyright's most fundamental justifications is that it provides benefits to the public. The theory of copyright which is embodied in current international frameworks and domestic laws appears to be that if the rights are taken care of, the public's benefits in the form of distribution and access

---

2   Sometimes copyright imposes additional positive duties: larger institutional users sometimes have positive duties to keep copies secure or ensure they are not used for unapproved purposes.
3   Although it is worth noting the mandatory requirement to make quotations permissible, found in Berne Convention, see n 7, Art 10.1.
4   See Rebecca Giblin, 'Is it copyright's role to fill houses with books?' in Susy Frankel and Daniel Gervais (eds), *The Internet and Intellectual Property: The Nexus with Human and Economic Development* (Victoria University Press, forthcoming) <ssrn.com/abstract=2853970>; Paul Harpur and Nicolas Suzor, 'Copyright Protections and Disability Rights: Turning the Page to a new International Paradigm' (2013) 36(3) *University of NSW Law Journal* 745.

will take care of themselves – after all, what rational copyright owner would refuse to make their material available on commercial terms? And yet we know for a fact that access to copyright material is *not* evenly distributed: work towards the Marrakesh Treaty highlighted the book famine suffered by those with print disabilities;[5] Ncube's chapter highlights the serious dearth of access to material for significant populations who do not speak English or some other dominant language, and the scale of the orphan works problem demonstrates that society regularly values and demands access to works in which their owners have no interest in exploiting.

This collection's authors wouldn't leave access so much to chance. Instead, they have imagined a much more distributed group of rights and duties and a greater engagement with issues of distributive justice. Geiger and Weatherall, for example, both suggest some form of positive duty of dissemination on copyright owners: Geiger as a standalone duty; Weatherall as a condition precedent to the application of public resources on enforcement. Ncube's proposals include a different kind of 'use it or lose it' principle, conditioning a continuing right to distribute translations on an owner's exploitation of that right. Both Gangjee and Giblin would require creators to positively demonstrate some minimal interest in continued protection after an initial fixed period in order to trigger additional rights, and Senftleben suggests a greater level of give and take as between authors: author's rights, he suggests, include a right to reuse and critique others' material. De Beer's chapter, while endorsing copyright as a market mechanism, nevertheless still recognises that other issues such as access may need to be addressed (albeit while arguing that the best mechanisms for so doing lie outside the copyright system).

Issues like distribution and access loom large when you place yourself, like Ho's Representative Individual, behind a veil of ignorance, and face a possible future where you are not endowed with the resources to thrive in a world of user-pays access to culture and knowledge.[6] It is easy to be blasé about questions of access from a position of privilege. If, however, you come at the matter from the perspective of having an even chance of belonging in the less-well-resourced half of the global population, would you be happy trusting entirely to the market and

5   See e.g. Giblin, above n 4.
6   For a more detailed exploration of this point see Giblin, above n 4.

the good offices of copyright owners for your ability to participate in global culture? Or would you ensure the benefits of copyright come with at least some minimal obligations to broader society? Try this *ex ante* approach on others, and see how quickly their focus switches from rights of protection to rights of access.

One size does not necessarily fit all

A third theme observable in a number of these collected chapters is the idea that one size does not necessarily fit all − and that one way to address this might be through 'phased' rights. Not all right holders have the same interests or concerns. Both Giblin and Gangjee, in seeking to design systems responsive to both the needs of commercial producers and distributors on the one hand, and individual creators on the other, proposed phases of copyright. Those two contributions independently proposed an initial short period of protection in recognition of creators' interests in their works, and as a way of levelling the playing field between individual creators and better resourced corporations. After this initial period, Gangjee's proposal would see protection for economic rights secured through obligatory registration for the remaining term of protection. Giblin's proposal, reflecting the reality that not all works *need* and not all creators *want* the same term, would set terms that march with their ongoing interests in their works. Recognising that creators' ongoing personal interests in works could outlast the economic, both contributions emphasised the need for moral rights (such as right of attribution and integrity) that would remain available regardless of copyright or registration status. Ncube's proposal also demonstrates how one size doesn't fit all, this time along the dimensions of access and development. With reference to the dire shortage of literature in neglected languages, she calls for greater rights over translation and use as a way of furthering human and economic development.

Are these impossible ideas?

The proposals collected here, then, imagine (to a greater or lesser degree) a differently conceived copyright: one that recognises the distinct interests of human creators, while also placing a higher importance on reciprocity and ensuring society gets its quid pro quo.

This leaves us with a very important question. The project started by asking contributors *not* to worry about the international legal framework. Now though, we do have to ask: how big a constraint is it on the ideas that we've proposed?

A great deal of the commentary in this area is premised on the idea that, as awareness grows about the inefficiencies and lost culture brought about by current approaches, change at the treaty level will follow. We very much wanted this book to end on a similarly positive and hopeful note. Ultimately though, the more deeply we explored these questions, the more our attempts to do so felt naive.

The truth of the matter is that the really significant changes mooted here – the ones that would bring about paradigmatic change in the way copyright operates, improving outcomes for creators and society as a whole – require rethinking longstanding international rules. Berne's minimum term of life plus 50 for copyright works dates back to 1948.[7] Its blanket ban on formalities as a condition of the enjoyment and exercise of rights was decided the year the first Model T's started rolling off Ford's production line.[8]

Today, these rules have been inextricably woven into the international economic order. When one actually sits down and tries to chart a pathway to treaty reform, it becomes apparent that the prospect of substantial change is illusory. No matter how much sense it might make to require copyright owners to assert some continuing interest in their works, or to rethink terms to better align with what copyright is intended to achieve, Berne's mandated minimum terms and prohibition on formalities simply. Won't. Budge.

---

7   *Berne Convention for the Protection of Literary and Artistic Works*, opened for signature 9 September 1886 (amended in 1914, 1928, 1948, 1967, 1971, and 1979) 25 UST 1341, 828 UNTS 221, entered into force 5 December 1887 ('Berne Convention'), Art 7(1). Shorter terms are possible for cinematographic works, anonymous and pseudonymous works, photographs and applied art (Art 7(3)–7(5)). For jointly authored works, the time clock starts ticking from demise of last surviving author (Art 7*bis*). The life + 50 minimum was first recommended in the *Berlin Act of 1908*, and became mandatory from the Brussels Revision in 1948.

8   Berne Convention, Art 5(2); introduced as part of the *Berlin Act of 1908*; *Marrakesh Agreement Establishing the World Trade Organization*, opened for signature 15 April 1994, 1867 UNTS 3 (entered into force 1 January 1995), annex IC (*Agreement on Trade-Related Aspects of Intellectual Property Rights*) ('TRIPS'), Art 9.

In large part that's because the treaty requires unanimity of votes cast for its substantive provisions to be revised.[9] Thus every single member nation effectively has a veto right, from tiny Portuguese-speaking West African nation the Democratic Republic of São Tomé and Príncipe to 170-odd others.[10] The difficulties associated with making law to bind so many countries with such divergent interests are hinted at in the current drought between revisions. Berne has not been revised since 1971. That's zero substantive changes in the digital and internet eras, and just one since we put a man on the moon. By contrast, there were seven revisions between 1971 and Berne's inception (averaging one every 12 years), and the longest pause before now was the 20 years between Rome (1928) and Brussels (1945), a time when the world was largely preoccupied with larger geopolitical concerns. But from where we stand right now, amidst increasingly fractious and polarised debates, it actually seems possible that Berne may never be amended again.

This reality forecloses even compromise solutions, such as Landes and Posner's proposal for 'indefinitely renewable copyrights'. The largest practical barriers to shorter terms are the interests of the authors and intermediaries whose works retain commercial value in the decades after creation (or who hope they will). Landes and Posner propose to give these interest groups more of what they want (copyrights that last more or less forever) in exchange for what society needs (freer access to more stuff, sooner). Their scheme would permit right holders with continuing interests in their works to renew them ad infinitum, enabling at least those unwanted or less valued works to enter into the public domain.[11] As Giblin points out, such a system is not justifiable on any recognised rationale for copyright protection, but it would

---

9   Berne Convention, Art 27. Note that the requirement of unanimity applies not only to the provisions of the 'Berne Convention Proper', but also to the Berne Appendix. This poses challenges to Ncube's proposals in this book for a radical broadening of the circumstances in which translations of under-exploited works may occur. This is exactly what the Berne Appendix was meant to do, but perhaps because the process by which the Appendix was developed was strongly influenced by first world publishers and authors, the resulting 'flexibilities' have proved so complex, unwieldy and unworkable in practice as to have been almost entirely forsaken by their putative beneficiaries (see also Giblin, above n 4). Whether the Berne Appendix could simply be 'abandoned' and a new treaty regarding translation written (in the style of the recent Marrakesh Treaty) raises interesting questions of international law well beyond the scope of this chapter.

10   See *WIPO-Administered Treaties Contracting Parties > Berne Convention* <www.wipo.int/treaties/en/ShowResults.jsp?treaty_id=15>.

11   William M Landes and Richard A Posner, 'Indefinitely Renewable Copyright' (2003) 70 *University of Chicago Law Review* 471, 517–518.

at least do *something* to address some of the worst wastages that flow inevitably from existing approaches. But even such a compromise simply wouldn't possible unless all Berne member states agree – or unless we walk away from Berne and start again.

That's where the rock comes along to join the hard place. Berne is impossible to amend, but walking away from it is scarcely more thinkable. TRIPS' express linking of Berne to membership of the WTO is one reason for that, and the loss of reciprocal rights – in an increasingly borderless digital world – is another. This is a hostage situation we can't see anyone walking away from.

It *is* possible, albeit with a great deal of difficulty, to create new treaties in this space. We saw this with Marrakesh's recognition of greater access rights for the blind and vision impaired, and before that, the WIPO Copyright and Performances and Phonograms treaties (WIPO Copyright Treaty and WPPT, respectively). Crucially though, Berne itself limits the possibility of new treaties to those that do not detract from its prohibitions and minimums.[12] This raises complex questions of interpretation of international law, but it seems likely that we could not even fix our formalities or duration problems via entry to a new multilateral agreement.

Cutting the Berne/TRIPS tie is also effectively impossible, because TRIPS itself is also practically unamendable. Proposals for amendments altering members' rights and obligations can be made, but require acceptance by two-thirds of the members (i.e. by 108 of the present 162 WTO members) in order to come into effect, and even then apply only to accepting members. To make an amendment effective for *all* WTO members requires the Ministerial Conference (i.e. all members in conference) to decide by a three-fourths majority that it is of such a nature that any member which has not accepted it within a specified period should be free to withdraw from the WTO or to remain a member only with the consent of the Ministerial Conference. As a practical matter, voting rarely occurs in the WTO system: most decisions are made by consensus.[13] The effectively unamendable nature of TRIPS is demonstrated by the fact that the TRIPS Amendment needed to make

---

12   See Berne Convention, Arts 20, 30.
13   Mitsuo Matsushita, Thomas J Schoenbaum and Petros C Mavroidis, *The World Trade Organization: Law, Practice, and Policy* (Oxford University Press, 2006), 12.

permanent the Doha Declaration accommodations to facilitate access to essential medicines for developing countries has still not garnered the needed two-thirds of member acceptances to come into force, despite being supported by a consensus in the General Council over a decade ago in December 2005 (WTO members in late 2015 voted themselves a fifth extension of the deadline for acceptance).

Note too that if TRIPS really is unamendable in any practical sense, this precludes even less significant changes to copyright, and even those for which a supportive industry coalition might be formed. For example, Reese suggested that computer software might be better protected via some sui generis regime than via copyright. There was in fact considerable debate over whether copyright was an appropriate source of protection given the functional nature of programming, and considerable dissatisfaction with software copyrights remains a generation later, shared across big business, individual programmers and the free and open source software communities alike. In these circumstances, the beneficiaries[14] of software copyright might, perhaps, be willing to abandon it in exchange for a better-tailored sui generis scheme. But TRIPS[15] and the WIPO Copyright Treaty[16] both require software (whether in source or object code) to be protected as a literary work in accordance with Berne: which feels like an end to the debate before it can even get started.

Treaty lock-ins severely curtail our ability to respond to changed circumstances in other ways as well. The key goal de Beer identifies for a reconceived copyright is to make copyright a better market facilitator, particularly by addressing fragmented copyright ownership, which imposes transaction costs which can prevent authors, owners and users from reaching mutually beneficial deals. Existing, extremely long-lived property rights stand in the way of any attempt to reduce fragmentation beyond a 'tinkering' via collective licensing. A number of the rules in the international legal framework would also require

---

14   William M Landes and Richard A Posner, 'Indefinitely Renewable Copyright' (2003) 70 *University of Chicago Law Review* 471, 483.

15   TRIPS, Art 10; *World Intellectual Property Organization Copyright Treaty*, opened for signature 20 December 1996, 36 ILM 65, entered into force 6 March 2002, Art 4 ('WIPO Copyright Treaty'). They also require the owners of computer programs to be granted a rental right, at least where the program is the essential object of the rental: TRIPS, Art 11; WIPO Copyright Treaty, Art 7.

16   The WIPO Copyright Treaty, which also mandates protection of software as a literary work, contains no provisions for its own amendment, although it can be denounced: Art 23.

amendment to fully achieve de Beer's vision, including, in particular, treaties such as Berne, TRIPS, the WIPO Copyright Treaty and the WIPO Performances and Phonograms Treaty, which grant identical, strong, exclusive rights to a series of different contributors to any given cultural product (authors, performers and producers).[17]

It is worth pausing a moment here to note another implication of our analysis. A great deal of concern has been expressed in the academic and policy literature about the way in which bilateral and regional trade agreements and rules have become more and more specific over time, with particular animus directed towards treaties such as the US trade agreements which export specific rules of US domestic law. It may be that the specificity of more recent treaties (as well as rapid technological change) is a reason why their constraints have been felt more rapidly. It took close to a century for mainstream copyright reform debates to progress to explicit criticism of Berne's prohibition on formalities, for example.[18] By contrast, some of the Australia–United States Free Trade Agreement's provisions have already caused problems within the first decade of the Agreement being signed.[19]

But some current literature would seem to suggest, at least implicitly, that we should be aiming for a return to the higher level principles embodied in older treaties, such as the Berne Convention. Free exploration by the authors in this book, however, suggests that this may be a misconception. In fact, longstanding, generally drafted provisions of the Berne Convention impose constraints at least as great as the new agreements.

---

17   Berne Convention, Arts 8, 9, 11*bis*, 11*ter*, 12; WIPO Copyright Treaty, above n 15, Arts 6–8; *World Intellectual Property Organization Performances and Phonograms Treaty* ('WPPT'), opened for signature 20 December 1996, 36 ILM 76 (entered into force 20 May 2002), Arts 6–8 and 11–13.
18   See Kimberlee G Weatherall, 'So Call Me a Copyright Radical' (2011) 29(4) *Copyright Reporter*, 123 and literature cited therein.
19   *Australia–United States Free Trade Agreement*, opened for signature 6 May 2004, signed 18 May 2004, [2005] ATS 1 (entered into force 1 January 2005) Kimberlee G Weatherall, 'The Australia-US free trade agreement's impact on Australia's copyright trade policy' (2015) 69(5) *Australian Journal of International Affairs* 538; notable in rewording of some US FTA provisions in the context of TPP negotiations and absence of certain provisions in TPP drafts.

Is it *all* impossible?

The forbidding practical barriers to many of the most interesting and important ideas in this book may not stand in the way of some smaller changes that would help improve the system. For the most part, implementing these would involve more fully exploiting existing flexibilities within Berne and TRIPS.

One area where there is obviously flexibility lies in exceptions and limitations. A number of contributors identified a need to expand these to better fulfil the public interest in copyright, and no doubt some steps could be taken in this direction. Of particular potential are fair uses involving quotation, which, as Senftleben points out, Berne positively obliges members to exempt from the copyright owner's control.[20] Senftleben argues that this could be interpreted as a positive right to transformative use[21] – a possibility that is worthy of serious thought and exploration, especially in light of our authors' desire to promote the interests of individual creators.

Outside of the quotation right (and a few other privileged categories), the ability of individual nations to introduce limitations and exceptions is curbed by the 'three-step test'. Originating in Berne,[22] then adapted and incorporated into a number of other international instruments including TRIPS,[23] the WIPO Copyright Treaty,[24] the WPPT,[25] various free trade agreements[26] and a swathe of EU Directives touching on IP-related rights,[27] this test limits most exceptions and limitations to 'certain special cases that do not conflict with a normal exploitation of the work and do not unreasonably prejudice the legitimate interests of the author'. This tends to preclude exceptions that would remove

---

20 Martin Senftleben, Chapter 2, this volume.
21 Ibid.
22 Berne Convention, Art 9.
23 TRIPS, Art 13.
24 WIPO Copyright Treaty, Art 10.
25 WPPT, Art 16.
26 See e.g. *Australia–United States Free Trade Agreement*, opened for signature 6 May 2004, signed 18 May 2004, [2005] ATS 1 (entered into force 1 January 2005) Art 17.4(10).
27 See e.g. *Directive 2009/24/EC of the European Parliament and of the Council of 23 April 2009 on the legal protection of computer programs* [2009] OJ L111/16, Art 6(3); *Directive 96/9/EC of the European Parliament and of the Council of 11 March 1996 on the legal protection of databases* [1996] OJ L077/20, Art 6(3); and *Directive 2001/29\EC of the European Parliament and of the Council of 22 May 2001 on the harmonisation of certain aspects of copyright and related rights in the information society* [2001] OJ L167/10, Art 5(5).

any given exclusive right or subsume substantial parts of a copyright owner's rights (even if they make objective sense, and indeed even if they cause little harm to copyright owners). Nonetheless, there remains considerable scope to develop the exceptions of most domestic laws to more fully take advantage of what *is* permitted – for example, by introducing flexible exceptions in the style of the US 'fair use'. That said, Giblin's proposal to progressively reserve a greater share of each work's value to the public over time, Ncube's call for broader exceptions to help rectify the failure of markets to produce works for the benefit of less advantaged language groups, and the broader approaches to users' and creators' rights proposed by Senftleben and Geiger may each fall foul of this rule, and thus simply not even be eligible for consideration or debate.

The enforcement area has perhaps the most interesting potential flexibility under current treaty arrangements. There is nothing in existing treaties barring governments from taking into account the degree of access their residents have to copyright works in establishing remedies for infringement, or directing their courts to frame remedies with degrees of access in mind. It might not be possible to foreclose the possibility of remedies entirely, even for works that are not made commercially available.[28] Nevertheless, flexibilities around enforcement could help ameliorate some of the big problems caused by current approaches, and reflect values such as reciprocity which are a theme in this collection.

Berne/TRIPS also has little to say about *ownership* of copyright. There is real potential, as Giblin points out, to design domestic systems that revert the above-incentive value of copyrights back to creators after some fixed period of time. The US already has one such system in place (though we would hope other countries considering whether to follow suit would adopt a more author-friendly, less formalistic model).[29] Reversion to authors would do much more than simply direct copyright's 'reward' component to its proper recipients. It would also

---

28   For a detailed discussion of this point, see Kimberlee Weatherall, 'Safeguards for Defendant Rights and Interests in International Intellectual Property Enforcement Treaties' (2016) 32 *American University International Law Review* 211 (discussing the degree of flexibility in the enforcement provisions of TRIPS).

29   See e.g. Lionel EF Bentley and Jane C Ginsburg, '"The Sole Right … Shall Return to the Authors": Anglo-American Authors' Reversion Rights from the Statute of Anne to Contemporary U.S. Copyright' (2010) 25 *Berkeley Technology Law Journal* 1475.

free up many of those works that had been languishing in the hands of intermediary owners with no further interest in commercially exploiting them, facilitating the transfer of rights to those who value them most. Furthermore, if authors were positioned to capture a greater share of the revenues from their works, it would open up new possibilities for socially valuable collective licensing arrangements (such as digital public libraries that pay fair remuneration to authors on a per-loan basis). Finally, reversion to authors would change the reform discourse. Currently, proposals to ameliorate the overreach of existing approaches are responded to with clockwork regularity by scare campaigns framed around the image of literary and artistic icons losing control of their masterworks. Focusing more squarely on the just deserts of authors could help the debate actually move forward, to identify where the interests of cultural intermediaries and authors cease to align, and better understand what we owe to each.

In addition, Berne/TRIPS' lack of hard rules on ownership might also allow de Beer's aims of limiting idiosyncratic divisions of ownership, and Ncube's suggestion that sometimes it might be appropriate to limit creators' assignments of copyright. Berne/TRIPS would also seem to have little to say about Senftleben's ideas for ensuring a right to fair remuneration, and *ex post* remedies in cases where remuneration appears disproportionately low in light of the market success of a work.

So not all the ideas in these collected chapters are impossible. In that, they complement some other recent projects which have done excellent work in seeking to frame a general and overarching agenda for *achievable* copyright reform such as Samuelson et al's *Copyright Principles Project* in the US or the Wittem Group Draft Model Copyright Code for the EU. To us though, these ideas for feasible change feel very much like mere tinkering at the edges of what's demonstrably a deeply flawed system.

Further, even more minor and creative suggestions not precluded by TRIPS or Berne may be in the process of being closed off by recent, more prescriptive trade agreements. For example, creative rules around ownership and non-assignability of rights, designed to protect individual creators, may be prevented by US-driven free trade agreement provisions stating that 'any person acquiring or holding any economic right in a work, performance, or phonogram ... may freely and separately transfer that right by contract'.[30] This provision appears to be designed precisely to counter European-style schemes for fair remuneration of authors and non-assignable rights to equitable remuneration.[31] And some of the existing flexibility around enforcement is under pressure in the context of recent bilateral and plurilateral IP negotiations.[32]

We are frequently told that the complex IP treaties being drafted today are acceptable because they merely reflect current levels of protection, and demand no changes to current domestic law. This is intuitively troubling: the problem with prescriptive rules is not just the changes they require right now, but also the changes they preclude in the future. But lost future opportunity does not feel like a loss: it needs to be made tangible. Some of the more achievable ideas in this collection give substance to what we might be losing right now.

Why entertain the impossible?

This brings us to our last big question: what is the practical significance of a collection of impossible ideas? Are these assembled chapters a mere requiem to what might have been?

We don't think so. Even apart from providing another position in the debate over current international treaty-making, for us, the exercise of reimagining copyright from a blank slate has proved a valuable lens for discovering fresh insights about the deficiencies of existing approaches. Thinking about redesigning elements of copyright from scratch necessarily involves deep thinking about what we want it to achieve. From there, new possibilities start to emerge.

---

30   See e.g. *Australia–United States Free Trade Agreement*, opened for signature 6 May 2004, signed 18 May 2004, [2005] ATS 1 (entered into force 1 January 2005), Art 17.4.6.
31   See analysis in Robert Burrell and Kimberlee Weatherall, 'Exporting Controversy? Reactions to the Copyright Provision of the U.S.–Australia Free Trade Agreement: Lessons for U.S. Trade Policy' (2008) 2 *University of Illinois Journal of Law, Technology and Policy* 259.
32   See generally Weatherall, above n 28.

Duration is again a useful example. Implicitly, debates over term generally compare long terms to ones of shorter duration, as if that were the entire universe of options.[33] Simple reductions in term, however, look like they're just taking away from already struggling authors. But this reimagination exercise – and the recognition that we have distinct goals for both authors and disseminators – leads one to recognise the possibility of more creative alternatives that could be good for a very wide range of stakeholders. Enter Giblin's proposal for different terms designed to satisfy our different rationales for copyright; where the author does not need to give up everything for all time before public exploitation of their creativity has even begun. Copyright is non-zero-sum. Unlike in a zero-sum game (where participants' gains and losses of utility are exactly balanced by those of the other players) a reallocation of copyright's rights – giving producers (only) what they need, and authors and society the rest – could potentially result in an enormous increase of utility for some in exchange for just a small reduction for others (or perhaps even no reduction at all). But with international constraints closing off many possible options, this potential is largely going unexplored.

Or take another example from enforcement: from the perspective of an individual creator concerned about rampant infringement, *any* new enforcement initiative, and any extensions or elaborations of the TRIPS provisions relating to enforcement, must seem inherently a good thing, even if in reality it creates only tools accessible to the largest, most organised right holders. But present that same creator with an alternative that halts the endless expansion of tools, but better and more effectively targets the public resources available, and it could well be more attractive. Similarly, copyright registration may look like an intolerable burden until you start imagining a system of streamlined digital deposit that gives access to enticing procedural or remedial advantages over the way that things work now.

---

33   There are some notable exceptions: see e.g. the well-known alternative proposed by Landes and Posner of indefinitely renewable copyright terms, William M Landes and Richard A Posner, 'Indefinitely Renewable Copyright' (2003) 70 *University of Chicago Law Review* 471; (and see also Giblin's criticisms of that approach in her reimagination of duration policy within this book).

Some hope for the future

As we mentioned above, when we really pushed ourselves to think about a path to useful reform, we couldn't find a politically feasible pathway to a reimagined copyright system in the public interest in the short to medium term. But despite the generally pessimistic tone of this concluding chapter, we *do* have some hope for change when we step back and take a longer view. As creators and the broader public become more aware about what existing rules force us to forsake, as global society moves further and further from the worlds which Berne and even TRIPS were formed in response to, it seems to us that something will simply have to give.

In some limited contexts we see faint evidence that this is starting to happen: in the voluntary registers of rights identified by Gangjee; in the increasing efforts of authors to reclaim rights or protect open access through organisations such as the Authors' Alliance (and those of academic and self-published authors to retain their copyrights and only licence to publishers the rights they need). Voluntary efforts will never be enough because so many issues with current copyright arise from the mass of unvalued material that's locked away by long terms and poor record keeping. But they are something.

Crucially though, we think that real change will only occur with serious support from the stakeholders at the very centre of the copyright equation: authors and creators, particularly those who rely on it in some way for their livelihoods. This book has shown how copyright fails its supposed primary beneficiaries. A system in which the lion's share of rewards goes to everyone *but* creators, and in which important non-economic interests such as attribution and integrity are promoted in only the most incomplete ways, doesn't meet creators' needs. In theory, if creators could be convinced that an alternatively framed system could genuinely offer them more of what they want and need, perhaps they might rethink the political support or cover they provide to the current system, and their resistance to changing it.

Based on some of the ideas presented in the this book, it is possible to imagine a more author-friendly kind of copyright: one that provides opportunities to recover and renegotiate exploitation rights and protects authors against being obliged to assign all rights for all time to obtain access to audiences and distribution channels (Giblin);

that provides mechanisms for sharing in the bounty of particularly successful works (Senftleben); that still protects rights of attribution and integrity for long periods regardless of formalities (Gangjee); that provides for much-simplified rights of remuneration or enforcement for registered works (Gangjee, Weatherall). A system that promoted (or even, consistent with the theme of reciprocity, *required*) access to material that was no longer commercially available could provide a plentiful supply of source material for future creation.

We see this as a long-term hope. We would not expect those creators succeeding in the current winner-takes-all system to advocate for change. Others will quite understandably be unwilling to give up whatever (measly) rewards they do eke out from current copyright systems: when you accrue but little directly from your creativity, giving any of that up is a big deal. With the intricacies of copyright law now largely inaccessible to all but lawyers heavily invested in the system, relatively few authors are ever likely to engage sufficiently with the detail of copyright law to be able to reach the conclusion that current settings so disserve their interests that they should lobby in favour of systemic change. We suspect that most creators have enough to worry about in developing their own creative practice, producing their music, or art, or words, and in managing the day-to-day business of a creative career. But we hope there will come a time when enough is enough: when enough creators will stop accepting that 'some copyright is good, so more copyright must be better' and start agitating for a system that genuinely serves their interests, rather than simply permitting their genuine claim to be used as a stalking horse for other economic interests.

Not an end, but a beginning

The strength of this collection – its highly skilled and hardworking team of international legal academics – is also one of its weaknesses.

The brief we started with is challenging for the legally trained thinker. Lawyers are accustomed to think within the framework of existing systems: to identify specific problems and propose incremental fixes and reforms that do not drastically challenge the foundations of the law. A blank slate is, frankly, both disconcerting and confronting. As lawyers, too, we tend immediately to see the problems with radical proposals, which can perhaps render us quick to dismiss, rather than embrace ideas that depart markedly from the norm. As Gangjee eloquently notes in his chapter, it is hard to let go of the edge of the pool and strike out for something new. We certainly had to push ourselves (and our colleagues, whom we thank for their tolerance) to think more radically, to be more adventurous, and to question preconceptions about the way things could and should be.

The proposals here reflect these challenges. They may put to one side the existing international and domestic legal framework, but it would be fair to say that most still operate within traditional understandings of what copyright is designed to achieve and accept the basic premise of achieving those goals within a framework of authors' proprietary rights, albeit, in some cases, with plenty of qualifications. So there is room to push our premise considerably further in the future. In particular, we have found in talking about these ideas and our initial premise with thinkers or audiences beyond the legally trained, that there's enormous scope for even more creative ideas to emerge.[34]

And so we invite the reader to try for themselves the exercise of trying to reimagine copyright without the safety net of current legal frameworks. We can certainly recommend it as an intellectual exercise. It may not be comfortable, or easy, but even the process of thinking up radical alternatives can not only spark some interesting ideas but it can also put existing problems in a new light. Copyright touches on all of our lives – and the conversations exploring how it might best achieve its aims should also be informed by a diverse range of perspectives and voices.

34   For example, one of the authors (Giblin) spoke on these ideas at the 2016 Annual Forum of the Australian Digital Alliance (March 2016), and invited a panel of non-lawyers to contribute their own ideas taking the same premise as a starting point. Their ideas can be seen in a video of the forum, available on YouTube at <www.youtube.com/watch?v=JsXWt7GrBbE>.

Made in the USA
Monee, IL
14 November 2019